# THE NEW PUBLIC SPEAKER

# THE NEW PUBLIC SPEAKER

## GEORGE RODMAN

Brooklyn College,
City University of New York

## RONALD B. ADLER

*Consulting Editor*

Santa Barbara City College

**Harcourt Brace College Publishers**

Fort Worth   Philadelphia   San Diego   New York   Orlando   Austin   San Antonio
Toronto   Montreal   London   Sydney   Tokyo

| | |
|---|---|
| **Publisher** | Christopher P. Klein |
| **Senior Acquisitions Editor** | Carol Wada |
| **Developmental Editor** | Laurie Runion |
| **Project Editor** | John Haakenson |
| **Production Manager** | Serena Manning |
| **Art Director** | Sue Hart |
| **Text Designer and Photo Permissions** | Janet Bollow |
| **Cover** | Design Deluxe |

*Address for Editorial Correspondence*
Harcourt Brace College Publishers, 301 Commerce Street, Suite 3700, Fort Worth, TX 76102

*Address for Orders*
Harcourt Brace & Company, 6277 Sea Harbor Drive, Orlando, FL 32887.
1-800-782-4479, or 1-800-433-0001 (in Florida)

Harcourt Brace College Publishers may provide complimentary instructional aids and supplements of supplement packages to those adopters qualified under our adoption policy. Please contact your sales representative for more information. If as an adopter or potential user you receive supplements you do not need, please return them to your sales representative or send them to:

Attn: Returns Department
Troy Warehouse
465 South Lincoln Drive
Troy, MO 63379

ISBN: 0-15-502708-5

Library of Congress Catalogue Number: 95-81786

Printed in the United States of America

6 7 8 9 0 1 2 3 4 5 032 10 9 8 7 6 5 4 3 2 1

# BRIEF TABLE OF CONTENTS

# TABLE OF CONTENTS

# PREFACE

Who is the new public speaker?

In one sense, the title refers to the reader of this book, who is probably inexperienced at speaking before an audience. But in an equally significant sense, the term "new" in this book's title suggests that changes in communication technology have transformed the nature of public speaking.

## PUBLIC SPEAKING IN THE MEDIA/INFORMATION AGE

This book suggests that the new public speaker, like his or her predecessors, must understand and possess traditional skills such as critical thinking, audience analysis, organization, research and delivery. At the same time, the book argues that in the late 20th century these skills alone are not sufficient to reach audiences who are bombarded with information from both the mass media and emerging technologies such as the World Wide Web. The new public speaker must recognize how to plan and present ideas in a form that will make the media-savvy audiences want to tune in. In many ways, the new public speaker is exemplified by some of the public figures whose portraits begin the chapters of this book: people such as Nelson Mandella, Mother Theresa, and General Norman Schwarzkopf; people who might never be described as media-slick and yet whose speaking has had a global impact, largely because their personal style projects their ethics, their credibility and their humanity.

The media age has affected speakers as well as audiences. A variety of scholars and teachers have pointed out that it is becoming increasingly difficult to inspire students to become effective speakers in the media age first described by Marshall McLuhan in his pioneering *Understanding Media: The Extensions of Man*.[1] James Chesebro, for example, has made clear that "media exert an independent and profound influence upon the nature of reality apprehended by human beings."[2] Chesebro explains that speechmaking, like reading and writing, "generates predominantly analytical, logical, sequential, and scientific modes"[3] of understanding, while

---

[1] Marshal McLuhan, *Understanding Media: The Extensions of Man* (New York: Signet, 1964).

[2] James Chesebro,"The Media Reality: Epistemological Functions of Media in Cultural Systems," *Critical Studies in Mass Communications* 1, June, 1984, p. 112.

[3] *Ibid.*, p. 119.

electronic media "generate predominantly synthesizing, holistic, pattern-recognition, and aesthetic modes."[4] W. Lance Haynes echoes this theme, pointing out that public speaking classes today are filled with "students whose thoughts and expression are increasingly shaped by electronic media."[5] The significance of this influence on the practice of public speaking has been widely debated.

The theme of this book is that media and information saturation have changed matters for the new public speaker—sometimes making speaking easier, and sometimes making it more difficult. Although this book looks at media critically, it also acknowledges that there is much to learn from media models. The new public speaker can learn from the way the media collect as much information as possible about their audiences, their expertise in making ideas visual, and, ironically, their ability to break through the clutter of messages that bombard consumers. One of the "hooks" in *The New Public Speaker,* therefore, will be the book's insight into how to succeed in an age dominated by technologies that were inconceivable to classical rhetoricians.

## THE BOOK'S APPROACH

The media/information age theme of this book is designed to wrap traditional content around an exciting idea, to allow students to appreciate the time-tested theory that will improve their speeches. To this end, key topics that are almost universally accepted as essential are developed in a recognizable form. The book also contains a typical blend of theory and skill-building, with perhaps 85% of content devoted to principles of effective speechmaking. The theory portion consists of equal parts of rhetorical/critical, classical and social scientific research—just enough of each for students to appreciate that the principles they are learning are based on sound scholarship.

*The New Public Speaker* also tries to balance the needs of the classroom with changes in society. Recognizing the time constraints of the typical public speaking class, the first chapter provides an overview to help students plan and deliver a first speech to their classmates. Ethics in face-to-face speaking is also so important that this topic is dealt with in an early chapter. Throughout the book, you will see these subtle approaches that adapt traditional public speaking to today's society.

The principles of speechmaking are illustrated whenever possible with examples that are interesting to read. Besides boosting student interest, the examples seek to encourage creativity in the student's own

[4.] *Ibid.*
[5.] W. Lance Haynes, "Public Speaking Pedagogy in the Media Age," *Communication Education* 38, April 1990, pp. 89–102.

speeches. By offering literally hundreds of examples of interesting topics and approaches, this text tries to show the new public speaker that it is possible to develop important ideas in new, interesting ways. This should result in more creative student speeches—a necessity in the media age, and usually a welcome development for both professors and students in this course.

Each chapter starts off with a list of chapter objectives, all of which pertain directly to the speechmaking process. Each chapter also contains at least one sample speech. Most of these speeches are by college students, although two are by professors and two are by celebrities. Each chapter ends with a summary, notes, and several exercises. These exercises, which stress critical thinking ethics as well as skill-building, are augmented and expanded upon in the instructor's manual.

## TEACHING AND LEARNING AIDS

*The New Public Speaker* comes with a comprehensive package of ancillary materials to help students and their professors:

▼ **Videotapes**   Three videotapes are available without charge to adopters of this book. *Public Speeches for Analysis I* includes student, business, and professional public speeches. Each speech illustrates a particular concept or technique with several of the speeches showing two versions as a way to demonstrate changes made for audience or improvement. *Public Speeches for Analysis II* contains all of the end-of-chapter sample speeches from this book. These videotaped speeches are given, for the most part, by the original speakers and appear on the video in their entirety. These performances are based on a wide assortment of types and qualities; although no professor will have time to show them all in class, every professor will find both positive and negative examples of every important trait. Finally, *Understanding Public Speaking Apprehension* features a lecture by Ron Adler on minimizing fear and shows students demonstrating techniques that help to minimize speech apprehension.

▼ **Instructor's Manual/Test Bank**   Written by Karen Krupar at Metropolitan State College, this comprehensive instructor's manual offers a wide range of teaching strategies. An extensive test bank was written by Darla Germeroth at University of Scranton.

▼ **Classroom-Ready Overhead Transparencies.**

▼ **Exammaster**   This computerized test-generating program makes the task of constructing and printing examinations quicker and easier than ever before. The program contains all exam questions printed in the *Instructor's Manual/Test Bank* and allows instructors to customize tests by adding their own questions. Available in DOS, Windows, and Macintosh formats.

▼ **Speech Grader Software**  This Macintosh software program is designed to enhance the instructor's grading of student speeches. Instructors simply check off descriptions of a student's speech and a personalized printout is created that refers the student to the textbook for work on problem areas. This enables professors to provide comprehensive feedback to students quickly and easily.

## Acknowledgments

I want to acknowledge the help of my friend and consulting editor, Ron Adler, who acted more like a co-author than an editor. His contribution of raw material and guidance in the ideas and writing of this book helped me to make it the best it could be.

The publishing of this book was superbly done by the professionals at Harcourt Brace. I would like to thank my editor Carol Wada, development editors Laurie Runion and Diane Drexler, production manager Serena Manning, project editor John Haakenson, and designers Janet Bollow and Sue Hart.

A team of experts lent guidance on all or parts of this book. I'd like to thank, therefore, the work and opinions of Don Ochs, University of Iowa; Joyce Ngoh, Marist College; Ralph Hillman, Middle Tennessee State University; Cynthia SoRelle, McLennan Community College; Gary Eckles, Thomas Nelson Community College; Deanna Sellnow, North Dakota State University; Bill Loftus, Austin Community College; Jacquelyn Buckrop, Ball State University; James Wolford, Joliet Junior College; Jill Voran, Anne Arundel Community College; Bill Poschman, Diablo Valley Community College; Jim Brooks, Middle Tennessee State University; Deborah Smith-Howell, University of Nebraska-Omaha; Clark McMillion, University of Missouri-St. Louis; Pam Joraanstad, Glendale Community College; Mark Morman, Johnson County Community College; Mary Haselrud Opp, University of North Dakota; Lawrence Hosman, University of Southern Mississippi; and Edward Pappas, Wayne State University. I'd also like to thank Deborah Borisoff of New York University and Charles Fleischman of Hofstra University for allowing me to test-run many of the ideas in this book in the courses I teach in their departments; Joseph Agolia and John Bosco, Jr. for their help at Garden City Library, and my research assistant, Lucia Lingua.

And, of course, I'd like to especially thank my family: My wife Linda, and my kids, Jenny, Alexandra and Dean Taylor. Especially Dean Taylor. He was born during the writing of this book and, with luck, will be able to use the 6th edition when he's in college.

# INTRODUCTION

## ▼ CHAPTER 1 OBJECTIVES

**After reading this chapter, you should understand:**

1. What we mean by the "media/information age," and its significance to public speaking.

2. Why public speaking, one of the oldest of academic subjects, is increasing in importance.

**You should be able to:**

1. Prepare a first speech following the guidelines presented in this chapter.

2. Begin to use the skills you acquire in your public speaking class for greater personal growth, academic achievement, and career success.

## ⬇ THE STUDY OF PUBLIC SPEAKING

Welcome to the college-level course in public speaking. By enrolling in this course, you are in good company. One survey suggests that some 300,000 college students take this course each year in the United States alone.[1] That number is especially impressive when you consider that this course has been a mainstay of the college curriculum since college began, more than 2,000 years ago.

The first academics, the ancient Greeks, placed the study of public speaking at the center of their curriculum. They did so for the same reasons we study this topic today: First, because public speaking skills often separate those who are successful in their careers from those who are not; second, because public speaking enhances personal development; and, third, because the study of public speaking develops communication skills that are essential in a democracy. Let's take a quick look at each of these objectives.

### Public Speaking and Careers

The ancient Greeks believed that speech training and leadership training were one and the same. The skills that were taught in the study of public speaking—skills such as the organization of information, effective language choices, critical decision making, and the analysis of logical arguments—are the same skills that lead to success in any field.

In modern times, study after study has confirmed the relationship between public speaking skills and professional success. Most people understand instinctively that training in public speaking is necessary for a communication-oriented career, such as teaching, law, public relations, or marketing. Research shows, however, that public speaking skills enhance career advancement in *any* job. They can help you get a job,[2] and, once you have the job, help you succeed at it.[3] In fact, the lack of public speaking skills has been identified as one of the causes of the "glass ceiling" that sometimes prevents women and minorities from advancing to the level of top management.[4]

In today's highly technological, information-oriented business environment, public speaking is more important than ever. More business conferences require oral presentations today than ever before. There is also more information that needs to be explained to specific groups of people in the communication-rich give-and-take of in-person speech presentations.

### Public Speaking and Personal Development

A wide range of skills are developed and sharpened in the study of public speaking. For example, giving speeches in the classroom helps build your

▼ Speech is civilization itself. The word, even the most contradictory word, preserves contact. It is silence which isolates.

Thomas Mann

▼ Self-confidence is the first requisite to great undertakings.

Samuel Johnson

confidence *in general*. Giving a speech is one of the most frightening things most people do; to do it and succeed in the classroom setting builds your confidence in the same way that a wilderness survival course builds your confidence in general (not just your confidence to survive in a wilderness). One of the great lessons of life is that this generalized confidence breeds success in *any* endeavor.

Personal growth is also enhanced by the types of personal analysis you will be required to do as a public speaker. You have to examine your own attitudes and you have to examine the way the audience perceives you. You also have to consider the needs and motivations of others. Perhaps most important, preparing speeches requires you to be creative. All these activities encourage personal growth. They are, in fact, as essential in personal growth as they are in the speech-making process.[5]

## Public Speaking and Democracy

Freedom of speech has always been a hallmark of the democratic form of government. People who are trained in thought and reason, who are well informed about the issues of their day, and who are allowed to speak out on those issues will be able to actively participate in their governance. In theory, as long as the people contribute in this way, they will in effect be governing themselves, and all social, political, and economic problems can be worked out, given time.[6]

When we think about the importance of public speaking in a democracy, we generally think in terms of historical or political figures: Franklin and Eleanor Roosevelt fighting to bring America out of the Great

Depression, Martin Luther King's fight for civil rights, even Bill and Hillary Clinton's battles for health-care reform. But the fact is, the most important battles are fought by "regular people" who use speech to fight for social improvement—people like Bill Walsh, a Florida resident whose son, Adam, was abducted and killed. Walsh became a prominent spokesperson for missing children, and eventually became the host of the television program *America's Most Wanted.* And there is Glogene Totechene, the first Native American principal of Mesa Elementary School in the Shiprock, New Mexico, area of the Navajo Reservation, who divides her time between giving motivational talks to Native American children and speaking to governmental and community groups to increase financial support for her school.[7]

Even for people within the government, public speaking is a cost-effective way to get things done. Take Ann Winkleman Brown, the head of the Consumer Product Safety Commission. Her federal agency has a huge job to do—protect consumers from dangerous products—with little budget. She informs the public about unsafe products by using press conferences, appearing on talk shows, and speaking to groups. According to the *New York Times,* "These tactics are designed to get the most attention and results with the least amount of difficulty—and the fewest dollars."[8]

The First Amendment stands as proof of how important the founders of the American democracy believed free speech to be. The First Amendment prohibited Congress from making laws that restricted free speech in order to encourage a "robust debate" about all political matters. Inherent within this freedom to speak is a freedom to *listen* to a wide range of opinions. Because there are few restrictions on claims in a free speech democracy, *critically analyzing the messages of others is essential.* This is especially true in the media/information age, when many of our politically motivated messages are slickly produced for distribution over the mass media.

## Public Speaking and Critical Thinking

One of the most important communication skills to be honed in this course is critical thinking. Using logic and reasoning, recognizing valid argument, and distinguishing discussion from manipulation are all part of this skill. In the media/information age, critical thinking involves the ability to test the validity of visual, emotional images used as evidence. For example, the healthy, active, eternally youthful people in cigarette and liquor ads are terrifically appealing, but a critical analysis of the implicit message of these images proves that they make no sense. There is even a movement in the world of education—the "visual literacy" movement—to train children in this type of critical thinking. Someone trained in "visual literacy" would be better able to point out the potential unstated meaning beneath the surface of media messages. A visually literate person would look at the people in the cigarette ads and recognize that, if they actually used those products being advertised, they would be less healthy and less active.

In your public speaking class you'll be expected to exercise critical thinking in planning your own speeches and in analyzing the speeches of others. Many of your instructor's comments will be aimed at improving the sharpness of your critical thought. Because this is especially important in the media/information age, and because we've already used this term a few times, it might be a good idea to take a closer look at it now.

## ▼ THE MEDIA/INFORMATION AGE

Social historians tell us that many countries have evolved, over the years, from agricultural economies to industrial economies to information economies. In an information economy, the thrust of national activity is not just what people grow or what they build; it is also the creation of, movement of, and recording of information. One symptom of the information age is the vast amount of information that people need to understand and react to. The effects of the information age are made even more powerful by the abundance of media in our lives. The mass media are so pervasive today that we are "plugged in" to one or more of them for a good part of each day. This involvement with radio, television, film, books, magazines, recordings, and computer networks means that we spend a huge amount of time *in* the information flow. We wake up to clock radios and use television as our evening's entertainment. Media tell us who our heroes are and what the important social issues are.

The media/information age has affected public speaking in a number of ways. It has, for example, brought with it a credibility problem for speakers. Each member of a

# Calvin and Hobbes
## by Bill Watterson

media/information society needs to wade through the glut of messages to determine which ones are true and meaningful. Today's public speaker thus faces skepticism much stronger than that faced by speakers of earlier times. Because of the media/information age, we are surrounded with so many conflicting messages that it's difficult for us to know what to believe. One moment, eggs are bad for us; the next, they are health food. One moment, all women should receive annual mammograms; the next day this practice is no longer recommended. The media seldom synthesize or summarize the information we receive over time, and, in spite of recent on-line developments, they are unable to adapt information to individual needs. In today's democracy, that's the job of the public speaker.

Today's public speaker often works against the audience perception that a speech packs less entertainment value than TV, movies, radio, recorded music, or a computer game. The constraints of public speaking, especially in a college class, make this form of communication seem boring in comparison with the mass media. Public speakers generally observe rules against rude and inappropriate language, for example, that would leave Howard Stern speechless. Moreover, compared to the shouting riots that occur on today's talk shows, public speaking can seem pretty tame. Perhaps the most important lesson that a student learns from the study of public speaking is that this form of communication can generate excitement also—excitement that comes from real human beings who are genuinely concerned about what they have to say.

In fact, in the media/information age, public speaking is more important than ever. It is through public speaking that we achieve something impossible to do through the media: We make human contact with an organized message, while taking advantage of face-to-face communication. We do this, as often as not, to help our audience make sense of some segment of the information glut.

## ⬇ GETTING STARTED: THE FIRST SPEECH

The process of speech planning could be thought of as having three phases. We'll call them *initial planning, rough construction,* and *finishing touches.* An outline of the steps involved in these phases can be found in Table 1–1.

### TABLE 1-1 CHECKLIST: THE PROCESS OF SPEECH PLANNING

A. Initial Planning
 1. Choosing a topic
 2. Defining a purpose
 3. Analyzing the speech situation
B. Rough Construction
 1. Doing research
 2. Organizing and outlining
 3. Choosing supporting material
C. Finishing Touches
 1. Introducing and concluding
 2. Making it visual
 3. Practicing delivery

### Initial Planning

As with most creative tasks, it's not easy to get started on a speech. This is because of the law of creative inertia: It takes a lot more effort to start rolling than to keep rolling. Your first task, generally, is to choose a topic.

### Choosing a Topic

The topic of the first speech is often chosen for you. For example, you might be asked to introduce yourself to the class. Or perhaps you have been asked to interview another student and introduce that student to the class. In that case your first task is to decide on the approach you will take to this topic.

Your *approach* is your way of dealing with your topic, the path you take through it. Your approach could be based on attitude (a serious approach versus a lighthearted one), organization (finding a new way to arrange information), or even new information about an otherwise familiar topic. For example, because you know yourself so well, in all your complexity, it is sometimes difficult to choose an approach to use in explaining yourself to others. You might say,

> The best way to get to know me is to look at the directories I keep on my hard drive . . .

or perhaps,

I'm from Sioux City, Iowa, home of the world's largest buffalo.

When introducing someone else, remember that a similar variety of approaches exists:

Allison Biddle is a dynamo of energy. Not only does she hold down a full-time job, she writes for the campus newspaper and maintains a 3.5 grade-point average.

or,

I'd like to introduce you to Allison Biddle. When I interviewed her I found out that Allison works full-time as a telephone sales rep. I guess that's why her right ear is three times bigger than her left.

If you're introducing a classmate, you might decide to approach the introduction through an interesting hobby, a personality trait, an opinion, or a belief. Your "approach" in this case would be your organizing principle, the main idea on which you hang the rest of your information. The process involved in choosing an approach is similar to the process of choosing a topic: You generate as large a list as you can based on your own interests, and then narrow the list down on the basis of your audience's interests.

## Defining a Purpose

▼ It's wise to know what you are going to say so you know when you've said it.

Gene Perret

The best way to achieve a goal—any goal—is to remain focused on what you want to achieve. This maxim is especially true in speech preparation, especially today. In the media/information age, the glut of messages makes it difficult to focus on anything.

Sometimes purposes are misunderstood or confused by the speaker, which results in a confusing presentation that is difficult to follow. The first step in keeping your presentation clear is to determine your *general purpose,* which is usually to *entertain, inform,* or *persuade.* You can see how these three general purposes can transform a topic by looking at the way the speech of introduction was approached by three different students with different purpose statements:

▼ To Entertain: I'm a goof, but I'm a good-hearted goof, and you ought to get to know me.

▼ To Inform: I'm an exchange student from Bosnia, and I can't separate my identity from the current struggles of my people. I'd like you to understand that struggle today.

▼ To Persuade: I'm a member of Sigma Chi, and I'd like to persuade you to become one, too.

*Specific purpose.*

Your next step in keeping your purpose straight is to formulate a *purpose statement*. A purpose statement tells what you expect your audience to know or be able to do following your speech:

> After listening to my speech, my audience will recognize at least three similarities between the dating rituals of today's college students and mating rituals of primates such as baboons and orangutans.

We will be taking an in-depth look at purpose statements in Chapter 4.

### Analyzing the Audience

As you plan your speech, you analyze your audience's attitudes, expectations, and needs. Once you analyze them, you adapt your message to them: You might adapt your approach to the topic or even the language you use to back up your ideas. Adapting does *not* mean that you sacrifice your integrity by telling your audience only what they want to hear. It *does* mean that you tell them what you want to tell them in the way that they are most likely to understand and accept.

In preparation for a speech of self-introduction, one student analyzed her audience as follows:

> There are 23 students in this class. The class is almost equally divided by gender, with 12 men and 11 women. Twenty of the students are of typical college age (between 18 and 22) and three (one of the men and two of the women) are older, returning students. The few students I've spoken to say they're taking the class because it's a requirement for their major. They admitted they're nervous, mostly about giving the speeches themselves but also about the work involved in preparing them. I think this audience will be very understanding about any nervousness or preparation problems I might have. Most of these students seem genuinely interested in meeting and learning about new people. I feel confident that I can be honest with them, and they'll accept what I have to say.

We will be looking at audience analysis in more depth in Chapter 5.

### Rough Construction

Whether you are working with bricks, silk, or ideas, there is a framework, a rough construction, to everything you build. In speech planning, your rough construction consists of research, organization, and choice of supporting material.

### Doing Research

When you speak before an audience, you have to be well informed, if only to make up for the combined knowledge of all the audience members. Research also helps build your credibility. It shows your audience that you've done your homework and you know what you're talking about. You research general ideas and specific facts to support those ideas. You generally perform your research in the library, through interviewing, or through on-line services.

If your first assignment is to introduce yourself, you might find it helpful to interview a few friends concerning their impressions of you, or to interview your parents concerning your personal or family history. If that first assignment is to introduce a classmate, your interview with that classmate counts as research. But you might also want to do some library research, finding out what you can about some aspect of that person's background, such as her religion, her parents' nationalities, perhaps even her hometown. (Sometimes people are so close to the things that have influenced their personalities that they don't recognize the influence.)

First assignments are designed to require minimal research; your instructor understands your time restrictions early in the term. As the term unfolds, your research responsibilities expand with the time available. Researching for information that will add impact to what you tell your audience is often the difference between a successful and an unsuccessful presentation.

We will discuss research in more depth in Chapter 6.

### Organizing and Outlining

Basic speech structure includes an introduction, a body, and a conclusion. This structure is reflected in an old aphorism for speakers: "Tell them what you're going to say, say it, then tell them what you said." Although this sounds redundant, research on listening demonstrates that receivers forget much of what they hear.[9] The clear, repetitive nature of basic speech structure reduces the potential for memory loss, because audiences have a tendency to listen more carefully during the beginning and ending of a speech.[10] Basic speech structure is summarized in the outline in Figure 1–1.

### FIGURE 1–1 BASIC SPEECH STRUCTURE

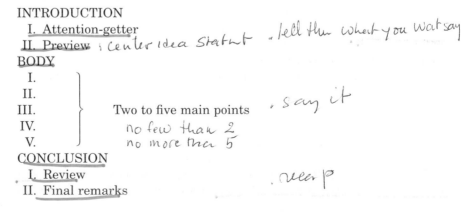

INTRODUCTION
  I. Attention-getter
  II. Preview *: Center idea Statmt* *"Tell them what you wat say*
BODY
  I.
  II.
  III.     Two to five main points *"say it*
  IV.       *no few than 2*
  V.        *no more than 5*
CONCLUSION
  I. Review
  II. Final remarks    *·reeap*

The organization of your main points is an ongoing process as you build your speech. You will start with a list of possible main points, arranged in what seems to you to be a logical and effective order. As you go through the research process and even, to a lesser extent, as you polish your final speech, you will be adapting your outline to your increased understanding of your topic. You might change points or the order of the points; you might divide them in some different way. You will go back and forth from research to outline, changing one from the other. You will probably present your speech from your finished outline, and that final outline will probably look quite different from its original version.

We will discuss organization in more detail in Chapter 8.

### Choosing Supporting Material

At this point you've completed your initial planning and most of your research. You've started to organize your ideas into a number of statements. In the formal analysis of public speeches, we call these statements "claims." A *claim* is an expressed opinion that the speaker would like the audience to accept. That acceptance usually depends on the material the speaker uses to support the claim. For example:

▼ Claim:  Returning students like me often feel out of place among younger classmates like most of you.

▼ Support:  An anecdote illustrating the claim

▼ Claim:  Besides the pay and tips, working in a local comedy club gives me plenty of jokes to tell.

▼ Support:  Tell jokes

▼ Claim:  Working for campus security has showed me that on-campus theft is a big problem.

▼ Support:  Statistics showing number and value of thefts

The main types of support are examples, statistics, and testimony. Definitions, descriptions, analogies, and anecdotes are also used to add substance to your claims. By "substance," we mean that your supporting material will be used to prove your arguments, to clarify your ideas, and to make them memorable and interesting.

We will discuss supporting material in more detail in Chapter 7.

### Finishing Touches  *Put together your intro sec 9*

The difference between a successful and an unsuccessful message is often a matter of perseverance. People who stick with the task until the speech is "right," until it "works," find success while those who give up prematurely don't. The three areas of finishing touches include preparing the introduction and conclusion, preparing visual aids, and practicing the speech.

### Introducing and Concluding

The introduction to a speech has to capture audience attention and give your audience an idea of what your speech is about. Simone Andrews, a student at New York University, began her self-introduction this way:

> I grew up in Los Angeles as a minority in a Mexican neighborhood. I have often been the only black child within my surroundings. One barrier that has hurt me, as significantly as any other, is the difficulty I have identifying with the community that society classifies me in: The African American community.[11]

Simone's introduction left no doubt what her speech was about. It grabbed her audience's attention with her startling statement about her problems relating to her ethnic community. It also set the mood and tone of the rest of her speech—her audience knew she was serious about what she was saying.

Your introduction is generally the last thing you prepare, because you can't preview what you're going to say before you've decided what that is. Your conclusion, on the other hand, will probably be the next-to-the-last thing you prepare. You want your conclusion to leave a powerful impression on your audience. This was Simone's conclusion:

> I still can't help but hear whispers from my past. But the blacks who call me whitewashed do so because they do not know me. I am not an Oreo. I am washed with many cultures and many ideas. My middle is not white but a combination of many colors, including one that I am proud to call my own.

Simone's conclusion leaves a strong impression. It also provides a sense of closure (letting the audience know the speech has come to an end) and repeats the main idea of her speech. We will discuss the functions and techniques of introductions and conclusions in more detail in Chapter 9.

### Making It Visual

Society's saturation with messages from the visual media has caused people to become much more visually oriented. Television viewers, filmgoers, magazine and newspaper readers, and browsers on the World Wide Web have become accustomed to ideas being backed up with high-impact visuals. One lesson from the media, therefore, is that a speech can be greatly enhanced by the use of visual aids. Visuals are especially useful for the first speech. Aside from being informative, they can take the audience's focus away from the speaker, which makes the speech less anxiety producing. Displaying them also gives you something to do with your hands and body. In a speech of self-introduction, you might consider visual aids like these:

▼ Slides of you involved in a favorite activity (the view from the top of the mountain at the ski resort, or that trophy picture of you at another exotic location).

▼ Demonstrations (actually performing a belly dance, juggling, or playing the saxophone).

▼ Models (like one of the cabin you built) or actual items (antique typewriters, or anything else you collect).

▼ Diagrams on posterboard (the route of last summer's bike race, or a map of that forest you got lost in).

▼ A chart on the chalkboard (showing the organization of your family or the division of your typical day).

We'll discuss visual aids in more detail in Chapter 10.

## Practicing Delivery

Your final step in speech preparation is to practice your delivery. One of the primary functions of practice is to enable you to come to terms with the stage fright that is a natural part of speaking.

You might have decided on a delivery style early on, or perhaps one was assigned. Most instructors will stress extemporaneous speaking.

An *extemporaneous* speech is planned in advance but presented in a direct, spontaneous manner. A speech presented extemporaneously will be researched, organized, and practiced in advance, but the exact wording of the entire speech will not be memorized. Because you speak from only brief, unobtrusive notes, you are able to move and maintain eye contact with your audience. Extemporaneous speaking is not

only the most effective type of delivery for a classroom speech, it is also the most common type of delivery in the "outside" world.

There are three other types of speeches that will be discussed in Chapter 11 on Delivery. An *impromptu* speech is given off the top of one's head, without preparation. If your instructor asks you to introduce yourself to the class during the first class period, this is the type of speech you will be giving. A *manuscript* speech is read word for word from a prepared text. Manuscript speeches are discouraged in most speech classes because of the lack of spontaneity and audience contact that usually result. A *memorized* speech—one learned by heart—is the most difficult and can result in even less spontaneity.

*No prepared*

*political media*

The best way to make sure that you are on your way to an effective delivery is to practice your speech repeatedly and systematically. The following rehearsal techniques are used by many speakers.

▼ To make arguments in my study and confute them is easy, where I answer myself, not an adversary.

Ben Johnson

1. Present the speech to yourself. "Talk through" the entire speech, including your examples and forms of support. In other words, you don't just say, "This is where I present my statistics"; you go ahead and present them just as you would during the speech.
2. Present the speech in front of a mirror, maintaining "eye contact" with yourself and watching your physical mannerisms. Admittedly, this technique is not for everyone.
3. Audiotape the speech, and listen to it. Because we hear our own voices partially through our cranial bone structure, we are sometimes surprised at what we sound like to others.
4. Videotape yourself giving the speech and, as you play the tape back, attempt to view it "objectively" as an audience member.
5. Present the speech in front of a small group of friends or relatives.
6. Present the speech to at least one listener in the same (or similar) room in which you will present the final speech.

Some of these techniques may be inappropriate for you; some people don't have access to video equipment and some feel downright silly talking to themselves in front of a mirror. But whatever technique you choose, practicing your speech is the most important step in controlling speech anxiety.

## ⬤ CONTROLLING SPEECH ANXIETY

Although speech anxiety is a common problem for many speakers, it is a problem that can be overcome. Interestingly enough, the first step in feeling less apprehensive about speaking is to realize that a certain amount of nervousness is not only natural but facilitative. That is, *facilitative* speech anxiety is a factor that can help improve your performance. Just as totally relaxed athletes or musicians aren't likely to perform at the top of their potential, speakers think more rapidly and express themselves more energetically when their level of tension is moderate.

It is only when the level of anxiety is intense that it becomes *debilitative,* inhibiting effective self-expression. Intense fear causes trouble in two ways. First, the strong emotion keeps you from thinking clearly.[12] Second, intense fear leads to an urge to do something, anything, to make the problem go away. This urge to escape often causes a speaker to speed up delivery, which results in a rapid, almost machine-gun style. As you can imagine, this boost in speaking rate leads to even more mistakes, which only adds to the speaker's anxiety. Thus, a relatively small amount of nervousness can begin to feed on itself until it grows into a serious problem. There are four fairly simple ways to overcome debilitative speech anxiety.

1. **Be Rational.** Listen to your thought processes, your internal voice, and try to figure out if the basis for your speech anxiety is rational. Then silently talk yourself out of any irrational beliefs. For example, it is irrational to believe you have to be perfect, or that everyone must approve of you, or that some type of catastrophe will result from your making a mistake in front of your classmates. It is also irrational to believe that your classmates aren't just as nervous as you are.

2. **Be Receiver-Oriented.** Concentrate on your audience rather than on yourself. Some experts suggest that you visualize the audience members in their underwear, to make them less intimidating.[13] Our suggestion is to worry about whether the audience members are interested, about whether they understand, and about whether you are maintaining human contact with them. You might find that most of your anxiety is based on an unnecessary (and basically unhealthy) self-absorption.

3. **Be Positive.** It is important to build and maintain a positive attitude toward your audience, your speech, and yourself as a speaker. Some communication consultants suggest that public speakers should concentrate on three statements immediately before speaking. The three statements are:

   > I'm glad I'm here.
   > I know my topic.
   > I care about you. ("You" being the audience.)

Keeping these ideas in mind can help you maintain a positive attitude. Another technique for building a positive attitude is known as *visualization.* This technique has been used successfully with athletes. It requires you to visualize the successful completion of a specific speech assignment.[14] You do this by taking a moment before your speech to close your eyes and picture yourself as a speaker. Visualize yourself from the perspective of an audience member as you present a confident, self-assured speech, achieving the desired audience response.

▼ There is no "secret" to being a successful communicator—just prepare, know your subject and care.

Leo Buscaglia

4. Be Prepared. If you are fully prepared, your speech will represent less of a threat.[15] Devote enough time to each step of speech preparation so that you can feel secure in your content and organization. And when it comes time to give your presentation, keep in mind that nervousness is normal. Expect it, and remember that its symptoms—even shaky knees and trembling hands—are more obvious to you than they are to the audience. Beginning public speakers, when congratulated for their poise during a speech, are apt to make such remarks as "Are you kidding? I was *dying* up there."

These four guidelines will enable most speakers to control their speech anxiety to the point where it will be facilitative rather than debilitative. We will discuss speech anxiety in more detail in Chapter 11, on style.

### ● LISTENING AND CRITICISM

The nervousness that you feel when you speak is the same nervousness that your classmates will feel. You can help them do their best by listening attentively during their speeches. Concentrate, take notes, and show them that you are listening by sitting up, looking at them and generally *looking* like you are interested. At the end of the speech you may have the opportunity to offer criticism; remember that "criticism" in this sense means what was done *right* as well as what was done *wrong*. In fact, most instructors suggest that students should precede each negative criticism with a positive criticism, and then follow it with another positive criticism. Chapter 2 will explore the concepts of listening and constructive criticism in greater detail.

### ● SAMPLE SPEECH

The sample speech for this chapter was prepared by Pearlita Peters, a student at Brooklyn College in New York City. She was asked to introduce herself to her class.

At first, Pearlita was reticent to expose much about herself, because her cultural background was different from that of most of her classmates. Eventually, however, she decided that this difference could work in her favor.

For research, she asked a few friends and family members what they considered unique about her. She then researched some of the history of her religious background, to make sure that whatever she told her class would be based in fact. She also tried to meet as many of her classmates as she could, so she could approach her own culture without offending theirs.

## ● Don't Call Them Dreadlocks

Pearlita Peters

Brooklyn College, New York

[1] My name is Pearlita Peters. I'm a dual major, in English and African Studies. I'm originally from the Caribbean island of Montserrat, a tiny island where everyone knows everyone else. I'm the youngest of three children, the daughter of a registered nurse who is a self-supporting single mom. My mother could serve as a role model for any female who believes in self-sufficiency.

[2] Following my mother's example, I am very independent. I live on my own, work, attend school, and still manage to spend time with my friends.

[3] I suppose in many ways I am much like you. I am a sister of Theta Phi Beta Sorority, an elected member of Brooklyn College's Student Government, a reporter for the *Brooklyn College Excelsior* newspaper. I love music: calypso, reggae, and African drum rhythms. I love to dance.

[4] In some ways, though, I am different. I am sure you've noticed, for example, that I am nearly six feet tall. You've probably also noticed that my hair is locked. I call it "locked" because I don't like the term "dreadlocks." I don't like the negative connotation of the word "dread." I wear it this way because I am Rastafari.

[5] Rastafarianism began on the island of Jamaica in the 1930s. It was inspired, in part, by Marcus Garvey's movement to reunite former slaves with their African culture. Rastafarians follow the tenets of the Ethiopian Orthodox church, which is a Christian church. Our name comes from the man who was crowned emperor of Ethiopia in 1930, whom the world knew as Haile Selassie. His original name was Ras Tafari.

[6] Rastafarianism is both a social movement and a religion. It is a social movement in the sense that members of mainstream society are straying from the "norm" to create their own community. The movement stresses economic independence. For instance, at the age of 19 I manage a very successful store specializing in Rasta merchandise—everything from the type of clothes I'm wearing now to the latest reggae music. The store is Rasta-owned. When I finish my education, I will look forward to opening my own business and being successful at it.

[7] Most people know Rastafarians only as the originators of reggae music. They see us, I'm afraid, as strange and mysterious people. I assure you, I am not strange. And the mysteriousness is easily explained when you understand the background and philosophy of Rastafarianism.

[8] Much of what we do is related to our cultural and spiritual identification with Africa. The "dreadlocks," for example, are modeled after those of the ancient Abyssinians. Rasta women are often referred to as "queen" or "princess," and men are called "king" or "prince," as a reminder of the royalty of our African ancestors. Some of our speech patterns are more modern, but are based on the objective of increasing pride and self-esteem among Africans of all types. For example, as a reminder of the importance of the individual we stress and sometimes repeat the word "I," referring to ourselves as "I & I" and using "I" when English grammar would require the word "me." We also avoid words that suggest subjugation, such as "under."

[9] So I & I hope you overstand I.

[10] Actually, I don't use those speech patterns when I'm away from my Rasta community. After all, I'm an English major. And there are other customs within the Rasta religion that I don't follow, either. Marijuana, which we call "ganga," is smoked as a religious tradition, much like the Native Americans smoke peace pipes. However, I don't smoke marijuana.

[11] Rastafarianism is a fairly new religion, as religions go. It is constantly changing and growing, but at its basis is a sense of community and identity. As I learn more about the other members of this class, I am amazed at the wide range of cultures and beliefs that we represent. I hope this brief introduction—to me, and to Rastafarianism—will encourage more of this type of understanding, and the tolerance that comes with it.

### ⬡ SUMMARY

We study public speaking today for the same reason the ancients did: to succeed in careers, to develop personally, and to make democracy work. But the media/information age has changed public speaking: In some ways, such as in the degeneration of audience attention spans, the media have made public speaking more difficult. In other ways, such as by providing models of visual effectiveness, the media have made public speaking easier. In all ways, however, public speaking has become more important in the media/information age. It is through public speaking that we make human contact with a specific audience, presenting a message that is tailored to their specific needs.

There are three areas to keep in mind for speech preparation. Within the area of initial planning, you have to choose a topic, define a purpose, and analyze the speech situation. Within the area of rough construction, you perform research, organize and outline, and choose effective supporting material. Within the area of finishing touches, you construct an introduction and conclusion, you consider the possibility of visual aids, and you practice your presentation. You will often move back and forth within the areas, and often you will find yourself doing two or three of these tasks at once. They are all necessary, however, to the successful completion of an effective speech. Each of these steps is introduced briefly in this chapter, and will be discussed in depth in subsequent chapters of this book.

## ▼ EXERCISES

1. In a free speech democracy, speakers are constantly trying to sway us toward a particular point of view. How good are you at discerning their effectiveness? Tape any television talk show that deals with a social issue. The issue might be women's rights, racism, sexism, civil disobedience, or any of a wealth of issues that are dealt with every day, sometimes responsibly, sometimes not. Of the "spokespeople" speaking on either side of the issue, which ones are effective and which are not? What criteria will you use to determine their effectiveness?

2. As you work on your first speech, keep a journal of the process. Which of the steps in the process were easiest for you? Which skills do you need to work on? As a guide, answer the following questions:

   I. Initial Planning
      A. Did you choose an effective topic, and/or an effective approach?
      B. Did you fulfill your purpose?
      C. Did you consider your audience members and adapt your speech to them?
   II. Rough Construction
      A. Did you do research? Was there any other research you *could* have done that would have made the speech more effective?
      B. Was the speech well organized? Did you use an outline in your preparation and presentation?
      C. Did you choose effective supporting material?
   III. Finishing Touches
      A. Were you satisfied with your introduction and conclusion? If not, how could you have made them more effective?

    B. Did you use a visual aid? If not, is there a visual that might have made your speech more effective?

    C. Did you practice your delivery? Were you satisfied with the final product?

**3.** It's not an easy thing to confront any type of fear. We tend to repress the causes of our fear and refuse to recognize them. In turn, this makes fears mysterious and difficult to overcome. As you prepare to give your speech, keep a journal in which you explore the root causes of your own speech anxiety: Perhaps these causes include some previous negative experience, or irrational thinking, or an inherent personality trait.

# NOTES

1. The 1994 survey by the publisher of this book confirms several other surveys made in recent years.

2. See, for example, Dan B. Curtis, Jerry L. Winsor, and Ronald D. Stephens, "National Preferences in Business and Communication Education," *Communication Education* 38 (January 1989), p. 11. Employment managers were asked which characteristics were most important in their hiring decisions. Out of a long list, oral communication skills ranked first. See also Richard Nelson Bolles, *What Color is Your Parachute? A Practical Manual for Job Hunters and Career Changers* (Berkeley, Calif.: Ten Speed Press, 1995).

3. See, for example, David Sharp, "Send in the Crowds," *Health* 6 (April 1992), pp. 66–70; or Kerry J. Rottenberger, "Can Anyone Become a More Effective Communicator?" *Sales and Marketing Management* 144 (August 1992), pp. 60–63.

4. Barbara Lyne, "The Executive Life," *The New York Times,* Business section, January 31, 1993.

5. We don't have the space here to fully develop the important relationship between communication skills and personal growth, but we invite you to read further in Ronald B. Adler and George Rodman, *Understanding Human Communication,* 6th ed. (Fort Worth: Harcourt Brace, 1997). See especially Chapters 2, 6, and 7.

6. It is one of the biases of this book that we live in an imperfect world and that problems will always exist. But in a functioning society we work on these problems, constantly seeking ways to solve them.

7. "Fred Rogers' Heroes: Who's Helping America's Children?" PBS television production, September, 1994.

8. Brian Steinberg, "Adding Some Prime-Time Sizzle to Product Safety," *New York Times,* September 11, 1994, p. F4.

9. R. G. Nichols, "Factors in Listening Comprehension," *Speech Monographs* 15 (1948), pp. 154–163.

10. See, for example, L. Stern, *The Structures and Strategies of Human Memory* (Homewood, Ill.: The Dorsey Press, 1985). See also C. Turner, "Organizing Information: Principles and Practices," *Library Journal* (June 15, 1987).

11. Crosscultural Communication classroom presentation at New York University, Spring 1995.

12. J. Borhis and M. Allen, "Meta-Analysis of the Relationship between Communication Apprehension and Cognitive Performance," *Communication Education* 41 (January 1992), pp. 68–76. This study demonstrated that there is a negative relationship between communication apprehension and cognitive performance (I.Q. tests, grade-point averages, course grades, assignment grades, and test scores).

13. See, for example, Ron Huff, *I Can See You Naked* (Kansas City, Mo.: Andrews & McMeel, 1992).

14. J. Ayres and T. S. Hopf, "Visualization: A Means of Reducing Speech Anxiety," *Communication Education* 34 (October 1985), pp. 318–323. See also S. Zarrow, "Picture Yourself Successful: Visualization Works," *Prevention,* March 1990, pp. 16–17.

15. Kent Menzel and Lori Carrell, "The Relationship Between Preparation and Performance in Public Speaking," *Communication Education* 43 (January 1994), pp. 17–26.

# CRITICAL LISTENING AND CONSTRUCTIVE CRITICISM

## ◉ CHAPTER 2 OBJECTIVES

**After reading this chapter, you should understand:**

1. How living in a media-saturated world affects your listening habits and skills.
2. That listening is an active process that requires effort.
3. That listening can be improved through study, practice, and awareness.

**You should be able to:**

1. Recognize and resist the causes of your own ineffective listening, using the methods outlined in this chapter.
2. Use the criteria in this chapter to evaluate speeches effectively.
3. Communicate your evaluation of another's speech in a way that is clear, accurate, and likely to be well received.

Jason was having trouble listening to today's lecture. He had a feeling he had forgotten something. He thought back to that morning.

He had awakened to the sound of his favorite station on the clock radio. He punched the "snooze" button and tried to get back to his dream, which had something to do with Cindy Crawford and Alicia Silverstone fighting over him.

Later, he stumbled into the kitchen, poured a cup of Folgers, and turned on the TV to catch the weather report. Smelling of Lever 2000 and wearing his best outfit from The Gap, Jason ran to the bus, found a seat, and plugged into his Walkman to enjoy his favorite tapes.

On his way into class, he picked up *USA Today* to catch last night's sports scores. After his second class Jason went to the student union with his girlfriend, Meagan, to catch *All My Children*. He calls it "Meagan's soap opera," even though he got hooked on it long ago and now looks forward to the daily installments more than she does. They had plans to study afterwards, but a "teaser" for the next program caught Meagan's attention, so they stayed to watch it. Jason barely had time to get to the class that he was sitting in now. And then he remembered: He forgot to set his VCR to automatically record David Letterman last night!

Now what was his professor saying? . . .

▼ Great ideas, it has been said, come into the world as gently as doves. Perhaps, then, if we listen attentively, we shall hear amid the uproar of empires and nations a faint flutter of winds, the gentle stirring of life and hope.

Albert Camus

## ● THE EFFECTS OF MEDIA ON LISTENING

Jason is exposed to an enormous number of messages during his media-saturated day. He has absorbed some of them, but he has ignored or forgotten many times more. He is often confused about details and even the main ideas of some of the messages he's heard. Did that health report on TV say Mexican food was bad for you? Or was that Italian food? He also knows bits and pieces of information without being completely sure where they came from. When he tells Meagan about a new software program he's heard about, he can't tell her *where* he heard about it.

Today's media saturation creates some listening problems with which people of earlier times didn't have to contend. Many of the messages to which Jason has been exposed have been designed for listeners and viewers with limited attention spans. In fact, throughout his life, from *Sesame Street* to MTV, he has been watching fast-paced programs made up of short segments with flashy production values, programming designed to capture his attention without much effort on his part. Perhaps the main effect of Jason's message-filled lifestyle, then, is that he has become passive in his reception. Each message was appealing, but there were just too many of them for him to make conscious choices about what

▼ We can communicate an idea around the world in seconds but it sometimes takes years for an idea to get through 1/4 inch of human skull.

Charles Kettering

to retain and what to let go. He just lets them all flow over him, leaving retention pretty much to fate and osmosis.

Most of the messages that we are exposed to today are designed by highly paid professionals. These messages are designed to encourage passive, uncritical listening. When it comes time to actively listen, to apply critical thinking to what is heard, many people today aren't equipped for it.

Listening deficiencies are a real problem when you consider how much time is spent listening. Research shows that most people communicate in some form about 80 percent of the time they are awake. For college students, about 60 percent to 70 percent of that time is spent listening.[1] A large proportion of our time is spent listening to professional communicators telling us who to vote for, what to buy, and generally how to live our lives. Obviously, it is important to learn how to listen *well* and to listen *critically*.[2] However, even though we spend a great amount of time listening, study after study suggests that we are not very good at it. For example, research suggests that the average person takes in only half of what he or she hears.[3]

It's a shame, when you think about it. There are so many advantages to good listening. In addition to making the best political, consumer, and

# Calvin and Hobbes by Bill Watterson

lifestyle decisions, good listeners are more popular (they are usually more in demand at gatherings than those who consider themselves the life of the party). They are also able to learn more, and they are more successful in their chosen professions.[4] For example, medical doctors who are good listeners have the most satisfied patients,[5] and are sued less for malpractice.[6] In any profession, from business management to creative writing, the best listeners tend to be the most successful. Perhaps most relevant to our purposes, students who are good listeners tend to get higher grades.

Unfortunately, there is no human behavior that is so difficult to do well yet so easy to fake. We fake listening to think about other things: What are you going to do after class? Will you ever finish that project you started? Does your significant other truly love you, or is this just a college dalliance? There are so many things to think about, and the easiest place to steal thinking time is in a nice, anonymous audience. Between media and the classroom, you spend a large amount of time as part of one audience or another. After a while, you learn how to look like you're listening when you aren't—you can keep your eyes wide open, your smile pasted on, your head nodding in more or less the right direction. This habit is especially unfortunate in a public speaking class, where listening critically to others' speeches will enable you to improve your own. As part of an audience in a public speaking class, you are entitled to be selfish; you have the right to seek out and take away from a speech ideas to improve your own speaking. In fact, it is your responsibility to do so. If you listen with what one expert calls "enlightened self-interest," you will probably become a better speaker as you become a better listener.[7]

Evaluating others' speeches in order to improve your own is, admittedly, a "selfish" objective. Nevertheless, the feedback that you give as both a selfish and a critical listener (sitting up, looking interested, looking back at the speaker) will help the speaker present a better speech. As

▼ No one cares to speak to an unwilling listener. An arrow never lodges in a stone: often it recoils upon the sender of it.

St. Jerome

Ralph Nichols, one of the pioneers in the field of listening, points out, "Nearly all of us have unconsciously developed a special set of senses that, in effect, measure the way people listen when we talk to them."[8] He sums it up this way: "The more we take from the speaker through listening, the more that speaker will give."[9] Anyone can learn to be a better listener. The first step is to understand the causes of ineffective listening.

## ● CAUSES OF INEFFECTIVE LISTENING

The problems associated with poor listening include *message overload, rapid thought, assuming message content, prejudice,* and *cultural attitudes.*

### Message Overload

*Message overload* is the mental exhaustion and confusion that sometimes occurs because of that glut of messages we mentioned earlier. The symptoms of message overload are probably familiar to you. They include that numb feeling you get when you try to read and carry on a conversation simultaneously, or study and pay attention to a TV drama. Perhaps more to the point, the symptoms include that buzz that you feel when you sit in a lecture after cramming all night for a test in another class.

There is only so much material that can be stored in either long-term or short-term memory. When you go beyond that capacity, trying to take in new information causes anxiety that is counterproductive to effective listening.

### Rapid Thought

Even though message overload might make you confused about the information you have stored, you have the capacity to think about it rapidly. Sometimes your thoughts are *too* rapid, jumping from one concept to the next, before you have had time to make sense of the first one. This tendency toward rapid thought makes listening to speeches especially difficult. Whereas you probably have the ability to *think* at the rate of 500 to 800 words per minute, on average speakers *speak* at only 150 words per minute.[10] This gap between thinking speed and speaking speed is usually detrimental to listening, because you have a tendency to start wandering off mentally in some direction other than the speaker's topic.[11]

### Making Assumptions

One thing people do with their excess thinking time during a speech is to make assumptions about what they are about to hear, rather than listen

▼ It is the province of knowledge to speak and it is the privilege of wisdom to listen.

Oliver Wendell Holmes

for new content. You might, for example, assume that the content will be too difficult. On the other hand, you might assume that it's too easy, that you've heard it all before. You might assume that the content won't be interesting, or that it won't relate to you personally. You also might assume that the speaker will say something wrong or inaccurate.

It is interesting to note that the more you know someone, the more likely you are to assume you know what he or she is going to say. This attitude becomes a factor in a public speaking class, in which you typically get to know your classmates fairly well. If a classmate speaks on the lighter side of things for most of the term, you might assume he's not being serious in one of his final speeches and fail to hear all that he has to tell you. You might have the same type of problem with another classmate who seemed only interested in one topic area—sports, fashion, media, computers—for the entire semester.

### Prejudicial Judgments

There are two types of prejudicial judgments: those based on cultural stereotyping, and those based on personal biases.

Prejudicial judgments that are based on cultural stereotyping are often made because of unconscious attitudes. These attitudes would be embarrassing to admit to consciously; they are deep-seated feelings that people who are different are somehow inferior, and therefore have nothing to say that will be of interest. There is also an element of fear in cultural prejudice: People fear what is different, and therefore feel threatened and act defensively toward someone who looks, dresses, talks, or thinks differently.

Other prejudicial judgments are based on dislike of an individual, rather than an entire culture. Perhaps someone's behavior has been generally obnoxious, or you take exception to the way someone has treated you, personally.

Prejudicial judgments lead to defensive listening, which is essentially the practice of "setting traps," in which people listen not for the main points but to details that they can refute. Noted psychologist Carl Rogers had defensive listening in mind when he said, "Most people are afraid to listen because what they hear might make them change."[12]

### Cultural Attitudes Toward Speaking and Listening

A second cultural bias that affects listening is the perception that, in our culture, talking has more apparent advantages. Talking is associated with intelligence, leadership, and power, whereas listening is mistakenly associated with passivity and inferiority. The reality, of course, is just the opposite; the most intelligent and powerful leaders are usually the best listeners.

##  IMPROVING LISTENING

The preceding problems do not make listening impossible. They do, however, make listening more difficult than we usually think it is. Keep in mind that *listening is an active process. It requires effort.* You don't just sit there and wait for it to happen. Five methods help make listening happen: being prepared, controlling distractions, withholding judgment, taking notes, and taking advantage of the thought/speech differential.

### Be Prepared to Listen

Some of the techniques involved in "being prepared to listen" might seem obvious. When you are listening as part of a college course or for an important business meeting, you should bring a pen and paper with you and be ready to take notes; when you're listening for *any* reason, you should have had enough sleep the night before so that you can remain mentally sharp.

One long-term way to prepare to listen is to work at improving your listening ability. The first step in this process of improvement is to be aware of your strengths and weaknesses as a listener. As a rule, do you concentrate well, or does your mind tend to wander? In what situations have you shown yourself to be a good listener, and in which situations could you use improvement?

You can improve your listening ability in a number of ways. You can *practice* listening by exposing yourself to challenging messages. Some experts suggest that you practice by listening to audiotapes of books.[13] Discussing complex topics with friends, attending lectures, and tuning in to documentaries on public radio and TV are all ways that you can exercise and improve your ability to listen.

Another way to prepare to listen is to find out what the topic of a speech will be and then do some reading or thinking about it in advance. If you know you are going to attend a seminar on "navigating on the Internet," for example, you might want to read up on the Internet and other routes of the information highway, or you might want to think about your own needs and how they might be met by using the Internet. This will give you the structure, perspective, and questions that help make for good listening.

Finally, you can prepare to listen by building up a positive attitude about listening. Remember, many speech topics might sound boring until you carefully listen to the speech itself. One recent college graduate entered the police academy and was surprised when he saw his classmate's reactions to a lecturer speaking about the counseling services that are available to police officers. The other recruits considered counseling a sign of weakness; they seemed to believe that police officers should be able to deal with their own ordeals. The recent grad used the listening skills that he had learned in his communication classes, and he left the lecture with information about the risks of alcoholism, depression, and suicide that could someday help him save lives.

## Control Distractions

Distractions can be either internal (within the listener's mind) or external (within the environment).[14] An effective listener has to make a conscious effort to overcome distractions, whether they be internal in the form of daydreams or personal worries, or external in any of its forms: the sound of a book closing, a whiff of cologne, or the sight of a speaker tripping over the podium on the way to the front of the room.

You can minimize the effect of some distractions by planning for them in advance. Recognize those distractions, both internal and external, that you can predict. Are you worried about your neighbors' complaints that your cat has been befouling their children's sandbox? Make a mental note of that worry, and resolve to concentrate on the speech instead. Do you have a social interest in one of your classmates? Make a mental note of that, too. Do you have a cold? Mental note: "possible sniffles." Just recognizing these distractions helps you to fight them. And, of course, you can take preventive action against some of them: If you have the sniffles, for example, you can take a sinus remedy before the speech starts.

Once you recognize potential distractions, you can *compartmentalize* them. In other words, put them away, into a separate compartment of your consciousness, and say to yourself, "I'll think about them later. For now I am going to concentrate on this speech."

## Withhold Judgment

▼ The human mind treats a new idea the way the body treats a strange protein; it rejects it.

Biologist P. B. Medawar

▼ It takes two to speak the truth—one to speak and another to hear.

Henry David Thoreau

As we mentioned earlier, evaluation is an integral part of the critical listening process. The listening process can be cut short, however, if evaluation takes place before understanding is complete. In other words, to listen effectively you should not judge too quickly. For example, you should not let your *initial* evaluation of the topic get in the way of comprehending a speech. Psychologist Carl Rogers has suggested that human beings have a natural tendency to evaluate a message before they hear all of it.[15] To truly listen you should withhold your evaluation of the message until your comprehension is complete.

To prevent premature evaluation, keep three things in mind: First, *do not dismiss a topic as "uninteresting" until you have heard all that the speaker has to say.* Some topics just do not sound interesting at first, but if looked at closely enough they can become fascinating. This was true for a speech given by Carol Rigolot, the executive director of the Humanities Council at Princeton University. One objective of the Humanities Council is to encourage an appreciation of the liberal arts in students of all levels. To this end, Dr. Rigolot traveled to Tulsa, Oklahoma, to speak to a group of high school students. The topic of her speech, "Why Read Books in an Age of Television," elicited groans from some of the students, who seemed to believe that they had heard all this before. The good listeners in the audience, however, soon found much to be interested in, as some of their notes on the lecture showed:

*60% of adult Americans have never read a book!*

*"We see what we have learned to expect is there." (Early Europeans missed the Crab Supernova.)*

*Minds can be conditioned to see "the widest variety of possibilities."*

*Literature gives us perspective...and a language to articulate our feelings.*

*Reality is plural and complex; we do not have sufficient perspective on our defeats. "Your dilemma has already been lived."*

*We're changing: from industrial to information society. Information doubles every eight years or less. Books are great organizers of this information.*

For this and any other speech, the key is to ask "What is of interest in this topic?" rather than "Is this topic interesting?" The difference between those two questions is crucial, because the first one presupposes that there will be *something* of interest if you listen closely enough. It might be the human side of the story, it might be something that relates to your own life, or it might be something that operates as a metaphor for life in general.

Remember also that the things that will be of interest to you might not emerge until the speaker is well into the presentation. For example, "The Budget Deficit" is a topic we've heard so much about that we might assume it would bore us. However, if we were to listen carefully to a well-researched speech on this topic, the possibility that this deficit might bring about the bankruptcy of our federal government could bring the topic to life. The possibility that, if left unchecked, it could bring about the end of the United States as we know it, might make the topic riveting.

Second, *keep your criticism of the speaker separate from your criticism of the speech*. Recognition of the speaker's delivery or physical appearance will be of use to you in improving your own speeches, but if you hold these things against a speaker you might "turn off" and miss the substance of what is being said. Do not let your feelings about the speaker interfere with your comprehension of the message.

Finally, *respect the speaker as a source of information.* Research shows that listening is measurably affected by the respect we feel for the speaker.[16] The more respect we feel, the better we listen. If you *don't* make a conscious effort to respect the speaker, you'll either fail to pay attention or you will argue mentally with everything that is said.

Take the case of the "class nerd." Every class has at least one. These studious nonconformists, who are often more withdrawn than other class members, might seem like complete social failures. But when they get up to talk about the area of their expertise, be it computers, electronics, or macrobiotic cooking, the results can be enlightening—if you can summon the respect that is necessary to truly hear what these speakers have to say.

Dismissing ideas you don't agree with is a problem that is made worse by today's media saturation. There are so many messages that some of them tend to contradict one another, making it easier to close our minds to new and different points of view than to wade through the glut and figure out what is true and meaningful.

The next method for enhancing listening, taking notes, will also help you to withhold evaluation and control distractions.

## Take Notes

▼ He listens well who takes notes.

Dante Alighieri
*The Devine Comedy*

Notetaking is not the norm in many types of listening. It would seem out of place to jot down the main ideas of a friend's problems when she's pouring them out to you, or to take note of interesting details in a church sermon. Notetaking in the classroom, however, especially the public speaking classroom, is essential.

Notetaking in the public speaking classroom is essential because, as several research studies have pointed out, one of the primary problems in ineffective listening is allowing insignificant details to distract you from the main points of the speech.[17] We've all experienced this type of distraction: While listening to a proposed local ordinance about noise control, you become sidetracked when leaf blowers (a particular gripe of yours) are mentioned. Or in a biography of our current president, you become distracted by a comment about his eating habits and miss the comments about his political philosophy.

To keep from being distracted by details you should "compartmentalize," as we suggested in our earlier discussion about controlling distractions. One way to compartmentalize is to jot down notes on various aspects of the speech that will help you remember it later. That way, you can critically evaluate the speech as a whole (as a group of related main ideas) rather than distracting details.

Along with the main ideas, you can jot down the details that you consider important and interesting as well as questions that you might want to ask at the end of the speech. Questions are particularly important in critical listening, because critical thinking is a process of asking questions: Does this make sense? Is this backed up with evidence? Is the evidence valid? It is impossible to keep all these matters in your head and listen at the same time. If you record them in notes you can keep your mind on what is being said *when* it is being said.[18] If the speaker does not answer your questions in the course of the speech, ask for clarification during the question-and-answer period.

Because your first responsibility is to listen to the speaker, it is important to keep your notes brief. Notetaking is not the same thing as *transcribing,* or writing word for word. If you take down too much you will be writing when you should be listening, which will be distracting for both you and the speaker. Listen for general ideas, jot them down briefly, and return your attention as quickly as possible to the speaker. You should write only enough to jog your memory at the end of the speech.

Sometimes you have to figure out general ideas from everything the speaker says. More often, though, the speaker will make a generalization about the idea before developing it. In fact, a well-organized speech will preview its main points in the introduction. This is what Ryan Siskow, a student at the University of Northern Iowa, did in his speech on how medical records are not kept confidential by hospitals. Part of his introduction went like this:

> In the effort to examine this threat to our medical confidentiality, we'll first look at how that confidence may be breached; we'll then look at how those threats make each of us vulnerable; and finally, we'll consider some solutions that may put an end to such intrusions.[19]

With an introduction like this, you could jot down the main points immediately, leaving room on the page to take notes on the ways these points are developed:

*Main Ideas*

*Confidentiality of Medical Records*

I. *How It's Breached*

II. *How We're Vulnerable*

III. *Solutions*

There are many methods of taking notes. Ralph Nichols, for example, suggests a split-page format, with "facts" on one side and "principles" on the other.[20] Other methods commonly used in speech classes include taking notes on an outline provided by the speaker and taking notes on a speech criticism form provided by the instructor (see p. 40 for an example of such a form). Many people use an apparently random method, drawing lines and symbols of their own choosing to keep track of ideas. The method of notetaking that you use is not terribly important. Research in the field of listening suggests that the best listeners know several different styles of notetaking, and they use the one that's most appropriate for a particular speech.[21] So use whatever method you like, but take notes.

## Make the Thought/Speech Differential Work for You ✗

Listening experts suggest a number of techniques for turning the gap between thinking speed and speaking speed into an advantage rather than a disadvantage.[22] Notetaking is one of them. Here are three more techniques:

1. Anticipate the speaker's ideas. It is sometimes helpful to think ahead of the speaker, to see whether you can predict the general direction in which the speech will move. If you find your mind wandering, you can make a game of it: See whether you can predict what the next point will be. Many jurors in criminal trials find this to be a useful tactic, because the defense and the prosecution will try to drum in their basic arguments by repeating them incessantly. Each witness will be asked to repeat those items that each side wants the jury to hear. The attentive juror, therefore, will anticipate each side's arguments and see if they are covered in a predictable sequence ("Okay, here's where they'll establish motive  . . ." "Here's where he'll remind us that this guy had a girlfriend and a gun collection . . ." In some of the longer trials, anticipating the speaker's ideas seems to be the only way to maintain both your consciousness and your sanity.

2. *"Fill in the blanks"* with your own ideas. When the speaker makes a point, expand on it, in your mind, from your own point of view. One way to do this is to add to the point with examples or other supporting material from your own experience. Some experts suggest that you fill in the blanks by "painting a mental picture" of what is heard.[23] Others suggest that you fill in the blanks with some critical thinking about what the speaker really means, by reading the nonverbal behavior of the speaker. Does the speaker's posture suggest deception? Are there voice patterns or mannerisms that suggest a lack of belief or confidence in the ideas being presented? Another way to use critical thinking to fill in the blanks is to think about the speaker's motivations, especially if there's some vagueness lurking.

   Political speeches tend to be good places for filling in the blanks as a listening technique. For example, Vice President Albert Gore has a rather slow, deliberate speaking style that some people find difficult to stay tuned to. In his 1992 vice-presidential debate with Dan Quayle (George Bush's running mate) and James Stockdale (Ross Perot's running mate), Gore first said it was a pleasure for him to be in Atlanta, and then he continued as follows:

> It's also a pleasure to be with my two opponents this evening. Admiral Stockdale, may I say it's a special honor to share this stage with you; those of us who served in Vietnam looked at you as a national hero even before you were awarded the Congressional Medal of Honor. And Mr. Vice President, Dan, if I may, it was 16 years ago that you and I went to the Congress on the very first day together. I'll make you a deal this evening: If you don't try to compare George Bush to Harry Truman I won't compare you to Jack Kennedy.[24]

That passage contains a lot of potential blanks to fill in. Among other things, Gore's motivation was to remind the audience that (1) he was a Vietnam veteran, whereas Quayle had avoided service there by joining the National Guard; (2) George Bush had been comparing himself to Harry Truman, a Democrat, on the campaign trail; and (3) Dan Quayle had been attacked in a debate during the previous campaign when his opponent told him, "You're no Jack Kennedy." If you were filling in all those motivations, Gore's slow speaking speed would actually enhance, rather than interfere with, your critical listening.

**3.** *Summarize* the speaker's ideas. A third way to make up for the thought/speech differential is to review in your mind the ideas that have been covered so far. You can, of course, consult your notes for this purpose, or you can review the speaker's main ideas mentally.

To return to our previous example, the 1992 vice-presidential debates went on for 90 minutes and sometimes, through interruptions and non sequiturs, became rather confusing. However, at many points during that debate you might have summarized the candidates' main ideas as follows:

Dan Quayle: Bill Clinton can't be trusted.
Albert Gore: President Bush's economic policies have been failures.
James Stockdale: Who am I? Why am I here?

By reviewing these main ideas, you would not only help yourself keep track of them, you could anticipate each candidate's development of these ideas and his opponents' rebuttal of them.

## OFFERING CONSTRUCTIVE CRITICISM be (+)

Critical listening results in well-reasoned opinions about what you have heard. In a public speaking class, you will usually be asked to

▼ A true critic ought to dwell rather upon excellencies than imperfections.

Joseph Addison

▼ A new idea is delicate. It can be killed by a sneer or a yawn, it can be stabbed to death by a quip and worried to death by a frown on a brow.

Charles Brower

communicate these opinions to the speaker. In fact, one of the traditional responsibilities of a member of a public speaking class is to offer constructive criticism of others' speeches.

We say that criticism is "constructive" when it helps the speaker improve. Constructive criticism depends on the critic's genuinely helpful attitude, and on that critic's skill in conveying suggestions in a way that the listener can understand and appreciate. There are three things to keep in mind when offering this type of criticism: be positive, be nonjudgmental, and be substantive.

### Be Positive

When we advise you to be positive in order to make criticism constructive, we mean that you have to point out what is *right* with the speech as well as what is *wrong* with it. There are at least two reasons for this advice. The first stems from learning theory: If you don't tell the speaker what was done right, you run the risk of extinguishing the *effective* aspects of that speaker's behavior.

The second reason we need to be positive is that purely negative criticism is often useless, because the speaker might become defensive and block out your criticism completely. It is a good idea, therefore, to offer your positive criticisms first, and then tactfully offer your suggestions for improvement. For example, rather than saying

"Your ideas about _____ were completely unclear and unsupported,"

you might say

"I really enjoyed your explanation of _____. It was clearly stated and well backed up with examples and details. Your explanation of _____ , however, left me a little confused. It might

# Calvin and Hobbes
### by Bill Watterson

be my own fault, but it just did not seem to be as well supported as the rest of your speech."

Some experts recommend a "plus-minus-plus" technique in offering criticism.[25] With this technique, you create a kind of "criticism sandwich" by pointing out something positive about the speech before *and* after the negative criticism.

To encourage constructive criticism, many instructors have their students use a speech evaluation form like the one in Figure 2–1. Notice especially the first two open-ended questions on the form: You are asked to discuss what was right with the speech before you go into what was wrong.

Your instructor might prefer a different evaluation form, or you might want to amend this one to your liking. Whatever type of form you use, make sure it allows for positive as well as negative criticism.

## Be Nonjudgmental

The second thing you have to be concerned with in constructive criticism is being nonjudgmental. Being nonjudgmental means making your critical statements in such a way that they do not provoke a defensive response. Three techniques are suggested for this:

**1.** *Be specific.* Use actual examples from the speech to suggest ways that the speaker might improve. Rather than saying, "You tend to use jargon and incomprehensible terms," say, "You used the terms _____ and _____ in your speech, and while I was trying to figure out what those terms meant, I missed what you said next. Are there more common terms you could use for those concepts?"

Once way to be specific in speech criticism is to concentrate on the speaker's behavior, rather than personality. You do this by centering your remarks on what the speaker *did* rather than what he or she *is*. This will keep you away from the dangerous area of personality traits, such as the speaker's intelligence, reasoning, and organizational skills. For example, rather than say,

"You are intellectually sloppy, especially in your use of statistics."

you would say,

"In your conclusion you said the problem costs us billions, but later you said millions. Could you clear that up for us?"

**2.** *"Own" your opinion.* When you criticize a speaker, you are expressing your *opinion,* not an absolute fact. You should not assume that everyone else will see things exactly as you do, and the way you word your criticism should reflect this. Don't say,

**FIGURE 2–1 SPEECH EVALUATION FORM**

Name _____ Topic _____
Assignment # _____ Date _____

What did you especially like? _____

_____

_____

_____

In your opinion, how could the speech be improved? _____

_____

_____

_____

Do you have any questions for this speaker? (If so, please jot them down here.)

What are the speaker's main points? (list)

What did you think of the
        Topic?
        Content?
        Speaker's style?

Did you find the speech to be
        Interesting?
        Informative?
        Well organized?

"You didn't cover that point sufficiently."

Rather, say,

"I felt confused about that third point. Perhaps I missed something, but does your argument logically support the conclusion you reached?"

This is sometimes referred to as using "I" language instead of "You" language because you are describing *your* opinion (*"I* feel that . . .") rather than the speaker (*"You* aren't very good at . . .").[26] The worst type of "you" language is that which includes an "allness" statement: "You *always* do _____ " or "You *never* do _____ ."

3. *Be flexible rather than dogmatic.* Dogmatic people—those who insist that they are absolutely right—usually inspire others to prove them wrong. There is something about the arrogance of dogmatism that makes the person being criticized become inflexible in return. Since the purpose of criticism is to help the speaker improve, a debate on who's right and who's wrong tends to be counterproductive.

When you are flexible in your criticism, you do not insist on being right. If you tell the speaker that you found a point confusing, and the speaker disagrees with you, you will move on to the next point. The fact that you have expressed your opinion (which you own) is enough. Perhaps it will sink in, perhaps it won't. And if you find some truth in the speaker's rejoinder, and mention it, you'll increase your credibility for the next comment you make.

### Be Substantive

The final thing to keep in mind in constructive criticism is to be *substantive.* Part of substance is the specificity mentioned above: Rather than saying just "I liked this" or "I didn't like that," you should provide substance by saying specifically what you liked or disliked, and you should make specific suggestions for improvement. (Sometimes your suggestion won't be right, either, but it can spur the creative process on to a better solution.)

## ⬤ SAMPLE SPEECH

The sample speech for this chapter was given by Carl Wayne Hensley, professor of Communications at Bethel College in St. Paul, Minnesota.[27] It was presented to a group of graduate students and professors at the Graduate School of Business at the University of St. Thomas in Minneapolis. The speech deals with developing style in public speaking (also the topic of Chapter 11 of this book).

The notes written in the margin are the notes that an audience member might take while listening to the speech. Notice they include main points, interesting details, and questions to be asked. The comments in parentheses are this hypothetical listener's thoughts about the notes: why certain notes were made or not made.

## ▼ SPEAK WITH STYLE AND WATCH THE IMPACT

By CARL WAYNE HENSLEY

Bethel College

(I'm listening for a statement of the main idea.)

[1] Early in my public speaking career, I discovered that one of the best ways to improve my speaking was to study speeches by outstanding speakers. So I read, and I listened. I examined how speakers developed organization; how they developed focus; how they developed their content with examples, quotations, and other types of support; and how they developed introductions and conclusions.

(Here's some key words:) *impact — precision—power—style.*

[2] Gradually, I realized that some speakers reached out to listeners, took hold of them, and pulled them into their speeches with greater impact and interest than others. So, I explored what made these speakers superior, and I found that they developed a dimension ignored by most—they used language with precision and power. They had style.

(Is this the main idea?) *style: carefully chosen language*

[3] Dressing ideas in carefully chosen language—this is the original meaning of the word "style." In the long march across public speaking history, style has walked a road which rises and falls between high peaks of precision and deep valleys of neglect. Unfortunately, in contemporary American speaking, style has been forced to build her home in the valley—ignored, if not forgotten. When it comes to style in American speaking—political, religious, reform, corporate—most speeches are about as exciting as a made-for-TV movie.

[4] If speakers (and speech writers as well) want to lift a speech to a higher level of interest and influence, let them work on improving their style. Fredrick Beuchner, a scintillating speaker and writer, expresses the value of style when he says:

> Words have color, depth, texture of their own, and power to evoke vastly more than they mean; words can be used to make things clear, make things vivid, make things interesting, and make things happen inside the one who reads them or hears them.

(Here it is: the central idea:)

\* *Style provides increased impact!*

(The first main point:)

1. *Language homicide. Bloating=unnecessary words*

[5] Thus, my claim, quite simply, is: *Style provides increased impact to a speech.* In order to help you improve your style, I want to give you three suggestions. Follow these suggestions and watch your speeches increase in impact.

[6] The first suggestion is: Guard against language homicide. Many speakers murder the English language by what Edwin Newman called "bloating"—adding unnecessary, redundant words to express an idea. Have you heard someone refer to "foreign imports," "imports into this country" and "exports out of this country"? How about "few in number" as if few were not number related?

7 Another common use of bloating is the "in . . . of" blight: in need of, in possession of, in hope of, in search of, ad nauseum. Drop the "in . . . of" and let the active verbs work for you: "we need," "we possess," "we hope."

8 Numerous other phrases contribute to this problem: two-way interaction, totally free, exact same, most unique, good success. Examine your speeches carefully, and, if you find bloating, remove it!

(Here's one I use myself:)

*"two-way interaction"*

*Jargon* (I know what he means.)

9 While some speakers murder the language by bloating it, others murder it by suffocating it with jargon. Kingman Brewster, U.S. diplomat, stated the case quite clearly: "Incomprehensible jargon is the hallmark of a profession." Consider some stifling jargon of the last few years: synergy (I think it means that we work together), proactive (we anticipate), wellness (what happened to the dependable "health"?), interface (computers may interface, but people talk to each other). In a cartoon a professor sits at his computer, looking puzzled. Another character asks, "What's the problem?" The professor replies, "It's a simple case of power source input interface inversion." Then, after a pause, he adds "It's not plugged in."

10 Not only do we murder our language by bloating it and suffocating it with jargon, but we also "age" and "ize" it to death. A few months ago, Tama Starr, president of Artcraft Strauss Sign Corp., tackled (or should I say "tackleized") this felon in a letter to the magazine, *Signs of the Time:*

*age—ize*

> We always thought we built signs. But, lately, we keep finding ourselves invited to bid on signage. What is signage? Is the simple, old, four-letter word "sign" too straightforward for this state-of-the-art day and age?
>
> Like rummage, tonnage, baggage, luggage, roughage, garbage and the Biblical "mess of pottage," signage sounds like something heavy, lifeless and full of lumps.

11 As a baseball fan, I was upset when the players went on strike in the fall and owners threatened a lockout in the spring. It gave me no consolation that it wasn't really a strike but merely a "work stoppage." Starr stated it succinctly when she wrote that "aging" the language "dulls the drama and dampens the ardor of our lusty mother tongue."

*"stoppage"*

12 No less deadly to our diction than "aging" is our propensity to "ize" words: politicize, utilize, calendarize, spiritualize, finalize, synergize, athleticize, problemize, and by all means, prioritize. One quickly concluizes that we have a surplussage of "ize-itis."

*"prioritize"*

13 Another method of murder relies on clichés such as back to the drawing board, track record, bottom line, touch base later, scenario (worst case/best case, of course), for all practical purposes, and flagship (I've yet to find a business type who knows the origin of this metaphor). Without a doubt, the corporate world (and the academic world and political world and athletic world) speak in wonderful ways, and communication becomes the casualty.

*Clichés—"bottom line"*

*(Second suggestion means second main point, right?)*

*II. Correct words and grammar*

*less-few — indiv.#/ quantity* (individually numbered) *(I get this one wrong sometimes)*

*between—among* (this one I know)

*may—can* (this one I remember from grade school. But is it still important? I guess it is.)

*grammar—self words* (here's another one I'm guilty of)

*obj/ subj pronouns: between you and me.*

[14] All of these lethal lesions on our language have drained its stamina and led to a steady decline in its health. Therefore, speakers and speech writers must guard against the widespread efforts to commit stylistic murder because *style provides increased impact to a speech.* In order to develop style for impact, I offer a second suggestion: Choose correct words and correct grammar. Mark Twain said,

> The difference between the right word and the almost right word is the difference between lightning and the lightning bug.

Choosing the correct word is crucial to using the right word.

[15] Consider some common choices. Do you use "less" when you mean "few" as in "less people attended the annual meeting this year"? When you refer to that which can be counted or numbered individually, use few—"fewer people attended." When you refer to quantity, use less. Thus, when my cup of coffee is half empty, I have less coffee than before, and I have fewer ounces of coffee.

[16] How do you use "between" and "among"? Do you say "between the four companies, we have the market covered"? Do you also say "between the two of us"? Which is correct? The second. Between always refers to two parts or people. Among always refers to more than two.

[17] How about "may" and "can"? People frequently ask, "Can I go? Can I sit here? Can I make an appointment with you?" They should ask, "May I go? May I sit here?" because they are asking permission. May, then, asks or grants permission. Can refers to ability or action, "We can increase profits this year."

[18] Walt Dziedzic, member of the Minneapolis City Council, demonstrated the importance of choosing the right word when the City Council was one of several groups trying to attract a professional hockey team to Minneapolis. When a reporter asked Dziedzic if the Council intended to do all it could in this effort, he replied, "We've gone from being the raided to the raidee. Are we looking for a team? You bet." Well, good luck, Mr. Dziedzic, since you haven't become the "raider" yet.

[19] Not only are correct words essential to strong style, but so is correct grammar. Using the "self" pronouns incorrectly is common. So we say, "Sarah and myself will chair the committee," or "Sarah and yourself will chair the committee." Instead, say, "Sarah and I will chair," or "Sarah and you will chair." The self pronouns are reflexive, used to reflect on a noun or another pronoun to add emphasis. "I myself will chair:" "You yourself will chair:" "They themselves created this crisis." James Kilpatrick suggested quite wisely that "the best thing to do with myself is to wrestle [it] to the floor and stomp on it. Be gone!"

[20] Another common error occurs when using objective and subjective pronouns. Bryant Gumbel of the *Today Show* referred to something "between

Jane and I." Speakers frequently say "to you and I," "for you and I," "with you and I." Between, to, for, with, and other prepositions require the objective "me" (or we, if plural). Hence "to you and me," "for you and me," etc. I and we are subjective pronouns. When you need a subjective pronoun, then say, "You and I received a bonus." I and we are always subjects of a sentence while me and us are objects.

[21] Another common error involves subject-verb agreement, such as using "media" as a singular noun. "The local media is an important ally." "Media" is the plural form of "medium." Consequently, "The media are important allies." When referring to individual media such as TV, newspaper, and radio, use a singular verb: "This medium is an important ally." Speakers make the same mistake with "data"—"the data supports our program," and "the data is correct." "Data," like "media," is a plural noun. Hence, "the data support our program," and "the data are correct."

*subj/verb agr:*
*media are*
*data are.*

[22] Do you want your speeches to rise above the mediocre, mundane messages which deluge our podiums, our conference rooms, and our training centers? Do you want your ideas to ascend beyond the lowly level of the majority of ideas in our culture? Then, by all means, guard against language homicide, choose correct words, and choose correct grammar.

(ah. Main points. Let me check my list of those.)

[23] Rescue style from her exile in the valley of neglect. Elevate style to her peak of precision. Honor style as a staunch ally. Because, beyond a doubt, style provides increased impact to a speech.

(Pretty good speech, I must say. Let me look back now and see about those questions I wanted to ask…)

## Notes Taken

Taken all together, the listener's page of notes at the end of this speech looked like this:

*Prof. Hensley*
*impact—precision—power—style*
*style: carefully chosen language*
*\*Style provides increased impact!*
*I. Language Homicide*
    *Bloating=unnecessary words*
    *"two way interaction"*
    *Jargon*
            *age—ize*
    *"Stoppage" "Prioritize"*
*Cliché's—Bottom Line*

*II. Correct Words and Grammar*
    *Less—Few*
    *quantity    indiv. #*
    *Between—among*
    *may—can*
    *Grammar*
    *Self words*
    *obj/subj pronouns: between you and*
    *subj/verb agr.: media are data are*

Notice how close the listener came to discerning the actual outline of this speech (paragraphs of the speech are in parentheses):

INTRODUCTION (1–5)
BODY
  I. Guarding against language homicide (6–13)
    A. Bloating (6)
    B. Jargon (9)
    C. "Aging" (10–11)
    D. "Izing" (12)
    E. Clichés (13)
 II. Choosing correct words (14–17)
    A. Less or few? (15)
    B. Between or among? (16)
    C. Can or may? (17)
III. Using correct grammar (19–21)
    A. "Self" words (19)
    B. Objective and subjective pronouns (20)
    C. Subject-verb agreement (21)
CONCLUSION (22–23)

In fact, the listener's notes suggest that this hypothetical audience member did a good job of listening. Every point was noted, and the listener came up with some reasonable questions. Of course, the example might be a little optimistic. The handwriting is neater than we might expect. There were no external distractions at all. The stream of consciousness is remarkably free of prejudice toward the speaker or assumptions about what's about to be said. It might not be entirely realistic, therefore, but it is an example to aspire to when you fight the causes of ineffective listening.

### ▼ SUMMARY

This chapter focuses on critical listening and constructive criticism, two activities that will occupy most of your class time.

Listening, especially critical listening, has become increasingly difficult in our media-saturated age. This chapter considered the primary causes of ineffective listening and strategies for improving listening.

The primary causes of ineffective listening include message overload (that feeling of exhaustion and confusion that is the result of information saturation), rapid thought (which causes concentration to wander), making assumptions (about message content), prejudicial judgments (both those based on cultural stereotyping and those based on personal biases), and cultural attitudes toward speaking and listening (such as the belief that speaking is more important than listening).

Strategies for improving listening include being prepared to listen, controlling distractions, withholding judgment until comprehension is complete, taking notes and making the rapid-thought/slow-speech differential work *for* you, instead of against you. We have discussed some specific techniques to put these strategies into action.

Finally, we discussed the necessity and techniques of offering constructive criticism on the speeches of others. When offering this criticism it is important to be positive, nonjudgmental, and substantive.

## ▼ EXERCISES

1. One point made early in this chapter was that media saturation has caused some people to lose the habit of critical listening. To analyze the effects of fast-paced media production values on the audience's ability to listen critically, try this experiment:

   Videotape a television commercial that catches your attention. This could be an advertisement for any product: automobiles, clothes, soap—even a political candidate. The only requirement is that it be the type of commercial that would normally capture your attention sufficiently to make you pay attention to it.

   As you tape the commercial, watch it carefully. Write a brief description of the commercial. Now play it back two or three times and look at it critically. Try to strip away the effect of the entertainment values, such as fancy editing and musical background. Did you miss anything in your first viewing?

2. To analyze your own listening abilities, try the following:
   Rank-order the following causes of ineffective listening as they pertain to your own listening behavior. List first the problem that you think most affects your ability to listen, then the next most powerful cause, and so on.
   A. Message Overload
   B. Rapid Thought
   C. Making Assumptions
   D. Prejudicial Judgments
   E. Cultural Attitudes toward Speaking and Listening
   Now think back to a time when each of these factors *might* have interfered with your clear reception of a message. Give an example of

how each one might have interfered with critical listening at some point in your life.

**3.** This chapter points out that you can practice your listening skills each time one of your classmates speaks. To help your classmates improve *their* listening ability next time *you* speak, try the following experiment:

Prepare in advance a list of questions on the content and critical issues of your speech. After the speech is completed (including a question-and-answer period, at the discretion of the instructor) give your classmates a quick quiz on these questions.

# NOTES

1. Lyman K. Steil, *Your Personal Listening Profile* (New York: Sperry Corp., 1980).

2. Theorists maintain that there are different types of listening, each with slightly different characteristics. These types include informational and empathic as well as critical listening. For a discussion of these types please see Ronald Adler and George Rodman, *Understanding Human Communication,* 5th ed. (Fort Worth, Tex.: Harcourt Brace College Publishers, 1994), pp. 111–153.

3. See Milt Reitzfeld, "Effective Listening," *Journal of Systems Management* 40 (August 1989), pp. 22–23. See also Thomas G. Devine, "Listening: What Do We Know After Fifty Years of Research and Theorizing?" *Journal of Reading* 21 (1978), pp. 296–304.

4. See, for example, Beatrice Hamilton, "Hearing, Analyzing, Empathizing, and Succeeding in Management," *Training and Development Journal* (August 1990), p. 16. See also Michael Shermis, "Listening Skills in Business," *Bulletin of the Association for Business Communication* 52 (June 1989), pp. 47–49.

5. Bernard L. Rosenbaum, "Rx for Better Doctors," *Training and Development Journal* 43 (August 1989), pp. 77–79.

6. Stephen F. Prather, "The Choice Is Yours: Communicate or Be Sued," *Medical Economics* 66 (April 17, 1989), pp. 90–96.

7. Ralph Nichols and Leonard Stevens, *Are You Listening?* (New York: McGraw-Hill, 1957), p. 42.

8. Ibid., p. 36.

9. Ibid., p. 42.

10. Florence L. Wolff, Nadine C. Marsnik, William S. Tracey, and Ralph G. Nichols, *Perceptive Listening* (Englewood Cliffs, N.J.: Prentice-Hall, 1983), p. 154.

11. Research suggests that this type of "inner speech" occurs constantly. See John R. Johnson, "The Role of Inner Speech in Human Communication," *Communication Education* 33 (July 1984), pp. 211–222.

12. Carl R. Rogers and F. J. Roethlisberger, "Effective Listening," *Harvard Business Review* 69 (November–December 1991), pp. 105–112. A large body of experimental research suggests that numerous other factors, such as our experience, expectations, and attitudes, affect how well we listen or observe. Two classic studies on this topic are A. H. Hastorf and H. Cantril, "They Saw a Game: A Case Study," *Journal of Abnormal and Social Psychology* 49 (1954), pp. 129–134; and G. W. Allport and L. J. Postman, "The Basic Psychology of Rumor," in Eleanor Maccoby, Theodore Newcomb, and Eugene Harley, eds., *Readings in Social Psychology,* 3rd ed. (New York: Holt, Rinehart and Winston, 1958), pp. 54–65.

13. Kate Moody, "Audio Tapes and Books: Perfect Partners," *School Library Journal* 35 (February 1989), pp. 27–29.

14. The problems of external/environmental distractions are analyzed in Augusta M. Simon, "Effective Listening: Barriers to Listening in a Diverse Business Environment," *Bulletin of the Association for Business Communication* 54 (September 1991), pp. 73–74. See also Jack E. Hulbert, "Barriers to Effective Listening," *Bulletin of the Association for Business Communication* 52 (June 1989), pp. 3–5.

15. Originally published in 1952, the classic statement on the effects of "premature evaluation" has recently been reprinted. See Rogers and Roethlisberger, *Effective Listening.*

16. See, for example, John S. Fielden and Ronald E. Dulek, "Matching Messages to Listening Styles," *Business* 40 (October–December 1990), pp. 55–57.

17. See Reitzfeld, "Effective Listening."

18. For a review of the literature on the effects of notetaking, see Robert N. Bostrom and D. Bruce Searle, "Encoding, Media, Affect, and Gender," in *Listening Behavior: Measurement and Application* Robert N. Bostrom, ed., (New York: Guilford Press, 1990), pp. 28–30.

19. Ryan Siskow, "The Double Indignity: Medical Confidentiality," *Winning Orations, 1991* (Interstate Oratorical Association, 1991), pp. 32–34.

20. Nichols and Stevens *op. cit.,* p. 113.

21. Ralph Nichols, "Do We Know How to Listen? Practical Helps in a Modern Age," *Speech Teacher* (March 1961), pp. 118–124.

22. Wolff et al., *Perceptive Listening,* p. 113.

23. John R. Ward, "Now Hear This: Without Listening, There Is No Communication," *Communication World* 7 (July 1990), pp. 20–22.

24. Albert Gore, in "Excerpts from the Debate among Quayle, Gore, and Stockdale," *The New York Times,* October 14, 1992, p. A20(L).

25. Laurie Schloff and Marcia Yudkin, *Smart Speaking* (New York: Plume, 1992), p. 172.

26. Adler and Rodman, *Understanding Human Communication,* pp. 244–245; see also p. 85.

27. Carl Wayne Hensley, "Speak with Style and Watch the Impact." A longer version of this speech is reprinted in *Vital Speeches of the Day,* September 1, 1995, pp. 701–704.

# THE ETHICS OF SPEECHMAKING

## ▼ CHAPTER 3 OBJECTIVES

**After reading this chapter, you should understand:**

**1.** The importance of examining ethics in the media/information age.

**2.** Why a public speaking class is an appropriate setting for the study of ethics.

**3.** The differences between ethical and unethical speech-making.

**You should be able to:**

**1.** Evaluate your own speeches in terms of ethics.

**2.** Evaluate the speeches of others in terms of ethics.

## ⬤ ETHICS IN THE MEDIA/INFORMATION AGE

We live in a time of considerable ethical confusion. As you read the following four case studies, consider what you might do if you were the speaker:

▼ Case #1: Brian Bown, a high school American government teacher in Snellville, Georgia, found himself in an ethical quandary when the state legislature passed a law requiring a moment of silence at the start of the school day. Bown believed that the law did not meet the constitutional requirement of the separation of church and state, because it was a thinly disguised form of state-ordered prayer. "I either violate my conscience and beliefs and follow a law that is patently unconstitutional, or I'm fired," Bown said at the time.[1]

▼ Case #2: Jerry Weissman was the chief financial officer of Empire Blue Cross and Blue Shield, a nonprofit company that was required to offer health insurance to all who could pay, no matter how old or sick they were. The company decided to mount a major lobbying campaign to convince lawmakers to also force for-profit insurers to offer policies to all applicants, thereby offering increased opportunity for hard-to-insure clients while at the same time removing some of the burden from Weissman's company. Looking at the company's books, however, he realized that his company's losses on high-risk customers weren't all that bad. However, it would be relatively simple for him to exaggerate the data a little, to make it conform to his argument. After all, it was for a good cause.

▼ Case #3: Raymond Cummings, salutatorian at North Miami High School, was told that his graduation speech should contain no controversial material. He was told to submit a copy of his speech for approval in advance. Cummings wanted to make some comments on racism in America that he knew his principal would not approve of.

Each of these cases presented the speaker with a moral dilemma because in each case "ethical behavior" could be defined differently. Sometimes it's ethical to listen to the voice of authority; sometimes it isn't. Sometimes the calls of your conscience are more important than externally imposed rules. Sometimes the ends of persuasion, such as saving human lives, justify the means, such as deception. Sometimes different ideas about morality are just different, not wrong.

Here is the outcome of each of these cases. Would your course of action have been different if you were the speaker?

▼ Case #1: Brian Bown decided to ignore the state law. Rather than using the time for a "moment of silence," he gave a speech on the topic of the new law instead. He was suspended from his job, and the school board instituted dismissal proceedings against him.

▼ Knowlege without integrity is dangerous and dreadful.

Samuel Johnson

▼ Case #2: Weissman decided to exaggerate the data, in a speech he presented before a Senate subcommittee. Somehow the lawmakers discovered the exaggeration, which they considered false testimony. Weissman immediately lost his job, and soon he was indicted by a federal grand jury on charges of perjury. He will very likely go to prison.[2]

▼ Case #3: Cummings submitted a copy of his speech with the controversial remarks removed. He then gave the speech he wanted to give, which included the controversial remarks. He said, among other things,

> In the movie *Menace II Society,* it was said that America's worst nightmare was someone young, black, and who just didn't care. But from what I have experienced, America's true worst nightmare is someone young, black, and educated—for education is the key that unlocks the door of oppression. So I say to all my African American peers, go to college, get your education, and take part in the uplifting of the African American race. It's time America realized that we are here and that we are not going anywhere.[3]

His principal accused Cummings of unethical behavior for not sticking to his agreed-upon speech. He tried to get Harvard University to take back Cummings's acceptance. Harvard refused to do so, believing that Cummings's actions were justified.

Ethics are defined as *the guidelines that help us determine right from wrong.* Communication is considered ethical if it conforms to accepted standards, but there is a considerable amount of confusion about what those standards are.[4] The preceding case studies concern people who committed ethical breaches, such as misleading their superiors or defying legal authorities. Yet two of the cases (Cummings and Bown) seem like heroes, and the other (Weissman) seems much less heroic.

There are many reasons for the confusing state of ethical standards. Many experts believe that the media are at least partly to blame.[5] There are so many messages out there that we become confused about what's right and what's wrong. Many of the messages seem to glorify ethical behavior: The blockbuster movie *Forrest Gump* exalted the power of decency, for example, and television magazine shows such as *60 Minutes* make a weekly practice out of uncovering and bringing down the unethical. But television sitcoms like *Roseanne* smirk at white lies and manipulation, and even cartoons such as *The Simpsons* celebrate antisocial behavior by both children and adults (Bart disrupts his classroom and vandalizes the town while Homer steals from his neighbors and sleeps through his new job as a safety inspector at the nuclear power plant). Meanwhile, in the world of popular music, "gangsta rappers" brag about rape, assault, and the murder of police officers.

Defenders of the media would point out that popular culture provides entertainment, not instruction. Just because a television program depicts a murder does not mean that it serves as an instruction manual for aspiring killers. Still, even the media's defenders would have to admit that a society is influenced by the way it entertains itself.[6] Part of the influence is caused by the sheer volume of the entertainment. We spend so much time being entertained that we have less time to think about the finer points of the conduct of our lives. We entertain ourselves so much, in fact, that the societal institutions that once regulated ethical thinking—institutions such as the church, family, and school—have had their authority eroded by the encroaching influence of the media.

Possibly the main reason the media have contributed to an era of confused ethics is they have created such a huge mass audience. Those who have to appeal to this audience, whether they be corporations, politicians, or activists, seem to feel that the stakes are so high that they simply cannot afford to tell the truth. Senator George McGovern, who was the Democratic presidential nominee in 1972, says that, because of television, "Politicians have learned not to bring bad news to the American people because if they do, they're going to get beaten politically."[7] By "bad news" McGovern means the truth about what politicians will do once they are elected. Most politicians seem to believe that voters don't want to hear about the cost and inconvenience of solutions to social problems. They don't want to hear about tax increases or sophisticated plans for change. They want simple answers that won't cost them anything. Whereas the ethical political path would be to educate voters about the truth, too many politicians choose the more expedient path of telling voters what they want to hear.

The use of deception by politicians—even politicians whom history views as ethical—is not new. Historians point out that both Thomas Jefferson and Franklin Roosevelt promised to decrease the government's powers when campaigning, and both expanded those powers as president.[8] But it does seem as if our political lies have become more outrageous. President Bush told us that he knew nothing about the transfer of funds from illegal arms

sales to fight an illegal war in Nicaragua, although records show he attended meetings where the scheme was discussed. And Bill Clinton told us all with a straight face that he had nothing to do with two women who accused him of sexual improprieties, in spite of the weight of the contrary evidence.

Politicians aren't the only ones with ethical problems, of course. An entire profession, that of public relations, has grown to be one that, according to one practitioner, "twists the truth to serve a specific need or interest."[9] Another major communication industry, advertising, makes a habit of misleading through the use of "weasel words," such as "virtually" ("Zitsaway will make your skin virtually clear"), which allow for the avoidance of truth without actually lying. (We'll have more to say about weasel words in Chapter 13, on Argumentation.) Advertisers also mislead in more subtle ways, such as visual distortion: through the use of trick photography, sometimes computer generated, they can make dolls look alive and wind-up cars look like supersonic racers.

Students today live in a complex world that provides few clear-cut ethical guidelines. Those guidelines you think you know don't always hold up when you look at them closely. Take the guideline, "Always tell the truth." Whereas this rule might stand you well in most circumstances, those who have been asked to give an opinion on their significant other's most recent clothing purchase ("Tell me the truth, what do you think of it?") know that absolute truth is sometimes ill advised. Take also the classic case of a victim seeking refuge from a murderer in your home; the murderer knocks on your door and says, "Is my victim in there?" Surely honesty is not the best policy in that situation. Obviously, then, to a certain degree ethics are complex and relative.

One of the reasons that the study of public speaking is important today is because it enables you to clarify your thoughts about what ethical communication really is. In this class you act as either a presenter or an evaluator of spoken messages. The feedback-rich environment of a college-level speech class provides the time and motivation for extended discussion into ethical questions. A few general guidelines will form a framework for these discussions.

## ⬇ ETHICAL GUIDELINES: GENERAL PRINCIPLES

For our purpose, we will define ethical communication as *communication that is honest and accurate, and serves the audience's best interests*. This definition will be most useful if we examine it within the context of a continuum of communication behaviors.

## The Ethical Continuum

It is useful, when discussing communication, to speak in terms of "ethical" and "unethical" behavior. In most cases, however, this is an oversimplification.[10] It is more helpful to think in terms of a continuum (that is, a continuous whole made up of "degrees of ethicality") than in terms of absolutes (such as ethical/unethical and moral/immoral). Asking if any act is "ethical" or "unethical" elicits a "yes" or "no" response, and the ensuing discussion becomes limited by black and white simplicity. Experts in the study of ethics point out that it is better to discuss these acts in terms of their "degree of ethical quality."[11]

At many points in this chapter we will use terms such as "ethical fault" or "ethical problem" to suggest a guideline for "more ethical" rather than "less ethical" behavior on the ethical continuum.

## Honesty

There are many types of dishonesty.[12] There is, for example, *deliberate lying,* which is usually an unambiguous ethical fault. When the Reverend Jim Bakker collected millions of dollars from his parishioners for various types of missionary work, he was fully aware that he was collecting the money only to build his personal fortune. Eventually he went to prison for it.

Of course, there are always exceptions. What happens, for example, when the captain of a cruise ship learns, in the middle of evening festivities, that the ship has sprung a major leak and is in the process of sinking? We could probably forgive him if he stands up in front of the bandstand and announces that there are some mechanical difficulties in the ship, and as a precaution he would like the passengers to assemble on the main deck, in their life jackets, next to the lifeboats. After all, he would seem justified in trying to keep panic to a minimum.

On the ethical continuum, however, we could still say that, all things being equal, it is generally more ethical to tell the truth than to lie. With that in mind, it is instructive to look at some of the more subtle forms of lying, such as *withholding information.*

▼ If you tell the truth you don't have to remember anything.

Mark Twain

## Withholding Information

It has been said that we all have different versions of the truth because we all have different stores of knowledge. In fact, it would be impossible to tell everything about anything. It's impractical, for example, to expect every candymaker to explain fully the dangers of cavities, fat, and empty calories in every ad. In public speaking, however, it is an ethical fault to withhold evidence or arguments that your audience would need to reach a logical conclusion about the arguments being presented. For example, the leaders of a religious cult, some of whom truly believe their mission is to save souls, might withhold information about their tactics as they try to recruit members and raise donations. That would be an ethical fault, however, if those tactics include sleep deprivation during the indoctrination of potential converts, and scare tactics when it comes time for members to donate all their worldly goods to the cult. Similarly, charity fund-raisers who do not disclose that most of the funds they raise will go to the costs of fund-raising are also at fault.

As these examples show, sometimes the information that is withheld in a speech would prove the unethical nature of the speech itself. Examining that information as a speaker might enable you to give up a topic on this ethical ground.

*Withholding opposing arguments* by presenting only one side of a controversial issue is not only considered an ethical fault, it will make your speech less effective with a reasonably intelligent audience.[13] Anytime you withhold (or fail to find) information that can help your audience make up its own mind, rationally and critically, you are on dangerous ethical ground.

Another common form of withholding information is *withholding the source of your evidence*. Where your evidence came from, of course, affects how reliable and valid it is. If your source might have a possible bias, you are ethically required to reveal it.

For example, let's say you wanted to present a speech on the benefits of eating chocolate. (There are many out there who would love to hear such a speech.) You find this terrific quotation:

> According to the Princeton Dental Resource Center, publisher of a newsletter for dentists, it's a good idea to eat chocolate. An article in last month's newsletter said, "The next time you snack on your favorite chocolate bar or bowl of peanuts, remember—If enjoyed in moderation, they can be good tasting and might even inhibit cavities."[14]

That's an actual quotation, but if you used it, you should also mention that the Princeton Dental Resource Center is financed to the tune of $1,000,000 per year by the M&M/Mars Candy Co.[15] This sort of information demonstrates the necessity of adequate research in ethical speaking.

Another form of withholding information is withholding information about yourself, as a speaker. One way to be guilty of this ethical fault is to *not disclose private motives or special interests* that conflict with the audience interest. Perhaps the worst form of withholding information about yourself is when by doing so you distort the true purpose of your speech (saying it's about financial planning, for example, when what you're really doing is selling life insurance). This doesn't mean that you always have to discuss all your motives with your audience. You might be speaking partially to

▼ Propaganda is the art of persuading others of what you don't believe yourself.

Abba Eban

impress new friends or to feel better about yourself—*those* motives you can keep to yourself, because they do not represent a conflict of interest with the audience. (We'll have more to say about conflict of interest in a moment.)

## Pandering

Another ethical problem in the realm of honesty is sacrificing conviction in adapting to an audience, or *pandering*. Whereas audience analysis and adaptation is an integral part of effective speechmaking, it is an ethical fault to pander to an audience by telling them what they want to hear, when what they want to hear is wrong or not what *you* believe in. Many people believe that former Governor Mario Cuomo of New York state is a good example of a strong ethical model in this respect. His political advisors told him that the voters favored the death penalty. Cuomo, however, did not believe in the death penalty. He was willing to speak for hours explaining his opposition, but he steadfastly refused to support a death penalty bill in any way—even though that refusal eventually helped cost him an election.

## Accuracy

Honesty and accuracy go hand in hand, but we consider them separately here because inaccuracies are often honest but careless mistakes in content. Although they are often not intentionally meant to mislead, they are still ethical faults.

### Ignorant Misstatement

There are many forms of inaccuracy. One is *ignorant misstatement*,[16] a type of inaccuracy that occurs when one is inaccurate without realizing it. This often happens when one's beliefs conflict with the facts. This is the type of inaccuracy that the media watchdog group Fairness and Accuracy in Reporting (FAIR) is continually on the lookout for. They found, for example, that the popular political commentator, Rush

without attention

▼ The best way I know of to win an argument is to start by being in the right.

Jooseph Roux

Limbaugh, often had trouble with facts.[17] The examples they cite include the following:

**LIMBAUGH:** "It has not been proven that nicotine is addictive."

**FAIR:** Medical reports of its addictiveness dating to the turn of the century were confirmed in the 1988 Surgeon General's study.

**LIMBAUGH:** "The poorest people in America are better off than mainstream families of Europe."

**FAIR:** Average income of the poorest 20 percent of Americans: $5,226; average income in four major European nations: $19,708.

**LIMBAUGH:** "Everybody in the world [except] the United States Congress" supported the Gulf War.

**FAIR:** Both houses of Congress authorized the Gulf War.

**LIMBAUGH:** "When the [black] illegitimacy rate is raised, Rev. Jackson and other black leaders immediately change the subject."

**FAIR:** For years, Jesse Jackson and others have decried "children having children."

**LIMBAUGH:** "Most Canadian physicians who are themselves in need of surgery scurry across the border to get it done right—the American way."

**FAIR:** Most Canadian physicians, like most other Canadians, much prefer their system to ours.

### Reporting Opinion as Fact

*Reporting opinion as fact* is another ethical fault based on inaccuracy. This happens when you say something that you truly believe but have no proof for. For example, if all the student newspapers disappeared from the student union before they could be distributed, you might hold a very strong opinion about who took them. However, if you said,

> Members of the opposition student government party have stolen the student newspapers that contained articles that exposed some of their mistakes . . .

without proof, you'd have an ethics problem.

Someone speaking on feminism might say, "Breast-feeding is just another male trick to keep women at home," and feel very strongly about it. But such an unprovable, opinionated statement is less ethical than a more carefully worded one. You can still express your opinion, for example, but you have to express it *as* your opinion:

> In my opinion, breast-feeding is just another male trick to keep women at home . . .

but then you would have to support that opinion rationally to make it effective with a nonpartisan audience.

## Reporting Rumors as Truth

*Reporting rumors as truth* is another form of inaccuracy. The media give us plenty of examples of this. Tabloid newspapers, for example, report rumors on everything from celebrity breakups to cures for cancer— sometimes in the biggest headlines they have. Even the mainstream media sometimes rely on rumors. Right after the attempted assassination of President Reagan, network television news reported that Reagan's press secretary, James Brady, had died. The report was based on a rumor, and it was inaccurate.

The media often get around their responsibility for accuracy by admitting that they are reporting rumors. In other words, they don't report that something, in fact, happened, but that rumors exist that something happened. Your responsibility as a public speaker is more rigorous—and your responsibility as an audience member is to hold the speaker to this rigorous standard. For example, if a speaker said,

> Everyone knows the rumors that are circulating about the college planning to eliminate the communications program, and where there's that much smoke, there must be some administrative fire . . .

you would be expected to call that speaker immediately on the ethical error of reporting rumors.

## The Audience Interest

The question of the audience interest derives from the concept of "the public interest," a term that appears repeatedly in the U.S. Constitution to differentiate legitimate actions of governmental officials from those that constitute a "conflict of interest." The audience interest question can be stated simply: In giving this speech, am I motivated by the best interests of my audience, rather than (or, at least, as well as) my own self-interest?

There are, of course, many happy occasions when what is best for you is also best for your audience. You might be in favor of your community purchasing some land to make a park, which will improve the quality of life for everyone in the community, including yourself. You're on solid ethical ground there. But if you're trying to get the community to sell you some land so you can establish a profitable toxic waste dump, and you know the project is not in the audience's interest, then you can't ethically speak in favor of it.

Of course, there are two sides (or more) to every story. Perhaps there are people who truly believe that the income derived from the toxic waste dump will benefit the community. Those who believe that, however, must recognize that their own short-term self-interest might affect the way they perceive the long-term audience interest.

Questions of the audience's interest are seldom cut and dried. But this perspective does provide us with one guideline for ethical behavior, as

Dilbert reprinted by permission of United Features Syndicate, Inc.

well as the ethical criticism of someone else's behavior. In fact, this might answer one of the questions posed earlier about the case studies that began this chapter. Perhaps what separated those speakers who seemed ethical from those who did not was their clearer conception of the audience interest.

Honesty, accuracy, and the audience interest provide three general guidelines by which you can judge your own speech tactics as well as those of others. There are also a few specific guidelines that are dealt with in every speech class.

## ▼ SPECIFIC GUIDELINES

### Plagiarism

One of the most common problems within the area of honesty is *plagiarism*. Plagiarism comes from the Latin word meaning "kidnapper." It is the act of kidnapping someone else's ideas or words and passing them off as your own.

The most common form of plagiarism is a simple failure to attribute the source of a piece of evidence. If you were speaking on the value of single-sex education, you might like to say the following:

> If too many coed classrooms are places where boys will be boys and girls will be girls, all-female classrooms are places where girls stand a better chance of getting to be people.[18]

This is a nicely worded statement, and anyone could be proud to have composed it. Unfortunately, someone already did. You could, however, use it like this:

> Judith Shapiro, the president of Barnard College, might have said it best: "If too many coed classrooms are places where boys will be boys and girls will be girls, all-female classrooms are places where girls stand a better chance of getting to be people."

Direct quotations are sometimes clumsy, however. To be absolutely clear, you often have to precede them with "And I quote" and attach "Unquote" at the end. Alternatively, you might still use the idea by *paraphrasing* it (stating it in your own words) and attributing its source:

> Judith Shapiro, the president of Barnard College, has pointed out that coed classrooms tend to be places where boys will be boys and girls will be girls. Implied in that statement is the idea that girls will participate less in the learning process when boys are the center of attention. According to Dr. Shapiro, in all-female classrooms girls stand a better chance of getting to be people.

Whether you quote directly or paraphrase, however, you avoid the ethical problem of plagiarism when you carefully attribute the source of the idea, information, or words. Tim Schultz, a student at Kansas State University, quoted directly in his speech on incorrect medical tests:

> Ironically, the same doctors who order all these tests know very little about how to interpret the results. The January/February 1993 *Consumer's Digest* interviewed international AIDS testing expert Klemenss Meyer. He exclaimed, "As an expert, I don't even know what quality controls are in place for the tests I order. I don't know enough to counsel my patients. And I know a lot more about this than most doctors, having written extensively on the subject."[19]

In that case, Tim took a quotation from an expert *who had been interviewed by someone else*. His attribution of the quotation makes that clear, and does so smoothly so as not to interfere with the flow of his speech.

Notice that he clearly stated the name and date of the publication in which the interview was published. This would be necessary for any form of support, whether it came from a newspaper, magazine, journal, or book.

*Reverse plagiarism* (saying someone said something, when he or she didn't) is also a problem. President Reagan's press secretary, Larry Speaks, got into trouble for this. When Speaks believed that Reagan *should* have said something, he had a tendency to simply make up the quotation for the president.[20] This same type of ethical fault surfaces occasionally in student speeches:

▼ Sigmund Freud was one of the first to point out that women are far more fragile psychologically than are men.

▼ Albert Einstein said that the atom bomb would make the United States the unchallenged leader of the world.

▼ Mother Teresa of Calcutta said it best when she said, "The best way to help our cause, my children, is to send a generous donation to Professor Rodman's Save the Elephants fund."

The fact is, Freud, Einstein, and Mother Teresa never said those things, and even if it's in the back of your head that they said *something* like that, at some time, you're on shaky ground ethically unless you make sure. This is also true if you claim general agreement in an authoritative community when none exists:

All economists agree on the effects of the current trade agreement.

An intelligent audience might be suspicious of your claim that any group of economists could agree on a specific treaty—or, for that matter, on anything.

One common form of plagiarism is to use a statistic without citing its source. This is just one of the ethical problems possible in the special case of statistics.

## Statistics

Statistics are often used to intentionally distort the truth. Because statistics are potentially powerful proof, you have the ethical responsibility to cite them exactly as they were published or tabulated. It's usually all right to round off a percentage or other figure, but it's considered an ethical fault to manipulate your statistics so they sound better than is warranted.

For example, the term *average* is often used to manipulate statistics. As there are actually three measures of central tendency, or "averages" (mean, median, and mode), it is important to be clear about which one you mean. Imagine that you had the following list of annual incomes for a group of five students:

1. $0
2. $40
3. $500
4. $750
5. $23,750

The mode (most frequent value) for that group would be $0, the mean (arithmetic average) would be $5,000, and the median (the point at which 50 percent of the values are greater and 50 percent are less) would be $500. Any of these could be cited as "average" by an unscrupulous speaker. Thus, the same set of statistics could be used to make any of the following statements:

1. The average student in this class has no income.
2. The average student in this class makes only $500 a year.
3. The average student in this class makes $5,000 a year.

Of course, an even *less* scrupulous speaker might decide that student 5 is just an "average" sort of guy, and state that the average student makes over $23,000 a year, but that would be classified as deliberate lying rather than manipulation. An ethical presentation of these statistics would require more careful wording:

1. The most common income in this class is $0, although some students do make some income.
2. The median income in this class is $500 a year, although some students make nothing and at least one makes considerably more.
3. The average income of students in this class is $5,000 a year, although the one student who made nearly $24,000 brought that statistic up considerably.

When using statistics as evidence you have to cite the complete source of your statistic along with any other information that would have a bearing on its validity. Established professional pollsters such as Gallup, Roper, and Harris, as well as the best magazines and newspapers, have reputations for accuracy. If you cite them, your audience can be relatively sure that your statistics are reliable.

## Being Rational

We speak often about the importance of critical thinking. As we mentioned in Chapter 1, critical thinking includes the use of logic and reasoning, the recognition of valid argument, distinguishing discussion from manipulation, and listening critically. The guideline of rationality means that the speaker has used critical thinking in the analysis of the topic, and that the audience is being encouraged to think critically about what is being said (by being given enough information, and so on.)

Being rational means providing logical proof. We will devote Chapter 13 on Argumentation mostly to logical standards of proof. For our purposes here we will say simply that *the claims you make, and the evidence that backs up those claims, should be logical and rational.*

Although it seems to go without saying that the claim itself should make sense, the media often discourage commonsense notions—ideas such as "people can't exist in two places at the same time," "animals live in one solid interval of time," and "two plus two equals four." These notions were described by one researcher as "the no-brainer stuff that encyclopedia editors assume their readers understand and that tabloid editors figure their readers either don't quite grasp or are willing to overlook."[21] It is these notions that allow tabloid newspapers to get away with stories about aliens landing from outer space, and human beings giving birth to some other species. Irrational claims have also allowed a string of fake religious leaders to persuade congregants to donate all their material goods, based on a prediction that the world would end in a month or so.

▼ When orators and auditors have the same prejudices, those prejudices run a great risk of being made to stand for incontestable truths.

Jooseph Roux

Jean Harris, a respected private school teacher, had the problem of an irrational claim several years ago when she was accused of killing her long-term companion, Dr. Herman Tarnauer, the "Scarsdale Diet Doctor." Her lawyers suggested that she plead temporary insanity—after all, Dr. Tarnauer had been abusive and unfaithful, and had been humiliating her in a variety of ways over several years. Ms. Harris refused the advice, however, and argued (quite eloquently) that she had shot Dr. Tarnauer by accident. The problem was, she had shot Dr. Tarnauer *five times, at point-blank range.* No matter how eloquently she argued, the jury simply could not believe that such an act could be "accidental." Ms. Harris was found guilty and sentenced to 25 years to life.

Within the realm of rationality, *it is an ethical fault to use emotional appeals to hinder truth.* Whereas it is an accepted practice to augment a logical argument with what we call "emotional evidence," it is unethical to use emotional appeals as a substitute or cover-up for a lack of sound reasoning and valid evidence. In the middle of the congressional campaign of 1994, for example, the press became obsessed with the case of Susan Smith, a young mother who murdered her two children and blamed the crime on an imaginary car jacker. At least one congressional candidate used that incident to insist that, if his party was in power, such crimes would not take place.[22]

Such an emotional appeal, and, often, the emotional language that goes with it, is an ethical fault when it is used to obscure the lines of argument that the audience needs to make up its mind logically.

## Ethical Listening

We mentioned the area of audience responsibilities earlier, when we spoke about how the audience has the responsibility to make sure that the speaker's forms of proof are within ethical bounds. Before we leave this list of specific guidelines for a public speaking class, we should emphasize that audience members cannot hold the speaker to any kind of ethical standard if they do not listen with all the care that was spelled out in Chapter 2. Audience members who use class time to read assignments from other classes, or to talk to a classmate, or to catch up on a nap have an ethical problem of their own. This happens to be an ethical fault that is especially annoying to the typical speech instructor.

## ▼ SAMPLE SPEECH

The following speech was presented by Dana M. Perino at the University of Southern Colorado.[23] Dana wanted to present a speech that was clearly in the audience's interest: She wanted to help make people aware of a widespread, unnecessary abuse of vitamin supplements. Dana had no particular self-interest in giving this speech—she wasn't selling a new diet plan to take the place of the vitamin tablets she was asking her audience to give up. She really wanted to help solve a problem that could be hurting people. To do so, she had to deal with possible ethical problems at several places in her speech. We think that Dana can be proud of the speech she gave; you'll find careful research here, for example, and no evidence of plagiarism. Still, each of her ethical choices leaves room for discussion. As you read the speech and attendant notes, see if you would have made the same choices Dana did.

## ▼ DEBUNKING THE VITAMIN MYTH

Dana M. Perino

University of Southern Colorado

[1] When baby Ryan Pitzer became colicky his mother, Susan Pitzer, decided to try a natural vitamin remedy she had read about in a book. The recipe called for potassium drops which Mrs. Pitzer gave in doses of 3,000 milligrams a day to her three-month-old baby. We can understand her desire to be a good mother and ensure her son's good health. She repeated the dose for two days until little Ryan stopped breathing. You see, this loving mother was administering a dose three times the daily amount needed

Dana starts off with a powerful piece of emotional evidence, which would be an ethical problem only if she used it to obscure the truth.

for an adult. Ryan died thirty-six hours later of acute potassium poisoning. Ryan's story was one of a series of horror stories reported by James DeBrosse in *The St. Petersburg Times* in November, 1990. His report prompted doctors to say that Ryan's death was a striking example of what can happen to people who become overzealous about food supplements.

[2] America's mind-set currently holds myths that vitamins are a miracle cure for colds, baldness, lack of energy, and hair and nail growth. All of these beliefs are false. The truth is that the body needs vitamins in small amounts that can be obtained through a balanced diet. An article entitled "The Real Power of Vitamins" in the April 6, 1992, issue of *Time* magazine suggests that misuse of and misconceptions about vitamins can be harmful and even deadly. In fact, the vitamin problem plagues many Americans. According to the October 23, 1991, issue of the *New York Times,* on any given day 80 percent of the American population will consume a vitamin, 37 percent will overindulge, and 19 percent will reach toxic levels. They go on to report that 1,752 people lost their lives in 1991 due to the overconsumption of vitamins. Clearly, this subject warrants further examination.

[3] We will first specify what a vitamin is and how it affects the body. Next, we will explore the multi-billion-dollar food supplement industry and will then consider alternatives to popping vitamins as a cure-all. Like the industry itself, I will use the word "vitamin" as a term that encompasses the 13 vitamins and the major and trace minerals.

[4] Basic information about vitamins is very simple. Vitamins can be divided into two groups: fat soluble and water soluble. A *Vitamin Fact Sheet* made available by Weight Watchers International in the fall of 1991 indicates that fat soluble vitamins include A, D, E, and K. They are stored in the liver and in body fat. In a 1989 text entitled *Personal Nutrition,* doctors Marie Boyle and Eleanor Whitney write that, "Fat soluble vitamins are not broken down easily and, therefore, they do not need to be consumed daily." For this reason, fat soluble vitamins are likely to reach toxic levels if consumed in high amounts. Water soluble vitamins include Vitamin C and the B vitamins. These vitamins are stored in the watery parts of the body and are excreted easily. In a 1981 publication entitled *Vitamins and Health Food: The Great American Hustle,* nutrition experts Victor Herbert and Stephen Barrett claim that because of their popularity, people overindulge in the consumption of water soluble vitamins.

[5] Minerals play their part in the body as well. Deficiencies in minerals such as calcium, iron, and zinc are more common in women. But the recent explosion of advertising relative to the minerals is the source of undue fear and has resulted in mineral toxicity cases in emergency rooms everywhere.

[6] You see, extra vitamins and minerals are not needed. Herbert and Barrett use this example: Imagine you are looking at an intersection (a vi-

---

**Sidebar notes (left margin):**

There's considerable evidence that vitamin C can help prevent colds. Should Dana have dealt with that?

Here she clarifies her claim and adds more evidence to prove the claim implied in her emotional introduction.

A preview of main points helps make clear the purpose of her speech. No hidden agenda here.

She makes the source of her testimony and statistics clear.

Calcium deficiency can be a serious health problem in women, leading to osteoporosis. Does Dana underplay that health threat?

tamin site) where one police officer (the vitamin) is making sure cars (food) move smoothly. Hundreds of cars go through the intersection (getting used up) but the police officer is replaced only once in a while. Bringing more officers (more vitamins) to the intersection only adds to taxpayer expense—in this case, the tax is levied against your body.

7 Vitamins are needed to help digest food, store energy, and form new blood cells. Barbara Bullock's 1989 text *Patho-Physiology* says that vitamins are catalysts which increase the rate of chemical reactions in the body, but toxic levels can cause liver damage, skin problems, severe pain, and even death.

8 Traditionally, Americans have taken vitamins according to governmental regulations commonly known as RDAs or Recommended Daily Allowances. The key word is "recommended." The Food and Drug Administration recalculates these figures every two years, but the numbers are set for an ideal height and weight. RDAs are calculated to meet the dietary needs of women who are 5'6" and weigh 120 pounds, and men who are 5'10" and weigh 160 pounds. If you do not meet either category exactly, you are ill advised to follow RDAs.

9 As consumers, we spend billions of dollars on vitamins, and that should prompt us to take a closer look at the vitamin industry. In his series about food supplements, DeBrosse reported that Americans pour $6 billion every year into the pockets of vitamin producers, purveyors, and publishers. Business is booming for the modern food quack in the form of countless vitamin products, sales, and numerous publications on vitamin magic.

10 A 73-year-old Floridian named Barbara Pletcher is only one of millions lulled into buying vitamins by unethical advertising and selling practices. For a fee of $750, Mrs. Pletcher stocked her cupboards with a year's supply of 50 different vitamins. She took them religiously with faith in the idea that she was doing her body nothing but good. But she stands as an example of the way the vitamin industry victimizes the sick and elderly.

11 DeBrosse even found one young man in a white doctor's jacket selling vitamins at a meeting of the American Association of Retired Persons. Further investigation revealed that he had been selling products, which were no more than generic multivitamins, to unsuspecting consumers for five years. Even worse is that the "scientist" never received a high school diploma.

12 Most people believe that quackery is easy to spot. It is not. The modern snake oil salesman wears a scientific disguise, will speak in scientific terms, will appear to be an expert, and will have people drawn to him like a moth to a flame. For some, qualifications will stem from distribution kits sold through the mail. With no special training in diet or nutrition, and for the low, low price of just $12.50, you, too, can buy into the "Shaklee Way of Life." But you might want to change your lifestyle when you hear that

Does Dana imply that vitamin and mineral supplements are *never* needed? Is this going too far?

How often is this problem fatal? Are we given enough information to use critical thinking about this?

Is the basic claim about RDAs being invalid strictly rational? Or are most people capable of factoring in the adjustments that make them handy guidelines?

One isolated example,

then another,

is used to further back up the idea that the problem exists. Combined with what she told us in paragraph 2, these examples rationally support the claim that the problem is widespread enough to warrant our attention.

Shaklee feeds you more than a line of promises with no guarantee. According to Herbert and Barrett, some Shaklee products contain addictive elements that ensure return customers—people who will sink as much as $10,000 in the vitamin pool over the course of 40 years. They might as well be eating their money—they'd get fiber from dollars, zinc and copper from pennies, and nickel from the trusty 5-cent piece.

[13] But Shaklee is not the only crook in the business. Even mall retail outlets like GNC and Vitamin World employ minimum wage workers and cloak them in the garb of nutrition experts. But they know no more than you or I. If they do know more, it's probably derived from reading works on food supplements along with promotional literature sent to retailers. But before these retailers start preaching their particular brand of religion, doctors Herbert and Barrett would say "Never fall into practicing unproven remedies found in books. There are no laws saying that they have to be true." And unfortunately, Ryan Pitzer's death reminds us that many claims made in such books are not.

[14] Evidently, the billions of dollars we are spending are going to unethical salespeople and false promises. It is time to reexamine our involvement in the vitamin industry, so let's consider alternatives to vitamin popping.

[15] First, people should break loose from the clutches of the vitamin demon that possesses them and arm themselves with information. The activities of the federal Food and Drug Administration can be obtained in the *FDA Consumer*. This reliable publication increases consumer awareness of nutritional rip offs and food supplement safety. It is readily available to the public at libraries and bookstores. The *FDA Consumer* also includes a list of legislation being advanced to Congress which will ultimately change the way we think about food supplements. Find the ideas you support and do just that.

[16] You can also save yourself from the perils of this industry by learning to differentiate between myth and fact. Stay away from the Avon Lady who has traded her cosmetics for food supplements and the minimum wage experts in white lab coats at retail outlets. Disregard advertisements and publications promising to cover a bald head, increase sexual potency, or help with weight loss "the natural way." These matters should be taken up with your doctor—the one who studied for and earned that white coat. He or she can tailor a nutrition schedule for you which may be complete enough that no vitamin supplements are necessary. If your doctor does suggest a vitamin supplement, he or she is likely to concur with Boyle and Whitney who say that one simple multivitamin a day will be sufficient. Even generic brands contain the essential elements and will cost much less. They note that it is senseless to waste your money on expensive food supplements that will often harm your body.

[17] Even without the help of your doctor, software is available which allows consumers to calculate the proper daily intake of vitamins for those of us

who don't fall into the RDA's ideal height or weight category. The computer will indicate deficiencies and overconsumption of certain elements.
[18] Clearly, the vitamin industry is large, prosperous, and confusing. To reduce the confusion we've defined what constitutes a vitamin and how it works in your system. We also discussed unscrupulous practices of the vitamin industry; and finally, learned how to ward off the beast that is the vitamin business. Our salvation lies in knowing where to go for complete, factual information about our dietary needs. Unfortunately, too many people have been ravaged by the industry's false claims. Vitamin awareness is a must if Americans are to fight back and win—like Susan Pitzer did by suing the author of the potassium remedy that took her son's life.

*Good review of main points, clarifying the purpose and thesis of this speech. But is all of the vitamin industry, in fact, a beast, guilty of false claims?*

 **SUMMARY**

The media/information age has ushered in a considerable amount of confusion and cynicism in the area of ethics. The glut of messages has made it extremely difficult to judge acceptable ethical guidelines in contemporary society. Providing a forum for the discussion of these issues is one of the things that makes the study of public speaking so valuable.

We propose a general set of ethical guidelines here. Ethical communication is defined as communication in the audience's best interest (as opposed to one's self-interest) that is honest (in other words, does not purposely intend to mislead) and accurate (which means that it provides correct information, without leaving out important information). Rather than using the terms *ethical* and *unethical* as blanket generalizations, however, we accept the idea of a continuum of ethical behaviors and use such terms as *more ethical, less ethical,* and *ethical fault* to describe communication behavior.

We also propose some specific guidelines to avoid plagiarism (by carefully attributing the source of ideas, facts, and words), statistical confusion (by carefully interpreting and wording statistical evidence), and irrationality (by using logic and encouraging critical thinking within the audience).

 **EXERCISES**

1. Prepare a three-minute speech on ethical choices that you have had to make in your own communications. These might be something as simple as a "white lie" told to keep from hurting someone, or telling a hard truth in the face of certain unpleasant consequences. If class time does not permit, this exercise can be completed as a 500-word essay.

2. Based on the guidelines presented in this chapter, prepare an ethical analysis of a printed speech. The speech might come from *Vital Speeches of the Day, Contemporary American Speeches,* the *New York Times,* or any other source. Try to find at least three or four possible ethical choices that had to be made in the speech, and tell whether you would have made the same choices, given as much as you know about the speech situation.

3. Using the same guidelines as exercise 2, prepare an ethical analysis of a televised message (videotaped, preferably). This message might be a commercial, an infomercial (that is, a program-length commercial), a segment from a tabloid news magazine show (such as *Hard Copy* or *A Current Affair*), or any other appropriate message.

# NOTES

1. "Teacher Ignores Georgia Law on Moment of Quiet," *New York Times,* August 24, 1994, p. B8.
2. Jane Fritsch, "Former Empire Blue Cross Financial Chief Indicted for Perjury," *New York Times,* October 19, 1994, p. B1.
3. "Veritas for One Student," *The Boston Globe,* August 10, 1994, p. 14.
4. Many twentieth-century philosophers believe that there are no universal moral codes. Others insist that although rules are not universal, dispositions toward morality are, and therefore all cultures share a tendency to form family and societal bonds that foster moral commitments. See James Q. Wilson, "What Is Moral, and How Do We Know It?" *Commentary* 95 (June 1993), pp. 37–44. One 22-year study showed a steady decline in integrity, honesty, and morality among adults. Cited in "Beyond Materialism: Dark Hearts," *Psychology Today* 26, January–February 1993, p. 9.
5. See, for example, George Will, "America's Slide into the Sewer," in *Mass Media Issues,* 4th ed., George Rodman, ed. (Dubuque: Kendall/Hunt, 1993), pp. 218–220.
6. For an expansion of this point of view, see Neil Postman, *Amusing Ourselves to Death: Public Discourse in the Age of Show Business* (New York: Penguin Books, 1985).
7. Quoted in John Makay, *Public Speaking: Theory into Practice* (Fort Worth: Harcourt Brace, 1992), p. 70.
8. Garry Will, "Dishonest Abe," *Time,* October 5, 1992, pp. 41–42.
9. David Finn, "Critical Choices Will Define Profession's Value," *Public Relations Journal* 49 (September 1993): p. 40.
10. James A. Jacksa and Michael S. Pritchard, *Communication Ethics: Methods of Analysis,* 2d ed. (Belmont, Calif.: Wadsworth, 1994).
11. Vernon Jensen, "Ethical Tension Points in Whistle-blowing," in *Ethics in Human Communication,* 3d ed., Richard Johannesen, (Prospect Heights, Ill.: Waveland, 1990), p. 281. Cited in Jacksa and Pritchard, *Communication Ethics,* p. 5.
12. For an incisive look into the problem of deception, see R. Hopper and R. H. Bell, "Broadening the Deception Construct," *Quarterly Journal of Speech* 67:3 (August 1984): pp. 288–302. These authors found six types of deception, which they called fictions, playings, lies, crimes, masks, and unlies. See also M. Osborne, "The Abuses of Argument," *Southern Speech Communication Journal* 49:1 (Fall 1983): pp. 1–11.
13. See, for example, Shearon Lowry and Melvin DeFleur, *Milestones in Mass Communication Research* (New York: Longman, 1988), p. 132.
14. "Nine out of ten dentists surveyed . . .", *Utne Reader,* November–December 1992, p. 44.
15. Ibid.
16. Ignorant misstatement is sometimes referred to as *misinformation,* to distinguish it from *disinformation,* which is purposeful misstatement.
17. Gregory Cerio, "Facts and Fantasy," *Newsweek,* July 11, 1994, p. 6, and "Rush to Judgment," *The Progressive,* August 1994, p. 9.
18. Judith R. Shapiro, "What Women Can Teach Men," *New York Times,* November 23, 1994, p. A23.
19. Tim Schultz, "Misgrading that Causes More Than Bad Test Scores," *Winning Orations* (Interstate Oratorical Association, 1993), p. 39.
20. Hugh Sidey, "Speaking Out of Turn," *Time,* April 25, 1988, p. 36.
21. Lawrence E. Joseph, *Common Sense: Why It's No Longer Common* (New York: Addison Wesley, 1994), p. 40.
22. The candidate was Newt Gingrich.
23. Dana M. Perino, "Debunking the Vitamin Myth," *Winning Orations, 1992* (Interstate Oratorical Association, 1992), p. 15. Dana was coached by Shawnalee A. Whitney.

▼ **CHAPTER 4**

# TOPIC, PURPOSE, AND CENTRAL IDEA

## ▼ CHAPTER 4 OBJECTIVES

**After reading this chapter, you should understand:**

1. The process involved in choosing an effective speech topic.
2. The importance of defining a clear speech purpose.
3. The relationship among topic, general purpose, specific purpose, and central idea.

**You should be able to:**

1. Choose an effective speaking topic.
2. Formulate a purpose statement that will help you focus and develop that topic.
3. Formulate a central idea that will help you further refine and focus your topic.

### ● CHOOSING A TOPIC

Glen Martin, a student at William Jewell College in Missouri, was having a bad semester. A close friend of his had been killed in a drive-by shooting, and since that time Glen had found it difficult to concentrate on his studies. When he was asked by his communications professor to come up with a speech topic, his initial response was, "I don't need this."

In this chapter, we are going to take a look at the process that Glen and every other student speaker goes through in choosing and developing a topic for a speech. The speech that Glen finally came up with will be the sample speech at the end of this chapter.

## Why Is Topic Choice Part of a Speech Assignment?

There's a paradox for student speakers: Choosing a topic will seldom be a problem for you outside the classroom. Generally you will be asked to speak on a topic because you are recognized as an authority in that area. Parents are asked to come into their children's classroom to talk about their jobs, police are asked to come to community groups to talk about safety, and the president of a sorority is asked to speak to freshmen about her organization. If you need to give a presentation as part of your job, such as briefing the sales force on a new product, your topic will essentially be assigned, either by your supervisor or by the needs of the meeting. In the rare instance in which you speak without being invited, you do so because of a deeply felt need. Perhaps you've been unfairly accused of a traffic ticket and you choose to speak up in court. Or perhaps you volunteer to inform your community about a problem, such as homelessness or teen suicide.

You might wish that your instructor would assign you a topic, since that's the way most speeches operate in the real world, but there are at

Dilbert                                                                    by Scott Adams

*Dilbert* reprinted by permission of United Features Syndicate.

least two reasons this task is left to you. First, it helps you to develop skills in goal-setting and analysis, skills that are valuable in any intellectual endeavor. Second, it gives you the chance to talk about a subject that fits *your* interests and knowledge.

Although topic selection is a rarity outside the classroom, it is a real problem within the classroom. Some students find it difficult to come up with a topic that they feel comfortable with and confident about. And the pressure is on, because the difference between a successful and an unsuccessful speech can depend on the choice of topic.

## ▼ TOPIC SELECTION IN THE MEDIA/INFORMATION AGE

In the media/information age, topic selection is largely a matter of focus. "To focus" means "to concentrate on one thing." Students often speak of the difficulties of "finding a topic," as though the world were a barren landscape of limited, carefully hidden topics. In fact, today's mediated world is a writhing confusion of limitless topics, and usually the problem involves focusing on one of them. The topics whirl by at a dizzying speed. Here, for example, are the topics that were mentioned or discussed in one randomly chosen, half-hour network television news report:[1]

▼ Health Care Reform

▼ How a Bill Is Passed in Congress

▼ The Working Relationship between Senate and House

▼ Congressional Lobbying

▼ Welfare Reform

▼ Campaign Fund-raising

▼ The Role of the First Lady

▼ Governmental Public Relations

▼ Liberalism vs. Conservatism

▼ The U.S. National Budget Process

▼ Deficit Financing

▼ The National Debt

▼ Congressional Hearings

▼ Governmental Scandals

▼ The Press-Government Relationship

▼ How the White House Works

▼ Abortion Clinic Violence

▼ The Abortion Controversy

▼ Radio Talk Show Commentators

▼ Tax-Exempt Violent Organizations

▼ I.R.S. Policies

▼ International Refugee Relief

▼ Cholera

▼ Dysentery

▼ U.N. Policies

▼ Doctors without Borders

▼ Antibiotics

▼ Water Purification Technology

▼ Army Corps of Engineers

▼ Military Coups

▼ Economic Blockades

▼ U.S. Military Intervention

▼ Freedom of the Press

▼ Political Editorial Cartoons

▼ Torture

▼ Human Rights

▼ Political Repression

▼ Spousal Abuse

▼ Domestic Violence

▼ Family Relations

▼ Interpersonal Control and Domination

▼ Mental Health Problems

▼ Economic Determinants of Violence

▼ Counseling Groups

▼ Child Rearing

▼ Robotic Technology

▼ The Study of Volcanoes

▼ NASA's Non space Studies

Without commercials, this program was 22 minutes long. The eight minutes of commercials suggested a list of topics nearly as long. And this list was generated only from the major stories of a national report. It contained none of the sports, weather, local crime, community affairs, movie reviews, and entertainment news of a local newscast. An even longer list could be developed from one issue of a daily newspaper, or one issue of a weekly newsmagazine.

One thing that makes the topics so plentiful is the "global village" created by the electronic media. The range of topics that interest today's audience come from all over the world. Global topics include far-off civil wars, famines, and even the extramarital affairs of the British royal family.

## ⬡ GUIDELINES FOR TOPIC SELECTION

▼ A good indignation makes an excellent speech.

Ralph Waldo Emerson

With media topics buzzing by so quickly, how do you go about focusing on one topic? Here are eight guidelines that make the process of choosing an effective topic easier.

### Start with Your Own Interests

One of the most clear-cut effects of the media is what is known as "agenda setting." Experts say that the media set our agenda, in the sense that they tell us what is important in society. If it's important, it's on the television news—and in the papers, in magazines, on the radio, and in films. In this sense the media might not tell us what to think (they offer too many competing arguments for that) but they do tell us what to think *about*.[2]

Keeping the agenda-setting function of the media in mind, it is important to remember that the topic of your speech can originate in either of two places: it can be externally generated, such as through the media, or it can be internally generated, from your own interests and experiences. It's a good idea to begin with your internally generated topics. Your personal interest will increase your motivation throughout your research and development of the topic.

## Choose a Topic You Know Something About

Some things interest us because of their mystery—because, in fact, we know so little about them. It is usually better to start with a topic that not only interests you but about which you already know something.

To choose such a topic, think about your activities, your hobbies, your special interests. The main problem for most people is realizing how much they know. It is a mistake to think that you have nothing new to say; your experiences, your thoughts, and your investigation of a topic will be, by definition, unique.

One student who felt he had no unique knowledge came up with the following list after reviewing his interests:

1. Cars: driving them, different types of safety features, and problems
2. Learning English as a second language: from his experiences as both a student and a tutor
3. Dealing with adoption (he was adopted)
4. Different forms of discrimination: age, sex, racial, and student discrimination, all of which he felt he had experienced firsthand
5. Religion: He was deeply involved with his own

Choosing a topic you know something about will make your research tasks easier. It will also increase your confidence when it comes time to deliver the speech.

## Move from Internally Generated to Externally Generated Topics

Sometimes it's difficult to pinpoint what your interests are—especially when you are being pressed to come up with a speech topic. If that happens to you, you might want to move from internally generated to externally generated topic choices by performing a quick "personal media review." You do this by reviewing your favorite newspapers, magazines, books, and television programs. You can see how "personal" a media review can be by looking at the lists generated by students with different preferences. For example, one student's favorite magazine was *Women's Sports and Fitness*. A quick review of one issue of this magazine provided her with the following list:[3]

- ▼ The Mind-Body Workout
- ▼ Antioxidants and Exercise
- ▼ Fitness Videos
- ▼ Massage Therapy
- ▼ Cross-Training
- ▼ Future Fitness: How We'll Be Working Out in the 21st Century

- ▼ Muscular Pain Relief
- ▼ Rock Climbing
- ▼ Diets that Prevent Injury
- ▼ Sports Bras
- ▼ Aerobic Shoes
- ▼ Healing Arts
- ▼ Nontraditional Medicines

Another student's favorite magazine was *The New Yorker*. Here's his list from one issue:[4]

- ▼ The "Hero Industry"
- ▼ Art Auctions
- ▼ Press Criticism
- ▼ The Clarence Thomas–Anita Hill Affair
- ▼ The Bosses of Organized Crime
- ▼ Cross-Dressing
- ▼ Sumner Redstone's Communi- cation Empire

- ▼ The Art of Lucian Freud
- ▼ Ronald Reagan's Farewell to the American People
- ▼ Why People Become Spies
- ▼ The Writers of the Beat Movement
- ▼ The Current Cinema
- ▼ Mozart's Demons
- ▼ The Role of Orphanages

When you perform a personal media review, make an "unedited" list of the topics that interest you. In other words, don't exclude topics from your first list as being inappropriate; these topics might remind you of a more appropriate topic as your list grows. It will also give you ideas to work with through analysis and combination.

## Multiply Topic Ideas Through Analysis

*Analysis is the process of taking something apart and systematically look-ing at each part.* Consider the way a speech topic can be selected purely on the basis of analysis. In looking for a topic that your classmates might find entertaining, you might analyze a typical day in the life of a student. Tak-ing the day apart, you might find that it basically consists of breakfast, classes, lunch, classes, dinner, library study, social functions, and sleep. That breakdown gives you a few topics right away. Eating brings to mind eating disorders, proper nutrition, cooking on a budget, and so on. Classes bring to mind required courses, new courses, needed courses, the quality of professors, notetaking, and so on. Even "sleeping" is a rich source of top-ics. You might realize that students often get too little sleep and find it challenging to stay awake in some of their classes. That might bring you to the idea of "sleeping problems and how to solve them." You could develop this topic through analysis by taking it apart according to types of sleep problems:

▼ Trouble getting to sleep

▼ Trouble sleeping soundly

▼ Trouble waking up

One type of analysis is performed through free association. To free-associate, you take any word from any one of your topic lists and write down whatever word it brings to mind, and then you write down whatever *that* word brings to mind, and so on. For example, the student whose favorite magazine was *The New Yorker* listed "Why People Become Spies" as a potential topic. This topic idea came from an article about Kim Philby, an aristocratic Englishman who was actually a spy for the K.G.B. during the Cold War. Free-associating from that topic idea, the student might produce a list like this:

▼ Why People Become Spies

▼ Explaining Thrill-Seeking Behavior

▼ Ethics in Public Life

▼ Kim Philby, Mata Hari, and Other Famous Spies

▼ Good Spies and Bad Spies

▼ Spy Novels

▼ Bond. James Bond

▼ Spies in the Movies

▼ The Role of Espionage in Modern Government

▼ The History of Espionage

▼ The Cold War

▼ Why Communism Fell

▼ The Fall of the Soviet Union

▼ Russia's Current Woes

▼ Global Economic Turmoil

▼ World Trade in Troubled Times

## Combine Topic Ideas to Create a Fresh Approach

In speaking about analysis and free association, we are really talking about techniques of enhancing creativity. One type of creativity is the ability to discover some new relationship between two or more things you already know. If you have both "racism" and "environmentalism" on your list of topics, you might be tempted to exclude them as too broad to be dealt with meaningfully in a speech. However, if you put these two topics together and think about them, you might realize that there is a relationship between the areas where people of a particular race live and the areas where solid waste disposal sites are located, and you might come up with "environmental racism" as a topic.[5]

Combining topics will help you avoid those topics that many instructors would perceive as "overused." In one survey, 300 college

professors were asked to list "overused" topics.[6] Here is the list (the number following each topic represents the number of professors listing that topic):

| | |
|---|---|
| Abortion 89 | Drinking Alcohol 24 |
| Gun Control 48 | Sports 22 |
| Drunk Driving 44 | Euthanasia 19 |
| Capital Punishment 42 | Recycling 17 |
| Drugs 29 | Health 16 |
| Exercise 28 | Child Abuse 14 |
| The Environment 27 | Current Events 11 |
| Smoking 26 | Stress 11 |
| Seat Belts 26 | Nutrition 10 |

The majority of the professors answered "none," pointing out that *no* topic was overused if an original or worthwhile approach was used. Still, the list should suggest some topics to beware of. Glen Martin, whose speech serves as a sample at the end of this chapter, came up with a fresh topic by combining guns, drugs, and gangs as a "tragic trilogy" that could be looked at as one problem.

## Look for a Topic Early

The best student speakers usually choose a topic as soon as possible after a speech is assigned. Saving time for adequate research, thought, and practice is essential to effective speechmaking. And yet the reasons for choosing a topic early run even deeper than that. Ideas seem to come automatically to speakers who have a topic in mind; this is partially because once you have focused on a topic you can begin to pluck ideas and facts out of the media stream that flows by you each day. Things you read or observe or talk about that might have otherwise been meaningless suddenly relate to your topic, providing material or inspiration for sources of material.[7] The earlier you decide on a topic, the more of these happy coincidences you can take advantage of.

## Stick with the Topic You've Chosen

Once you decide on a topic, stick with it. If you feel that the topic is not working, adapt it, but don't junk it completely. For example, if you were working on a speech on violence in the media, the research process might lead you to believe that there was not enough new to say on that topic. Rather than begin from scratch, you could adapt the speech to violence in society. If you find that topic too broad, you could adapt it to "Teen-Age Homicide" (a class of crime that has risen alarmingly in recent years).[8]

## Keep the Audience in Mind

It is important to consider the audience—their interests, their knowledge, their attitudes—throughout the topic selection process. In fact, audience considerations are so important, throughout the entire speech preparation process, that all of Chapter 5 will be devoted to audience analysis and adaptation.

These guidelines suggest that a quick media-use profile, some conversations with friends and family members, and perhaps some quiet introspection will help you choose a topic quickly. With the huge number of topics buzzing by, you have to reach out and grab one of them and slow it down enough to get into it. You "get into" it through research, a topic we will devote more time to in Chapter 6.

Once you have chosen your topic, you can turn to the first step in developing it: determining your purpose.

## ▼ DETERMINING YOUR PURPOSE

No one gives a speech, or expresses any kind of message, without a reason. Purpose is easy to see in messages that ask for something: "Pass the salt" or "How about a movie this Friday?" or "Excuse me, that's my foot you're standing on." But even in more subtle messages the speaker always

▼ Even if you're on the right track, you'll get run over if you just sit there.

Will Rogers

▼ There is no such thing as an uninteresting subject. There are only uninterested people.

G. K. Chesterton

▼ The secret of success is constancy of purpose.

Benjamin Disraeli

has a purpose, which is to evoke a response from the listener. When purposes are misunderstood or confused by the speaker, the speech preparation process becomes more difficult and the final speech runs the risk of confusing the audience.

The first step in understanding your purpose is to formulate a clear and precise statement of that purpose. You focus first on the *general purpose*.

### General Purpose

Most students, when asked *why* they are giving a speech in a college class, quickly cite course requirements. But you have to analyze your motives more deeply than that to develop a complete speech purpose. Even if you are only giving your speech for the grade, you still have to affect your audience in some way to earn that grade.

If your motive for speaking is to learn effective speech techniques (as we hope it is), you still have to influence your audience to accomplish your goal. After all, that is what effective speaking is all about.

When we say you have to influence your audience, we mean you have to *change* them in some way. If you think about all the possible ways you could change an audience, you'll realize that they all boil down to three options, which happen to be the three *general purposes* for speaking.

**1.** *To Entertain.* To relax your audience by providing them with a pleasant listening experience.
**2.** *To Inform.* To enlighten your audience by teaching them something.
**3.** *To Persuade.* To move your audience toward a new attitude or behavior.

A brief scrutiny of these purposes will reveal that no speech could ever have *only* one purpose. These purposes are interrelated because a speech designed for one purpose will almost always accomplish at least a little of the other purposes; even a speech designed purely to entertain might change audience attitudes or teach that audience something new. In fact, these purposes are *cumulative* in the sense that, to inform an audience, you have to make your remarks entertaining enough to hold their interest—at least long enough to convince them your topic is worth learning about. And you certainly have to inform an audience (about your arguments) in order to persuade them.

Deciding your general purpose is like choosing the "right" answer on one of those multiple-choice tests in which *all* the answers are right to a certain degree, but *one* answer is more right than the others. Thus, we say that any speech is *primarily* designed for one of these purposes.

A clear understanding of your general purpose gets you on the right track for choosing and developing a topic. It is a refinement, a narrowing of the broad general topic; you're not just dealing with an idea anymore, but an idea that is being used to move your audience in a particular direction. Understanding your *specific purpose* continues that process of refinement.

## Specific Purpose

Whereas your general purpose is only a one-word label, your *specific* goal is expressed in the form of a *purpose statement*—a complete sentence that describes exactly what you want your speech to accomplish. The purpose statement usually isn't

used word for word in the actual speech; its purpose is to keep you focused as you plan your speech.

If you were giving an informative talk on small claims court, your purpose statement might be worded something like this:

> After listening to my speech my audience will be able to list the five steps for preparing a small claims case.

Keep this example in mind as we summarize several characteristics of effective purpose statements:

1. *A Purpose Statement Is Audience-Oriented.* Since every speech seeks some response from a receiver, the desired response should be reflected in the purpose statement. For your talk on small claims court, the preceding purpose statement would be more effective than if you had said "My purpose is to talk about small claims court," or "My purpose is to tell my audience about small claims court."

   If your purpose is "to tell" an audience something, that would suggest that the speech could be successful even if no one listens. Your purpose statement should refer to the response you want from your audience: It should tell what the audience members will know or be able to do after listening to your speech. That is why the statement begins,

   > After listening to my speech, my audience will . . .

and then continues with a verb that tells what your audience members will understand, know, or be able to do:

▼ understand the meaning of . . .

▼ be able to list . . .

▼ be able to recall . . .

▼ be able to make . . .

▼ know the steps involved in, etc.

Telling what your audience will be able to understand, know, or be able to do often suggests an organizational pattern for the speech ("the five steps").

**2.** *A Purpose Statement Should Be Specific.* To be effective, a purpose statement should be worded specifically, with enough detail so that you would be able to measure or test your audience, after your speech, to see if you had achieved your purpose. To say "After listening to my speech, my audience will know more about small claims court" is too vague. To be able to "list the five steps of preparing a small claims case," however, is specific enough to be testable. This doesn't mean you *have* to give your audience a quiz after your speech. In fact, most audiences would resent that. The testable nature of the audience response is used to keep *you* focused.

**3.** *A Purpose Statement Should Be Realistic.* You must be able to realistically accomplish your purpose as stated. Some speakers insist on formulating purpose statements such as, "My purpose is to convince my audience to make federal budget deficits illegal." Unfortunately, unless your audience happens to be a joint session of Congress, it won't have the power to change United States fiscal policy. But any audience can write their congressional representative or sign a petition. Similarly, an audience will not "learn how to play championship tennis" or "understand the dangers of business regulation" in one sitting. You must aim for an audience response that is possible to accomplish. In the small claims court speech, it would be unrealistic to say, "After listening to my speech, my audience will be able to win a case in small claims court." It would be impossible to be sure that each member of an audience has a winnable case.

Consider how each of the following sets of purpose statements become more effective when they meet the criteria we have been discussing:

| LESS EFFECTIVE | MORE EFFECTIVE |
|---|---|
| To tell my audience about day-care centers (not result-oriented) | After listening to my speech, my audience will be able to identify the three basic types of day-care centers. |

| LESS EFFECTIVE | MORE EFFECTIVE |
|---|---|
| After listening to my speech, my audience will understand solar power. (not realistic) | After listening to my speech, my audience will understand how solar power can be used at home, in business, and in government. |
| To tell my audience about contact lenses (not specific) | After listening to my speech, my audience will be able to identify the three basic types of contact lenses. |

## ⬤ THE CENTRAL IDEA

So far we have discussed how to select a topic and how partially to focus that topic through its general and specific purpose. Your next step in the focusing process is to formulate a statement of your central idea. The statement of your *central idea,* sometimes called the *thesis statement,* tells you the one idea that you want your audience to remember after they have forgotten everything else you had to say. It is the one idea that everything else in your speech relates to. If your purpose statement tells you what you expect from your audience, your central idea tells you what you expect to say. The statement of central idea for your small claims speech might be worded like this:

> Arguing a case on your own in small claims court is a simple, five-step process that can give you the same results you would achieve with a lawyer.

It's possible that there will be some overlap between your purpose statement and your central idea, especially if your purpose statement is to help your audience be able to recall or use the essential information in your speech. You can always keep the two devices separate, however, by remembering that the purpose statement is audience-oriented and the statement of central idea is message-oriented.

The progression from topic to purpose to central idea is another focusing process, as you can see from the following examples:

▼ Topic: Why Must an Injured Horse Be Destroyed?

▼ General Purpose: To inform.

▼ Specific Purpose: After listening to my speech, my audience will understand why certain types of equine injuries cannot be healed.

▼ Central Idea: If a horse cannot recover, it is more humane to destroy it than to let it suffer a slow, agonizing death.

▼ Topic: Plastics Recycling

▼ General Purpose: To persuade.

▼ If you can't write your message in a sentence, you can't say it in an hour.

Dianna Booher

▼ Specific Purpose: After listening to my speech, at least half my audience members will sign my petition to the governor supporting a state plastics recycling bill.

▼ Central Idea: Recycling plastics reduces litter, creates new employment, and saves resources.

▼ Topic: Saving Water

▼ General Purpose: To persuade.

▼ Specific Purpose: After listening to my speech, audience members will use less water in their daily activities.

▼ Central Idea: Conserving water is a relatively simple process that will save us from much greater inconveniences in the future.

Remember that the preceding topics, purposes, and central ideas did not spring fully formed from the mind of the prospective speaker. Each of these focal points evolved, and very often changed radically, during the speech planning and research process. Moreover, the progression from topic to general purpose to specific purpose to central idea is cumulative in nature. Whereas the choice of topic is made early in the speech preparation process, the central idea will tend to evolve much later, as a result of your having thought about and done some research into your topic. Also, this is a progression of specificity, from a general, abstract statement to a much more specific, focused one.

## ⬤ SAMPLE SPEECH

You might remember that we introduced this chapter with the case of Glen Martin, a student at William Jewell College in Missouri.[9] Ever since a close friend of his had been killed in a drive-by shooting, Glen had found it difficult to think about anything else. A trauma like losing a close friend to violence has a tendency to shape all your perceptions. For several months, everything that Glen saw or heard seemed to suggest that society, in general, was falling apart. His speech assignment seemed particularly trivial in a world that was in such sorry shape.

Back in his room, Glen followed his instructor's directions and reviewed his interests and personal experience, but everything he came up with paled in significance when compared with his friend's death. Glen also performed a personal media review, but even in that he seemed to come up with endless lists of societal problems that culminated in violence.

Then Glen realized that his ideal speech topic was not only a potentially effective one, but one that he *needed* to talk about. He needed to make some sense of violence among young people, and he needed to think about some real solutions. It would almost be a form of therapy for him.

Not that his involvement in the topic made it easy for him; the topic was too broad for him to get his mind around, and the problem was made worse by the pain Glen felt in trying to make sense of his friend's death. But Glen stuck with the topic, adapting it through analysis and combining different facets of the general topic, and it slowly began to take shape. His general purpose, specific purpose, and thesis statement began to shape up like this:

▼ General Purpose: To persuade

▼ Specific Purpose: After listening to my speech, my audience should want to support social programs that help stop violence.

▼ Central Idea: Gangs, drugs, and guns form a "tragic trilogy" that are ruining society.

As you read this speech, decide for yourself if Glen chose an effective topic and purpose. Our comments will follow.

## ⬢ TRAGIC TRILOGY

Glen Martin

William Jewell College, Missouri

1 "All right, men. Good practice today. Listen, be careful getting home. Don't get caught in the wrong place at the wrong time tonight. I want to see you in class tomorrow morning and I want to see you at practice. I want to see you alive."

2 Those are the words Willie Stewart uses to close each of his football practices. He is Head Coach at Anacostia High School in California. In the past 10 years, over 100 of his players have been shot and killed by gangs. In the 1993 season Coach Stewart lost four of his players to bullets.

3 "Thank God", you might say, "my friends, my brother, my kids don't have to hear those words every day." No matter where you live, or where you go to school, you can only thank God they don't have to hear them yet.

4 We have dropped the ball. We have committed a great fumble of responsibility. We must halt the proliferation of violence. We must recognize and remedy the tragic trilogy of gangs, drugs, and guns.

5 I, like most of us, had become desensitized to the violence, the shootings, the mindless, motiveless drive-bys with which we are bombarded every day. At least, I was until that fumble rolled to my feet. It happened when Joshua died. He was my friend.

⁶ We grew up together, played high school sports together. He pursued his only dream, which was to play in the NFL. He was a prize recruit, receiving a full scholarship to the University of Houston to play middle linebacker. Halfway through his freshman year, he was playing. He was living his dream.

⁷ His dream came to an end as he walked down a Houston street wearing a red Kansas City Chiefs hat. He was in the wrong part of town, wearing the wrong color and he was shot and killed from the window of a moving car. That was when the fumble rolled to my feet. My friend could be any of yours, anytime, anywhere. It could even be one of you. That fumble continues to roll everywhere, because we've all dropped the ball. The tragic trilogy of gangs, drugs, and guns has become a crisis threatening our future.

⁸ In *U.S. News & World Report,* April 8, 1991, we learned another young man's story. Kevin was taken from drug-addicted parents in Massachusetts and sent to live with his grandparents in Texas. His grandfather let him shoot a gun and Kevin loved the feeling. As an early teen, Kevin would shoot out the window at a day-care center to show off for the members of the gang he had just joined. He became a petty thief in the gang and eventually became an enforcer for a Jamaican drug-trafficking posse. One day, some of the drug money was missing, and Kevin suspected an acquaintance. "I figured if I shot him," said Kevin, "the Jamaicans wouldn't think I'd taken their money. I shot him in the face, point blank. Parts of his head wound up in the doorway and there was blood everywhere. Thing is, if I'd just pulled the gun, I could have gotten the money. I shot him anyway."

⁹ Kevin's story is a perfect example of exactly how we've dropped the ball. The gang gave Kevin the attitude of a killer. The drugs gave Kevin the motive of a killer. The gun gave Kevin the weapon of a killer. Before we can even begin to pick this fumble up, we must recognize how each of these three issues has caused us to drop the ball.

¹⁰ The first component of our trilogy is the growth of gangs. Gangs are growing like a cancer. The Crips and the Bloods were the original gangs, starting in Southern California about 20 years ago. They now have affiliations in 32 states and 113 cities. Gang membership doubles every five years nationwide. Remember, the gang gave Kevin his attitude.

¹¹ The second component of our trilogy is drugs. According to *Time* magazine's Elaine Shannon, "While the U.S. has made significant progress in curbing casual drug use, it has made far less headway on the problems that most trouble the public: hard-core addiction and drug-related violence." Drugs are a part of our discussion today precisely because of the violence they cause. Violence is a by-product of the sale of drugs. Simply stated, drugs finance the guns which arm the gangs who sell the drugs. Truly, this is a vicious cycle. Remember, drugs gave Kevin his motive.

¹² Gangs and drugs pose serious threats. The real killer, however, is the third component of our trilogy, guns. When speaking about the problem of

violence in our nation, Boston Police Commissioner Francis M. Roache said simply, "The immediate problem is the availability of firearms in general." A 20-state survey of adolescent boys reported that 84 percent of them could obtain a handgun if they wanted it. The National School Safety Center suggested that in 1987, 135,000 students carried guns to school daily. They believe that number is much higher today. To put that number in perspective, there are more guns in our nation's schools, every day, than were on the battlefield at Gettysburg. Every day.

13 Kids have always faced difficult challenges. Substance abuse, violence, poverty, poor education, and an uncertain future have existed for generations. The new variable in the equation in recent years is the presence of so many guns. But, guns don't kill people, people kill people, right? We've all heard that, but I submit to you that nothing helps people kill people so quickly, efficiently, or decisively as a gun. Remember, a gun gave Kevin his weapon. Sadly, the number of Kevins grows every day.

14 We have seen how the three components of our trilogy, gangs, drugs, and guns, have become a crisis threatening our future. We have seen that the number of Kevins (and fallen friends like Joshua) grows every day. We have seen that we've dropped the ball.

15 We must pick it up. We must devise a game plan. The suggestions I am going to offer come from combining the results of two personal interviews I conducted with law enforcement officials. The first was with Edward Allen, a former police officer in Richmond, Missouri. The second was with the deputy sheriff of Ray County, Missouri, Janet Connor.

16 The first step of our game plan is to eliminate the need for gangs. To do this, we must improve the education of at-risk youths. We must also improve the legitimate economic opportunities for at-risk youths. Most importantly, we must re-emphasize family values in our society. "Family Values" has become a much-maligned catch phrase in recent months. I'm not suggesting we return to a distorted image of America as the *Donna Reed Show.* I'm simply suggesting that we must recognize and foster such values as hard work, fair play, striving for excellence, pride, and self-esteem. These are essential values gained primarily from the family. The breakdown of the family unit has much to do with the moral decay found in many of today's youth. Kids are finding in gangs that which society, school, and their family no longer provide.

17 The second step of our game plan is to wage a true war on drugs. We must destroy drugs at their source and prevent them from entering our country. We must severely punish the distributors of drugs. Increased sentences, up to and including the death penalty for drug murders, must be handed down as disincentives. We must rehabilitate addicts. We need to distribute fewer clean needles and more clean lives.

18 The third step of our game plan is gun control. Obviously, gun control is also a catch phrase that means many different things to different people. Clearly, the passage of the Brady Bill in recent weeks is a step in the right

direction, but even its staunchest supporters would have to admit that it is not nearly enough. Even as we have established that guns do indeed kill people, it is indisputable that people pull the trigger. In addition to the values mentioned earlier, we must emphasize the importance of respect for human life. Attempting to take guns out of people's hands is meaningless unless we also attempt to improve and educate those hands that continue to hold guns.

[19] Certainly, well-educated, motivated, morally stable youths, free of the influence of drugs, unable to obtain guns easily, and unwilling to waste human life, would not only pose less of a threat to our society, they would become an asset. These are the goals of our game plan. No game plan is foolproof. It will take hard work, considerable time, and certainly more youths will die before we reach our goal. It is precisely because of that last fact that we must score this touchdown.

[20] You may be thinking, "Can he guarantee all these wonderful things will happen?" No, I can't. I can, however, guarantee exactly what will happen if we don't pick up this fumble. The number of Kevins and Joshuas will continue to grow and, eventually, the ball will roll to your feet as it did mine.

[21] We can look back and see that the tragic trilogy of gangs, drugs, and guns has indeed become a crisis threatening our future. We must eliminate the need for gangs, wage a true war on drugs, and control the use of guns through education and legislation.

[22] Here is what you can do to execute the game plan. Emphasize the importance of hard work. Next, find out how your elected officials intend to vote on issues such as crime, education, and urban renewal. Finally, vote. If your elected officials are not willing to help execute our game plan, kick them off our team.

[23] A few days ago, I heard Kansas City Mayor Emanuel Cleaver give a speech. In it, he told a story about attending a funeral for two teenage boys who had been killed in a drive-by shooting. He said that he became angry while looking at the weeping mother of the two boys. Angry, he said, because while so few wept for the death of these two boys, so many of us were being held spellbound by the events surrounding a young woman who had been hit on the knee.* "Scandal and trivia," he said, "have become more important to the people of this nation than the death we see every day." He paused, shook his head, and asked the audience, "What is wrong with us?"

[24] If we decide to execute this game plan, we can begin to answer the mayor's question. We can only answer it, however, if we decide to get in the game.

---

*A reference to the attack on figure skater Nancy Kerrigan by associates of her rival Tonya Harding. This case had obsessed the national media for weeks preceding Mayor Cleaver's speech.

## Comments

The topic was a good one. This is an important societal issue, and it was certainly one in which Glen's personal experience added to the power of his words. He used analysis and focus to come up with a relatively new approach on this important topic.

Both the purpose statement and the central idea, however, could be improved with more specificity. Remember, the progression from topic to purpose to central idea is a refining process that should lend the speech a specific focus. In Glen's speech, by the time he gets to the discussion of solutions (paragraphs 16 through 19), he seems to be throwing in everything except the kitchen sink. The mind reels. Some of these solutions are highly ambiguous: "Family values" (paragraph 16), although Glen tries to define it somewhat, is still too broad a concept. Other solutions offered by Glen are controversial: "We must distribute fewer clean needles and more clean lives," for example (paragraph 17), could in itself be the topic of another speech, but is offered here without development. If Glen had zeroed in on one anti-crime program—a local gang outreach program, for example— the speech would have been more effective.

If the focus in Glen's purpose statement and central idea had been stronger, both the desired audience response (paragraph 22) and conclusion of the speech (paragraphs 23 and 24) would probably have been stronger, also. He might have asked his audience to sign a petition in support of a local program, for example. (Not that Glen did a bad job here. This is a good speech, but it's part of the philosophy of this course that there's always room for improvement.)

### ▼ SUMMARY

This chapter dealt with your first tasks in preparing a speech: choosing a topic, determining your purpose, and expressing your central idea.

Some guidelines for choosing a topic are: Start with your own interests; choose a topic you know something about; move from internally generated (personal) topic ideas to externally generated (media-based) ideas; multiply your topic ideas by using analysis to reduce general ideas to their component parts; combine other topic ideas to form a fresh approach; look for a topic early; and, finally, stick with the topic you've chosen by adapting it as you go along.

One of your tasks is to understand your purpose so that you can stick to it as you prepare your speech. General purposes include entertaining, informing, and persuading. Specific purposes are expressed in the form of purpose statements, which must be audience-oriented, precise, and realistic.

Your next step is to formulate the statement of your central idea, which is the one basic idea that you want your audience to remember after they have forgotten everything else you tell them.

## ● EXERCISES

1. Perform a "media use survey" as suggested in this chapter. Specifically, list your favorite newspapers, magazines, television programs, and books. Review them and generate a possible list of topics based on your media use.

2. Write a specific purpose statement for each of the following speeches:
   a. An after-dinner speech at an awards banquet in which you will honor a team that has a winning, but not championship, record. (You pick the team.)
   b. A classroom speech in which you explain how to do something. (Once again, you choose the topic—rebuilding an engine, cooking a favorite dish, playing a guitar, or whatever.)
   c. A campaign speech in which you support the candidate of your choice.

   Is each of your purpose statements audience-oriented? Is it precise?

3. Determine the central idea for each of these sets of main points:

   Grade inflation constitutes false promises to students whose work is average or inferior.
   Grade inflation demeans the accomplishments of students who truly excel.
   Grade inflation is basically dishonest, and therefore weakens the basis of a university.

   Motorcycle helmets prevent injuries and deaths.
   Motorcycle helmet laws work when they are enforced.
   Motorcycle helmet laws are supported by the public.

   Eating red meat increases the risk of heart disease.
   Eating red meat increases the risk of colon and prostate cancer.
   Eating red meat increases the risk of osteoporosis.

## NOTES

1. ABC "World News Tonight," August 2, 1994. The main stories for the night were as follows: Congress debates a health-care bill; Whitewater hearings continue; abortion doctor murdered by "pro-life" activist; Rwanda refugees die of dysentery; possible U.S. invasion of Haiti; counseling for spousal abusers; robotic exploration of volcano by NASA.

2. Maxwell E. McCombs and Donald L. Shaw, "The Evolution of Agenda-Setting Research: Twenty-Five Years in the Marketplace of Ideas," *Journal of Communication* 43:2 (Spring, 1993), pp. 58–67.

3. *Women's Sports and Fitness,* January 1995.

4. *The New Yorker,* January 16, 1995.

5. This is, in fact, what one student at the University of Illinois did. See Steve Osunsami, "Environmental Racism—Solving Our Nation's Waste Problems by Abusing the Disadvantaged," *Winning Orations, 1992* (Interstate Oratorical Association, 1992), p. 28.

6. This survey was conducted by the Communications Texts department of Harcourt Brace College Publishers during 1994.

7. Those interested in further reading on the topic of stimulating creativity about speech topics, or any task, will want to read Bill Backer, *The Care and Feeding of Ideas* (Times Books, 1993), which presents ideas about stimulating creativity, using the development of one award-winning TV commercial as its extended example.

8. Fox Butterfield, "Teen-Age Homicide Rate Has Soared," *New York Times,* October 14, 1994, p. A22.

9. Glen Martin, "Tragic Trilogy," *Winning Orations, 1994* (Interstate Oratorical Association, 1994), pp. 74–77. Glen was coached by Tom Willett and presented his speech at the annual contest of the Interstate Oratorical Association at the University of Alaska, Anchorage, in April 1994.

# AUDIENCE ANALYSIS AND ADAPTATION

## ▼ CHAPTER 5 OBJECTIVES

**After completing this chapter, you should understand:**

1. The importance of audience analysis.
2. The psychological, demographic, and situational elements of audience analysis.

**You should be able to:**

1. Create psychological, demographic, and situational profiles of an audience.
2. Use your audience analysis to develop an ethical speech strategy.

## ▼ AUDIENCE ANALYSIS IN THE MEDIA/INFORMATION AGE

▼ If you don't aim at the audience, they may take aim at you.

Alan J. Parisse

At the age of 36, Stephen Chao had everything an ambitious executive could want. He was considered a genius at audience analysis. He seemed to have a "sixth sense" for what the American public wanted to watch. He had developed several enormously successful low-budget TV "reality" hits, including *America's Most Wanted, Cops,* and *Studs.* Although critics panned his tabloid approach, Chao's ideas brought in millions of dollars in revenue and earned him promotion to president of Fox Television.

But in early 1992 Chao's unerring sense of audience analysis apparently failed him. The scene was a Snowmass, Colorado, conference on trends in the media industry. The audience consisted of 200 Fox News Corporation executives and their spouses, along with other VIPs, including National Endowment for the Humanities chief Lynne Cheney and her husband, Dick Cheney, the U.S. Secretary of Defense. Chao was delivering a speech defending free expression of controversial ideas. As he began his remarks, a young man with a blond ponytail entered the room, walked to the podium, and began to strip. After completely disrobing, the man exposed himself to the audience for a full 30 seconds while Chao grinned at his planned spectacle and said to his boss Murdoch's wife, "Pay attention, Anna!"

The audience was stunned, and Murdoch left the program in a cold rage. Four hours after the spectacle, he fired Chao by telephone. Analysts said that Chao had seriously misjudged his boss's tolerance for such a controversial stunt. Murdoch was well known to be a staunch conservative who had been trying to shed his image as a tabloid publisher, and Chao's audacious ploy flew in the face of this bid for respectability. Chao should have taken some of his wisdom from mass media audience analysis and applied it to his public speaking.

# Calvin and Hobbes                    by Bill Watterson

In spite of Chao's problems, we can learn a lot from observing the way that media experts concentrate on their audiences. Take the case of an advertiser introducing a new product: Such an advertiser will devote huge amounts of time and money to researching how the audience will respond to the product. Before the product is ever produced a team of marketing professionals will conduct surveys (in shopping malls and over the telephone) to try to determine if there is a market for the product. They will run controlled laboratory experiments to see if consumers will pick their product against its competition. They will run focus groups of retailers who are interviewed in-depth to see which style of packaging is most appealing. They will run more focus groups (of consumers, this time) to test the advertising that will help sell the product. They will place observers in the store to measure how many people buy the product, how many look at it but don't buy it, and how many ignore it completely.

These practices of the typical advertiser have been adopted in recent years by television executives trying to determine whether their new sitcom will be a hit; by newspaper and magazine publishers trying to determine which features will increase their readership; by film producers looking for the next box office smash; by politicians looking for ways to sell their message; and by every media professional whose goal is success. Your task as a public speaker is the same: Get to know your audience, and adapt your product (your speech) to them.

## Collecting Information About Your Audience

You can collect information about your audience in much the same way that media professionals collect information about the mass audience. The first way is simple *observation:* Look at your class members—what they wear, how they spend their time, the kinds of things they talk about. The second way is an *interview,* although in a speech class interviews tend to be very informal. A classroom "interview" usually consists of talking to one or two class members after class. Ask them what they know about your topic, how they feel about it, how it touches their lives. Test out different approaches on them. At this level, a *focus group* is also an informal affair: Get three to five class members together over a cup of decaf and let the group dynamic cook as you talk about each other's topics. You can also hand out a written *survey* to your class members. Several versions are suggested in the next chapter.

Your interpretation of data about your audience requires common sense, logic, and a respect for the law of probabilities. In other words, there are no mathematical certainties with audience analysis. People are individuals first, and individuals are notoriously unpredictable. Still, there are ways to discern patterns and trends within an audience and make some assumptions about how they affect your message.

### The Importance of Audience Analysis

Adapting your approach to the situation isn't just a technique for media moguls and public speakers. Ordinary people do it all the time. You think about your audience before telling a joke, realizing that the story that will make a hit at an end-of-the-year party would probably get you thrown out of church. You think about the others who will be attending an occasion before choosing the way you will dress, knowing that the outfit you wear while bumming around home on the weekend would earn you glares at a funeral. Likewise, you realize the good-natured insults you trade with a friend might cost you your job if you tried them with your boss.

Even with the same person, smart communicators alter their approach depending on the situation. There's a time to be quick and a time to tell your story in a leisurely manner. There's a time for bluntness and a time for tact. There's a time to be dramatic, and a time to be matter of fact. The same principles apply in public speaking. You need to fit the subject you've chosen (or been assigned) to the audience who will hear it.

Communication experts have always understood the importance of analyzing the audience. Over two thousand years ago, in his *Rhetoric,* Aristotle wrote:

> Of the three elements in speechmaking—speaker, subject, and person addressed—it is the last one, the hearer, that determines the speech's end and object.[1]

You can appreciate the importance of adapting to the audience by considering a few examples of what can happen when speakers fail to take this critical step:

▼ One student described an almost foolproof way to live rent-free and earn thousands of dollars at the same time. His listeners were very interested until it became clear that the method required a $40,000 investment—not an amount of money most could lay their hands on.

▼ A visiting journalist explained what life was like in the strife-ridden Middle East. But in the process of telling his gripping story, he offended his audience by accusing them of being pampered, self-centered Americans. After a few minutes of his speech, the audience was so defensive that they were in no mood to consider anything he said.

Just as it's possible to bungle potentially interesting topics, a speaker can also breathe life into subjects that seem deadly dull.

▼ A biology professor made the potentially boring subject of human digestion more interesting by taking her listeners on a guided tour of what was happening to their morning's breakfast while they were listening to her lecture. For the non-science-minded students, this approach personalized a subject that otherwise would have been much less interesting.

▼ A Civil War enthusiast got his audience to appreciate the struggles of that period by having them imagine that they had been drafted to serve in a military campaign. He described in graphic detail the battles, physical effort, medical care, equipment, clothing, and food that his audience would have experienced if they had served during that time.

Examples like these show that you should consider audience analysis throughout the speech preparation process as well as during the actual presentation of your speech.

Like media practitioners, public speakers have two ways to look at audience analysis—through *demographics* and *psychographics*. Demographics are audience characteristics that can be observed, such as age and gender; psychographics are "internal" characteristics, such as attitudes, values, and beliefs. Media practitioners use probability estimates and common sense in their interpretation of demographics and psychographics. You have to do the same for the audience you will face.

## DEMOGRAPHIC ANALYSIS

Demographics are the relatively straightforward characteristics of your audience. They can be observed, quantified, and labeled.

Television ratings are a good example of demographics. When the ratings services look at who watches what, they take special note of the gender, age, economic status, education, ethnic origin, family size, occupation, and place of residence of their audience.[2] In public speaking, you can make a similar profile of a given audience, and then use that profile to become "rhetorically sensitive" to all

members of your audience. One student wanted to speak about buffalo as a food source, but his audience was not of an age or income bracket to care much about bison steaks as a dining delicacy. He adapted his speech to stress ecological concerns: how large sections of the Great Plains would turn into depopulated zones without buffalo ranching, and how "animals that people eat do not become extinct."[3] We'll take a look at how you might adapt to demographic factors, including gender, age, economic status, ethnic and cultural background, membership in social and professional groups, and religion.

## Gender

In this relatively liberated age it's a mistake to assume that men and women can be counted on to be different as audience members. Take the case of audience interests: Men raise children and cook, and women take an interest in athletics and careers. Most topics can work for both sexes if you spend enough time finding a way to link them to both men and women.

For example, one student's goal was to inform her listeners about the problem of date rape on campus. She realized that the subject was a more immediate threat to women, but she wanted to find a way to make it just as important to her male listeners. After all, the men in the audience needed information on what constitutes date rape, so they wouldn't cross the line. Still, she couldn't expect much sympathy from the males in her audience if they felt that she was accusing them of being potential rapists. She adapted her speech by pointing out the concern each of the men had for the welfare of a friend, sweetheart, or family member, and urged that they share the information she was presenting with women they cared for.

The main guideline for audience adaptation in terms of gender might be this: *Do not exclude or offend any portion of your audience on the basis of sex.* Every speech teacher has a horror story about a student getting up in front of a class composed primarily, but not entirely, of men and speaking on a subject such as "Picking Up Chicks." The women, once they realize that the speech is not about methods of handling poultry, are invariably offended. And most of the men will feel the same way.

## Age

An approach may work well with one age group and fail completely with another. Aristotle once observed that young people "have strong passions," that "their lives are spent not in memory but in expectation," and that they have high ideals "because they have not been humbled by life or learnt its necessary limitations."[4] Even though some social security recipients have younger attitudes than their conservative grandchildren, it is safe to

say that, as a group, younger audiences are likely to have perspectives that differ from those of older listeners. Failure to acknowledge these differences can lead to trouble.

For example, one student wanted to inform his classmates about the health benefits of an enzyme present in certain foods. He presented an impressive amount of evidence showing how the enzyme can prevent the risk of heart disease. Despite the quality of this evidence, his audience was indifferent. Most of them were in their late teens and early twenties, and the prospect of suffering from heart disease was too remote for them to worry much about.

Another example: The recruiter for an international hotel chain was having little success in persuading the graduates of top colleges to consider her organization. During her first round of visits to college campuses she emphasized the generous retirement plan that was part of her company's benefits program. After several months she realized that the plan just didn't have much appeal for graduating students in their twenties. She had much better luck attracting candidates when she highlighted the company's policy of offering free lodging around the world for employees. Even though the dollar amount of the retirement benefits was far greater, the immediate payoff of longer, cheaper vacations had more appeal to her young listeners.

## Economic Status

The financial status of your audience can make a big difference in how you treat a topic. One student wanted to convince her audience to vacation in San Sebastian, Spain. Her speech showed that the town was a holiday paradise: sunny climate, beautiful beaches, friendly people, great shopping, and wonderful food. But she realized that the biggest question for most of her listeners was "How can I afford a European holiday?" She devoted a large part of her speech to showing the class that the combination of economy airfares and the low cost of living in Spain made the trip no more expensive than many similar ones closer to home.

### Ethnic and Cultural Background

Details that might have little meaning to members of one group might mean a great deal—either positively or negatively—to others. For instance, a speaker's choice of the terms "black" or "African American," "white" or "Anglo," can win the approval or hostility of members of each group. A little research in advance can help you decide which terms are most acceptable to your listeners.

Speakers who fail to consider the ethnic and cultural perspectives of their listeners can get into trouble. In a speech on changes in the English language, one student discussed the "problems" caused by the immigration of large numbers of Latin Americans into the United States. Several Mexican-American audience members were offended by his choice of words. They argued that many influences of Spanish weren't problems at all, but ways of enriching the language and culture.

In fact, in many parts of the southwestern United States, cross-cultural communication classes focusing on improving communication between North Americans and Mexicans are extremely popular. One video for such a course includes this advice for speakers:

> Don't keep your emotions close to the vest. Cultivate drama in your style. Use your hands, facial gestures, vocal inflections. Avoid being too cool, distant, rational. What's a professional attitude in the U.S. seems distant there.[5]

In today's global economy, business executives are learning how important it is to adapt to their audience's cultural background. Anthony Hollway, who manages a branch of an American company in China, points out the following examples:

▼ Don't use a clock as a visual aid; the Chinese word for "clock" sounds like the word for "death," so clocks are considered unlucky.
▼ Don't use white flowers, either. The color is associated with funerals.
▼ If you're speaking at a banquet, don't leave early, even for an urgent appointment. It's considered insulting to the guests.

Hollway offered a final example of an American who was giving a training presentation. To build team spirit, he gave out hats with the company logo and in the company color, green. But the trainees, all men, would not wear the hats. Finally one trainee admitted, "In China, wearing a green hat means your wife is cheating on you."[6]

Cultural background can make a big difference in how gestures are interpreted, also. For Americans, a "V" sign made with two fingers usually represents victory. Australians equate this gesture with a rude American gesture usually made with the middle finger.[7] In the United States, "making a circle with one's thumb and index finger while extending the others is emblematic of the word 'OK'; in Japan (and Korea) it signifies 'money' (*okane*) and among Arabs this gesture is usually accompanied by a baring of teeth, and together they signify extreme hostility."[8] The same gesture has a vulgar connotation in Mexico and Germany, and to the Tunisian it means "I'll kill you." In Argentina, one twists an imaginary mustache to signify that everything is OK.[9]

## Membership in Social and Professional Groups

It would be helpful to know how many members of your audience are members of fraternities and sororities if you're planning a speech on the merits (or drawbacks) of the Greek system. In fact, group membership is often an important consideration in college classes. Consider the difference between "typical" college day classes and night classes. At many colleges the evening students work full time during the day and are often older than the day students. They tend to belong to civic groups, church clubs, and the local chamber of commerce. Daytime students tend to belong to sororities and fraternities, sports clubs, and social-action groups.

Group membership can help you understand audiences in the outside world, also. For example, if you were speaking to a meeting of the local chamber of commerce, you could make some confident predictions about the listeners' attitude toward business issues. By examining the groups to which they belong, you can surmise an audience's political leanings (College Republicans or Young Democrats), religious beliefs (CYO or Hillel), or occupation (Bartenders Union or Speech Communication Association).

When Stephen Middlebrook, an insurance company executive, was asked to speak before a civic club in Connecticut, he knew that his audience members were mostly members of the legal and medical professions. He also knew that many of them might be sensitive about his topic:

> Today I want to talk to you about something that's broken—
> namely, our civil justice system, and about some ways to fix it.
> Voltaire once said of the Holy Roman Empire that it was neither
> holy, nor Roman, nor an empire. The same might also be said of the
> civil justice system in the United States: that it is neither civil, nor
> just, nor a system.

Middlebrook adapted his next remarks to the physicians in his audience:

> After all, can it rightly be called "civil," when enormous costs and
> interminable delays deter citizens from using it? Is "justice" the

right word to describe it, when 80 percent of physicians who are sued for malpractice are not negligent and 40 percent of those pay damages anyway? And can we accurately call it a "system," when it has so few standards? For example, so-called expert witnesses helped convince a jury to award one million dollars to a Philadelphia soothsayer who claimed that a CAT scan robbed her of her psychic powers.

His next remarks were adapted for the lawyers:

Even though that verdict was eventually overturned, the point remains valid: Expert witnesses don't have to be experts, juries are unpredictable, and the aggregate costs of trying the suit, I suspect, ran well over $100,000.

My talk today will not be an exercise in lawyer-bashing. I am, after all, a lawyer myself, and see the problems going far beyond lawyers' involvement in the process.[10]

## Religion

Few topics arouse more passion than religion. When a speaker's religious values match those of the audience, this passion can be an advantage. But discussing religious issues calls for a cautious approach when there is a difference between the religious beliefs of speaker and listeners.

One student was a committed member of an evangelical church. One of her biggest reasons for taking a public speaking class was to become

more effective at sharing her deeply held faith with others. In her first speech, she shared the moment of her religious awakening with the class and encouraged them to open themselves to the same experience. She was stunned to find that many of her listeners were offended by this approach, viewing it as an attempt to impose her faith on them.

An experience like this explains why some instructors discourage students from tackling religious topics in speech classes. If you do decide to discuss religion with an audience of skeptics, it's important to find an approach that won't put them on the defensive.

One student was a geology major and a committed Christian. He decided to explain his faith in a way that wouldn't seem like an attempt to convert others. "I'm headed for a career in science," he explained. "And at the same time I accept the Bible as true. Now that probably sounds to you like a difficult position to hold. I know I used to think that you had to choose between science and religion. But I've found out that a lot of scientists—including even Albert Einstein—believe that science and religion don't conflict as much as they complement one another. Let me explain what I've learned."

Gender, age, economic status, cultural background, membership in social and professional groups, and religion are only a few of the factors that might shape your audience analysis. Others might include educational level, political attitudes, place of residence, recreational interests, family status, and political viewpoints. Although it's rare that all these factors will shape your remarks, identifying the key ingredients can help you plan your remarks to achieve your goal.

## PSYCHOGRAPHIC ANALYSIS

*Psychographics* is an advertising term for psychological information about an audience, including such attributes as deep-seated beliefs, unconscious motivations, attitudes, and values. Psychographics are not as readily observable as demographics. In fact, psychographic characteristics are sometimes unrecognized by the audience members themselves. This makes psychographics tricky, but they are still useful. If you can make some logical assumptions about what's going on in the minds of your audience members, you can tailor your message to them. This could be used in the adaptation of a speech in much the same way that media practitioners use it to adapt their messages:

> When Merrill Lynch learned through psychographics that the bulk of its clients saw themselves as independent-minded, upwardly mobile achievers, the investment firm changed the image in its commercials. Instead of the familiar thundering herd of bulls from the 1970s, Merrill Lynch ads portrayed scenes of a solitary bull: "a breed apart."[11]

Psychographics can also be used to help determine the psychological groups within your audience. Once again, a lesson from the media:

When the current walking-shoe boom began, the athletic-shoe industry assumed that most walkers were simply burned-out joggers. Psychographic research, however, has shown that there are really several different groups of walkers: Some walk for fun, some walk with religious dedication, others walk to work, and still others walk the dog. Some really want to exercise, and some want the illusion of exercise. As a result, there are now walking shoes aimed at several groups, ranging from Nike Healthwalkers to Footjoy Joy-Walkers.[12]

Psychographic analysis is performed by looking at such attributes as types of audiences, audience knowledge about your topic, attitudes, values, and specific motives.

### Types of Audiences

▼ If you want an audience, start a fight.

Gaelic proverb

Your first step in psychologically analyzing your audience is to determine how they see themselves. Do they recognize themselves as a group? If so, what kind of group? Some audiences consist of what might be called **passersby,** people who aren't initially interested in hearing a speech. A crowd hanging around the student union between classes or pedestrians walking by a street corner orator fit into this category. When you are faced with an audience of passersby, the first task is to capture their attention. A low-key approach probably won't work here: Sheer volume is necessary for potential listeners to notice, and you may need to present your ideas in some sort of catchy way to hold your listeners' interest—particularly if the topic isn't inherently interesting.

Unlike passersby, **captives** view themselves as an audience, although not a willing one. Consider the example of a "traffic school" where students are present only because attendance is an alternative to losing their driver's licenses. You might face a situation almost this difficult if you are scheduled to speak in class on the last day of a speaking round, especially if this date falls immediately before a vacation. The class might be tired of hearing speeches, perhaps even fed up with the whole idea of school in general. Capturing the attention of groups like this is certainly possible, but it takes some extra effort. In one sense captives are easier to deal with than passersby, since you don't have to make them aware of you as a speaker. On the other hand, you will have to work especially hard to convince reluctant listeners that your remarks are worth listening to.

The final type of audience consists of **volunteers**—people who have willingly come to hear a speaker. Friends attending a "roast" honoring a popular colleague come to the event expecting to have a good time, and an audience who voluntarily chooses to attend a talk on trekking in the Himalayas or on tax-sheltered investments are seeking desired information. While an audience of volunteers is certainly ideal, you can't take willing listeners for granted. You may *start* with the volunteers' interest, but *keeping* it will require giving them something new.

## Knowledge

You give your audience something "new" by analyzing their **knowledge:** what they know—or think they know—about your speech topic. Sometimes your audience will already be familiar with the subject: the shortage of on-campus parking, the high rents in your town, or the pressures of too much to do and too little time to do it. In cases like this you can launch into your remarks without providing much background.

On the other hand, if your listeners don't know much about your topic, you may need to start with a more basic explanation. With topics like Freud's sexist attitudes toward women or the significance of the Tibetan Book of the Dead, you will probably need to educate your audience before you try to change their viewpoints. For example, one employee of the Body Shop, a chain of natural cosmetics stores, was convinced that the mainline cosmetics industry tortures animals, exploits women, and pillages the earth in search of profits. Before she could persuade her audience that the industry should be regulated, she had to educate them to the abuses.

Sometimes your listeners *think* they know about your topic when they really don't. In cases like this, setting them straight may become your first task. One physical activity buff wanted to motivate her listeners to exercise outdoors in the winter. In order to edge them toward her enthusiasm for running in the rain, she began by correcting the mistaken belief that wet feet and cold weather cause colds. She explained that colds are caused by contact with people who carry the virus—a risk that is greater indoors than outside.

▼ People are generally better persuaded by the reasons which they have themselves discovered than by those which have come into the mind of others.

Pascal

## Attitudes

Besides thinking about what your listeners know (or don't know), you need to consider their attitudes—how they *feel*. **Attitudes** are emotional predispositions that listeners bring to a speech.

Attitudes fall into three categories. Some relate to the speech *topic*. Do your listeners find it interesting or boring? Do they support your point of view, disagree with it, or are they indifferent? An audience that doesn't care about the Federal Reserve system or Parkinson's disease won't listen very attentively. Attitudes toward the subject can be positive, too. The audience might already share your interest in such topics as how to buy products at rock-bottom prices or easy steps to bodybuilding. Even if they aren't clamoring to hear about a topic like Darwin's "missing link" or the hobby of collecting celebrity autographs, most group members are likely to listen attentively once you introduce it.

▼ When we wish to correct with advantage, and to show another that he errs, we must notice from what side he views the matter, for on that side it is usually true.

Pascal

Audiences may also have attitudes toward you, the speaker. Sometimes they have this impression before you begin to speak. Rhetoricians call this *initial credibility*. These attitudes can come from your reputation, from having heard you speak before, or from being introduced by another speaker. Initial credibility can be a strong factor in a public speaking class, both for the instructor who grades your speech and the other students who listen to it. As the semester or quarter goes on, your behavior in initial speeches and class discussions will shape the group's attitude about you. This was the case for one student whose first two classroom speeches were weak. He chose frivolous topics: how to "score" with a date and choosing the best brand of beer. In addition to speaking on poor topics, his delivery was careless and sloppy. When he decided to get serious about the class in his third speech, his classmates considered him to be a "flake"—a tough image to overcome.

Even if your prior ethos isn't high, you can win the audience's respect during your speech by showing that you are sincere and knowledgeable. Another student was a single parent. In a class speech she proposed several changes in adoption laws, basing her arguments on personal experiences as a mother who had considered giving her child up for adoption and on an impressive amount of information she collected from authorities in the field. Her credibility was high, both as a knowledgeable researcher and as someone who had experienced adoption firsthand.

## Values

**Values** are deeply rooted feelings about the worth of certain basic principles. The principles on which values are based are high-level abstractions, such as honesty, fairness, equality, and freedom. Values are the bedrock upon which all attitudes are based. Consider two examples:

▼ Value: Education should have application in everyday life.

▼ Attitude: Courses that don't have demonstrated value are worthless.

▼ Value: All life is sacred.

▼ Attitude: Medical researchers who use animals in their experiments are cruel and insensitive.

Sometimes a speech is persuasive because it shows that one value is more important than another:

▼ Central idea: The United States should not sell arms to other countries.

▼ Implied values: Peace is a higher value than profit.

▼ Central idea: Leash laws in public parks should be abolished.

▼  Implied values: Individual freedom of action is more important than the right to absolute peace and quiet.

These examples show how fundamental and important values are. They are usually formed over a long period, and are not easily changed. Since values are so hard to alter, the best way to reach your audience is to show how your position is consistent with values they already hold.

For example, a dermatologist wanted to convince her audience not to spend too much time in the sun. She knew that one appeal was to the value of health, since no one wants skin cancer. But she also realized that the value of attractiveness was important to her listeners, and so she described how to get an attractive tan *and* reduce the risk of skin problems by using sunscreens and spending less time in the midday sun.

Two speakers arguing opposite sides of the same issue might base their appeals on different values. For example, two students disagreed about a proposed law that would require motorcyclists to wear helmets. The first student favored the law, and based her case on economic values. She argued that, since public funds supported the hospitalization and rehabilitation of motorcycle accident victims, society has a right to protect its resources by requiring riders to wear helmets. The second student opposed the law. He appealed to the value of freedom of choice, arguing that if people want to risk injury, it was their business.

Chapter 13 has more advice about how to analyze values when planning a persuasive speech. For now, the important point to realize is that identifying those values is a key step in planning *any* successful speech that gets the attention and support of your audience.

## Specific Motives

One branch of psychographics is "motivational research." Motivational research is an investigation into what "moves" an audience—what makes them act in a particular way. When you look at specific motives, you assume that people almost always listen to speeches because the information will do something for *them,* not as a favor to the speaker. Therefore, you can succeed by showing them how your ideas fit with their interests and needs. Consider two examples:

▼  The enrollment of a preschool was declining because some anxious parents feared its emphasis on play was leaving their children ill prepared for success in elementary school. The school's director was committed to the philosophy that young children should not be put into an academic environment too early; but instead of trying to persuade the parents that they were pushing their children too early, she developed a presentation showing that the school's approach gave young children a love of school that would help them do better later in elementary school.

▼ Volunteers planning a fund-raising triathlon emphasized the challenging course and valuable prizes to attract competitors, realizing that most participants were not interested enough in the charitable cause to attend just to support it.

The strategy you use to achieve a speaking goal might change according to the motives of different audiences. Consider the different approaches you might take when persuading listeners to buy a personal computer. To an audience of students, you might appeal to the need for convenience, showing them how a computer can save time on school projects. To an audience of business people, you could appeal to the motive of profitability, showing how computers can reduce costs and increase productivity. To an audience of parents, you could stress the advantages their children could gain by becoming computer literate at an early age.

Health educators used the same principle of appealing to values an audience already holds to persuade high-school-age students to adopt a healthier lifestyle. The educators realized the folly of lecturing teens on long-term health risks, since "long term" to most adolescents means the upcoming weekend. Instead, they appealed to the strongly held motive of vanity to discourage smoking and promote exercise.

## SITUATIONAL ANALYSIS

A third way to analyze an audience, besides demographics and psychographics, is to look at the situation surrounding the speech. In this way you get an idea about audience expectations surrounding the occasion. Why is the speech being delivered? Where will it be given? How much time is available? What is the physical setting?

Situational factors like these can play an important role in shaping the content and style of an effective speech. For instance, the situation of being enrolled in a public speaking class is probably the main reason you are spending so much time and energy planning speeches at this point in your life. Likewise, the situation of a funeral is what leads people to deliver eulogies, shaping what they say and the way they say it. The same principle holds for most speaking situations: Job interviews, graduation speeches, religious sermons, political campaigns, and courtroom pleas are all shaped by the circumstances that surround them. If those circumstances didn't exist, there would be no need for a speech in the first place.

Furthermore, the characteristics of each situation govern the kind of remarks a speaker will make.

There are several factors to consider as you try to make your speech fit the situation.

## The Nature of the Situation

Different situations call for different approaches—both in what you say and how you say it. When your speech doesn't fit the occasion, you can embarrass or offend your listeners.

▼ The best man at a wedding dinner toasted the bride and groom by making explicit joking references to the romantic details of the upcoming honeymoon. While this humor might have been appropriate at a bachelor party, it didn't belong at an occasion with family members of all ages.

▼ The principal of a high school spent most of his graduation speech bemoaning the decline of American students' academic skills. While most of his listeners might have agreed with these ideas, they were offended by the downbeat, critical tone of the speech on an occasion that called for praise and recognition of the graduates' achievement.

For classroom speeches it is just as important to consider the occasion. We spoke about the importance of a clear speech purpose in the preceding chapter. Most speaking assignments call for a certain type of purpose. For one speech you might be told to inform your audience, while the goal for another one may be to persuade them. Don't make the mistake of doing more—or less—than you've been told to. One class was assigned to deliver a round of demonstration speeches that would teach the class how to do something. Despite the topic, one student—a committed feminist—spoke on "how to change a male-dominated, sexist society." The subject of female oppression certainly was worth discussion, but it did not fit the assignment.

## The "Rules" of the Situation

Many occasions have their own set of customs. They may not be written in any rule book, but speakers who violate them still suffer. Most public speaking classes have their own cultures and rules. Do students dress differently on their speaking days? Are any subjects off limits? Are certain types of humor acceptable? The most dramatic way to learn the importance of rules is to break them. For example, an earnest but basically insecure student might distract his listeners in a classroom speech by using overblown vocabulary and reading his remarks from a manuscript instead of speaking extemporaneously, as he had been instructed. Such a speech would be more appropriate for a State of the Union address than for a talk to his classmates.

Like public speaking classes, most other groups have their own customs. Do audience members interrupt a speaker with questions and comments, or do they wait until the end of a talk? Are they used to a formal or an informal approach? Do they mind speakers running over the allotted time, or are they fanatical about punctuality? Knowing the answers to questions like these can make the difference between being welcomed and rejected by an audience.

## Time Available

▼ What some orators lack in depth they make up to you in length.

Montesquieu

Listeners usually won't mind if a speech is a little shorter than expected, but running over the allotted time will often cause problems. In the classroom, the problems of taking too much time are obvious. If your six-minute speech turns into a nine- or ten-minute lecture, the students who are scheduled to speak after you might not have a chance to speak. Even if they appreciate the delay, you won't win the gratitude of your instructor, who probably has to juggle an already crowded schedule.

Staying within time limits is just as important outside the classroom. Most speeches are part of a larger event, and hogging the stage can leave other speakers short of the time they need and deserve.

▼ The sales representative for an office equipment company bungled the chance to make a big sale by expanding a half-hour presentation into almost an hour. By the time she was finished, several potential customers had walked out, and most of the remaining ones were impatient and irritated.

▼ A disgruntled customer took a claim against an unscrupulous auto repair shop to small claims court. His case was good, but he ignored the judge's instructions to make his arguments brief. After running over his time limit, the judge cut him off before he made his strongest arguments, causing him to lose a case he should have won.

## Size of the Group

Speaking to two or three people calls for a different approach than addressing a large audience. The biggest difference will probably be in your style of delivery, since the relatively formal approach you might use with a large audience would sound foolish with a smaller one. The group's size will also influence the way you dress, the kind of visual aids you use, and a variety of other factors.

One student's speech opposing censorship of rock music lyrics was so effective that she entered it in a contest sponsored by the local chamber of commerce. But the conversational style that worked so well in a classroom with 25 students wasn't appropriate for an audience of almost 400 spectators at the contest. Besides adopting a more formal speaking style, she dressed differently at the contest. She also replaced the album covers she used as examples in her classroom speech with slides that could be viewed easily by all audience members in the contest auditorium.

## Physical Setting

The physical setting in which you speak can influence how you plan and deliver a speech. Some speakers learn the hard way that the setting can make a difference. One speaker had wanted to explain the role dress plays in making impressions. She had carefully edited and organized a series of slides to illustrate her remarks. But when she began to set up her projector, she found that the nearest electrical outlet was too far away for the cord to reach. There wasn't time to find an extension cord, and without the slides a potentially successful speech turned into a mediocre one.

This speaker could have overcome the limitations of her environment by bringing along an extension cord. Likewise, you can discover ways to make the place you speak work for, not against, you. You might be able to adjust the seating, moving yourself closer to your audience or shifting chairs around so everyone can see and hear you. You may be able to reposition yourself to keep the sun out of your eyes, or those of your listeners.

Sometimes you won't be able to improve the physical environment. The space may be too small for the crowd; the lighting or ventilation might be inadequate; or there may be distracting noises. Even in these unhappy circumstances it's best to discover beforehand the limitations facing you so you won't be surprised by them.

## Context

*Context* refers to the events surrounding your speech. These events can make a big difference in your approach. For example, referring to the remarks of other speakers can help you reach your goals. One student wanted to persuade his classmates to boycott veal, since veal calves were raised in inhumane conditions. He began his speech by building on the success of a classmate who had spoken the day before:

> Leah talked to you about the miserable lives of unwanted dogs and cats who roam the streets until they die of starvation, attacks by other animals, or in car accidents. I'm going to tell you about animals who suffer in a different way. They are doomed from the day of their birth, and their short lives are filled with more misery and pain than the strays Leah described. I'm talking about veal calves.

Other events familiar to your audience can also give you a way to connect your speech to the experience of your listeners. John Bull, an editor at the *Philadelphia Inquirer,* began his speech before a civic club this way:

> Today is marked on my calendar as "Traditional Columbus Day," which seems a particularly good time to take stock of our legacy from that adventure of 500 years ago.
>
> A consequence of that journey was the creation of the United States of America, a nation that *Time* magazine last week called "a daring experiment in democracy that in turn became a symbol and a haven of individual liberty for people throughout the world."[13]

Mr. Bull went on to relate Columbus Day to the topic of his speech, which was the survival of free speech.

Even ordinary events can influence your approach. The joke that works well at 10 A.M. might not get a laugh from your sleepy audience in an 8 A.M. class. A speech about following a healthy diet would be especially easy to introduce right before or after lunch. Arguments about changing public policy are probably better in the months before elections, when your listeners can vote to bring changes about, than afterwards, when there may be little they can do to change policies.

## ● GUIDELINES FOR USING YOUR ANALYSIS

By now the value of adapting you speech to the audience should be clear. The following guidelines will help you use your analysis effectively.

### Avoid Demographic Stereotyping

A demographic analysis can give you valuable insights into how to reach an audience, but it's important to realize that real listeners don't always fit demographic profiles. One local politician addressed a meeting at the Knights of Columbus hall and gave a spirited attack on abortion, assuming that all his listeners were Catholics who would support his position. He failed to realize that the gathering was merely hosted by the Knights to honor community volunteers—many of whom were not Catholic and not against a woman's right to choose.

Remember that demographic characteristics are usually averages: When taken to extremes, they become stereotypes. Not all women like to cook, and some men aren't football fans. Science majors can enjoy literature and drama. Assuming that listeners all fit statistical profiles can lead to a mistaken analysis—and an unsuccessful speech.

### Consider Audience Diversity

As the size of your audience grows larger, the number of generalizations you can accurately make about them decreases. If, for example, you are speaking to a few teenagers, your research will probably reveal some useful information about their interests, knowledge, values, and so on. But if you were speaking to fifty or a hundred teenagers, the same assumptions probably wouldn't fit them all.

How should you develop a speech when you face a variety of listeners? Whenever possible, it's best to take an approach that stresses the common ground shared by all your listeners. This is what one student did in her speech about premarital counseling:

> If you've ever experienced divorce firsthand, you know how painful that experience can be. And if you haven't, I'm sure you'd like to keep it that way. You'd support anything that could make sure that

couples only get married for the right reasons, and that those who do marry have the communication skills that will keep them married. That's why I know you'll endorse the idea of mandatory premarital counseling.

When you can't find a single approach that reaches everyone in your audience, you can still succeed by addressing each segment of your audience, one at a time:

▼ If you're an in-state resident, here's how the tuition changes will affect you . . .

▼ If you're from out of state, the changes will work this way . . .

## Identify the Target Audience

Sometimes one or more listeners are especially important to the objective of your speech. In these cases it's important to identify the person or persons whose approval matters most, and make sure your speech succeeds with them. One student described how this approach works on the job:

> I work in a restaurant, and I like to suggest ways of changing the menu to improve business. Any menu changes have to be approved by the two owners and the chef. But the owners will okay almost anything that the chef will support, so he's really the person I have to persuade.

In a public speaking class you always have two audiences: your classmates and the instructor who will be grading your performance. With enough thought, you should be able to please them both, but you may need to consider different factors when you think about how to reach your professor. For example, most instructors spend a good deal of time explaining the criteria for a good speech, so their students will realize that speech grades are not based on personal whim. Still, some instructors stress some principles over others; for example, some are especially concerned with principles of organization, while others are extremely interested in good delivery. Some

The Far Side                     by Gary Larsen

"OK, everyone, we'll be departing for Antarctica in about 15 minutes. . . . If anyone thinks he may be in the wrong migration, let us know now."

instructors are tired of hearing about certain speech topics that have become worn out over the years. By learning about these preferences you can plan a speech that will be right for you, please your fellow students, *and* earn the grade you're seeking.

## Avoid Antagonizing Listeners

You may not be able to persuade all your listeners, but there's rarely a need to annoy any of them. Despite this fact, speakers sometimes unnecessarily antagonize some audience members. One student wanted to convince her listeners that *in vitro* fertilization was a justifiable option for couples who were unable to conceive a child naturally. In her effort to consider possible audience concerns, she disputed the objections "Catholics and right-to-lifers" might have to the method.

After her speech, some students identified themselves as Catholic and others as opponents of abortion. They stated that they had no strong objection to *in vitro* fertilization, but that they felt defensive when the speaker criticized their beliefs.

Even when you are trying to convince listeners to change their minds, it's possible to acknowledge their beliefs and to appeal to them in a respectful way:

> I know it might seem impractical to vote for a third party candidate who has almost no chance of winning the election, and I can see why you'd ask "Why waste my vote?" I don't blame you for thinking about the campaign this way. But let me explain how a vote for my candidate *won't* be a waste. After I'm done, I hope you'll consider changing your mind.

An approach like this treats your listeners as intelligent people who have reasonable grounds for disagreeing with you. Besides the strategic wisdom of respecting your audience, this approach is ethically sound. There are other ethical considerations that will help your speeches be more successful and, just as important, morally sound.

## ▼ THE ETHICS OF ADAPTING TO YOUR AUDIENCE

Adapting your approach to the occasion might seem sneaky or dishonest— a case of telling people what they want to hear. There are cases where an analysis can tell a cynical speaker what approach to take, regardless of whether he or she believes it. Two researchers demonstrated this type of technique more than 20 years ago when they asked a cross-section of citizens from Peoria, Illinois, to respond to a number of statements about American foreign policy.[14] The researchers also had the respondents rate their liking of certain political phrases, and then fed the responses into a computer. Their computer was programmed to use the findings to write a seven- to nine-minute speech on foreign policy—the kind of speech a candidate could deliver at a typical airport rally. Some excerpts from that speech:

> The Middle East is again in a no-war, no-peace stalemate and is likely to remain so for some time. Step-by-step diplomacy, treating all parties with an even hand, is the only means for maintaining a delicate peace.
>
> I do not believe that we should dismantle the CIA, for many times it is the CIA's covert capability that stands between a do-nothing policy and nuclear confrontation. I oppose unnecessary secrecy, but I believe in a strong national defense. And, unfortunately, in today's world, the CIA is needed.
>
> On terrorists, my position is clear. International terrorism, such as bombings and hijackings, is deplorable. Yet, the U.S. should not put itself in a position committed to meet such actions whenever and wherever they might occur. I will go to the United Nations and get an international law against terrorism.

Positions like these are not surprising. After all, they were scientifically generated to reflect the precise attitudes and values of the audiences who heard them. What is significant is that the positions do not reflect the beliefs of any candidate. They were chosen by a machine to please the greatest number of people and offend the fewest.

It is alarming how much the computer-generated speech resembles today's political speeches. As one of the researchers remarked at the time, "We hope it will spark enough controversy for someone to ask the candidates why their speeches sound so much like our computer's. Maybe that will get them to say what they really think for a change."

Tailoring your speech to your audience doesn't require you to sacrifice your principles. You don't have to deceive your audience, and you don't have to be purposely ambiguous. Audience adaptation should only be a tool for presenting your ideas in a way that the receivers will understand and appreciate. Community organizer Saul Alinsky put it this way:

> If the real radical finds that having long hair sets up psychological barriers to communication and organization, he cuts his hair. If I were organizing in an orthodox Jewish community I would not walk in there eating a ham sandwich, unless I wanted to be rejected.
>
> As an organizer I start from where the world is, as it is, not what I would like it to be. That we accept the world as it is does not in any sense weaken our desire to change it into what we believe it should be—it is necessary to begin where the world is if we are going to change it to what we think it should be.[15]

Alinsky emphasizes that the goal of any speech is to achieve some purpose. He also points out that it is possible to design a message in the best way to achieve that purpose without sacrificing your principles. If your goal is to get the agreement and respect of your audience, quoting Martin Luther King, Jr. to an audience of predominantly African American listeners and the pope to a group of Roman Catholics wouldn't be sneaky or deceitful. Using sports heroes as examples when you're facing an audience of athletes and citing popular entertainers to a group of their fans makes good sense.

For an ethical speaker, the question isn't whether to adapt your remarks to the audience, but how to do so *honestly*. One test of whether you are using your analysis ethically is to decide whether you would share your strategy with your listeners if asked to do so. If you wouldn't be embarrassed to explain what you've learned about them and how you have used that information, there is little danger of being overly manipulative.

## ⬡ SAMPLE SPEECH

Our sample speech for this chapter is a hypothetical one. Imagine a typical student (we'll call her Gina) who has been hired as an intern at the local YMCA. Her first job is to help plan a speaking program in which representatives of the Y will visit various community groups. The club is willing to provide the lectures as a public service, but the main reason for offering the program is to get new members.

Gina has received two invitations to speak. One is to a group of high school students enrolled in a "Self-Esteem for Young Women" class. The other is to an evening meeting of the local Newcomers Club, a group of couples who have moved to town within the past year. Even though she has the same speaking goal for both groups—to encourage listeners to join the YMCA—Gina recognizes the importance of tailoring each talk to its audience. As she plans the presentations, Gina considers several demographic variables.

## ⬡ THE YMCA AND YOU
### ("Self-Esteem for Young Women" Class)

It's a pleasure to be here today. As I look around your school today, I see some things have changed and some things haven't. Fashions have changed, for one thing. I notice that the boys are wearing pants that you could fit the entire basketball team into. And when I went to high school just a few years ago, the only computer was in the principal's office, and I don't think even he knew how to use it. Today, it seems like there are as many computers as books in your classrooms. But I'm glad to see that one thing hasn't changed: You still have classes for just young women, where you can discuss those things you don't want to discuss in front of men. Like men, for example.

Now, you might not think that the YMCA is a great place to get away from men. After all, everyone knows those initials stand for "Young Men's Christian Association." But the association has changed faster than the name. Not only is membership open to young women (and people of any religion or race, of course), but there are many programs for you exclusively. You have your own hours for the pool, for the exercise room, for the paddleball and tennis courts. And then there are other hours when the facilities are open to both sexes, which is a good time to mingle. In fact, some of our high school members find that's a good time to meet students from other schools, students they wouldn't meet otherwise, except as crosstown rivals at a ballgame.

I'd like to show you some of our facilities. [slide 1] This is our exercise room. As you can see, we have all the latest equipment: treadmills, step machines, free weights, and weight-resistance machines. [slide 2] And this is Scott, one of our trainers. We have both men and women trainers who are trained to set up individual workout programs to help you make the most of what you have. They can help you shape up and trim down in safe, gradual ways, all year long. This type of consistent training, by the way, makes crash diets and fasting unnecessary. In fact, our trainers are very sensitive to the problems of anorexia, bulimia, and obsessive dieting. We offer special classes on how to avoid these eating disorders, by stressing reasonable dieting and good health. We also sponsor makeup and fashion classes whose theme is maximizing your assets. [slide 3] This is one of the meeting rooms where those classes take place.

[slide 4] Here are the indoor, all-weather tennis courts. We have same-sex and both-sexes hours at these courts, and tennis lessons are available. The same is true for our paddleball courts [slide 5], our swimming pool [slide 6], our steamroom [slide 7], which is great for cleansing the skin as well as steaming out the stress of the day, and our indoor running track [slide 8]. As you can see from this picture, the young men who use the facility tend to be the type of young men you like to meet: active, well-conditioned, and smart enough to stay that way.

The final point I'd like to leave you with today is that the Y is inexpensive, especially with our low student rates. [show chart] This chart shows you how your Y membership fee compares to the fees at the private health clubs in the area. And this includes the local Living Well Lady, which excludes men, and the Jack LaLanne, which offers no same-sex hours. And the Y's monthly installment plan allows you to pay your dues in small installments. Even better, if you get your families to join for our low family rate, you'll be included for free, and you'll have the same privileges as an individual member. You might be surprised at how receptive your parents are to the idea. One father told me that he would much rather spend money on a healthy activity like the YMCA than on overpriced clothing and jewelry.

If you are undecided, I strongly recommend that you give it a try. These are free passes for an introductory workout. [hand out passes] You can use your pass at any time for a free workout, alone or with a friend. And there's no risk to a Y membership. If you decide you don't like it you can drop out at any time and get a full refund for unused membership.

Let me close by saying that a Y membership fits in perfectly with the self-esteem theme of this class. One way to feel better about oneself is to become healthier and more physically fit, and that's what the Y is all about.

I'll take some group questions now. I'll be available for individual questions after class.

## ◉ The YMCA and You
## (Newcomers Club)

Thanks for that warm welcome. And I should welcome you to the community, also. If you're like most of our new residents, you have moved here for a number of reasons: the fine schools, rated among the highest in the state; the well-run municipal government; the convenient shopping and work centers; the easy commute into the city. High on the list of reasons is the recreational facilities, and I'm here to introduce you to one of them: the YMCA.

A lot has changed at the YMCA since the Village People sang about it in the 1970s. You probably remember that they sang about how much they liked to stay there—the cowboy was always my favorite. Today, our local Y no longer rents rooms. It is also open to women and people of both sexes, all ages, religions, and races. About half of our membership is made up of families and couples: people like you. Over the years, we have listened to what this part of our membership wants in the Y, and we have tried to provide it. We now make it easy for both men and women to use the facilities, alone or with friends of the same sex. But we also have hours when couples can spend time together and get in shape as well.

For those who want to work out with members of the same sex, our exercise room is open during convenient daytime hours. [slide 1] This is our main exercise room. As you can see, we have all the latest equipment, including treadmills, step machines, free weights, and resistance machines. [slide 2] During men's, women's, and couples' hours, we have trainers on premises. They'll show you the latest techniques in pre-workout stretching and warm-up, and the latest techniques to maximize workouts while avoiding injuries. Our trainers are experts in developing individual fitness programs to suit the age and condition of each member. On weekdays we have "For Women Only" aerobics classes and a men's basketball league.

For those who want to spend time together as couples, we have our swimming pool [slide 3], our steam room [slide 4], our tennis courts [slide 5], which are also open for lessons, and our indoor track [slide 6], which has evening hours for jogging.

[slide 7] We also have meeting rooms that are used for a wide range of couples' activities. There's a gourmet cooking club that's very popular. [slide 8] And here's another facility that I know many of you will be interested in. The Y's child-care center provides low-cost day care and evening care with qualified, licensed child-care workers. You can drop the kids off while you work out, or while you shop in the nearby downtown shopping district. And for older children there are youth groups that meet during couples' exercise hours.

One of the best things about the Garden City Y is that it is such a bargain compared to the private health clubs in the area, especially with our special rates for first-time members. [show chart of comparisons] As you can see from this chart, the whole family can take advantage of all the Y facilities for just a fraction of the fees at the three nearest private clubs. And here's another interesting comparison. [show chart] Monthly fees are about a third of what one movie night costs with a modest dinner, babysitting, and parking, not counting the cleaning bills if you happen to sit on another patron's leftover popcorn butter. And one last comparison: The daily fee is actually less than staying home and renting a videotape, and that's without the cost of snacks that you would be munching while you could be working out!

There are so many reasons to get involved in a steady fitness program. Most of you know them. You know the studies that relate physical fitness to extra productivity in your careers. But I'd like to remind you that the Y is also a great place for networking. You meet other professionals from the area, and many of them will be some type of business contact. In fact, between the advantages of employees who are healthy and employees who are plugged into a wider network, many business owners pay for memberships for their employees. Among other things, they like the flexible hours we offer for workers and commuters. So check with your bosses about supporting your membership. Unless you are the boss, of course, in which case I encourage you to support memberships for your employees. If you are interested in that program, I'll have information for you after today's meeting.

I urge you to come try out our facilities. I'm distributing free passes for an introductory workout. [hand out passes] You can use your pass at any time, alone or with a spouse or friend. And a Y membership is truly risk-free. If you have to drop out at any time—whether it be an unexpected transfer or you just decide you don't have the time to use the facilities— you can withdraw, no questions asked, and get a full refund for unused membership. We doubt that you'll ask for this refund, though. Most of the people who try the Y turn out to be like the Village People: They'd rather stay there.

Does anyone have any questions? I'll be available after the meeting, as I said, for individual questions.

## Speech Analysis

Notice the way Gina adapted this speech for different audiences:

### "Self-Esteem for Young Women" Class                    ### Newcomers Club

#### Gender

Since this is an all-female audience, Gina adapts her approach to suit the interests of young women. Most of the slides she uses in her program illustrate women using the Y's exercise areas, dressing rooms, swimming pool, and other facilities. Nonetheless, Gina realizes that high school girls are interested in high school boys, so she makes sure to include some pictures of young men in her program.

Gina has learned that most Newcomers' Club members join as couples. Market research has also shown that these couples use the Y in several different ways. During the daytime, both men and women are likely to use the facilities alone or with friends of the same sex. But on weekends, couples often spend time together swimming, jogging, and so on. Armed with this information, Gina highlights both ways to use the club.

#### Physical condition

Gina has learned that many students enroll in the self-esteem class because they are unhappy with their physical appearance.

The members of the Newcomers' Club certainly aren't senior citizens, but they are older than the girls in the high school program.

## Physical condition—cont'd

Knowing this, she emphasizes activities that help members get into shape: exercise classes, weight training, diet programs, and so on. In choosing slides, Gina is careful to show pictures of women in all sorts of physical condition. She knows that showing only photos of slim, beautiful women might make the members of her audience feel self-conscious.

Gina adapts her approach to this group by mentioning programs that are likely to interest adults: classes that promote cardiovascular fitness, keep a person limber, and won't cause injuries. She describes how the Y's staff is trained to develop an individual fitness program to suit the age and condition of each member.

## Marital and family status

Gina knows that the YMCA can be a good way to meet members of the opposite sex. She emphasizes this fact to the young, unmarried listeners in the self-esteem class, pointing out that the tennis court or running track can be a terrific place to get acquainted with boys from other schools in the area, who they wouldn't otherwise meet.

Since the Newcomers' Club members are all married couples, Gina downplays the courtship angle. Instead, she points out that the YMCA is a place where a husband and wife can exercise together, combining the twin goals of spending time with one another and keeping in shape. She also discusses how the Y's child-care program and youth groups provide childcare for couples while they exercise.

## Economic status

Gina suspects that some members of the high school class will pay for a membership themselves, so she stresses the affordability of the Y's special student rates. She also points out that the club's monthly installment plan allows members to pay their dues in small installments. She knows that the parents of other students would probably consider paying the membership fees, so she mentions the club's family rates, which make it eco-

nomical for both the high school girls and other family members to use the club for one low fee.

With the couples group, Gina emphasizes that the YMCA is a bargain by comparing its fees to the price of a modest dinner and movie—activities most of her listeners can afford. She also emphasizes the club's special promotion that offers first-time memberships at reduced rates.

## Occupation

Gina knows that the high school students have already learned about the relationship between physical health and performance in school, so she reminds them that exercising at the YMCA can be a way to improve their appearance as well. She links the benefits of membership to the self-esteem theme of the class, suggesting that one way to feel better about oneself is to become healthier and more physically fit.

Since many Newcomers' Club members are business people, Gina stresses the flexible hours at the Y for workers and commuters. She also describes the relationship between physical fitness and productivity on the job. In addition to showing her listeners that they can become more efficient at work, she hopes some business owners in the group will support memberships for their employees. Knowing that there are parents in her audience, Gina also mentions the YMCA's many activities for young people.

 **SUMMARY**

Identifying the characteristics of an audience is among the first and most important steps to take when planning a successful speech. One way to analyze an audience is to consider its demographic characteristics. Some of these characteristics are physiological: age, gender, physical condition, and so on. Other features are socioeconomic: religion, economic status, ethnic background, occupation, and political viewpoint are a few examples. Analyzing according to "psychographics," or psychological attributes of an audience, can also make a speech more effective. One such attribute is audience "type": Some listeners are passersby, while others are either captives or volunteers. Each type of audience has a different psychology and therefore requires a different approach. The same can be said for audiences with different knowledge, attitudes, values, and specific motives.

Understanding the nature of the speaking situation is one way to judge audience expectations. What circumstances call for a speech? What are the explicit and unwritten rules that govern this situation? How much time is available? What is the size of the group? What other events relate to this occasion? The answers to questions like these will suggest ways to construct a speech that suits the event.

Understanding the audience can provide valuable information, but it is important to use the results of this analysis thoughtfully. It is usually a mistake to stereotype listeners on the basis of a demographic profile, since not all members of a group are identical. In fact, most audiences aren't homogeneous, but are made up of subgroups of listeners with different characteristics. In some cases it is possible to appeal to different audience segments; at other times the best approach is to focus appeals on the target audience—one or more key listeners whose reactions are especially important. In any case, the best approach will not unnecessarily antagonize any listeners.

Analyzing the audience and situation is a strategic act, but it can also be an ethical one. As long as a speaker is willing to share his or her strategy if asked to do so, there is probably nothing unethical or manipulative about tailoring a message to suit its recipients or the occasion.

## ● EXERCISES

1. You can develop your skill at identifying what an audience knows, thinks, feels, and wants by trying this exercise. For each of the following topics, identify the knowledge, attitudes, and values of your classmates.
   a. Laws protecting endangered species, even at the expense of owners' rights to develop their property as they desire.
   b. The trend toward increasingly explicit sexual television programming during late afternoon and early evening hours, when young children may be viewing.
   c. Today's negative attitudes toward people who are not physically fit.
   Describe how you could build an argument consistent with your beliefs on each of these topics in a way that does not antagonize your classmates.

2. Conduct a demographic analysis of your classmates (or any other audience) for a speech you will be delivering in the near future. Use the following list to identify and consider the factors that will be important for your topic. (Other factors may also be important, depending on your topic and goal.)
   a. Gender
   b. Age
   c. Physical condition
   d. Economic status
   e. Ethnic/racial/cultural background
   f. Group membership
   g. Membership in social groups
   h. Religion
   i. Educational level

3. For practice in analyzing audience motivations, try the following: For each goal in Column A, identify the appeals you could make for the different audiences listed in Column B.

COLUMN A: GOAL

1. Use the local rapid transit system instead of driving.

2. Donate to the United Way fund-raising drive.

3. Buy domestic products instead of imported ones.

4. Volunteer for work in the local homeless shelter.

COLUMN B: AUDIENCE

1. Students at your college or university

2. A group of senior citizens

3. Employees at local businesses

4. The congregation of a church or synagogue

## NOTES

1. Lane Cooper, *The Rhetoric of Aristotle: An Expanded Translation with Supplementary Examples for Students of Composition and Public Speaking* (New York: Appleton-Century-Crofts, 1960), p. 136.

2. Sydney W. Head, C. Sterling, and L. Schofield, *Broadcasting in America: A Survey of Electronic Media,* 7th ed. (Boston: Houghton Mifflin, 1994), p. 410.

3. The quotation comes from the director of the American Bison Association. See Clifford D. May, "The Buffalo Returns: This Time for Dinner," *New York Times Magazine,* September 26, 1993, p. 30.

4. Aristotle, *Rhetoric,* translated by W. Rhys Roberts (New York: Modern Library, 1954), pp. 122–123.

5. Instructional videotape cited in Allen R. Myerson, "Texans Want to Get Closer to Mexico," *New York Times,* November 27, 1994, Section 4, p. 1.

6. Anthony Hollway, "Culture Follies: Our China Strategy," *New York Times,* December 25, 1994, p. 9.

7. Larry A. Samovar and Richard E. Porter, *Communication between Cultures,* 2d ed. (Belmont, Calif.: Wadsworth, 1995), p. 79.

8. Robert G. Harper, Arthur N. Wiens, and Joseph Matarazzo, *Nonverbal Communication: The State of the Art* (New York: Wiley, 1978), p. 164.

9. Samovar and Porter, *Communication between Cultures,* p. 191.

10. Stephen B. Middlebrook, "Reforming the Civil Justice System," *Vital Speeches of the Day,* August 1, 1992, p. 631.

11. Berkeley Rice, "The Selling of Lifestyles," in *Mass Media Issues,* George Rodman, ed. (Dubuque: Kendall/Hunt, 1993), p. 289.

12. Ibid.

13. John V. R. Bull, "Freedom of Speech: Can It Survive?" *Vital Speeches of the Day,* December 1, 1991, p. 117.

14. The experiment described in this section is reported in John F. Cragan and Donald C. Shields, *Applied Communication Research: A Dramatistic Approach* (Prospect Heights, Ill.: Waveland Press, 1981). It was originally reported in John F. Cragan and Donald C. Shields, "Foreign Policy Communication Dramas: How Mediated Rhetoric Played in Peoria in Campaign '76," *Quarterly Journal of Speech* 63 (1977) pp. 275–289.

15. Saul Alinsky, *Rules for Radicals* (New York: Vintage, 1972), p. xix.

# RESEARCHING THE TOPIC

## ▼ CHAPTER 6 OBJECTIVES

**After reading this chapter, you should understand:**

1. The value of your own knowledge and experience as a source of material for a speech.

2. The kinds of authoritative organizations that can furnish you with materials for a speech.

3. The range of library resources available as you develop a speech.

**You should be able to:**

1. Identify one or more experts and conduct interviews to gather materials for a speech.

2. Use resources such as surveys and personal observation as speech material.

3. Follow the research strategies listed in this chapter to gather materials efficiently.

## 🔵 RESEARCH IN THE MEDIA/INFORMATION AGE

### The Good News About the Information Explosion

The information proliferation of the media/information age has been called an "explosion." Recorded information is expanding at a breath-taking rate. One group of experts estimates that the entire amount of knowledge generated by the human race since the beginning of time will have more than doubled from 1990 to 2000.[1] There are literally millions of research projects generating and recording volumes of data annually. Just one of these projects, the Digital Sky Survey, will produce a three-dimensional map of one million galaxies and a million stars in the earth's own galaxy. This survey will store and analyze ten million megabytes of information.

The information explosion is made possible by the technical advances in computer technology. Today's palm-sized organizers can store more information than a roomful of first-generation computers, at a fraction of the price. A single CD-ROM disk can replace two thousand library card catalog drawers. Satellite technology makes it possible to instantly share, and restore, all this information worldwide.

▼ Integrity without knowledge
is weak and
useless.

Samuel Johnson

### ... And the Bad News

The information explosion has not necessarily made speech research easier. Edward Tenner, contributing editor of *Harvard Magazine,* suggests that what is actually occurring is not an explosion but an *implosion,* or "bursting inward." His analogy suggests that, as the amount of information has increased, it has become more difficult to find the information that you really need. Tenner suggests that there are at least two ways that the media/information age has made your research task more difficult:

# Calvin and Hobbes                           by Bill Watterson

*Calvin and Hobbes* © 1992 Watterson. Dist. by Universal Press Syndicate. Reprinted with permission. All rights reserved.

**1.** *Access.* Budget-crunched libraries often cut back on subscriptions and acquisitions, meaning that searches in sophisticated databases can result in long bibliographies of materials that are simply not available. Cutbacks affect personnel, also, resulting in fewer qualified librarians to help retrieve information.

**2.** *Clarity.* Much of what is available must be read on video display terminals and microfilm readers, which aren't as easy to read as print media. And, because of the proliferation of print media, much of what is recorded there is printed on the cheaper grade of high-acid paper that disintegrates quickly with use or in storage.

We might add a third problem: Much of the information that is generated in the information age is "tainted" by its source. As Cynthia Crossen points out in her book, *Tainted Truth: The Manipulation of Fact in America,* much of our information is generated by "sponsored studies," paid for by various commercial interests.[2] The findings of these studies often reflect the sponsor's intentions: The Tobacco Institute's study will find that people aren't really bothered by secondhand smoke, and the Cotton Growers' Association's studies will find that most people are slightly allergic to wool. As Christopher Lasch pointed out, much of the tainted information appears as "fact" in news stories:

> Most of the "news" in our newspapers—40 percent, according to the conservative estimate of Professor Scott Cutlip of the University of Georgia—consists of items churned out by press agencies and public relations bureaus and then regurgitated intact by the "objective" organs of journalism.[3]

The tainted nature of information-age "facts" requires extra work: It means that research must be verified from more than one source, and then tested against logic and common sense. Critical thinking is an important part of the research process in the media/information age.

This chapter is designed to help you work around the detriments and take advantage of the benefits of research in the media/information age. These benefits are not just for your public speaking class. The research skills that you hone in this class will enhance all your college studies as well as your subsequent personal and professional life. For the purposes of this chapter, however, keep in mind that speech research *is* unique in certain ways.

## The Unique Task of Speech Research

You have been doing research for years, of course. In fact, you have been doing research, formally and informally, all your life. But as an academic public speaker, you have to practice a higher level of research. Whereas for a term paper you might need to find information to cite, you don't need to become comfortable or conversant with it. In speechmaking, you do. Usually you will be presenting your speech from brief notes; there will probably be slight differences in wording each time you give the speech, either as practice or in the classroom. There may also be a question-and-answer period following your speech. Under those circumstances, you have to be comfortable with your information, to believe in it, and be able to use it in different contexts and from different points of view.[4]

There are three types of information you need for a speech. The first category, which we discussed in the preceding chapter, is information about the audience and the occasion. In addition, you need information about the ideas you use, and you need facts to substantiate and help develop your ideas. By this time, of course, you are familiar with library research as a form of gathering information. Sometimes, however, speakers overlook some of the less obvious resources of the library; more often they also overlook interviewing, personal observation, and survey research as equally effective methods of gathering information. We will review all these methods here and perhaps provide a new perspective on one or more of them.

▼ Eloquence is the child of knowledge. When a mind is full, like a wholesome river, it is also clear.

Benjamin Disraeli

▼ Nothing's so hard, but search will find it out.

Robert Herrick

## ⬤ SOURCES OF INFORMATION

For most people, the term *research* means library time. And while we won't disparage the importance of library research, we'd like to suggest some additional sources of information.

## Personal Experience and Knowledge

On some topics you might not qualify as an expert. You probably don't have much to say personally about the federal deficit or lifestyles of Australian aborigines, for example. But your personal experience does qualify you as an authority on other subjects. In a single public speaking class it's likely that at least one person is able to speak authoritatively on topics like

▼ Challenges facing single parents

▼ The rewards and costs of college athletics

▼ Problems with the high school educational system

▼ How ethnic minorities feel about discrimination

▼ Why 1930s films are worth viewing

▼ Coping with stress in academics

Your personal experience probably isn't broad or deep enough to serve as the *only* source for speeches like these. Your presentation will be stronger if you back up your own information with examples, testimony, statistics, and other supporting materials that you have collected from other sources. But your own knowledge can be a good starting point.

Including your own experience can not only make research easier, it can make a speech more credible. One student delivered a speech describing how young men abused steroids in order to look better and excel in sports. In addition to citing statistics showing the growth of steroid use and quoting medical authorities about the drug's dangers, he told a personal story. "I know about the pressure to abuse steroids," he claimed. "Until a few months ago I used them myself." He went on to describe the pressures that led him to start using steroids, and he explained the problems they caused in his life. This student's personal testimony made a powerful impression on his classmates—much stronger than citing outside sources alone.

## Information in Your Possession

In our earlier chapter on topic selection, we suggested a personal media review. A similar type of review can be a good start for research. Your personal library might not look very impressive, but the materials you have on hand can be more useful than they appear. One student proved this point by coming up with the support for several speeches from the publications in his apartment:

▼ From a *Sports Illustrated* magazine: How mountaineers have demonstrated the human capacity for endurance by climbing Mt. Everest without bottled oxygen.

▼ From a current edition of a metropolitan newspaper: How unrest in Tibet illustrates the difficulties communist governments have in suppressing the desire for religious freedom.

▼ From a reader used in English composition: Guidelines for using non-sexist language.

▼ From an almost-forgotten *Boy Scout Handbook:* How the handbook can be a single-volume guide to surviving in and enjoying the outdoors.

These examples show the value of a personal library. Of course it's unrealistic to buy every book you might need and save every piece of reading material you get. One way to strike a balance between having nothing and becoming a pack rat is to start with a small personal library of reference books and files on areas of special importance to you. A good personal library would probably include:

| TYPE OF BOOK | EXAMPLE |
|---|---|
| dictionary | *Webster's New Collegiate Dictionary* |
| thesaurus | *Roget's Thesaurus* |
| book of quotations | *Bartlett's Familiar Quotations* |
| guide to English usage | *The Elements of Style,* by Strunk and White |
| guide to public speaking | This book! |
| single-volume encyclopedia | *New Columbia Encyclopedia* |
| almanac | *World Almanac* or *Information Please Almanac* |
| introduction to fields of personal interest | *Dictionary of American History, Cassell's Encyclopedia of World Literature, Harvard Dictionary of Music, Encyclopedia of Psychology* |
| Books on weird topics that, according to your friends, appeal to no one but you. | You name them |

Of course, some of these references, especially the encyclopedias and almanacs, are available on CD and on-line for personal computer, for those who prefer cyberspace to shelf space. In addition to reference books like these, keeping files of clippings on topics that are important to you can prove tremendously useful. Besides having personal value, they can provide much of the material for use in a successful speech. These files can cover a wide range of topics, such as:

▼ Reviews on consumer products (cars, musical equipment, etc.)

▼ Career opportunities in your area of interest.

▼ Information about people important to you (entertainers, athletes, etc.)

▼ Statistical surveys from newspapers such as *USA Today* on topics of interest.

▼ Quotations that have personal significance or that might be useful in writing assignments.

▼ Recreational opportunities (vacation spots, travel discounts, etc.)

Videotaped television programming from your personal collection can be used as research also. A TV documentary on a subject that interests you can contain a wealth of information. If you missed a program, you can call the Viewer Relations Office at the local station and they'll give you the address to purchase a transcript or videotape. Audiotapes of radio documentaries, such as those heard on National Public Radio, can also be used.

### Personal Observation

Personal *experience* is one of the basic ingredients of any speech; personal observation is like a personal experience that you experienced specifically *for* the speech. For example, if you were suggesting to an audience that the TV sets in your student union should be removed, you might say this:

> I think people would interact more here if the televisions were removed from the student union.

But all you have there is personal opinion, which could be based on anything, including a purely emotional hatred of television or of college students. The use of systematic personal observation, however, allows you to take a more objective stance. Using it, you might be able to say something like this:

> Last Wednesday I spent 7 to 10 P.M. in the lounge of the student union. Only three times during the evening did anyone attempt to start a conversation. Two of those attempts were met with a request for silence in deference to the television.

If you wanted to prove your point further, you could do what social scientists call "manipulating a variable":

> This Wednesday I received permission to remove the television from the student union. During those same hours, 7 to 10 P.M., I observed the following behavior in that lounge, this time without television:

1. Thirty conversations were begun.
2. Twenty-four of these conversations continued, in depth, for more than ten minutes.
3. Seven groups of students decided on alternative entertainment for the evening, including table games, dancing, and going to the library.
4. Four new male-female acquaintances were made, one of which resulted in a TV date for the following Thursday night.

Personal observation has been used profitably in hundreds of student speeches, including talks on how dress affects people's perceptions of you, people's reactions to dogs, reactions to panhandlers and the homeless, library etiquette, and what people throw away.

## Survey Research

Survey research is one of the mainstays of media professionals. Advertisers, programmers, publishers, and producers are constantly conducting surveys as a form of audience analysis. A public speaking class is a good place to introduce yourself to this type of research.

Survey research involves asking a number of people an identical set of questions. You can ask these questions in person, over the telephone, or on printed questionnaires. You can use survey research to find out how your class members feel about your topic. You can use that data for your audience analysis as well as for supporting material in your speech. One advantage to survey data as supporting material is that it gives you answers that are up to date and tailored to a specific group of people. Consider the following ideas, which might be presented in a speech on "How to Handle Stress":

▼ According to a *Time* magazine article published in 1989, five out of ten college students will suffer from stress-related illness during their stay in college. (library data)

▼ According to a survey I conducted last week, nine out of ten students in this class have experienced symptoms of stress within the last two weeks, and fully half of you can expect to suffer from a stress-related illness by the end of this term. (survey data)

### Types of Survey Questions

There are basically three types of survey questions: those that can be answered "yes" or "no," multiple-choice questions, and open questions that can be answered any way the respondent wants.

***Yes-or-No Questions*** The yes-or-no question is best asked when you need a quick statistic. For example, if you were speaking in Wyoming or Idaho on the federal government's plan to reintroduce wolves into nearby national parks, you might want to be able to say, "More than half the students in this class are involved in the ranching industry, or have family members involved in ranching." A yes-or-no survey question could be used to produce this statistic; such a question produces responses that can be easily tabulated and expressed as percentages. However, a yes-or-no question also requires you to "lead" the respondent and does not encourage detail that might be important. For example, if you asked the question, "Are you in favor of reintroducing gray wolves into Yellowstone Park? Yes _____ No_____", the respondents would not have the opportunity to explain that they might be in favor of the proposal under certain conditions, and against it under other conditions. For example, they might be in favor of the reintroduction *if* they would be allowed to hunt any wolves who wandered off the park into livestock areas. Of course, this type of question might be handy when you are trying to avoid long-winded responses by forcing a simple "yes" or "no."

***Multiple-Choice Questions*** As a rule, the more detail you ask for in your questionnaire, the more difficult the answers will be to tabulate and explain. One way to ask a question so the respondent can give some detail, without making tabulation difficult, is to establish the choices yourself. You might follow up a yes-or-no question such as "Do you have home exercise equipment?" with a multiple-choice item, such as:

▼ If so, do you use it

_____ every day

_____ at least once a week

_____ only occasionally

_____ never

_____ other

You should arrange your choices so only a minimum number of responses will appear in the "other" slot, because those responses will be the most difficult to tabulate.

One useful type of multiple-choice question is the *scale question*. These questions are particularly useful when you are investigating the strength of a respondent's attitude. Scale questions allow the respondent to answer anywhere along a continuum, such as:

▼ Do you agree or disagree that criminal defendants currently have too many rights?

| ▼ Strongly Agree | Mildly Agree | Undecided | Mildly Disagree | Strongly Disagree |
|---|---|---|---|---|
| _____ | _____ | _____ | _____ | _____ |

Notice that scale questions will always have an odd number of choices (usually five or seven) so there will be a point "in the middle" to represent neutrality on the question.

**Open Questions**   To encourage detailed, complete responses, you might want to use open questions: "What do you think is the number one health hazard in the United States today?" or "How much do you know about the relationship between dietary fiber and the risk of cancer?"

A typical questionnaire will contain five to ten questions, usually including all three types.

## Interviews with Experts

Even if you don't have the information you need on hand, there's a good chance someone nearby does. People in your community can be useful sources of information—and most of the time they are happy to share it if you ask. (This is especially true in a college community—a sort of collection of experts.)

### Types of Experts

There are several kinds of experts. One type can provide the *specific facts* you need. Have stiffer penalties for drunk driving reduced the number of alcohol-related accidents? The local police or highway patrol can tell you. How bad is the air pollution in your area? A call to the air quality management district will give you the answer. Are there many job openings in the field of computer programming? Asking the personnel managers at several companies can give you an idea.

Asking experts may not be the only way to get facts, but it is often the easiest. Often a quick phone call or visit to an accessible, knowledgeable person can provide just the data you need.

Sometimes experts will give you even more information than you hoped for. One student needed to know the vacancy rate in local apartments for a speech on the local housing shortage. The director of the board of realtors supplied him with this information as well as up-to-date figures on the average cost of rents, the number of new units under construction, and five-year trends on the supply and demand for housing units. In a five-minute conversation, this student was able to get most of the information he needed to deliver an excellent speech.

Besides supplying you with facts, some experts can give you *quotable testimony*—opinions that will add a useful perspective to your speech and boost your credibility. A veteran teacher can give you insights about how today's students measure up against their predecessors. The contestants in a beauty pageant can talk about whether the experience left them feeling like objects rather than human beings.

▼ Somewhere, sprinkled out amongst the best minds of the century, are clues. And someone's tongue is bound to slip.

Digby Diehl

▼ I have more understanding than my teachers: for thy testimonies are my study.

The Book of Common Prayer

Testimony from experts can be an ideal supplement to the facts you uncover in more traditional research. Combining a quotation from a credible person is an excellent complement to impersonal facts and figures. One student, a third-generation Japanese-American, wanted to speak about the injustices suffered by members of her grandparents' generation who were interned in "relocation camps" during World War II. A visit to the library produced details on the number of people who were forced to live in the camps, the legal justifications used by authorities to put them there, the harsh living conditions, and the struggle to gain an official government apology for the internment program. But an afternoon's conversation with her grandmother, who had spent almost four years at the Manzanar camp, gave new meaning to the dry facts. This student's audience listened spellbound as she quoted her grandmother's recollections of how it felt as an American citizen to be treated like a wartime prisoner.

In addition to personal insights, meeting new people in research interviews can lead to valuable career opportunities. One student interviewed several local landscape architects to get an idea of career opportunities for women in the field. Besides finding the information she needed for her speech, she wound up making such a positive impression in one firm that she was invited to work there as an intern, and later as a paid employee.

### How to Interview Experts

***Planning the Interview***   Most good interviews begin long before the first question is asked. You will get the best results if you follow these steps:

▼ *Define your goal.* Ask yourself exactly what information you need. Try to define your goal as specifically as possible. For example, instead of saying "I want to learn more about autism," say "I want to learn about the causes of autism and the characteristics of its victims." Instead of stating "I want to learn about teen suicides," say "I want to find out why teens take their own lives and what can be done by teachers, family, and friends to prevent suicides."

▼ *Conduct background research.* Consider who can give you the information you need. Learn enough about the expert and about the topic to avoid wasting time or asking foolish questions. For example, you can read a great deal about the Peace Corps before interviewing a former volunteer.

▼ *Plan your questions.* Organize the questions by topic area. Make sure all of them are focused on your goal. Word your questions clearly, and make sure they aren't hostile ("How do you feel about torturing helpless laboratory animals?") or leading ("Aren't you interested in giving minorities the breaks they deserve?").

***During the Interview***    A good interview may sound like an ordinary conversation, but successful outcomes usually depend on following several steps.

▼ *Preview your approach.* An introduction is just as important in an interview as it is in a speech. Your expert can be most helpful if he or she knows how you want to use the interview time. Explain your goals for the interview and the topic areas you will be covering. Clarify the amount of time you hope to spend.

▼ *Keep the interviewee on target.* There are several ways in which an interview can get off track. You may get so interested in one topic that you run out of time before you get to other important areas. The expert may go off on tangents, telling stories and making comments that don't give you the information you need. As the interviewer, it's your job to keep the conversation on track by diplomatically but firmly steering the conversation back to your agenda.

▼ *Keep notetaking to a minimum.* Inexperienced interviewers feel obligated to scribble down almost every word their subjects utter. Besides being physically impossible, this approach can be distracting for both the expert and the interviewer. It's far better to record important ideas and specific facts, but to keep most of your attention focused on the expert. After the interview you can fill in details.

   One way to keep notetaking to a minimum is to use a tape recorder. But be forewarned: Despite the advantage of having a word-for-word record of your conversation, a tape recorder can make some interviewees feel uncomfortable. A tape recording can also use up a large amount of time, since you have to replay large parts of the conversation to find the information you are looking for. Whether you use a recorder will probably depend on the type of information you seek. If you are looking for broad ideas and inspiration, you probably don't need a recorder. If you are seeking specific, word-for-word testimony, then a tape recorder is a necessity. If you do decide to use a recorder, make sure to get advance approval from the person you are interviewing.

***After the Interview***    In order to get the most out of your conversation, you need to follow these guidelines after the interview.

▼ *Review your notes promptly.* The best time to make use of the information you collected is immediately after your interview. Review your notes (or the tape recording if you made one) and decide how to fit the information into your speech. Waiting even a few hours can result in your forgetting key points or losing insights that struck you during the conversation.

▼ *Thank the interviewee.* If interviews are important enough to set up in advance, it is probably a good idea to write a note of thanks to the people who have given you their valuable time. Writing thank-you notes may not be common, but that makes them even more appreciated when they arrive. Besides being good manners, a note of appreciation increases the odds that the interviewee will remember you if you need to make contact in the future.

Even the most helpful interview may not give you all the information you need to plan an effective speech. It's not common for a single person to have all the facts on a subject; and when you are seeking opinions, one person's point of view may not be enough. Sometimes you can meet your information needs by interviewing several people. But in other cases you can get the best results by contacting an organization.

## Authoritative Organizations

It is hard to imagine a topic that does not have at least one organization dedicated to it. A look at the phone book of a midsize city reveals over 75 listings, including:

▼ African-American Community Services

▼ Alzheimer's Disease Association

▼ American Civil Liberties Union

▼ Associated General Contractors

▼ Audubon Society

▼ Better Business Bureau

▼ Children of the Americas

▼ County Medical Society

▼ Developmental Disabilities Board

▼ Junior Chamber of Commerce

▼ League of Women Voters

▼ National Association for the Advancement of Colored People

▼ National Automobile Club

▼ National Foundation of the Blind

▼ Peace Resource Center

▼ Retired Senior Volunteer Program

▼ Sierra Club

▼ Society for the Prevention of Cruelty to Animals

▼ Trust for Historic Preservation

▼ United Nations Association

Because they have the interest and talent to study a subject in depth, these organizations can be a gold mine of information about your speech topic. Helpful organizations fall into two categories. Some of them are advocates for a cause, while others are more impartial.

### Advocates

Because there's power in numbers, people who favor or oppose a subject usually unite. If the cause is important enough, they raise financing, conduct research, and develop a campaign to convince others that their position is right. Because they have spent so much time and money exploring a subject, interest groups can be a useful source of information for your speech. For example, if you were preparing a speech on any type of allergy, you would find the following organizations in the *Encyclopedia of Associations:*

▼ The American Academy of Allergy and Immunology

▼ National Allergy Bureau

▼ The American College of Allergy and Immunology

▼ The Allergy and Asthma Network/Mothers of Asthmatics

▼ The Asthma and Allergy Foundation of America

▼ The Food Allergy Network

Many of these organizations have local branches you can visit, and most of them have 800 numbers you can call. Because there are two sides to most issues, it's likely that for every organization that advocates a controversial cause there is another one that opposes it. Consider a few examples:

| | |
|---|---|
| National Right to Life | National Abortion Rights Action League |
| Smoke Enders | The Tobacco Institute |
| Partnership for a Drug-Free America | National Organization for the Reform of Marijuana Laws |
| National Rifle Association | Handgun Control |
| Young Democrats | Young Republicans |

If your goal is to advocate one side of an issue, you might be tempted to contact only groups that support your position. After all, advocates will supply you with the most powerful evidence they have. They might even offer you the other side's "arguments," but, unfortunately, they will seldom cast those arguments in the best light or offer the best evidence to back them up. So don't dismiss organizations on the other side too quickly. At the very least they can tell you what arguments your opponents are likely to use. And who knows—the information you receive may even change your mind!

## Impartial Sources

Some groups don't take a position for or against an issue. Instead, they analyze it impartially. Local governments often publish reports on topics of local interest: urban development, health hazards, crime statistics, and so on. Universities and foundations study everything from acid rain to television programming. The Better Business Bureau mediates between businesses and consumers. A letter to organizations like these can produce materials useful for many speeches.

Probably the largest source of impartial information is the U.S. government. Its various departments and agencies produce literally thousands of publications every year, and there is a good chance that at least one of those pieces contains information you can use.[5]

Sometimes finding the right organization can seem like the most difficult part of your research, but with enough thought you can usually find a shortcut to the groups you are looking for. Often the easiest way is to find an expert who can direct you to groups that have an interest in your topic. For example, your doctor may be able to put you in touch with organizations concerned with health issues, and a conservation-minded friend may be able to tell you about groups that support environmental causes. You can find authoritative organizations with on-line searches using any of the Internet searching devices that use key words. You'll also find organizations mentioned in the published books and articles about your topic, which is one of the many reasons it's time to brush up your library skills.

## Library Resources

▼ A library is a sacred place. For four thousand years, humanity has gone through dreadful horrors, dreadful turmoils, varied glories. How do we distill the past? How do we retain the memories? Libraries.

Vartan Gregorian

Library research is probably the type of research you're most familiar with. You've been doing this type of research since elementary school, although, as we explained earlier, some of the side effects of the information age might be fewer librarians, more database searches, and information that is difficult to locate. One purpose of library research in the media/information age is to use limited time most effectively. To save time in the long run, you have to learn the layout and system of the library or libraries that you have at your disposal.

Perhaps the best way to get acquainted with a library is to take one of the tours that are usually offered on a regular basis. This tour will show you what resources the library has and where these resources are located. A tour will also show you that library personnel are usually friendly people who want to help you find the information you are seeking.

### Library Staff

It is ironic but true that human beings can be the first and best source of information in the media age. Library personnel are the logical guides to introduce you to the many resources they manage, and they can be lifesavers when you get lost in a sea of information.

Even after you are familiar with the library and its collection, reference librarians can be a source of help when you hit a dead end in your research. They can suggest new strategies—and, if time permits, even do a little digging for you. Many people have the mistaken idea that librarians resent requests for assistance. In fact, most of them enjoy helping serious patrons search for the facts they need. After all, librarians are skilled "information detectives" who enjoy solving a particularly difficult case. This doesn't mean you should expect librarians to do *all* your research for you. The following pages describe many tools you can use on your own before turning to them for help.

## The Library Catalog

Library catalogs can be contained on cards, microfilm or computer files. Despite these different formats, the basic methods of organizing books have changed little. Whether you look in a card catalog or a microfilm catalog, you will find the books cataloged three times: by subject, title, and author. Some catalogs are physically separated by these three divisions, while others mix all three from A to Z. Each system allows you to search for materials in whatever manner is most convenient for you. Regardless of its type, every catalog card tells you what the book is about, how many pages it has, when it was written, and who wrote it, and gives ideas for other items to look up on the same subject.

On-line catalogs generally have a *Boolian capability*. In a Boolian search, you don't need to know a particular author, title, or even subject; you give the computer two or three key words and it searches the library's entire collection for you. If, for example, you wanted to research frivolous lawsuits by prisoners, you could input "Suits/Prisoner/Frivolous" into a Boolian search and the computer would tell you any book that includes those three words, in any order, within its description on its catalog entry.

The library catalog can be used to find more than one book at a time. You can locate, through a "subject" search, the section of the stacks that holds the books related to your topic. Once you find the general area, you can review the tables of contents and indexes of several of the books there. This perusal of the library stacks is especially useful when you are looking for inspiration for topics, and for general overviews. It will also guard against the heartache that occurs when that one specific book you were looking for is checked out by someone else.

Despite its usefulness, the card catalog is not always the best place to look for speech materials. Sometimes the information you are looking for is too recent to have been published in a book. In other cases it won't be easily found by scanning book titles or authors' names. Even the subject catalog might not be specific enough to help you locate easily the information you need. At times like these, the best place to look is in the library's reference section.

### Reference Materials

The library's reference section is especially useful when you are seeking specific facts: the most recent work published on the techniques of terrorism, the dates of Millard Fillmore's presidency, winners of last year's Academy Awards, and so on. The reference section also is a good place to find overviews of most subjects.

***Dictionaries*** The library's reference section has unabridged dictionaries that contain far more information than the book you keep handy on your desktop. These dictionaries, such as *Funk and Wagnall's New Standard Dictionary* and *Webster's Third New International Dictionary* try to define as much of the entire language as possible, including an average of 12,000 new terms that arise each year. The *Oxford English Dictionary* gives a history of each word's development and usage. You may only need an unabridged dictionary occasionally, but it's good to know that several are ready for your use in the reference section of the library.

In addition to the general dictionaries, many specialized volumes are published whose entries concentrate on particular areas of study. Foreign language dictionaries fall into this category, as do reverse dictionaries (those organized by meaning, rather than word), picture dictionaries, and dictionaries for acronyms, initials, allusions, slang, and new words. The following dictionaries and directories appeal to readers in specialized knowledge spheres:

- ▼ *Dictionary of American Biography*
- ▼ *Dictionary of American Immigration History*
- ▼ *Dictionary of Computing*
- ▼ *Dictionary of Jargon*
- ▼ *Dictionary of Religious and Spiritual Quotations*
- ▼ *Dictionary of Scientific and Technical Terms*
- ▼ *Dictionary of the Environment*
- ▼ *Dictionary of Women's Biography*
- ▼ *International Dictionary of Medicine and Biology*
- ▼ *New Harvard Dictionary of Music*
- ▼ *The Nonsexist Wordfinder: A Dictionary of Gender-Free Usage*

***Encyclopedias*** Since the time of Aristotle, encyclopedias have attempted to bring all existing knowledge together in one place. This undertaking produces a productive source for speech planning. The coverage in an encyclopedia will lack the depth you need to plan an entire speech, but it will provide a good overview of topics and give you ideas for other topics to explore.

Several encyclopedias are available for personal computers equipped with CD-ROM drives. The current best-sellers are *Compton's,* Microsoft's *Encarta,* and *Grolier's,* all of which provide moving images, sound, and dictionaries that will give you the definition of an unfamiliar word with a click of the mouse control.

Although many families have either a CD-ROM or home encyclopedia, a library trip is sometimes necessary to get the best coverage on a topic. Writing an encyclopedia is much like paving an interstate highway or washing the windows on the Empire State Building: Once the job looks finished, it's time to start all over again. When Volume Z is ready for the printer, Volume A needs modernizing. Even in this system, each new edition of an encyclopedia is not entirely rewritten. Some of the articles are only rewritten every three to five years, a further reason to be careful when researching topics whose technology changes rapidly. The yearly supplements that update some encyclopedias help only marginally in this regard. Most libraries have the yearly supplements to update their editions.

With today's information explosion, it is impossible to collect knowledge comprehensively. Many modern encyclopedias focus on one particular subject area, such as the following:

▼ *Concise Encyclopedia of Science & Technology*

▼ *Encyclopedia of American Facts & Dates*

▼ *Encyclopedia of Arts & Crafts*

▼ *Encyclopedia of Associations*

▼ *Encyclopedia of Business Information Sources*

▼ *Encyclopedia of Censorship*

▼ *Encyclopedia of Crime, Occult and the Supernatural*

▼ *Encyclopedia of Education*

▼ *Encyclopedia of Popular Music*

▼ *Encyclopedia of Religion and Ethics*

▼ *Encyclopedia of Television*

▼ *Encyclopedia of World Literature*

▼ *Encyclopedia of World Mythology & Legend*

▼ *Encyclopedia of American History*

▼ *International Encyclopedia of Communications*

▼ *Prentice-Hall Encyclopedia of Information Technology*

▼ *The Sports Encyclopedia*

**Periodical Indexes**   Some topics demand the most current information available. A magazine article written two months ago on discoveries about black holes in the universe might have more up-to-date material than even a book published recently on the same subject. Indexes are especially important when you are speaking about fast-breaking events. You can't rely on last year's publications for information about Middle Eastern politics or federal legislation; indexes are the way to find out what has been written lately on topics like these.

▼ *Reader's Guide to Periodical Literature* This venerable index is the best known tool of most library users for good reason. It provides a quick, easy way to search over 200 popular magazines by topic. A computerized version makes searching even easier and quicker.

▼ *Newspaper Indexes* Print indexes for many leading newspapers are available in libraries. Computerized searching of newspaper indexes is also available in many libraries, as well as via online services and on the Worldwide Web. Many libraries have actual issues of key newspapers available on microfilm or microfiche.

▼ *Other Printed Indexes* Indexes are published on many areas of special interest. If you are lucky enough to find one for your speech topic, you will be able to locate a wide assortment of published material on the subject. Some indexes include:

▼ *American Statistics Index*
▼ *Applied Science and Technology Index*
▼ *Book Review Index*
▼ *Business Periodicals Index*
▼ *Computer Literature Index*
▼ *Education Index*
▼ *Historical Abstracts*

▼ *Psychological Abstracts*
▼ *Science Index*
▼ *Social Sciences and Humanities Index*
▼ *Technology Index*
▼ *Who's Who* (separate volumes published for leaders in many fields)

**Biographies** Biographies can help you locate information about specific individuals, either as the subject of a speech or as illustrations of a point you want to make. For example, suppose your thesis is "it's possible to make a fortune in the computer industry . . . if you're a man." A Boolean search of the card catalog under the categories "Biography" and "Computer Industry" would identify a list of books that support your claim, including the stories of Bill Gates, Steve Jobs, Bill Millard, William Hewett, Ken Olsen, and An Wang.

The media/information age makes it necessary to include a note of warning about the accuracy of biographies. Always consider the authorship: Autobiographies and biographies written by loved ones often attempt to sanitize and glamorize the life under scrutiny. (This includes the brief summaries in *Who's Who,* which are often contributed by the subject of the entry.) On the other hand, many biographies that are written for commercial gain look for something to sensationalize, and tend to be inaccurate in the opposite direction.[6] The best approach to biography, therefore, is to read more than one author's account.

*Information Digests*   Summaries of recent developments are published in many fields. These digests provide a useful way to keep informed on the latest news, or to find out what was happening at a specific time in the past. Some of these make excellent sources of speech topics. The following is a partial list of available digests:

▼ *The Congressional Researcher* This weekly digest explores the background, outlook and analysis of "hot button" issues, any one of which could serve as a speech topic. This digest includes up-to-date bibliographies on each issue.

▼ *The Congressional Quarterly Weekly Report* This digest summarizes congressional activities both on the floor and in committee. The backstage drama of the legislature in action is also included. For information on the Washington political scene, CQ provides an excellent overview. Each weekly issue has a table of contents and an index.

▼ *Editorials on File* A biweekly collection of selected newspaper editorials on issues of widespread interest. Over 150 newspapers nationwide are searched for these editorials, which always contain interesting, well-informed points of view.

▼ *Facts on File* This weekly publication of current events covers a broad spectrum of topics, such as world news stories, sports, the economy, and the arts. *Facts on File* is widely respected for its accuracy and ease of use. Its coverage is worldwide although its emphasis is on the United States. When you need to locate or verify a fact quickly, *Facts on File* is one of the best indexes available.

▼ *Social Issues Resources Service (SIRS)* This digest consists of looseleaf volumes covering 32 social issues, such as Crime, Communications, Defense, Health, etc. Each volume is devoted to a single issue and contains reprinted articles that are supplemented during the year. This is another excellent resource for topic selection, as well as supporting material.

*Almanacs*   Almanacs are usually published annually, and contain a great variety of material on economic, political, geographic, and other topics in addition to summaries of the year's events. The three major almanacs published in the United States are the *Information Please Almanac,* the *Reader's Digest Almanac and Yearbook,* and the *World Almanac and Book of Facts.* There are dozens of other almanacs, all of which are designed to make it easy to look up facts. If you can formulate the question in statistical terms (How many convicted murderers were executed last year? How much does the government spend on prisons?) you can find the answer in an almanac.

### Computerized Reference Services

Computer databases are one of the blessings of the media/information age. They are an ideal medium for storing and organizing information. They allow a user to search literally millions of documents quickly and thoroughly. Just as important, they make it possible to sort through information in a multitude of ways. Like a card catalog, databases allow searches by title, author, and subject. But users can also use Boolian searches of key words as well as search by publication date, language, type of publication (book, journal, newspaper), and in many other ways.

Some databases operate as on-line services. Using a personal computer or terminal, searchers make contact over phone lines with a mainframe computer. These databases are accessible over popular on-line services such as America On Line, Prodigy and CompuServe, as well as more specialized information services such as Dialog, EasyLink, and Nexis.

The Dialog information service contains over 300 databases holding more than 120 million records. Dialog searches can uncover a variety of information: directory-type listings of companies, associations, or famous people; financial statements; citations with bibliographic information and abstracts summarizing an article; and even the complete text of some works.

Other computerized databases are self-contained on CD-ROM disks similar to ones used for home encyclopedias (or, for that matter, to record music). Self-contained databases are usually easier to use than on-line services, and many libraries make them available for their patrons. Infotrac, for example, has a general magazine index on one CD-ROM, and a business index, a health index, and an academic index on others.

On-line computer services can also be used to search for recent news and magazine articles. Also, electronic discussion groups can be used as a form of research. These discussion groups are formed by people with similar interests who are eager to share knowledge, so you can pose a question ("How is plastics recycling handled in your town?" "Any ideas about tax reform?") and collect a wide range of answers.

As exciting as they are, computer services and databases do have their drawbacks. Some types of information are better retrieved from standard sources such as books. For example, consulting the dictionary on your shelf makes a lot more sense than booting up your computer just to define a word, and looking in your library's newspaper index is probably a better way to find the publication date for a recent article.

### ▼ RESEARCH STRATEGIES

Knowing where to look for materials is certainly important, but knowing *how* to conduct your research is just as critical if you are going to develop an effective speech. The following tips will help you use your time most effectively and produce the best results.

## Get an Early Start

Regardless of the sources you are using to gather material, give yourself enough time to conduct thorough research. Remember Murphy's first law—"Whatever can go wrong will go wrong." Assume that your first efforts will fail for one reason or another. Early research—if only for inspiration and approach to a topic—will at least give you an idea of how much time you need to budget to complete the task.

## Be Systematic

It is also wise to be systematic in your search. Your "system" can be either general to specific or specific to general. In other words, you can start out with a broad search for information, and gradually narrow your focus as you get a clearer idea of the final form your speech will take, or you can start with a specific idea and move systematically to broader key words. When you work from the general to the specific, your starting point could be a general idea that seems to have potential for satisfying both your interests and the audience's needs. When this is your plan, you take this general and sometimes fuzzy subject and gradually narrow it down to something concrete. If you were interested in the idea of alternative automobile fuels, that general idea might lead you to the idea of hydrogen as a fuel, in a progression like this:

▼ Automobile Fuels

▼ Alternative Fuels

▼ Alternative Energy

▼ Future Fuels

▼ Hydrogen

▼ Hydrogen Fuel

At each stage of your exploration, new information should emerge and new ways of looking at the topic should become apparent. The research itself is a learning experience in seeing the dimensions of the topic, isolating different possibilities, finding out what facets of it may be easy or difficult to illustrate and, finally, deciding on a sharply focused purpose.

If you move from specific to general key terms, you can still do so systematically. For example, if you wanted information on what has come to be known as "The Russian Mob" (a new form of organized crime in America), you could start with the name "Marat Belugula," who has been identified as the "Russian Godfather." If you don't find enough under that key term, you can move to more general terms:

▼ The Organizatsiya

▼ The Russian Mob

▼ Russian Organized Crime

▼ Russian Criminals

▼ Russian Emigrés in America

▼ Organized Crime in America

▼ Organized Crime

When you've focused your topic and begin looking for specific information on it, you can still move from either general to specific or specific to general key words in your search. The key is to work with a consistent, systematic list. This is true whether you are searching through the library or through an interviewee's memory.

## Be Methodical

With an early start and a systematic approach, you may find scores of publications on your topic. You might find dozens of books and articles, interview several experts, and receive thick packets of material from authoritative organizations. Even enthusiastic researchers surface from this sort of information binge with the information overload that we discussed in Chapter 2. Researchers suffering from information overload have pleasant but fuzzy recollections of useful material for their speeches, but they can't remember exactly what they found or where it is located.

Although no system is perfect, a few guidelines will help you get the most out of your research.

1. Record each usable bit of information you collect on a separate sheet of paper. This will allow you to shuffle your notes around as you try out different organizational plans.

2. Immediately jot down every idea you have about how to use the material you collect. For example, if the comments of an expert you inter-

viewed reinforce statistics you found in library research, make a note
of the fact so you can use the two bits of information together.

3. Build your rough outline as you go. In this way you can "compose" parts
of your speech as you go.

4. Keep your work neat. The scribbles you understand today may look
like gibberish tomorrow when you are trying to build a final outline. No
matter how rushed you feel, proofread your notes on each resource before you put that resource back on the shelf.

5. Whenever possible, photocopy research materials. In fact, duplicate
any materials you *think* might be useful. The small amount of money
you spend is a bargain when you consider how much time you'll save
by not transcribing long passages from printed materials. It's also better to have a copy of information you might need on hand than to go
back to the library to find it later.

A reminder about ethics is in order at this point. It is important to
carefully cite the sources of any information you have collected for your
speech. In the rush of gathering facts and opinions, don't forget to record
exactly where they came from, and offer credit within your speech where
it is due. Aside from being the ethical course of action, citing sources will
boost your credibility in the eyes of your audience. Showing that you have
collected material from reputable sources is an implicit way of saying,
"Don't just take my word for this. I've taken the time to research the topic
and find out what experts have to say."

## Sample Speech

Our sample speech was presented by Sara Hessenflow when she was a
student at Kansas State University.[7] Sara got the idea for the speech
when watching *60 Minutes*. She later sent away for the transcript of
that program, and that transcript became an important part of her research.

Sara did her library research in Farrell Library at Kansas State
University. Farrell has a reputation among the student body as being a
difficult library to work with, both because of its enormous size and the
constant modifications that are made to adapt to new materials and
databases. As Sara did her research, she faced the additional problem of
remodeling, so material was often in the process of being transferred. Still,
she managed to find appropriate books in the card catalog. She consulted
the *Washington Post Index*, the *Reader's Guide to Periodical Literature*,
the *New York Times Index*, and the computerized *Academic Index*. She
then contacted some of the people mentioned in the articles, and they recommended people for her to interview, one of whom proved particularly
helpful.

It is interesting to note that Sara used only about a third of the information she actually uncovered about this topic. The rest contributed to the background knowledge that gave her the confidence to interact freely with her audience about this topic. The methodical elimination of less effective material was one of the things that made Sara's speech so effective. She presented the speech at the 1993 Interstate Oratorical Association Contest, and won first prize with it.

## ▼ TRANSRACIAL ADOPTION

By Sara Hessenflow

Kansas State University

[1] When Recee came up for adoption, he wanted to stay with his foster family, and they wanted to adopt him. While no one could find anything wrong with the foster family's desire or ability to care for the child, the adoption agency went to court to block the adoption. The court gave the agency 30 days to find an alternative home. On day 29, one was found, four states away, and Recee had to move to his new home. Six months later, Recee was dead of child abuse. Apparently in the rush to find an alternative home, the agency was not interested in a thorough background check.

[2] But what was so wrong with Recee's original foster family? It was clearly demonstrated that they could provide the kind of home any child would want. What did the agency find so objectionable? According to the October 25, 1992, broadcast of *60 Minutes,* the foster family's problem was their race. They were white, Recee was black.

[3] Transracial adoption is a controversial issue that has unfortunately placed misguided theories of race above the welfare of many children. In a perfect world, blacks would adopt blacks, Hispanics would adopt Hispanics, and whites would adopt whites. But in a perfect world, children would never face the issue of adoption. The fact is, we do not live in a perfect world, and in the world we do live in, limiting children to homes of their same racial background is not in their best interest.

[4] Many of us will never deal personally with the issue of adoption. But if we believe that every child has the right to grow up in a secure and loving home, then we should all be concerned with the barriers to trans-racial adoption. Today, I hope to encourage you to help drop these barriers. To do so, we will need to first examine the problem of transracial adoption, next look at why it is occurring, and finally, understand what we can do to ensure the best family situation for adopted children.

[5] To begin, the problem of transracial adoption is fairly easy to understand. Adoption agencies, which wield an understandable amount of power in deciding which families can adopt, are against placing a child in a home

where the child and the parent are not of the same race. Unfortunately, this runs into the problem of supply and demand. According to the April 5, 1992, *Washington Post,* 38 percent of the children who are up for adoption are black; and according to the January 5, 1992, *New York Times,* there are more black children up for adoption than there are black families to take them in.

6 More often than not, the problems barring transracial adoption face white families wanting to adopt black children, because of the strong objections made by black social workers. But it should be made clear that these problems face any family wanting to adopt a child of a different race. So while it may be rare, the same situation faces black families wanting to adopt white children. The simple fact is: In a nation trying to dedicate itself to the principle that your skin color does not matter, it obviously does matter . . . when it comes to adoption. But why is placing a child in any same-race home more important than placing that child in a good home? To answer this question, we must next look at why the problem of transracial adoption exists.

7 First, when push comes to shove, the courts favor the opinions of adoption agencies, so many times, qualified parents are simply denied. According to Dr. Rita Simon and Howard Alstein's book *Transracial Adoptees and Their Families,* although transracial adoptions are legal, if pursued in a court of law because of a challenge made by an adoption agency, these adoptions are oftentimes denied on the basis of race alone. The argument cited is that the best interest of the child is not being served. And then there is the second objection to transracial adoption: that it is unnatural. Simon and Alstein report that many social workers feel there will be many social problems after these children leave home. They will feel rejected by their race, and they will not fit into either world.

8 Contrary to these opinions, there are documented studies that prove transracial adoption to be beneficial. For example, the *Washington Post* article noted a 20-year study done on black adoptees placed in white homes and found that they "overwhelmingly reported that they love their white parents, have high self-esteem and feel black." Simon and Alstein also found in their study of 206 families that adopted transracially that two-thirds of the parents significantly changed their lifestyles after adopting their children. They moved to transracial neighborhoods, sent their children to transracial schools, even attended transracial churches.

9 It is a shame that we are letting unsubstantiated fear stand in the way of healthy home environments for children. It becomes tragic when you realize that by denying children transracial adoption, we are putting them at a higher risk of becoming homeless later on in life. According to the October 13, 1991, *New York Times,* foster care and institutionalization were

set up to be temporary measures of child placement. When they are used on a permanent basis, as is the case many times when children are denied transracial adoption and their agencies cannot find same-race homes, these children are more likely to end up homeless. That is because children cannot form the type of bonding in an institution that they would in a family, and when they leave these institutions they have no home to come back to. Consequently, many of them end up on the streets. Now, it is bad enough that any child would be at risk for becoming homeless … but it is pathetic when you realize that transracial adoption could avoid much of this problem.

[10] Well, we have seen the problem of transracial adoption, and we know why it is occurring. But what can we do? First, an incentive needs to be created to open up the transracial option. Judy Etkin, the co-founder of Child Placement Services, an adoption agency that works extensively with transracial adoptions, stated one way to do just that. In a November 5, 1992, personal phone interview, she told me about the national Coalition to End Racism in America's Child Care System and their success at persuading the state of Michigan to withhold federal funding from adoption agencies that automatically bar transracial adoptions. That is great for the state of Michigan, but we need to adopt this policy nationwide. We must provide qualified parents with some recourse from the powerful prejudices of private agencies.

[11] To ease the potential problems of transracial adoption, we should consider another local solution. The August 10, 1990, *New York Times* chronicles a court case in Cincinnati that could help us achieve this aim. In this case, a judge ordered a white couple wanting to adopt a black child to enroll in racial and ethnic courses on that child's background. This seems like a reasonable request for all transracial adoptions. By expanding this policy nationwide, we not only create more well-informed parents, we also help to silence critics of transracial adoption.

[12] These two solutions will both require legislative action. Now, we all know, legislative action does not just happen. At the very least it requires public support. Now if you want to write your representative, I'm not going to complain, but there is an easier way to get personally involved in this solution. When I spoke to Etkin, she told me that the single most important thing any of us can do is to spread the word about transracial adoption. Etkin explained to me that by explaining transracial adoption for what it is—a legitimate option for children who have very few options rather than one culture trying to subdue another—we are creating a society that is more informed and, therefore, more accepting of transracial adoption.

[13] Today we have seen the problem of transracial adoption, we recognize the misguided theories that are perpetuating it, and we know what has to be done to work toward a solution.

[14] When we look at cases like Recee, as tragic as they are, the fundamental problem is that it did not have to happen. For all the Recees in the world, there are warm and loving homes, many of them being barred simply because skin colors do not match. We must do all we can as a society, for our own future stability, to make sure children are going to good homes—not just politically correct ones.

## ▼ SUMMARY

Sometimes the speaker's own resources can provide useful material. Personal experience and knowledge can make a speech more interesting and clear, and boost the speaker's credibility. A personal library can also furnish useful material. But it is important to remember that speakers need to base their claims and conclusions on more than just their own opinions, and they need to go beyond their own perspectives to look at what others with wider perspectives have discovered.

Experts on your topic can be a useful source of information. Some can supply factual information. Others can provide the kind of quotable testimony that makes a speech more persuasive. You may already know some experts, and it is likely that you can contact others without much difficulty. Getting the information you need from an expert will usually call for a carefully planned and conducted interview.

Authoritative organizations can supply useful material on many speech topics. Some organizations are advocates for one side of an issue, while others are impartial. In either case, contacting them can be a rich source of information for a speech. The library's staff can provide advice about how to locate materials, and computerized reference services give you quick access to a tremendous amount of information stored in databases.

Regardless of the information sources you use, several research strategies will make your efforts most successful. The first is to get an early start, since delays and obstacles are common. It is also wise to be systematic in your search: You can start out with a broad search for information, and gradually narrow your focus as you get a clearer idea of the final form your speech will take, or you can start with a specific idea and move systematically to broader topics. Finally, it is important to conduct a methodical search, keeping careful records of all your ideas and the material you examine in your explorations.

## ▼ EXERCISES

For the following exercises you can research the topic of your next speech, or one of the following topics:

    A. How a washing machine works

    B. The problem of employee theft

    C. Outpatient surgery (prevalence of, risks of, guidelines for)

    D. Can you trust a child's testimony (in child molestation and devil worshipping cases)?

    E. What is—and isn't—rape?

    F. Do animal rights activists go too far?

    G. Should standardized tests be the main criteria for college admissions?

For your chosen topic:

**1.** Find a form of personal observation that can be used in your speech.

**2.** Compose a survey, using all three types of survey questions, to be given to your audience members. Design the survey to be used for audience analysis as well as speech material.

**3.** Identify one person who could be interviewed on this topic. Compile a question list for the interview.

**4.** Find at least one authoritative organization in the *Encyclopedia of Associations* from which you could request information.

**5.** Make up a systematic list of at least five key words or phrases. Perform at least one computerized reference service search; identify one book from the library catalog, one magazine article from *Reader's Guide to Periodical Literature,* and one item in a reference book that could be used in your speech.

# NOTES

1. Edward Tenner, "The Impending Information Implosion," *Harvard Magazine,* November/December 1991, pp. 30–34.
2. Cynthia Crossen, *Tainted Truth: The Manipulation of Fact in America* (New York: Simon & Schuster, 1994).
3. Christopher Lasch, "Journalism, Publicity and the Lost Art of Argument," in *Mass Media Issues,* 4th ed., George Rodman, ed. (Dubuque: Kendall/Hunt, 1993), p. 375.
4. What we are talking about here is the difference between "writing-based" and "interaction-based" rhetoric. See W. Lance Haynes, "Public Speaking Pedagogy in the Media Age," *Communication Education* 38 (April 1990), p. 92.
5. Your librarian can help you locate useful government publications. You may also order the *Consumer Information Catalog,* a listing of 200 free and low-cost government publications on jobs, health, money, housing, cars, and a wealth of other topics. The catalog is available free from the Consumer Information Center, Department 94, Pueblo, Colorado 81009.
6. See, for example, Steve Weinberg, "The Kitty Kelley Syndrome," in *Mass Media Issues,* pp. 149–160.
7. Sara Hessenflow, "Transracial Adoption," *Winning Orations, 1993* (Interstate Oratorical Association, 1993), pp. 34–37. Sara was coached by Craig Brown.

# SUPPORTING MATERIAL

## ▼ CHAPTER 7 OBJECTIVES

**After reading this chapter, you should understand:**

**1.** The functions of supporting material in an effective speech.

**2.** The importance of supporting material in the media/information age.

**3.** The guidelines for evaluating support.

**You should be able to:**

**1.** Look for a variety of types of support to lend clarity and interest to your speech, to prove your ideas, and to help your audience remember them.

**2.** Use facts, examples, statistics, and quotations effectively in your own speeches.

**3.** Evaluate the supporting materials used by others.

### ▼ SUPPORTING IDEAS IN THE MEDIA/INFORMATION AGE

Supporting materials are the details that make a speech come alive. They include facts, examples, statistics, and quotations. (Visual aids are also considered a form of support; Chapter 10 will be devoted to them.)

In the media/information age, so much information flows by so quickly that people seldom analyze how it catches their attention or why it affects them the way it does. Because of this, people seldom realize the amount of care that goes into the planning of message details. Political speeches, ads, news reports, and every gag in every sitcom are agonized over by the media professionals who produce them.

Real media professionals, like David Letterman, make their presentations look so spontaneous that it's easy to believe that all that brilliance is coming off the top of their heads. It isn't. Many of those spontaneous little bits of "support" that Letterman comes up with, such as pulling a tourist out of the restaurant next door to prove that anyone can be a cohost, or sending out a man in a bear suit to get hugs to prove how friendly New Yorkers are, are written by a team of writers and chosen over many other potential "bits."

Your first question in determining the effectiveness of support is, "Does it perform the desired function?"

### ▼ FUNCTIONS OF SUPPORTING MATERIAL

The four traditional functions of support are: *to clarify, to make interesting, to make memorable,* and *to prove.*

# Calvin and Hobbes          by Bill Watterson

## To Clarify

As we pointed out in Chapter 2, people of different backgrounds tend to attach different meanings to words. For example, if you were talking about the emotional problems of young people, every member of your audience could have a different idea about what you meant. To some, "emotional problems" mean a lack of discipline in holding one's temper; to others, the same term might mean severe psychological problems.

You clarify an idea by adding supporting material to it. As you do so, the idea becomes more specific:

▼ Least specific/clear:
Kids suffer from emotional problems today.

▼ More specific/clear:
Kids suffer from a wide range of emotional problems, including social problems, attention disorders, delinquency, and depression.

▼ Most specific/clear:
According to psychologist Daniel Goleman, there are four areas of emotional problems for children seven to sixteen years old. The first are social problems, which are characterized by an inability to get along with others; the second is attention disorders, which are characterized by an inability to concentrate; the third is delinquency, which manifests itself in children who get into trouble with authority figures and/or associate with kids who get into trouble; and, finally, depression, which is characterized by feelings of sadness, worry, and a lack of energy.[1]

This progression from general, unclear statements to specific, clearer statements is one of the attributes of well-chosen support.

## To Make Interesting

A second use of support is to make an idea interesting by catching your audience's attention.

Brian Swenson, a student at Dakota Wesleyan, wanted to capture his audience's attention when he spoke to them about "Gun Safety and Children." His least specific statement might have been, "Kids as young as nine have murdered other children." A more specific statement might be, "In a small town in Pennsylvania, a 9-year-old boy shot a 7-year-old girl with a hunting rifle." But notice how Brian used highly specific supporting material (in this case, a descriptive anecdote) to capture audience interest:

At first, police feared a sniper was loose.

It was March 6 and, up on Hideaway Hill, 7-year-old Jessica Ann Carr had been shot once in the back as she and a friend rode a snowmobile. Terrified neighbors screamed for other children to

▼ It is a luxury to be understood.

Ralph Waldo Emerson

come inside, then cried and prayed as ambulance workers tried in vain to save the little girl.

That night, police officers found a suspect with a bloody, crescent-shaped gash on his forehead. It matched the telescopic sight of a Marlin .35-caliber hunting rifle in an upstairs bedroom. Soon, the suspect confessed that he had fired the gun.

But tragedy is still tearing at this tiny Poconos Mountain community. Police say the killer is Cameron R. Kocher, a 9-year-old Cub Scout, Bible-class leader, and honor-roll student. And, if prosecutors have their way, Kocher may be the youngest person ever tried for murder in a U.S. adult court.[2]

The detail that Brian used to show the horror of a 9-year-old murderer creates the type of "human interest" at which mass media excel.

### To Make Memorable

We reviewed in Chapter 2 the problems audiences have in remembering the information they have heard. You use supporting material to help alleviate that problem.

You make information memorable by choosing details that create a vivid image in the mind of the listener. C. Haydon Cherry, a student at Western Kentucky University, used a vivid description to begin his speech denouncing the deforestation of marijuana crops in Latin America:

> Fetal malformations, intense headaches, vomiting of blood, and shivering all over until death. Sounds like a description of chemical warfare using nerve gas, doesn't it? But I'm not talking about war. What I've just described is even worse because the United States government is responsible.[3]

Supporting material can also make an idea memorable through the force of your language. Tracy Schario, a student at Ohio State University, not only chose her own language carefully, but also found a quotation with memorable language to use in her speech about discrimination against gays in the military:

> Let's hope sometime during the 1990s gay men and lesbians will be assured their right to fight for their—our—country. Unfortunately, until then, there will be more cases like decorated Vietnam veteran Leonard Matlovich, discharged in 1975 after 12 years of military service. He stated: "When I was in the military, they gave me a medal for killing two men and a discharge for loving one."[4]

We'll have more to say about language use in Chapter 11.

## To Prove

Finally, supporting material can be used as evidence, to prove the truth of what you are saying. This use of support would be most important in a persuasive speech; however, you will be making claims in any kind of speech, and whenever you make a claim it is important to back it up. For example, if you said, "There are more youth murders in the United States than in all the other nations of the world combined," your audience might not want to take your word for it. But supporting material makes it less easy to disagree:

> According to an international study conducted by UNICEF, the United Nations children's organization, fully 90 percent of the youth homicides in the industrial world occur in the United States.[5]

If you were speaking about the deforestation of the rain forests, you would want to prove your claim that these forests are disappearing at an alarming rate. That's what Laura Oster, a student at North Dakota State University, did in her speech on this topic:

> Rain forests are lush tropical forests, existing primarily in the rich Amazonian River Basin and covering 2.7 million square miles—an area approximately equal to the size of the continental United States. According to a report prepared by the Senate Committee on Agriculture, Nature, and Forestry, from April of this year, "each year an area of trees slightly larger than New York and Vermont combined is lost."[6]

We will discuss four major types of supporting material in this chapter: facts, examples, statistics, and quotations.

## ▼ TYPES OF SUPPORTING MATERIAL

An examination of each type of supporting material allows us to consider how each type performs its desired function. It also allows us to consider specific rules for the evaluation of each type. In practice, however, they can be combined; examples can contain facts and quotations might include statistics, for example.

### Facts

▼ Facts are to the mind what food is to the body.

Edmund Burke

As we mentioned before, no matter what type of speech you are presenting, you will make a series of claims. A claim is an assertion that something is true, which will then be backed up with facts and other forms of support.

A sample speech will be presented at the end of this chapter. Claims from this speech need to be backed up with facts:[7]

▼ Claim: Teens are under more stress today than ever before.

▼ Fact: According to psychiatrist Glenda Taber, in her book, *Suicide: The Teenage Death Syndrome,* "Teens are under more stress today than ever before."

▼ Claim: Suicide kills thousands of high school teenagers every year.

▼ Fact: The American Suicide Prevention Association says that over 3,000 teenagers died in 1993 from suicide.

▼ Claim: Suicide prevention programs work.

▼ Fact: According to the *San Francisco Tribune,* March 1993, North High School in San Francisco had the highest suicide average in a ten-year period. Their average death rate was five deaths a year with an additional 15 attempts. A new principal came in and decided to stop the deaths and initiated a program. In the past three years their average death rate has dropped from five deaths a year to less than one and from 15 attempts to about three.

### Facts, Inferences, and Opinions

It is important to distinguish among facts, inferences, and opinions. An *inference* refers to something that cannot be measured objectively, such as someone's emotions (Lucy hates Charlie Brown) or any other internal state. Inferences add to the facts, such as when someone makes a prediction about the future. An *opinion* is a statement that interprets facts or adds a value judgment to the facts. For example, if you said, "The center of Hoop U's basketball team is a bum," you would be stating an opinion, not a fact.

Facts are more specific than inferences or value judgments. You might be able to say, as a statement of fact, that the center of Hoop U's basketball team is 7 feet 6 inches tall. That is something you can measure objectively, given a ruler and a stepladder. If you added something to that statement that could not be measured objectively, you would be making an inference, as in "The center of Hoop U's team hates our center." Because we cannot get inside someone else's brain, human emotions are something that we have to infer. After all, the center of Hoop U's team might act as if he hated our center, but he might actually love him, deep down inside. To be specific in that case, you might use a quotation: "The center of Hoop U's basketball team said recently that he hates our center's guts." That is a specific statement of fact, in that you have merely reported a statement made by another.[8]

When you state an opinion, you also add something to the facts of the case. If you said, "The center of Hoop U's basketball team is a bum," you would be telling more about your own feelings than you would about Hoop U's center. Generally speaking, the more opinions you use, the more facts you need to back them up. When you call someone a bum, you might need to define the term "bum" or describe the particular behaviors that make the basketball player, in your estimation, a bum.

Notice the different levels of specificity in the following:

**OPINION:** I think too many puppies are put to sleep by our local animal shelter.

**INFERENCE:** The local head of the Society for the Prevention of Cruelty to Animals thinks that too many puppies are put to sleep at our local shelter.

**STATEMENT OF FACT:** In an interview I conducted last week, John Atmos, head of our local SPCA, stated that the euthanasia rate for puppies at our local shelter is 85 percent.[9]

## Examples

An example is a specific case that is used to demonstrate a general idea. Examples can be either factual or hypothetical, personal or borrowed.

Karen Kimmey, a student at Arizona State University, spoke about types of employee time theft. To back up her idea that unauthorized use of the office computer is one type of employee theft, she used the following example:

> Financial consultant Michael Nolan tells of one marginal employee who was not quite ready to be fired but was certainly not a top worker. But all of this changed when the firm computerized. The formerly listless employee began to spend hours in front of his computer and management was encouraged—until they discovered that he had become so familiar with the computer that he had

▼ Example is the school of mankind, and they will learn at no other.

Edmund Burke

created a game program and was spending his hours on the job playing blackjack.[10]

*Hypothetical examples* are fictional. They can often be more powerful than factual examples, because hypothetical examples ask the audience to imagine something—thus causing them to become active participants in the thought. If you were speaking on the subject of euthanasia (mercy killing), you might ask your audience to imagine that someone they loved was suffering and being kept alive by a machine. If you were dealing with street crime, you might begin by saying, "Imagine you're walking down a dark street and you hear footsteps . . ." Jeni Pruitt, a student at Kansas State University, used a hypothetical example to clarify her point that unfunded federal mandates are unfair:

> Let's say that I ask a man out for dinner, he accepts and off we go. We have a great time and really enjoy the meal, but when the check comes, I insist that he pay—even though I'm the one who asked him out.
>
> Now, if I really did this, not only would I soon no longer have a social life, but we would also consider my actions to be extremely rude. Unfortunately what we call rude, our federal government calls "a normal business practice," or more specifically, a federally unfunded mandate.[11]

If you use a hypothetical example, you have to make it clear that the example *is* hypothetical, by using such expressions as "Let's say that . . ." or "Imagine that . . ." or "I'd like you to visualize this scene: . . ."

Examples take many different forms. They appear, for example, as descriptions, analogies and anecdotes.

### Descriptions

An example presented through detailed description becomes a type of "word picture." Martin Luther King, Jr. used description in his famous "I Have a Dream" speech, when he described the plight of the African American in 1963:

> There are those who are asking the devotees of civil rights, "When will you be satisfied?" We can never be satisfied as long as our bodies, heavy with the fatigue of travel, cannot gain lodging in the motels of the highways and the hotels of the cities. We cannot be satisfied as long as the Negro's basic mobility is from a smaller ghetto to a larger one. We can never be satisfied as long as our children are stripped of their selfhood and robbed of their dignity by signs stating "for whites only."[12]

▼ A single death is a tragedy, a million deaths is a statistic

Joseph Stalin

Dr. King's description helps us to imagine pain and fatigue as well as the sight of a sign that says "for whites only." These things can be truly perceived only through the senses, but he manages to give us an image of them by capturing their essence in a few words. In his description, as in all good description, it is the choice of details that makes the difference.

## Analogies

Another effective form of example is the analogy. We use analogies, or comparisons, all the time, often in the form of figures of speech such as similes and metaphors. A simile is a direct comparison that usually uses *like* or *as* whereas a metaphor is an implied comparison that does not use *like* or *as*. So if you said that the rush of refugees from a war-torn country is "like a tidal wave," you would be using a simile. If you used the expression "a tidal wave of refugees," you would be using a metaphor because you have only implied the comparison.

Comparisons are often briefly stated, but they can still pack emotional power. When referring to "deadbeat dads," or any absent parent who does not pay child support, you could use this comparison:

> According to the Children's Defense Fund, absent parents are more likely to pay for their cars than pay for their kids.[13]

Analogies are extended metaphors. We run across analogies all the time. Cynthia Tucker, the editorial page editor of the *Atlanta Constitution,* used several analogies when she was given a Human Rights Award by the American Federation of Teachers. At the award ceremony, she chose to speak out against the disrespect and contempt different ethnic groups hold for one another on college campuses:

> Perhaps most bewildering is the expressions of stark bigotry from some African Americans. Given the racism, the contempt, the hatred, and the inhumanity to which black people have been subjected, it would seem that we would be most careful not to turn that same bigotry and hatred on other racial or ethnic groups.[14]

Not everyone would appreciate Tucker's comparison of the bigotry of some African Americans to the bigotry that they themselves had experienced, but that comparison would give her audience something to think about.

Analogies can be used to point out a relationship that the audience might not have otherwise been familiar with. You could, for example, begin a speech on homelessness by showing a picture of the Pilgrims arriving in America, and say:

> With a little help, there's no telling what a group of homeless people can accomplish.
> The plain fact is that the homeless built this country.[15]

Analogies can be used to compare or contrast an unknown concept with a known one. For example, if you had difficulty explaining to a

▼ Analogies prove nothing, that is quite true, but they can make one feel more at home.

Sigmund Freud

public speaking class composed mostly of music majors why they should practice their speeches out loud, you might use this analogy:

> We all realize that great masters often can compose music in their heads. Beethoven, for example, composed his greatest masterpieces after he had gone deaf and couldn't even hear the instruments play out his ideas. However, beginners have to sit down at a piano or some other instrument and play their pieces as they create them. It is much the same way for beginning public speakers. When composing their speeches, they need to use their instruments—their voices—to hear how their ideas sound.

For an audience of music majors, this analogy might clarify the concept of a speech. For a class of electrical engineers who may not know Beethoven from Hootie and the Blowfish, this analogy might confuse rather than clarify. It is important to remember to make your analogies appropriate to your audience.

### Anecdotes

An anecdote is a brief story with a point, often (but not always) based on personal experience. (The word *anecdote* comes from the Greek meaning "unpublished item.") Anecdotes can add a lively, personal touch to your explanation.

To fully appreciate anecdotes as a type of example you should understand the difference between narration and citation. *Narration* is the telling of a story with your information. Narration means putting your example in the form of a small drama, with a beginning, middle, and end. *Citation* is a simple statement of the facts. Citation is shorter and more precise than narration, in the sense that the source is carefully stated. Citation will include such phrases as, "According to the July 25, 1994, edition of *Time* magazine," or "As Mr. Smith made clear in an interview last April 24, . . . " From a functional point of view, citation tends to add proof, whereas most forms of narration add clarity and interest.

President Ronald Reagan was famous for his use of anecdotes. In his Farewell Address, when he wanted to make the point that America stood as a symbol of freedom to people in other lands, he used the following anecdote:

> It was back in the early eighties, at the height of the boat people, and a sailor was hard at work on the carrier *Midway,* which was patrolling the South China Sea. The sailor, like most American servicemen, was young, smart, and fiercely observant. The crew spied on the horizon a leaky little boat—and crammed inside were refugees from

Indochina hoping to get to America. The *Midway* sent a small launch to bring them to the ship, and safety. As the refugees made their way through the choppy seas, one spied the sailor on deck, and stood up and called out to him. He yelled, "Hello American sailor—Hello Freedom Man."

A small moment with a big meaning, a moment the sailor, who wrote it in a letter, couldn't get out of his mind. And, when I saw it, neither could I.[16]

Anecdotes based on your personal experience can be particularly effective. Chris Fleming, a student at Western Kentucky University, used a personal anecdote to enliven his speech on car insurance:

Part of every teenager's "Great American Dream" is to someday get a driver's license, and more importantly . . . to own some wheels. Since there are nine children in my family, to realize my dream I knew that I would have to earn the money for a car. The day finally arrived when I could go to our local car dealer with checkbook in hand. I found a six-year-old candy apple red Mustang that was well within my price range. My dream was shattered when I discovered that I would have to pay more for insurance coverage than my car would be worth on the resale market.[17]

Anecdotes, descriptions, and other types of examples can be effective in clarifying information and making it interesting and memorable. They are sometimes used as "proof" in the mass media, especially when the example is highly visual and/or emotional. But in the more critically thought-out world of public speaking, examples aren't a powerful form of proof. That's because they refer only to isolated instances that might not be representative. Any audience member might bring this up to show the logical fallacy behind a single example used as proof. In a speech, to prove an idea with examples, you have to collect a number of them; at that point they become statistics.

## Statistics

Statistics are numbers that are arranged or organized to show significant information. Statistics are important in the media/information age, because they can be used to show how a fact or principle is true for a large number of cases. They are reality checks in a world where the media present life in terms of constant crises and emergencies. When media reports scream out to us, "Killer bees are taking over the state!" or "Pesticides on cherries are turning large numbers of brown eyes blue!" we can verify the extent of the emergency by examining the statistical proof. Statistics are a good form of evidence; they can be used to correct false assumptions and contradict myths. They are especially effective at showing trends.

▼ Numbers are intellectual witnesses that belong only to mankind.

Honore De Balzac

Statistics are actually collections of examples, so they can be more effective as proof than are isolated examples. If you wanted to develop the idea that American youth are not well informed about the American economic system, the following example would be insufficient proof:

> I asked my younger brother the other day if he knew the difference between collectivism and a free-enterprise society, and he had no idea. He didn't even know that the U.S. economy is based on free enterprise.

Proof based on *lots* of people's younger siblings would be more effective:

> A 1995 study by the Joint Council on Economic Education showed that 50 percent of high school students could not distinguish between collectivism and a free-enterprise society, and 50 percent did not know the U.S. economy is based on free enterprise.

## Statistical Confusion

▼ There are three kinds of lies—lies, damned lies, and statistics.

Benjamin Disraeli

In Chapter 3 we spoke about some of the ethical problems involved with statistics. Our main point there was that statistics are sometimes used to intentionally distort the truth, so you have to be careful about where you get them and how you express them.

Unfortunately, you also have to be careful about statistics that come from seemingly reliable sources, because sometimes they are abused *unintentionally.* For example, when the Shell Oil Company announced plans to sink an oil platform at sea, Greenpeace, the environmental organization, publicized that the rig still contained 5,500 tons of oil. They had run their own tests on the rig, and, since Greenpeace is a highly credible source among environmental groups, the statistic was widely publicized. After Greenpeace's campaign was victorious, they had to admit that their sampling procedure had given them the wrong statistic (the sampling device had been in the pipe leading to the storage tanks, rather than in the tanks themselves). Therefore, the organization had no idea how much oil, if any, was contained in the rig.[18]

It's easy to see how statistics get abused and misinterpreted. For example, several best-selling authors have claimed that 150,000 women die annually from anorexia.[19] This was apparently a misinterpretation of a study that found 150,000 *cases* of anorexia a year. However, almost none of those cases was fatal.[20]

Sometimes a statistic becomes inflated simply because the crime it describes is so horrible. For example, the Center for Women's Policy Studies claimed that "each year, 4,000 women are killed by husbands or partners who have abused them." Not long after that, a fact sheet published by the American Medical Association asserted that family violence "kills as many women in five years as the total number of Americans who lost their lives in the Vietnam War." Around 50,000 Americans were killed in Vietnam, so the AMA statement implies that around 10,000 women a year die from family violence. FBI statistics, however, which are extremely reliable in cases of homicide, place the figure at 1,400.[21]

Everyone agrees that even *one* battered wife, or one death from anorexia or family violence, is too many. But people are hesitant to attack statistics that come from advocacy groups for good causes. The lesson here is that the credibility of the organization does not necessarily guarantee the credibility of the statistic. As *Newsweek* magazine pointed out, "Once a fake statistic is floated by an apparently credible source, it can be picked up and repeated until it seems like common knowledge."[22] It bears repeating that, in the media/information age, you should check your statistics with a second source, and use critical thinking to make sure it makes sense.

It is also important to point out that there are two types of statistics: descriptive and inferential. The preceding examples are descriptive statistics. Descriptive statistics are collections of numbers that are based on verifiable observations of some type. Inferential statistics, as the name implies, go beyond observation to refer to something that cannot be measured objectively (those "inferences" we spoke of earlier). Inferential statistics include predictions. There are famous examples of the failure of predictive statistics. In 1948, virtually every poll predicted that Harry Truman would lose the presidential election to Thomas Dewey. The press was so sure of these predictions that they printed their front pages with huge headlines about Dewey's victory before all the returns were in. Truman, of course, won the election. In 1992, early polls suggested that George Bush would be unbeatable in that presidential election. He lost.

Another type of inferential statistic is the correlation. A correlation tells you that two things occur at the same time. This does not, however, prove that one thing caused the other. For example, the correlational statistics about television violence seem very powerful. In the 40 years of network television, the depiction of crime and violence has gone up steadily. At the same time, violence in society has gone up by a similar proportion. This statistic would suggest (but not prove) that there is a relationship between these two trends. On first glance, the suggestion would be that television violence has caused societal violence. But even if there were a cause-effect relationship, it would be difficult to say which is the cause and which is the effect; perhaps violence on television has gone up *because* violence in society has gone up, rather than vice versa. Because of the tenuous nature of the relationship, you have to be careful not to place too much burden of proof on inferential statistics.

▼ It has been said that numbers rule the world. Maybe. But I am sure that figures show us whether it is being ruled well or badly.

Goethe

## Rules for Using Statistics

One rule about the use of statistics is based on effectiveness rather than ethics. If possible, you should reduce the statistic to a concrete image. For example, $1 billion in one-hundred-dollar bills would be about the same height as a 60-story building. Using concrete images such as this will make your statistics more than "just numbers."

A second rule is to round off unwieldy numbers. For example:

▼ Rather than saying the U.S. population is 249,932,206, say "around 250 million" or "nearly a quarter of a billion."

▼ Instead of 25,142 deaths from alcohol-related automobile accidents, say "approximately 25 thousand," or "around 25 thousand."

▼ Rather than saying that it is estimated to cost $11,580 to support an adopted pet over its ten-year life span, say "more than $11,000."

▼ Rather than citing annual welfare costs of $59,965,000,000, say "around $60 billion."

Of course, there are cases in which precision is necessary and helpful. If you were briefing a group of engineers about specifications for rocket engine parts, you wouldn't want to fudge on the 0.0000096 tolerance for the bolt that holds the turbine blades together. Generally, however, the preferred medium for such precise detail is some form of written communication.

## Quotations

▼ Next to the originator of a good sentence is the first quoter of it.

Ralph Waldo Emerson

Using a familiar or artistically stated quotation will enable you to take advantage of someone else's memorable wording. For example, if you were giving a speech on personal integrity, you might quote Mark Twain, who said, "Always do right. This will gratify some people, and astonish the rest." A quotation like that fits the eighteenth-century poet Alexander Pope's definition of "true wit": "What was often thought, but ne'er so well expressed."

You can also use quotations as *testimony,* to prove a point by using the support of someone who is more authoritative or experienced on the subject than you. Janet Martin, a bank vice-president, used a quotation for this purpose in her speech "Room at the Top: Women in Banking":

> Careers are limited by a glass ceiling that enables women to glimpse but not grasp top executive positions. . . . Might the glass ceiling exist because the personal trade-offs and sacrifices women must make are greater than their male counterparts? John Kenneth Galbraith once told writer Michael Bliss that, "in the modern world, women's liberation consists of submerging a personality to a corporation rather than a husband."[23]

Martin's use of testimony by the well-known economist John Kenneth Galbraith added authority to her support. An effective source for testimony will be authoritative (Galbraith has written widely on employment issues) and unbiased (Galbraith is known as an economist, not a feminist). Because Galbraith would have been instantly recognized by Martin's audience, she did not have to introduce his testimony with "According to world-famous economist John Kenneth Galbraith . . . ," although for a different audience, she might have.

Besides expert testimony, there is also the person-on-the-street variety. The media use this type of testimony for two purposes. First, it gets the reaction of the common person, the type of person with whom the mass audience can identify. This type of reaction is a staple of television news: "What do you think of the home team's chances tonight?" "What do you think of the mayor's new proposal for cleaning up the town?" "Do you think men and women are natural enemies?" It's a time-honored tradition, and not a bad one when the person-on-the-street's opinion is truly representative of that of a large portion of the viewing public. You could use this type of testimony in a speech, provided that the person on the street makes a well-thought-out and well-worded statement that is both representative of the real world and relevant to your speech. House Democratic Leader Richard Gephardt used this type of testimony in a speech on unemployment:

> A few weeks ago, I met a man in Jefferson County, Missouri, who had lost his job, and couldn't find a way to earn a living. His economic crisis shattered his marriage, as well as his self-confidence. He had loaded all of his worldly possessions into his car, and was headed down the road to nowhere. He looked at me with tears in his eyes, and said, "They took away more than my paycheck. They took away my *pride*. And that was all I had left to give."[24]

The person-on-the-street reaction is also the life-blood of the talk-show circuit; ironically, though, on talk shows the less expert the person is, the more his or her opinion is desired. Ignorant opinions, after all, help fuel the shouting matches that these shows thrive on. This type of person-on-the-street testimony is less useful in public speaking; it's another example of the higher standard required for public speaking support.

The second purpose of person-on-the-street testimony is to get information from someone who witnessed an event (an "eyewitness"). The Gephardt example could also be used for this type of testimony, since the man he quoted was an "eyewitness" to unemployment. This type of testimony might be useful to the public speaker:

> During my trip to Cambodia, I asked one farmer what it was like to live there 20 years ago. He told me, "I was a boy during the Pol Pot times, and I still remember how they would line up people— 10 people, 100 people—and tie their hands and shoot them in the back. You don't forget this."[25]

A third type of testimony that is often found in the media is celebrity testimony, exemplified by the soap opera actor selling aspirin by admitting

▼ Despise not the discoveries of the wise, but acquaint thyself with their proverbs.

Bible, Ecclesiasticus 8:8

up front, "I'm not a doctor, but I play one on TV." In celebrity testimony, the celebrities don't have any particular expertise in the area under discussion. They are just there to grab the audience's attention by taking advantage of the public's obsession with celebrities. This obsession is one of the symptoms of the media/information age. Like the ignorant opinion of the person on the street, it's one more example of something that the media can get away with, but the public speaker can't.

If the exact words of your quotation are not important, you can quote the idea through the use of *paraphrase*. This is what business executive James Carr did in a speech about the problems of inner-city youth:

> A recent issue of *The Atlantic Monthly* discusses the "Code of the Streets." Many inner-city environments foster a need for respect and a self-image based on violence. In these communities, knowing the code is not a way to be "with it," it's a means of survival.
>
> For example, the article suggests that wearing something like a fashionable, expensive pair of tennis shoes could make a person vulnerable to attack: You are willing to possess things that might require defending. Stated otherwise, wearing a nice pair of sneakers could get you beaten, if not shot.[26]

A word on the ethics of quotation would be in order here. We discussed in the ethics chapter the idea of reverse plagiarism, which is defined as claiming that someone said something that she or he in fact had not said. A related problem is *quoting out of context,* as in the old joke about the movie ad that quotes a reviewer out of context. The review stated that the star's performance was "the best example of bad acting I've ever seen." In the ad the quotation over the reviewer's name reads, "The best . . . acting I've ever seen." You should be careful to use your quotation only in the same context in which it was originally offered.

The major types of support dealt with here can be combined, divided, and dealt with in innovative ways. A consideration of the individual types provides you with some guidelines for evaluating their effectiveness for various purposes. There are four other guidelines that relate to any type of support.

## ▼ GUIDELINES FOR EVALUATING SUPPORT

### Ethics

As we discussed in Chapter 3, there are three general guidelines for ethical speechmaking. These guidelines can also be used to evaluate support:

Is it honest, is it accurate, and is it in the audience's best interest? An example from the mass media is instructive here. A few years ago a reporter for the *Washington Post* needed a strong example in her investigation of drug abuse among inner-city kids. She made up a fictional character, a 9-year-old heroin addict named Jimmy. But she presented Jimmy as a real person, and the series of articles she wrote about him won a Pulitzer Prize. When her deception was discovered, she lost her job as well as the prize. Her supporting material was effective, but dishonest.[27]

Inaccuracy can be an ethical fault even when it is unintentional. If you were giving a speech on the same topic as Janet Cooke's—heroin addiction among kids—and you misinterpreted a statistic and stated that more kids were addicted than really were, you would be guilty of this fault even if it was unintentional.

In terms of ethics, the audience interest is especially important. To cite another example from the media, a "Mickey Mouse Club" actor wanted to demonstrate the sound of a revolving tire on a car. He put a BB into a balloon and rotated it, and encouraged his home audience to do the same. An eleven-year-old followed his advice, and the balloon burst and the BB blinded him in one eye.[28]

The large audience that was reached over the mass media made this example devastating. But similar concerns have to be kept in mind in the public speaking context. One student, when speaking on ways to finance a college education, used the example of an investment scam in such a way that she might have encouraged members of her audience to behave in a way that was clearly not in their best interest—and not legal.

In the choice of supporting material, as in any aspect of speechmaking, a careless disregard for the audience interest tends to be an ethical fault.

## Currency

Currency deals with *how recent your supporting material is*. Some support doesn't have to be current. You can, for example, quote the wisdom of one of the writers of the U.S. Constitution, and not have to worry about its age:

▼ The problems of marital discord are nothing new. As Benjamin Franklin pointed out in 1734, "Where there's marriage without love, there will be love without marriage."[29]

▼ Those who are upset by protest should remember the words of Thomas Jefferson: "A little rebellion, now and then, is a good thing, and as necessary in the political world as storms in the physical."[30]

Some supporting material, however, needs to be up-to-date. One student gave a speech on "sweatshops" employing illegal, underpaid immigrants. He quoted Jacob Riis, who had many important things to say about the problem. Unfortunately, Jacob Riis was a turn-of-the-century reformer, speaking about the sweatshops of a different era. Because his testimony was not backed up with current support, it lacked relevancy.

Currency of support is especially important in an area in which facts change rapidly. Several industries, such as telecommunications and computing, change almost daily. A statement about "the state of the art" or "the most successful corporation in the industry" would have to be checked carefully for currency. Another example of this is in our legal system, where decisions are often appealed and overturned. One student gave a speech on libel and used three cases as examples of successful libel suits. Unfortunately, all three cases had been overturned on appeals. It was downright embarrassing when one of his audience members pointed this out.

### Relevancy

The first test of relevance is *whether the supporting material relates to the matter at hand.* It is easy to be seduced by a powerful piece of support that is simply not pertinent to a particular point. One student wanted to make the point that student loan defaults were costly to the taxpayer. She spoke at length about how college students are graduating deeply in debt, averaging 10,000 per student with debts of $50,000 being fairly

common. The numbers were inherently interesting to her audience, but they didn't prove her point. A better choice might have been:

> Since 1990, many graduates have been unable to repay their student loans. Since that time, the student loan default rate has been 22 percent. These defaults have cost the government—and the taxpayers—close to $3 billion a year.[31]

The guideline of relevancy requires that supporting material have a close logical relationship with the matter under consideration. Critical thinking is an important tool in testing relevancy. In the preceding example, the better choice for relevant support deals strictly with the burden on the taxpayer caused by student loan defaults. Relevance also suggests that the support should be *important* to that particular point. In this example, the fact that the loan defaults cost taxpayers a huge amount of money makes it important.

Support also needs to be relevant to the time and place in which the speech is given, as well as to the audience.

## Reliability

The question to ask in terms of reliability is, can the support be trusted? We mentioned earlier in this chapter that one ramification of the media/information age is that you have to consider the source of any information that you use in a speech. For example, both Coke and Pepsi have run studies proving that their product "tastes better." The question that has to be asked in a situation like that is whether the source (which might, by the way, be an individual or an organization) has its own agenda. For example, if you were speaking on the safety of your local transit system, you would have to be careful of information derived from someone who was suing over an injury sustained on a local bus. The rule in a case like that would be to verify the information from a second source, preferably one without a conflict of interest.

Along with the absence of conflict of interest, you also have to ask if the source is credible. The two major components of credibility are competence (Does he know what he's talking about?) and character (Is she generally honest as well as impartial?).

You also need to use critical thinking to test the internal reliability of your support. That is, exclusive of the source and the original context, does the support, as presented in your speech, make sense? For example, in a speech on the car theft epidemic, you might be tempted to use the following information that actually appeared in a major newspaper:

> Eight billion cars are stolen annually in the United States. In the U.S., a car is stolen every 20 seconds.[32]

That is an impressive statement, but it makes no sense. If a car is stolen every 20 seconds, that would be 3 per minute, or 180 per hour, or 4,320 per day, which totals 1,576,800 per year, not eight billion. Eight billion car thefts would be 32 thefts for each man, woman, and child in the United States. If this statistic were true, the average family of four would suffer 128 car thefts each year. More than 10 a month. Two or three a week. Talk about an epidemic.

Remember that the rule is to check your information from more than one source whenever possible.

The guidelines of ethics, currency, relevancy, and reliability were all considered by the student who presented the sample speech for this chapter. See if you agree with the way support is used in this speech. Compare your evaluation with the comments on the left.

### Sample Speech

The sample speech for this chapter was presented by Rebecca Witte, a student at the University of Missouri–St. Louis.[33] It deals with teen suicide, the same topic as the hypothetical example that began this chapter. The outline for this speech (showing the basic claims) is as follows:

OUTLINE
Introduction
  I. Teen suicide is a serious problem.
 II. There are solutions.
Body
  I. Why teenagers commit suicide:
    A. Teens are under considerable stress.
    B. Suicide is the easy way out.
 II. Some schools do nothing.
III. Some schools have programs that work.
IV. What you can do.
    A. Know the suicide hotline number.
    B. Support prevention programs.
    C. Know the signs.
Conclusion

## ▼ AMERICA'S YOUTH IN CRISIS

Rebecca Witte

University of Missouri—St. Louis

A description, worded to capture audience attention. This device might seem overly dramatic or stagey for some audiences, however. If so, another form of support could be used for the same purpose.

[1] I am a seven-letter word. I destroy friends, families, neighborhoods, and schools. I am the biggest killer among teenagers today. I am not alcohol. I am not cocaine. I am suicide.

[2] According to the American Suicide Prevention Association, 85 percent of all teenagers between the ages of 15 and 18 consider committing suicide. Of that 85 percent, 50 percent of them will attempt and roughly 32 percent will succeed.

[3] Obviously, suicide kills thousands of high school teenagers every year. In fact, the ASPA says that over 3,000 teenagers died in 1993 alone from suicide. Why is it then that the high schools aren't doing anything? Why is it that high schools do not have mandatory suicide prevention programs as a part of their everyday curriculum? Those are very good questions and that is why I am here today. First, we'll establish why teenagers commit suicide; next, we'll compare the schools that have a prevention program to those that do not; and finally, we will look at what we can do to help decrease the number of suicides every year.

[4] According to psychiatrist Glenda Taber, in her book, *Suicide: The Teenage Death Syndrome,* "Teens are under more stress today than ever before." This stress stems from such things as drug and alcohol abuse, abusive parents, an abusive boyfriend or girlfriend, pressure to have sex, failure, be it on the job or in school, even homosexuality. Taber says that when these teens are so low that they are actually considering suicide, they have what is known as tunnel vision, meaning that they can see no option other than the one in front of them. They can't even see the light at the end of the tunnel. Dr. Michael Gleason, a psychiatrist at Christian Northwest Hospital in St. Louis, Missouri, says that suicide is such an easy option for teenagers because they aren't taught the correct ways to deal with the stressors in their lives. So they don't. Instead, they continue to build up one stressor on top of another until they all come toppling over. Suicide then becomes an easy, permanent answer to a difficult temporary situation. Dr. Gleason puts it this way: "Picture it. These teens are dealing with multitudes of problems every day, and one little thing promises to take it all away." A national organization called TREND, or Turning Reactional Excitement in New Directions, has published a pamphlet entitled, "Getting Out or Getting Help." In this pamphlet it states that teens need to be taught that there are other options besides suicide. It goes on to say that every community across the United States has a suicide hotline number. Unfortunately, for these troubled teens the primary place for them to get this vital information is at school.

Does this statistic make sense?*

Compare this statistic with the one above.**

Suggestion: A more in-depth narrative of one tragic teen suicide would have added emotional power.

"Tunnel vision" is defined. The testimony from Dr. Gleason might have been even more powerful if it was established that it came from a personal interview with Gleason, conducted by the speaker.

*Would that mean 27 percent or even 13 percent of all teens between the ages of 15 and 18 die by suicide? What's the real statistic? According to *American Almanac: Statistical Abstract of the United States, 1994–1995,* there were 4,800 suicides in 1991 in the 15–24 age group. That was the highest number in a decade. For that same year, there were 36 million people in that age group. That would suggest that suicides occur in 0.01 percent of this population.

**Those 3,000 suicides are out of a population of approximately 30 million teenagers. Once again, that's one in ten thousand, or 0.01 percent.

Statistics and quotation.

⁵ Then why is it that high schools refuse to do anything? TREND itself has given them two options of what to do: publish the community suicide hotline number and teach teenagers other options besides suicide. What is holding them back? According to a study conducted by *Newsweek,* June, 1992, superintendents and principals seem to possess a fear of suicide. They interviewed over 2,000 high school principals. Only 22 percent of those interviewed claimed to discuss suicide in any way, shape, or form. This includes prevention programs in class, assemblies, publication of the community's suicide hotline number, and any advertisement that the school has suicide counseling available. That leaves 80 percent of the high school students in America to fend for themselves. One superintendent went so far as to say, "Hey, if we discussed everything that affects teenagers today, we'd have to add on another month to the school year." What he doesn't understand is that unless he decides to face this problem he will lose many of his students before the year 2000.

The unnamed superintendent is in effect a person-on-the-street. Is his statement representative of superintendents in general?

⁶ This fear that high school authorities have of suicide often snowballs into disaster. According to the *St. Louis Post Dispatch,* August, 1992, a newspaper editor of a small school in St. Charles County, Missouri, wanted to publish an article about suicide in her school's paper. She dealt with the issues honestly and carefully, providing some statistics, some things to look for in friends, and their community's suicide hotline number. The principal, however, would not allow the article to be published, saying his school did not have a problem with suicide. The article went unpublished, as did the suicide hotline number. Later that year, the editor graduated. And two days after her graduation, her best friend shot himself in the head. Two weeks after that, an alum from the school from two years before shot himself in the head. And two weeks after that, the principal's son shot himself in the head. Three suicides from a school where "suicide is not a problem."

A striking example.

⁷ The real problem is that the story is true and is happening to schools all across the country. Another problem is that the story does not end here. The small community found out about the editor's article and demanded the principal's resignation, blaming him for the three deaths. He resigned and moved on to another high school, initiating a suicide prevention program there.

⁸ Admitting the problem is the first step. Unfortunately, most programs are not initiated until after the school has suffered great suicidal loss. According to the *San Francisco Tribune,* March, 1993, North High School in San Francisco had the highest suicide average in a ten-year period. Their average death rate was five deaths a year with an additional 15 attempts. A new principal came in and decided to stop the death and initiated a program. In the past three years their average death rate has dropped from five deaths a year to less than one and from 15 attempts to about three.

An example of one school where a suicide prevention program worked.

9 Obviously, these programs work. And they work for three reasons. The first is because most often these programs are interspliced with health class. Health class is a mandatory class every public high school student must take in order to graduate. By making it mandatory, the schools are guaranteeing these students will take the class. I mean, what student is going to pick "Death 101" over Home Ec or Shop? The second reason they work is because the books that deal with suicide do so in a down-to-earth personal manner. [A] This appeals to teenagers, making them want to learn. So, they do. The final reason they work is because teenagers are able to keep this new information throughout the rest of their lives. This is beneficial to you and me because these students are graduating with this vital information. They know the statistics, they know the signs to look for in friends, and they know the community's suicide hotline number. They know what to do when suicide comes knocking not only at their doors, but at our doors as well. [B]

It's not so obvious that all such programs work. Our only evidence is the example found in paragraph 8, and one example might not be sufficient to prove the claim.

This first hypothetical example ("What student . . .") works well, but one is needed here [A] . . .

. . . and some form of support is needed here [B].

10 The programs work, but it takes a superintendent who is willing to face the issues. Without our help this could take years and many lives. So what can we do to help decrease the number of suicidal deaths? There are many things, but first and foremost, make sure every person you know knows your community's suicide hotline number. It's very easy to find—simply open up the Yellow Pages and look up "suicide." Secondly, check with the high schools in your area and see if they have a suicide prevention program. If they don't, make them. We all know that with enough arguing, enough petitioning, enough phone calls, action will be taken. Talk to the parents, talk to the students, talk to the school board if you have to, but do something to stop the deaths in your area. Remember, just because you don't hear about it, doesn't mean it doesn't happen.

Examples: What to do.

11 Finally, because suicide does not just affect teenagers, because it affects every age group across the spectrum, check for some of these possible suicide signs in friends of yours as published in *Health* from Health Publishing in 1993:

1. Severe depression
2. Giving away personal possessions
3. Buying a weapon
4. Talking about suicide
5. A decrease in energy
6. A sudden increased use of drugs or alcohol
7. Wanting to continually be alone

List of examples: Behaviors to watch out for.

12 We all know why teens commit suicide. We all know what happens to the schools that do nothing compared to those that do. And now, we know what we can do to decrease the number of suicides every year. The next suicide victim could be someone you know. You may hold their life, their future, in the palm of your hand.

Again, for some audiences this conclusion might seem like a cliché. If so, other support could be found.

## ▼ SUMMARY

Supporting material flows by so quickly in the media glut that it is sometimes difficult to recognize the care that has to go into the choice of this material. Supporting material is used to clarify (in which ideas are made more specific), to make interesting (by involving the audience's attention), to make memorable (through vivid details and other memory devices), and to prove (to verify the truth of a claim). These functions provide one perspective for evaluating the support you choose for a speech. Other guidelines for evaluation include the material's ethicality (honesty, accuracy, the best interest of the audience), its currency (the appropriateness of the age of the material), its relevance (how it relates and how important it is to the point under consideration), and its reliability (how well it can be trusted). We have concentrated in this chapter on four types of support: facts (as opposed to claims, assertions, and opinions); examples (specific cases in which a point was true), which include descriptions, analogies, and anecdotes; statistics (numbers arranged to prove a point); and quotations (which include testimony).

These forms of support can be provided as narratives (stories, with a beginning, middle, and end) or as citations (brief identifications).

## ▼ EXERCISES

1. Technically, an example is a less powerful piece of proof than a statistic. And yet an example can be powerful *emotional* proof. As you collect supporting material for the speech you are currently working on, find one piece of statistical proof and one example for any point. Compare the logical power of the statistical proof to the emotional power of the example. If class time permits, share your findings with your class.

2. Review the four functions of supporting material, along with the types of supporting material discussed in this chapter. In your opinion, which types of supporting material best perform each function? (Remember, of course, that any instance of support *could* perform more than one function.)

3. Devise one piece of hypothetical support for each of the following claims:

   ▼ Statehood for Puerto Rico would financially benefit the United States.

▼ Outpatient surgery is less risky than hospitalized surgery.

▼ There are entirely too many jokes about drugs on prime-time television.

▼ Silicone breast implants are a serious health threat.

▼ The dinosaurs were probably wiped out by the collision of a comet
with the earth.

# NOTES

1. See, for example, Daniel Goleman, "New Study Portrays the Young as More and More Troubled," *New York Times,* December 8, 1993.

2. Brian Swenson, "Gun Safety and Children," *Winning Orations 1990* (Interstate Oratorical Association, 1990), p. 101. Brian was coached by Mike Truchen.

3. C. Haydon Cherry, "Los Doce del Patibulo," *Winning Orations, 1991* (Interstate Oratorical Association, 1991), p. 41. C. Haydon was coached by Judy Woodring.

4. Tracy A. Schario, "Discrimination in Defense," *Winning Orations, 1991* (Interstate Oratorical Association, 1991), p. 84. Tracy was coached by Lisa Phillips.

5. Reported in Ron Howell, "U.N.: 90% of Youth Murder Is in the U.S.," *Newsday,* September 26, 1993, p. 4.

6. Laura K. Oster, "Deforestation: A Time for Action," *Winning Orations, 1990* (Interstate Oratorical Association, 1990), pp. 79–80. Laura was coached by Theresa Krier.

7. There are two types of facts. *Prima facie* ("at first sight") facts, in the legal sense, need no additional support. They are the established facts and common knowledge that we all accept. The second type of facts, those that need additional support, are more common in speeches.

8. Fudging on statements of opinion by attributing them to the person who said them is a potential ethical problem, in the same way as fudging on rumors by calling them rumors, as discussed in Chapter 3 on ethics.

9. This horrifying statistic was true for one Indianapolis shelter. It was alleviated by airlifting pups to Las Vegas, where the supply of adoptable pups could not keep up with the demand. See "For Indiana Puppies, It's Viva Las Vegas," *New York Times,* February 9, 1995, p. A20.

10. Karen Kimmey, "Time Theft: The Silent Thief," *Winning Orations, 1990* (Interstate Oratorical Association, 1990), p. 5. Karen was coached by Clark Olsen.

11. Jeni Pruitt, "Federal Freeloading," *Winning Orations 1994* (Interstate Oratorical Association, 1994), p. 41. Jeni was coached by Craig Brown. We assume

that her example about a date with a man in a speech about mandates was purely coincidental.

12. Martin Luther King, Jr., "I Have a Dream," speech at civil rights rally, Washington, D.C., August 28, 1963.

13. "The Big Payback," *Los Angeles Times,* July 20, 1994, editorial page.

14. Cynthia Tucker, "An Unhappy American Tradition," *On Campus,* September 1994, p. 19.

15. This example was adapted from an ad run in several major newspapers by the National Alliance to End Homelessness, whose telephone number is 1-800-230-DREAM. The ad was run the day before Thanksgiving. See, for example, the *New York Times,* November 23, 1994, p. A17.

16. R. Reagan, "President's Farewell Address to the American People," *Vital Speeches of the Day* (February 1, 1989), p. 226.

17. Chris Fleming, speech on car insurance (title unknown), *Winning Orations, 1994* (Interstate Oratorical Association, 1994), p. 50. Chris was coached by Judy Woodring.

18. "Greenpeace Apologizes to Shell Oil Company," *New York Times,* September 6, 1995, p. A11.

19. Jerry Adler, "The Numbers Game," *Newsweek,* July 25, 1994, pp. 56–58.

20. Christin Hoff Sommers, *Who Stole Feminism* (New York: Simon and Schuster, 1994).

21. Adler, "The Numbers Game."

22. *Ibid.*

23. J. Martin, "Room at the Top: Women in Banking," speech delivered to the North Toronto Business and Professional Women's Club, December 4, 1991. Reprinted in *Vital Speeches of the Day,* March 15, 1992, pp. 347–350.

24. Richard A. Gephardt, "The Democratic Challenge in the 104th Congress," *Vital Speeches of the Day,* January 15, 1995, p. 199. The speech was delivered before the Center for National Policy, Washington, D.C., December 13, 1994.

25. Testimony of Buntha Krouch quoted in Philip Shenon, "Rebels Still Torment Cambodia 20 Years After Their Rampage," *New York Times,* February 6, 1995, p. 1.

26. James H. Carr, "Restoring Opportunities for Urban Communities," *Vital Speeches of the Day,* January 15, 1995, p. 217.

27. "On the Pulitzer Prize Hoax," in *Mass Media Issues,* 2d ed., George Rodman, ed. (Chicago: SRA, 1984), pp. 193–199.

28. Case cited in Juliet Dee, "Heavy Metal, Hit Men, Dial-a-Porn, and the First Amendment", in *Mass Media Issues,* p. 8.

29. From *Poor Richard's Almanak,* May 1734. Cited in *Bartlett's Familiar Quotations,* 15th ed. (Boston: Little, Brown, 1980), p. 347.

30. From a letter to James Madison, January 30, 1787. Cited in *Bartlett's Familiar Quotations,* 15th ed. (Boston: Little, Brown, 1980), p. 388.

31. David Lipsky, "Young, Eager, and Deep in Debt," *New York Times,* December 29, 1994, p. A21.

32. *Newsday* (Long Island), September 21, 1994.

33. Rebecca Witte, "America's Youth in Crisis," *Winning Orations, 1994* (Interstate Oratorical Association, 1994), pp. 77–79. Rebecca was coached by Sherry LaBoon and Tom Preston.

# ORGANIZATION AND OUTLINING

## ▼ CHAPTER 8 OBJECTIVES

**After reading this chapter, you should understand:**

1. The advantages of clear organization in the media/ information age.
2. The process of and patterns for organizing speech material.
3. The principles of effective organization and outlining.

**You should be able to:**

1. Identify the organizational pattern of a speech.
2. Choose the most effective organizational pattern for speech material.
3. Construct effective outlines for speech preparation, for speaking notes, and for presentation to your instructor.

## ▼ ORGANIZATION IN THE MEDIA/INFORMATION AGE

▼ Our problem is not that we don't have enough information. . . . The problem lies elsewhere, and I think it is a loss of meaning. People don't know what to do with the information.
They have no organizing principle.

Neil Postman

Austin was an avid baseball fan, so he welcomed the chance to explain his favorite game to a group of foreign students who had just arrived in the United States from around the world.

"Baseball is really simple," he began. "You get three strikes before you're out. A pitch is a strike if you swing at it and miss, or if you *don't* swing at it and the ball is between your armpits and knees and over the plate. But if you don't swing and the ball isn't in the strike zone, then it's a ball. Are there any questions?"

"The ball is a ball?" one student asked, looking confused.

"Right," Austin answered. "The word has two meanings. That *is* weird, isn't it? Anyway, if you get four balls before three strikes, then you walk. That means you get to go to first base without having to hit the ball. That's the only way you can do that. No, wait. There's one other way to get on base without getting a hit. If you get hit by a pitch, then you also can go to first."

Most of the students nodded politely, but they didn't look confident as Austin went on with his explanation.

After it was over, several students confessed that they knew less about baseball than they had before the explanation began.

Austin's problem might be connected to a characteristic of the media/information age: It is difficult to structure messages in an age in which messages seem to be strangely unstructured. Because many mediated messages aren't organized for the kind of clarity most speeches aim for, contemporary speakers don't have the abundance of well-organized messages to use as models that their counterparts had when oratory was more valued. To make matters worse, mediated messages come at you so quickly, so "all at once," that, even if they are well organized, they seem chaotic and random.

In fact, most mediated messages are carefully organized for effect. They only *seem* unorganized because there are so many of them and the messages are so diverse. The glut of messages makes it difficult for most people to *recognize* organization, and the problem is aggra-

"I just can't seem to get myself organized this morning!"

Reprinted by permission of Gahan Wilson.

vated by the way people acquire messages from the media. That is, people have a tendency to sample bits and pieces of messages in the media stream. Listeners "graze" restlessly among radio stations, looking for the best song. Viewers "channel surf" through dozens of television channels, while browsers leaf through magazines and newspapers looking for random items of interest, putting together a "message" out of a mosaic of bits and pieces.

All this makes media messages *seem* unorganized, but if you closely scrutinize them, you can see how carefully organized they are. Take radio programming, for example. What sounds like random D.J. patter, random album cuts, and an occasional news report is actually planned out, second by second, to keep the listener listening for as long as possible.

It is the same in every mass medium.[1] Take television: Every second of programming is carefully organized, even if that organization is not readily apparent. Everything is *produced,* which means that it is selected from the buzzing confusion of reality, edited, shaped, and organized. Media practitioners understand how essential organization is in the media/information age. No message will make sense within the glut of information that vies for our attention unless it is organized.

Organizing your ideas for a speech takes the same kind of advance planning that media practitioners use. For most speeches, you will use this planning to come up with a more traditionally logical organizational style than many media messages use. Although this traditional style of organization might seem difficult at first, it is the style that has proven itself most successful in developing ideas in depth. Research into public speaking has proved that organization promotes audience understanding[2] and persuasiveness[3], as well as speaker confidence.[4]

▼ Order is heaven's first law.

Alexander Pope

## ⬤ OUTLINING

You begin your organization, and you stay organized throughout the speech preparation process, through the use of outlines. You are no doubt familiar with the general idea of outlining, as well as outline form. A review of the principles and types of outlines, as they are used in speaking, will be provided here.

▼ Good order is the foundation of all good things.

Edmund Burke

### Types of Outlines

A speech outline is like a diagram of the organization of your speech. It shows your main ideas and how they relate to one another and to your central idea. Speech outlines come in all shapes and sizes, but they can generally be classified in one of three categories: formal outlines, working outlines, and speaking notes.

## Formal Outlines

A formal outline uses a consistent format and set of symbols to identify the structure of ideas. Formal outlines can be composed of either key words or complete sentences. A full-sentence outline on the topic of breast cancer might look like this:

  I. The Threat of Breast Cancer Is Growing.
      A. One in nine women has a lifetime risk.
      B. Certain factors increase this risk.
          1. The risk increases if a family member had the disease.
          2. The risk increases if a woman hasn't had a child by age 30.
          3. The risk increases for those with an "apple" rather than a "pear" body type.
 II. The Causes of Breast Cancer Are Largely Unknown.
      A. One suspected cause is dietary fat.
      B. Another suspected cause is the hormone estrogen.
      C. A third suspected cause is the environment.
          1. Agricultural toxins accumulate in food.
              a. Pesticides are used on fruits.
              b. Herbicides are used on vegetables.
          2. Industrial pollution accumulates in the air.
              a. PCBs are by-products of manufacturing processes.
              b. Other toxins are by-products of chemical processes.
          3. Electromagnetic fields are a new potential problem.
III. Your Protection from Breast Cancer Depends on Early Detection.
      A. Begin monthly self-exams at age 20.
      B. Begin regular doctor exams every three years at age 20, every year after age 40.
      C. Begin mammograms every 1 or 2 years after age 40.

A key-word outline on the same topic might look like this:

  I. Growing Threat
      A. One-in-nine lifetime risk
      B. Other risks
          1. disease in family
          2. childless by 30
          3. "apple" body types
 II. Causes
      A. diet
      B. estrogen

        C. environment
            1. agriculture
                a. pesticides
                b. herbicides
            2. industry
                a. PCBs
                b. other chemical waste
            3. electromagnetic fields
III. Protection
    A. self-exams
    B. doctor exams
    C. mammograms

A speech outline might combine full-sentence and key-word formats, with main points in full sentences and subpoints in key words.

A formal outline serves several purposes. In simplified form, it can be used as a visual aid (displayed on a poster board, for example, or distributed as a handout). It can serve as a record of a speech that was delivered. Many organizations send outlines to members who miss meetings at which presentations were given. In speech classes, outlines are often used by the instructor to analyze student speeches.

## Working Outlines

Working outlines are construction tools used in building your speech. Unlike a formal outline, a working outline is a constantly changing, personal device. You begin organizing your speech material from a rough working outline; then, as your ideas solidify, your outline changes accordingly.

A working outline is for your eyes only. No one else need understand it, so you can use whatever symbols and personal shorthand you find functional. In fact, your working outline will probably become pretty messy by the time you are ready to create a formal outline for others to see.

## Speaking Notes

Like your working outline, your speaking notes are a personal device, so the format is up to you. Many teachers suggest that speaking notes should be in the form of a brief key-word outline, with just enough information listed to jog your memory but not enough to get lost in. Special reminders about delivery ("slow down!") are also appropriate here.

Many teachers also suggest that you fit your notes on one side of one 3-by-5-inch card. Other teachers recommend that you also have outlines for your introduction and conclusion on note cards, and still others suggest that your references and quotations be written out on them. Your notes for a speech on breast cancer might look like this:

Eye Contact!
    I. Threat
        A. 1 in 9
            Quote #2
        B. Greater Risk:
            1. Family member
            2. Childless at 30
            3. Apples, not pears
Slow down!
    II. Causes
        A. Fat
        B. Estrogen
        C. Environment
            Quote #3
    III. Protection
        A. Self
        B. Doctor
        C. Mammograms

## Principles of Outlining

▼ Art and science cannot exist but in minutely organized particulars.

William Blake

Over the years, rules or principles for the construction of outlines have evolved. These rules are based on the use of a set of standard symbols and a standard format.

### Standard Symbols

A speech outline generally uses the following symbols:

    I. Main point (Roman numeral)
        A. Subpoint (capital letter)
            1. Sub-subpoint (standard number)
                a. Sub-subsubpoint (lowercase letter)

Usually the major divisions of the speech—introduction, body, and conclusion—are not given symbols. They are listed by name, and the Roman numerals for their main points begin anew in each division. Your outline helps you make sure that each section of your speech accomplishes its purpose. As we mentioned in Chapter 1, the introduction should attract the attention of your listeners and orient them to the message that follows. The body develops your ideas. The conclusion reviews the material and provides a sense of closure. The outline for a basic speech format, therefore, looks like this:

Introduction
  I. Capture attention of audience
 II. Introduce central idea
III. Preview main points
Body
  I. Main point 1
 II. Main point 2
III. Main point 3, etc.
Conclusion
  I. Review central idea
 II. Review main points
III. Signal end of speech

Introductions and conclusions will be covered in depth in Chapter 9.

## Standard Format

In the sample outlines in this chapter, notice that each symbol is indented from the symbol of the next highest order. Besides keeping the outline neat, the indentation of different-order ideas enables you to structure and coordinate your ideas. If the standard format is used in your working outline, it will help you create a well-organized speech. If it is used in speaking notes, it will help you remember everything you want to say.

## Guidelines for Choosing Points

Your outline lists both main points and subordinate points. There are a number of guidelines for distinguishing between the two, and choosing the ones that will be most effective.

## Divide Points into at Least Two Parts

In formal outlines main points and subpoints always represent a division of a whole. Because it is impossible to divide something into fewer than two parts, you always have at least two main points for every topic. Then, if your main points are divided, you will always have at least two subpoints, and so on. Thus, the rule for formal outlines is: never a I without a II, never an A without a B, and so on.

## Limit the Number of Points

Research reveals that people are best able to understand and remember information when it is grouped into no more than seven categories.[5] Most rhetorical experts agree that the best way to make your ideas clear and memorable is to limit the body of your speech even further, to a maximum of five main points.

Even if you have a large number of ideas to communicate or plan to speak for a long time, you can cover almost any topic within the five-point limit. For example, suppose you wanted to describe a number of dinosaurs to your audience. You might want to talk about twenty or twenty-five different creatures. You could keep the number of main points manageable by grouping the animals in categories. You might organize the speech according to the age in which the various creatures lived:

I. Cretaceous Period
II. Jurassic Period
III. Triassic Period
IV. Permian Period
V. Devonian Period

You could also discuss the dinosaurs according to habitat:

I. Land dwellers
II. Sea dwellers
III. Flying dinosaurs

A third approach would be to group the animals according to diet:

I. Meat eaters
II. Plant eaters

No matter what the topic, you can probably find at least one organizational plan that accomplishes your goal and contains no more than five main points. We will discuss organization plans in more depth later in this chapter.

### Limit Each Point to One Idea

Don't confuse your audience by lumping two ideas together in one main point. You can see the problem with combining ideas in this outline:

*Thesis:* Throughout history, any group lacking power has been victimized by discrimination.

 I. The aged
 II. The young
 III. The poor
 III. Women and minorities

It is easy to see that women and minorities are different groups, each of which should be given a separate main point.

There are occasions where it makes sense to include more than one item in a single main point. As long as the items are part of the same category or idea, you aren't violating any rules of logic:

*Central Idea:* Views of the afterlife vary from one religion to another.
*Main Points:*
 I. Judaism is extremely vague about the afterlife.
 II. Christianity and Islam portray the afterlife as a paradise.
 III. Buddhism characterizes the afterlife as a state of enlightenment.

Because Christianity and Islam share similar concepts of heaven, it makes sense to discuss them in the same point. Indeed, it would be repetitive and illogical not to do so.

## Balance the Coverage of Points

It isn't necessary to spend exactly the same amount of time on each point, but it is important to keep your treatment balanced. If you spend five minutes on one point and five seconds on another, you create certain problems. Your audience may not remember the points you treat briefly. Even if they do recall the less prominent points, listeners might think they are less important due to your lack of emphasis. Even worse, your listeners might interpret the skimpy coverage as a sign that you don't know what you are talking about. It's far better to restructure your points so that each one gets a similar amount of coverage. If there is no way to restructure your ideas, you may decide to eliminate one or two of them, at least as separate points.

## Use Parallel Wording for Points

The structure of your ideas will be clearest when you use similar wording for each main point. Consider this outline for a speech against capital punishment:

 I. Crime did not decrease during the 1950s, when capital punishment was enforced.
 II. The Eighth Amendment to the U.S. Constitution protects against cruel and unusual punishment.
 III. Most civilized countries have abandoned the notion of capital punishment.

The relationship of those points might seem obvious to you as a speaker, but chances are they would leave the audience confused. Similar, parallel wording of main points helps to guard against this confusion:

I. Capital punishment is not effective: It is not a deterrent to crime.
II. Capital punishment is not constitutional: It does not comply with the Eighth Amendment.
III. Capital punishment is not civilized; It does not allow for a reverence for life.

When you phrase each main point in the same way, your arguments take on a kind of symmetry that makes them more interesting and memorable. It isn't always possible to use parallel wording, but when you can do so your ideas will be clearer and more memorable.

## Other Parts of the Speech Outline

Many instructors require formal speech outlines to list the purpose, the central idea, and the topic or title. (It may be a good idea to title your speech, since a title often helps your audience understand your approach.) Most instructors also require a bibliography of sources at the end of the outline. The bibliography should include full research citations. The correct form for these citations can be found in any style guide, such as Kate Turabian's *Student's Guide for Writing College Papers*.[6] Many instructors also like to have supporting material listed on a speech outline, to remind students to back up their ideas with support. When support is listed in this way, it is not given one of the standard symbols. It is identified by type:

▼ Example:

▼ Visual Aid:

▼ Quotation:

Because supporting material is not always divided into subpoints, it *is* possible to list only one item under a particular point.

Some instructors like to have connectives, such as transitions, listed on student outlines. These also are not given standard symbols. Like supporting points, these connectives are not divisions of an idea, so it is possible to have only one of them under a point. We will discuss connectives later in this chapter.

With all the extra components added, a formal outline handed in for the speech on breast cancer might look like this:

Topic: Breast Cancer
Purpose: After listening to my speech, audience members will plan to protect themselves against breast cancer through regular self-examinations, doctor exams, and mammograms.

Central Idea: Breast cancer is a serious threat that we can protect ourselves against.
Title: "Protecting Ourselves from the Puzzling Plague"
Introduction
  I. Breast cancer is a tragedy for individuals.
     Example: Betty Comden
  II. Breast cancer is a tragedy for society.
     Statistics: Harold Maxwell
     Preview of main points
Body
  I. The threat of breast cancer is growing.
    A. One in nine women has a lifetime risk.
    B. Some women run an even greater risk.
      1. If a family member had the disease
      2. Women who haven't had a child by age 30
      3. "Apple" rather than "pear" types of body fat distribution.
    Preview of next main point
  II. The causes of breast cancer are largely unknown.
    A. One suspected cause is dietary fat.
    B. Another suspected cause is the hormone estrogen.
    C. A third suspected cause is the environment.
      1. Agricultural pollution
        a. Pesticides
        b. Herbicides
      2. Industrial pollution
        a. PCBs
        b. Other chemical waste
      3. Electromagnetic fields
    Preview of next main point
  III. Your protection from breast cancer depends on early detection.
    A. Begin monthly self-exams at age 20.
    B. Begin regular doctor exams every three years at age 20, every year after age 40.
    C. Begin mammograms every one or two years after age 40.
Conclusion
Review of main points
  I. Remember Betty Comden
  II. Visit the campus health center

▼ Order and simplification are the first steps toward the mastery of a subject.

Thomas Mann

### ▼ BIBLIOGRAPHY

Eliot Marshall, interview at Michigan State University, December 7, 1995.
Cathy Perlmutter and Gloria McVeigh, "Your Best Breast Protection," *Prevention,* May 1996, p. 36.

I. Raloff, "Breast Cancer Rise: Due to Dietary Fat?" *Science News,* April 21, 1995, p. 245.

"Study Sees Risk in Breast Cancer Therapy Falling," *New York Times,* June 25, 1996, p. A10(N), p. A28(L), col. 1.

Survey on audience health history conducted in class, September 15, 1996.

John Vitto, "Breast Cancer in Young Women," *Patient Care,* April 15, 1996, p. 28.

Claudia Wallis, "A Puzzling Plague: What Is It About the American Way of Life that Causes Breast Cancer?" *Time,* January 14, 1996, p. 48.

## ▼ PATTERNS OF ORGANIZATION

Patterns of information are important to public speakers because of the way the human mind works. We know, from knowledge both ancient and modern, that the mind will seek out patterns in information, and if it doesn't find them, it will tend not to make sense of the information. Patterns therefore help you make your ideas comprehensible. They also help you, the speaker, figure out what your points are: They enable you to determine how a central idea should be divided into main points, and how main points should be divided into subordinate points. Patterns of organization also help you place your ideas into a sequence, or order, that will be easiest for both you and your audience to remember.

### Chronological Patterns

Chronological patterns are based on time. The units of time could be anything from seconds to centuries. This is essentially the way we organize our lives, so chronological sequencing is usually familiar and easy for listeners to follow. A chronological approach is well suited to describing historical trends. The term *historical* can involve events that change the course of human affairs, but it also includes less momentous subjects: the events leading up to a brawl at last week's football game or an account of your experiences trekking through Nepal. The body of a historical speech would look like this:

*Central Idea:* Once it began, the collapse of communism in central and eastern Europe accelerated with a speed that few had predicted and no individuals or governments could control.

*Main Points:*
   I. In Poland, the struggle against communism took several years.
  II. In Hungary, the rebellion took several months.
 III. In Czechoslovakia, the struggle took several weeks.
  IV. In Romania, the struggle took eight days.

A chronological approach is usually the best way to describe a *process*—any phenomenon that changes over time. Processes involve everything from how chewing gum is made to how a bill becomes a law. The main points in a speech describing the process of adjusting to the death of a loved one might look like this:

*Central Idea:* Before coming to terms with the death of a loved one, it is necessary to experience several stages.
*Main Points:*
   I. The first stage is denial.
  II. The second stage is bargaining.
 III. The third stage is anger.
  IV. The fourth stage is depression.
   V. The fifth stage is acceptance.

A final type of chronological plan is the *narrative,* which is used to tell a story or anecdote. Most narratives follow a *climax pattern* that tells a story from start to finish:

*Central Idea:* Locating and exploring the sunken ocean liner *Titanic* was a feat that illustrated the best scientific and human qualities.
*Main Points:*
   I. From 1914 to 1960, reaching the *Titanic* was a scientific impossibility.
  II. In 1985, the wreck was finally located in 2,000 feet of water, but it might as well have been on another planet.
 III. In 1991, the first serious effort to reach the ship ended in failure.
  IV. In 1993, an exploration team finally achieved the goal that had eluded adventurers for over two-thirds of a century.

Another type of narrative is the *anticlimax,* which begins with the conclusion and then backtracks to describe the events leading up to it. This approach is especially useful when you need to capture the attention of a disinterested audience early in your speech.

*Central Idea:* Teresa Jackson's death was caused by the failure of school and community support.
*Main Points:*
   I. Last month, 14-year-old Teresa Jackson was found beaten to death in an alley on the west side of town. (climax)
  II. Teresa's death was caused by the failure of school and community support. (central idea)

III. Her parents abused her from the time she was a child until she ran away from home at age 13. (beginning of story)
IV. Once on the street, there were no social or church agencies to care for her. (continuation of story)
 V. To stay alive, Teresa turned to the only method she could think of: prostitution. This choice led to more abuse, and ultimately to her death. (continuation of story)

### Spatial Patterns

Spatial patterns are organized according to space, or area. The area could be stated in terms of continents or centimeters or anything in between. If you have divided your ideas from a spatial perspective, you have to choose an order such as closest (to the audience) to farthest away, or most familiar area to least familiar area. For example:

*Central Idea:* Most ordinary "American" cuisine is based on food from around the world.
*Main Points:*
  I. The majority of everyday meals are European in origin.
 II. Asian cuisines show up in surprisingly familiar foods.
III. Africa was the inspiration for some common dishes.

Along with geography, other spatial organizing schemes can develop a topic clearly: bottom to top (the structure of a tree), left to right (descriptions of people in a photograph), inside to outside (the moons of Jupiter), and so on. As these examples suggest, speeches that deal with concrete subjects are ideally suited to spatial order. The physical scale could be small (the structure of an atom) or large (the diversity of cultures in China).

Spatial order isn't limited to physical topics. Another organizing scheme is the *spatial metaphor,* in which you use the image of a physical object to represent an idea.[7] As this example shows, spatial metaphors can help make a potentially confusing subject clear:

*Central Idea:* John Donne's claim that "no man is an island" reflects Carl Jung's idea of the collective unconscious.
*Main Points:*
  I. People appear to be individuals, like islands.
 II. But, like islands, much of our identity is invisible, lying "below the surface."
III. Like the earth that connects islands below the surface, each of us is connected by a "collective unconscious."

### Causal Patterns

As its name suggests, an idea organized in *causal order* establishes a relationship between the causes and effects of the subject. Causal plans can be used in informative speeches to explain how a certain condition has arisen. For example, you could describe the factors (causes) that have led to the extent of drug abuse facing society today. But a causal approach is used more often in persuasive speeches, to convince listeners that the conditions that have caused or will cause a problem need to be changed. For example, you might use a causal approach that the decriminalization of drug use (the cause) would lead to greater problems (the effect).

Causal speeches can take two forms. *Cause-effect* order shows how one set of events follows from another. For example:

*Central Idea:* Rock music is leading to the decline of important values.
*Main Points:*
  I. Much rock music idealizes antisocial themes. (cause)
 II. As rock music has become raunchier, antisocial activities have increased. (effect)

A second causal plan is *effect-cause*. It begins by describing the results, and then explains the forces that created them.

*Central Idea:* The tenure system contributes to poor teaching.
*Main Points:*
  I. Many professors have no apparent desire to teach or counsel their students well. (effect)
 II. The tenure system removes any pressure for unmotivated professors to perform. (cause)

## Problem-Solution Patterns

As its name suggests, a *problem-solution* plan is a two-part organizing scheme that begins by outlining a state of affairs that needs to be changed, and then goes on to offer a remedy. By its nature, the problem-solution approach is ideally suited to persuasive speeches. For example:

*Central Idea:* Rent control laws are needed to protect tenants from greedy landlords.
*Main Points:*
  I. Many tenants are victimized by greedy, unfair landlords. (problem)
 II. A rent control law would protect tenants and still give landlords a fair profit. (solution)

## Topical Patterns

Topical patterns are based on types and categories. Generally, if a pattern is not chronological, spatial, causal, or problem-solution, it will be categorized as a type of topical organization. Most subjects divide into natural categories. For instance:

| TYPE OF DIVISION | EXAMPLES |
|---|---|
| Parts of a whole | Ethnic groups in the community |
| | Types of instruments in a symphony orchestra |
| Pros and Cons | Living together before marriage |
| | Taking longer than four years to earn a bachelor's degree |
| Reasons | For electing a candidate |
| | For following a vegetarian diet |
| Customary divisions of a topic | Male and female |
| | Assets and liabilities (in a financial report) |

Along with these standard topical schemes, some subjects seem to suggest their own unique but logical topical division. Consider this example:

*Central Idea:* As consumers, we can preserve the environment by patronizing only organizations that carry out environmentally safe practices.
*Main Points:*
  I. We can avoid companies that damage the environment.
 II. We can buy products and services from companies that preserve the environment.

A topical approach works especially well when your main points are a list of items, since it breaks a potentially long and unwieldy mass of information into categories that are easier to grasp. If you wanted to discuss some of the technological breakthroughs that have transformed life in the last half of the twentieth century, you might want to cite the following items:

▼ cellular telephones      ▼ laser technology

▼ videotape recorders      ▼ microsurgery

▼ compact disc recordings  ▼ antibiotic drugs

▼ virtual reality games    ▼ multimedia computer systems

▼ genetic engineering      ▼ magnetic image scanning

Rather than rattle off this long list, you could organize it into three topical categories:

*Central Idea:* A variety of technological breakthroughs have made our lives different from those of our parents and grandparents.
*Main Points:*
  I. Entertainment has been revolutionized.
 II. Communication has become quicker, easier, and cheaper.
III. Medical advances have given us longer, healthier lives.

Sometimes the subtopics that make up a topical organization will be obvious. If you were explaining the structure of the federal government to a visitor from abroad, the nature of the topic would dictate the structure of the body:

*Central Idea:* The federal government consists of three parts.
*Main Points:*
  I.  The legislative branch writes the laws.
 II.  The executive branch enforces the laws.
III.  The judicial branch interprets ambiguities or questions in the laws.

In other cases your purpose will suggest the main points. If the goal of your speech is to recruit volunteer tutors in a local adult literacy program, then your main points might be the reasons they should volunteer. The purpose statement and the main points of the speech might look like this:

*Specific Purpose:* After hearing my speech, at least some members of my audience will volunteer as adult literacy tutors.
*Main Points:*
  I.  Service as a volunteer looks good on a job resume.
 II.  The people you meet as a tutor are interesting.
III.  Teaching an adult to read will give you a tremendous feeling of satisfaction.

A knowledge of patterns of organization gives you a range of options when you are deciding what the main points of your speech should be. Organizational patterns also allow you to place those points, and all the information in your speech, in an order that will be most effective. Your final step in speech organization will be to demonstrate to the audience how your ideas fit together. You do this through the use of connectives.

## CONNECTIVES

It is easy for listeners to get lost in a speech. A spoken message doesn't have paragraphs, headings, italics, and other devices that help clarify the structure of written text. It's impossible for listeners to stop a speaker in mid-sentence the way they can pause while reading a book, article, or letter. They can't pause to think about the importance of an idea, or even sneeze without missing something. For an audience, the message keeps coming, whether or not they are ready.

Because an oral message is harder to understand, you need to use some special devices to make the structure of your message clear. You have to spell out ideas in far more detail than you would in writing, so that listeners can always see where you are now, where you have been, and where you are headed.

*Connectives* help make your ideas clear. They are devices (sometimes statements, sometimes just words and phrases) that establish the relationship of ideas in a speech to help listeners understand its structure. Connectives take several forms, including transitions, internal previews, internal reviews, and signposts.

## Transitions

Transitions are statements that help the audience understand the relationships among ideas in a speech by showing the connection between two points. Transitions form a sort of verbal bridge, helping listeners span the gap between two pieces of information. And like a bridge, the best transitions provide a clear link between ideas by being anchored at both ends. They refer to both the preceding and the upcoming points, showing the relationship between them:

▼ Our look at the history of immigration has shown that virtually every group of newcomers to the country has suffered discrimination at the hands of the people who came before. Unfortunately, the same sad story is true today.

▼ Now that you understand just what the balance of payments is, let's take a look at how it affects our everyday lives.

These examples show how transitions function as a kind of glue, holding the important parts of a speech together so that listeners can understand how they relate. To do this, transitions occur in a number of places throughout the speech: between the introduction and body, between main points, between the body and conclusion—anywhere listeners might become confused about the relationship between ideas. In long speeches, transitions might even be necessary to connect subordinate points within one or more main points.

Rhetorical questions can be used to increase the effectiveness of a transition. By posing a question and inviting the audience to consider an answer, you create involvement that keeps listeners interested:

Suppose you were the victim of this kind of sexual harassment. What would you do? Would you complain at the risk of losing your job? Would you grit your teeth and put up with the abuse? Neither of these alternatives sounds very good, so let's take a look at some other ways of coping with illegal sexual harassment.

## Internal Previews and Reviews

*Internal previews* tell an audience what points are coming up next:

Now let's take a look at the real truth about the American cowboy and see just how closely it matches the legends we've seen on television and in the movies.

*Internal reviews* summarize the material that was just completed. For example, an internal review in a speech criticizing the American educational system might sound like this:

> By now you can see that the state of high school education in this country is pretty dismal. Reading scores are down. Most students can't write more than the simplest ideas clearly. Math abilities are among the lowest in the developed nations. Most high school graduates don't know much about world geography, and they know even less about current events.

Although this sort of restatement might seem to insult the intelligence of an audience, listeners who have to understand ideas without the benefit of a written text often need the redundancy offered by internal summaries, especially for ideas that are at all complicated. Of course, internal summaries also help pound the material into audience members who weren't listening the first time around.

In many speeches, the best transitions combine internal previews and reviews:

▼ By now you can see that crash diets have plenty of problems. They rarely produce lasting weight loss, they can lead to malnourishment, and they make it harder to lose weight the next time a dieter tries. But there are two kinds of diets that do work. Let's take a look at them now:

▼ The videotapes you just saw prove that swing dancing can be fun, and you can see that it's a terrific form of exercise. So now that you have some good reasons for learning to swing dance, let's take a look at how to do it. In the next few minutes I'll show you a simple step that is easy to learn, and that will have you looking good on the dance floor.

## Signposts

*Signposts* are phrases that help orient listeners to the structure of a message. They are like brief statements to the effect of "this is important" or "this is where we are now." They include the following:

▼ The first thing to consider is . . .

▼ A second reason . . .

▼ For example . . .

▼ In addition . . .

▼ Finally . . .

Signposts are useful for highlighting the relationship between main and subordinate points. Used this way, a signpost says "Here's a piece of information that will make my point clear."

▼ Not all young teens who run away from home come from terrible family backgrounds. For instance, take Katie . . .

▼ Supreme Court precedents have supported the constitutionality of flag burning as "free speech." In one case—Tinker vs. Des Moines Independent School District—the Court said . . .

Signposts also help an audience keep track of material you present in a list. As every student who has tried to take notes in a lecture knows, signposts can make the difference between getting a speaker's ideas straight and getting lost in a sea of detail.

▼ There are several kinds of computer operating systems in use today. First, there's the IBM personal computer standard called Disk Operating System or "DOS," for short. Second, there's IBM's newer system, "Warp 2." Third, there's Apple Computer's Macintosh operating system. And fourth, there's Microsoft's Windows . . .

▼ To get the best videos using the camcorder, follow a few simple guidelines. First, don't zoom in and out rapidly. Second, try to get closeups of the people you are taping. Third, use a tripod whenever possible to keep the picture steady.

Connectives like transitions, internal previews, internal reviews, and signposts can provide verbal clues that convey the structure of your ideas to an audience. Listeners need this kind of help. Especially in the real world, where audience members don't have a written outline or text to follow, your verbal clues will keep them oriented as you present your speech.

### ⬤ SAMPLE SPEECH

The sample speech for this chapter was presented by Andy Wood, a student at Berry College in Georgia.[8] With it, Andy won first prize in the 1994 Annual Contest of the Interstate Oratorical Association at Anchorage, Alaska.

The organization of this speech could be represented in the following outline (numbers in the outline refer to the numbered paragraphs of the speech):

Introduction (1–2)

I. We all get sick from common diseases.
II. We all use antibiotics.
III. We are all at risk.
    Statistics: diseases
    Testimony: Dr. Cohen
  Preview of main points (2)
BODY (3–12)
  I. The superbugs are deadly.
    A. Tuberculosis has killed 22,000. (3)
      Stats: cases and deaths
    B. Streptococcus kills 15,000 a year. (4)
      Example: Jim Henson
      Stats: cases and deaths
    C. Staphylococcus aureus is almost impossible to kill. (5)
      Testimony: journals
  II. Our defenses have failed. (6)
    A. There is limited national surveillance. (6)
      Testimony: Dr. Joseph, Dr. Gaynes
    B. There is faulty hospital infection control. (7)
      Statistics: CDC report
    C. There are dangerous public perceptions. (8)
      Testimony: Dr. Platt
      Statistics: JAMA
  Preview of next main point (9)
III. We need a new offensive strategy.
    A. We need to redesign our national surveillance system. (10)
      1. Increase funding for NIH and CDC
      2. Alliance for the Prudent Use of Antibiotics
    B. We need to limit the use of antibiotics in the medical com-munity. (11)
      Testimony: journals
    C. We need to increase our vigilance. (12)
      1. Ask for alternatives to antibiotics.
      2. Stick to the prescribed treatment.
Conclusion (13)
  Review of main points
  I. Victory requires vision and foresight.
  II. In this war, we are all enlisted.

This speech makes a good example for organization, but of course not all speeches are this clearly organized or this easily analyzed in a straight paragraph-for-paragraph manner. After all, Andy is speaking for other "forensicators" at a speech contest.

## ◉ SUPERBUGS: SCOURGE OF THE POST-ANTIBIOTIC ERA

Andy Wood

Berry College

[1] It always happens when you're the busiest. Your body gives out on you. Like any forensicator, you don't have time to get sick. So you see a doctor, grab an antibiotic, and feel better. Problem solved . . . or created. You see, every year 15,000 people die of pneumonia caused by a form of strep throat. Nineteen thousand die of hospital-acquired infections. And so far, a deadly form of tuberculosis has killed 22,000 people. Now you may be thinking, "Wait a minute. I take one antibiotic and all these people die? What's the connection?" The connection is that the more we use antibiotics, the stronger these diseases become. They're called superbugs and they're growing out of control. In *Newsweek,* March 7, 1994, Dr. Mitchell Cohen of the Centers for Disease Control warned: Superbugs threaten us all. He said: "Many of the diseases we once had under control are coming back."

[2] Now is the time for us to adopt a new strategy in this biological war. First, we must examine the emergence and the dangers of superbugs. Then we'll explore why our defenses fail against them. Finally, we'll outline a new offensive strategy that works.

[3] Three of the deadliest superbugs are tuberculosis, streptococcus, and staphylococcus. The critical connection is that these infections have developed resistance to antibiotics. Thus, our only resistance to them is luck. Consider TB. At the turn of the century, tuberculosis killed over a third of all U.S. adults between age 20 and 45. With antibiotics, we discovered what appeared to be a magic bullet to fight this menace. However, according to *Science News,* February 6, 1993, 36 states have reported cases of TB that is resistant to antibiotics. In fact, *Medical World News,* January 1993, reports 30,000 cases of drug-resistant TB nationwide. Of those cases, 22,000 people have died.

[4] But TB isn't the only threat. Resistant streptococcus pneumonia is so dangerous, any delay in treatment is fatal. That's why on May 16, 1990, in one of the world's most advanced hospitals, a team of doctors could do nothing to save the life of a man with what appeared to be a simple infection, but was actually a deadly form of strep. Dose after dose of antibiotic failed. His name was Jim Henson. And his tragedy is not uncommon. According to *The Atlanta Constitution,* May 18, 1993, resistant streptococcus causes 500,000 cases of pneumonia a year. Of those cases, 15,000 people die.

[5] But, perhaps the most dangerous resistant strain is staphylococcus aureus: one superbug that's almost impossible to kill. According to the journal *Antimicrobial Agents,* March 1993, staph can attack and grow on any surface and can carry resistance to other bacteria. Ironically, its favorite

breeding ground is the hospital. During the '50's, methicillin and vancomycin put the bug on the defensive. But according to *Science Magazine,* July 16, 1993, 95 percent of all staph infections are now resistant to methicillin. If reports of vancomycin resistant staph are accurate, we face a real-life andromeda strain that can't be stopped. These three examples prove we're fighting superbugs on a post-antibiotic battleground in which our big guns no longer work.

[6] There are three reasons why our defenses have failed: limited national surveillance, faulty hospital infection control, and dangerous public perceptions. Dr. Steven Joseph writes in *The American Journal of Public Health,* May 1993, that with the apparent success of antibiotics, America practically dismantled its infectious disease surveillance system. As a result, superbugs usually go undetected until they reach a hospital. Even then, it's often too late. In a June 24, 1993, personal interview, Dr. Robert Gaynes, Director of the CDC, said, "We track resistant bacteria in only 160 out of 5,000 hospitals. There could be a strain of vancomycin-resistant staph out there and we wouldn't know it."

[7] Surprisingly, much of this threat comes from hospitals themselves. Their indiscriminate use and abuse of antibiotics leads to a selective killing of weak bacteria, allowing the strong to thrive. Without natural enemies, these bugs are free to concentrate on developing resistance. In fact, the *Buffalo New York News,* January 25, 1993, quotes a CDC report stating: Of the 35 million Americans admitted to hospitals every year, 2 million catch something new after they check in. And in 60 percent of the cases, those infections are resistant to one or more drugs. These infections kill 19,000 people directly and contribute to another 58,000 fatalities a year. Of course, this problem isn't confined to hospitals. Any doctor who overprescribes antibiotics helps bacteria develop resistance.

[8] At this point, one may assume that reckless doctors or unscrupulous drug companies are behind all of this. (There are plenty of both.) But in truth, we are all part of the cause when we demand antibiotics for all that ails us. Dr. Richard Platt writes in *Harvard Health Letter,* April 1993, that doctors often prescribe antibiotics even for viral infections (when they'd be ineffective) because patients "have a strong expectation that when they see a doctor, they should come away with a drug prescription." As a result, the *Journal of the American Medical Association,* April 14, 1994, reports that of the 220 million prescriptions written for oral antibiotics every year, one-half are unnecessary. Certainly doctors are the ones writing these prescriptions. But all too often they are reacting to our assumptions about what antibiotics can do. As we've seen, these assumptions expose us to bacteria that can kill us—but can't be killed.

[9] Refortifying our antibiotic defense against superbugs requires three steps: redesign of our national surveillance system, disciplined response by the medical community, and increased vigilance on all our parts.

[10] The Public Health Service Act of 1993 increased funding to the National Institutes of Health, as well as the Centers for Disease Control—two essential watchtowers that protect us from superbugs. However, if you read the *Congressional Quarterly,* July 24, 1993, you'll find no increased funding for research on antibiotic resistance in either the NIH or CDC. While it would be easy to just ask for more money this year, there is a better solution in the private sector. It's called the Alliance for the Prudent Use of Antibiotics. As the *APUA Newsletter,* Spring 1993, explains, this group is a network of physicians, microbiologists, and public health workers sharing information on emerging superbugs in 95 countries. Hospitals, testing labs, even medical schools should build on this skeleton, creating an effective surveillance body. Such a network would focus on surveillance, putting the NIH and CDC in better positions to attack superbugs that threaten us.

[11] The second step involves hospitals, doctors, and their use of antibiotics. Last September, the CDC released the first new guidelines on hospital-borne infections in over a decade. Obviously, the medical community should implement these standards without waiting for another outbreak of resistant staph or TB. But that's not enough. This next step requires that hospitals and doctors discipline their use of antibiotics. According to the *Annals of Internal Medicine,* April 1, 1993, the Infectious Disease Society of America is establishing guidelines on antimicrobial drug use. These guidelines limit the prescribed length of antibiotic treatment in non-life-threatening cases. The *Lancet,* February 27, 1993, illustrates this concept, noting that meningococcal meningitis—a recent killer of college students—can, itself, be killed by a single dose of long-acting penicillin as opposed to the commonly used seven-day treatment cycle. Limiting the use of antibiotics in this manner limits the opportunity for bacteria to develop resistance.

[12] But, if all this talk about national surveillance and hospital infections seems a bit remote, remember: Our use of antibiotics is our front line of defense against superbugs. That's why there are two things you should do. First, if your doctor prescribes an antibiotic, ask why. Ask whether there are alternatives like vaccines. Because they are harder to resist, vaccines are successful against diseases like strep and, according to *Nature Magazine,* July 1, 1993, research is underway for a TB vaccine. Second, if you must use an antibiotic, stick to the prescribed treatment. After all, when we use antibiotics as "home remedies" or share them with friends like they're cough drops, we increase the risk of resistance. By serving as individual gatekeepers of antibiotic use, we can fight superbugs without tearing down our best line of defense.

[13] In the past few minutes, we've examined how superbugs threaten our health, why we've lowered our defenses, and how America can answer this call to battle. In doing so, we've learned about the dangerous relationship

between antibiotics and superbugs. It's ironic isn't it? Our most powerful medical tool used against us by a simple life-form. Clearly, victory in this war demands more than brute force. It requires vision and foresight. And not just from doctors and scientists—but from all of us. After all, in the battle against resistant bacteria there are no volunteers. In this war, we are all enlisted.

## ▼ SUMMARY

Mediated messages can be models of effective organization, and yet, because of the random way we process most messages, it is difficult to recognize organization in the media/information age. Media practitioners recognize that a well-organized message will make your ideas more understandable as well as boost your personal credibility and the persuasiveness of your message. In addition to these benefits, knowing that your ideas are well organized will help you feel more confident and boost your ability to deliver your remarks smoothly.

The principles of organization are based on the limitations of human information processing. Principles of information processing require you to structure your speech by dividing it into three parts: introduction, body, and conclusion. Although listeners will hear the introduction first, the best way to begin organizing a speech is to plan the main points in the body. After identifying the main points, you can go on to add subordinate points and supporting material.

Principles of information processing also require you to break up complex information into a small number of ideas. In speeches, the recommended number of ideas is two to five, whether you are dividing topics into main points or main points into subpoints.

There are several ways to order main points. A chronological plan follows the development of ideas over time. A spatial approach uses physical properties to organize the material. Causally organized speeches link the causes and effects of a subject, while problem-solution speeches describe one or more needs and then propose one or more ways of satisfying them. Topically organized ideas are broken up into subtopics and arranged in some logical way. All of these patterns are enhanced by connectives, such as transitions, internal previews, internal reviews, and signposts.

Sometimes the nature of the material will determine which plan to use, and sometimes your purpose for speaking will determine the best plan. In other cases the interests and knowledge of the audience or the dictates of the situation will help you choose the best approach.

The structural components of a speech are planned out and demonstrated on a speech outline, which is like a diagram of the organization of your speech. Speech outlines include formal and working outlines, as well as outlines used as speaking notes.

## ▼ EXERCISES

1. Choose an effective written statement at least three paragraphs in length. This statement might be an editorial in your local newspaper, a short magazine article, or even a section of one of your textbooks. Outline this statement according to the rules discussed in this chapter. Was the statement well organized? Did its organization contribute to its effectiveness?

2. For practice in selecting main points, divide each of the following into 2–5 subcategories:
   **a.** clothing
   **b.** academic studies
   **c.** crime
   **d.** health care
   **e.** fun
   **f.** charities

# NOTES

1. Media messages are often organized according to rules different from the ones discussed in this chapter. Examples would include flashbacks and "flash forwards" in films and jarring juxtapositions in music videos. These types of organization are designed for psychological effect, and work because they *break* the rules of traditional organization. It is worthwhile to notice that even this type of organization is carefully planned by media practitioners.

2. Ernest Thompson, "An Experimental Investigation of the Relative Effectiveness of Organization Structure in Oral Communication," *Southern Speech Journal* 26 (1960), pp. 59–69. See also Arlee Johnson, "A Preliminary Investigation of the Relationship between Message Organization and Listener Comprehension," *Central States Speech Journal* 21 (Summer 1970), pp. 104–107.

3. See also J. P. Parker, "Some Organizational Variables and Their Effect upon Comprehension," *Journal of Communication* 12 (1962), pp. 27–32; and D. L. Thistlethwaite, H. de Haan, and J. Kemenetzky, "The Effects of 'Directive' and 'Non-directive' Communication Procedures on Attitudes," *Journal of Abnormal and Social Psychology* 51 (1955), pp. 107–113.

4. See, for example, James C. McCroskey and R. Samuel Mehrley, "The Effects of Disorganization and Nonfluency on Attitude Change and Source Credibility," *Speech Monographs* 36 (March 1969), pp. 13–21. See also R. G. Smith, "An Experimental Study of the Effects of Speech Organization upon Attitudes of College Students," *Speech Monographs* 18 (1951), p. 292.

5. See George A. Miller, "The Magical Number Seven, Plus or Minus Two: Some Limits on Our Capacity for Processing Information," in *Readings in the Psychology of Cognition*, Richard C. Anderson and David Ausubel, eds. (New York: Holt, Rinehart and Winston, 1965), pp. 242–267.

6. K. L. Turabian, *Student's Guide for Writing College Papers* (Chicago: University of Chicago Press, 1995).

7. See George Lakoff and Mark Johnson, *Metaphors We Live By* (Chicago: University of Chicago Press, 1982); and Philip Wheelwright, *Metaphor and Reality* (Bloomington, Ind.: Indiana University Press, 1964).

8. Andy Wood, "Superbugs: Scourge of the Post-Antibiotic Era," *Winning Orations, 1994* (Interstate Oratorical Association, 1994), pp. 23–25. Andy was coached by Randy Richardson.

▼ **CHAPTER 9**

# INTRODUCTIONS AND CONCLUSIONS

## ▼ CHAPTER 9 OBJECTIVES

**After reading this chapter, you should understand:**

1. The functions of a speech introduction.
2. The functions of a speech conclusion.

**You should be able to:**

1. Plan an effective introduction.
2. Plan an effective conclusion.

## ⬤ LESSONS FROM THE MEDIA

Media practitioners know the importance of the beginning and ending of any message. We can see this in the way a commercial attempts to grab our attention in the first five seconds, and stresses the main selling point or the product name in the last five seconds. We can also see it in the way a television sitcom invests so much energy in its "tease," its opening graphics, or the promotional spot (promo) that is aired right before it comes on.[1]

You know how it works. You're relaxing in front of your TV after a hard day, grazing through the channels, when a promo for an upcoming show catches your attention. Perhaps it arouses your curiosity with a perplexing question or piques your interest by mentioning a problem you've experienced personally. Whatever the device, it's probably given you a fairly good idea of the content of the program you're about to see, and it's made you want to see it. You've been sucked into the vortex of a professionally produced media introduction.

Conclusions are also vitally important to the media. We see this most easily in drama: You're watching a movie like *Casablanca* and, just when the various conflicts seem unresolvable, Humphrey Bogart puts Ingrid Bergman on the plane and tells her, "We'll always have Paris." It's shocking but somehow inevitable, and, most of all, unforgettable. And yet you don't have to look to classic films to find examples of how important conclusions are. Commercial producers often put a "zinger" at the end of their ad to help you remember the basic message.

Media professionals are taught the importance of introductions and conclusions. Robert L. Hilliard, in *Writing for Television and Radio,* reminds fledgling commercial writers of the importance of introductions:

> Keep in mind that the television audience is prone to use the commercial break to head for a bathroom, a beer, a phone call, or food. If you don't get their attention in the first few seconds, before they leave the area of the television set, you've lost them.[2]

Like other media mentors,[3] Hilliard also points out that a commercial should build to its most dramatic or humorous effect in its conclusion, to be memorable to its audience.

What is true for media writers in this respect is equally true for public speakers. In fact, media writers learned their theory from public speaking history and research.

## ⬤ THE INTRODUCTION

In earlier chapters we've mentioned certain basic functions of introductions, such as gaining the audience's attention and previewing the central

# Calvin and Hobbes

## by Bill Watterson

UFOs! ARE THEY REAL ?? HAVE THEY LANDED IN OUR TOWNS AND NEIGHBORHOODS?

DO THE CHILLING PHOTOGRAPHS BY AN AMATEUR PHOTOGRAPHER REALLY SHOW A SINISTER ALIEN SPACESHIP AND THE GRIM RESULTS OF A CLOSE ENCOUNTER, OR ARE THE PICTURES AN ELABORATE HOAX?

LISTEN TO AN EXPERT ON SPACE ALIENS SPECULATE ON THEIR HIDEOUS BIOLOGY AND THEIR HORRIFYING WEAPONRY! ALL THIS AND MORE...

...ON CALVIN'S SHOW AND TELL ... NEXT!

CALVIN, WILL YOU COME HERE PLEASE?

5-28 © 1990 Universal Press Syndicate

idea of the speech. Here we'll discuss these and other functions of the introduction, including previewing the main points, setting the mood and tone of the speech, establishing credibility and goodwill, and demonstrating the importance of the topic.

## Gain Audience Attention

There are several ways to capture an audience's attention in the introduction of your speech. Let's take a look at some of the devices.

***Refer to the Audience*** As we mentioned in our opening chapters, you should always be "audience-oriented" in your choice of topic. Your introduction is an effective place to demonstrate to your audience that you have them in mind. An effective audience reference, therefore, is a statement that reflects how the topic relates directly to your audience members and how important it is for them.

For example, if you were speaking on the topic of sleep deprivation, you might begin like this:

> As college students, we all experience sleep deprivation. It seems like the TV programs directed toward our age group come on late at night, and our classes start early in the morning. Socializing keeps us up late, work commitments get us up early. And this time of year, when final exams and final papers combine with the championship playoffs, it gets especially bad . . .

Being human, audience members are interested in themselves. They are also flattered to hear some evidence that you're thinking about them. Often, your reference to the audience can be in the form of a thank you: for being invited, for contributing in some way, or just for putting up with you and listening to you when they could be doing something else. Margaret Milner Richardson, the commissioner of the Internal Revenue

Service, used this technique when she spoke before the New York State Bar Association Tax Section:

Good afternoon. Thank you for the warm welcome. It is an honor and pleasure to be here. I would like to first offer my thanks to the New York Bar Tax Section for your support. From the fine quality of your comment letters, the dedication of your members is obvious, and it is apparent that much time, talent, and thought goes into each of the projects your committees and subcommittees undertake. I also thank you for your recent support on some difficult issues.

I know we will not, cannot, and should not always agree, but I also know we have a common interest in having clear tax rules and a tax administration system that works efficiently, effectively, and fairly. I hope, therefore, that you will continue to provide your support and your comments for many years to come.[4]

Richardson thanked her audience for their "comment letters," even though such letters are almost exclusively complaints. By doing so, she showed that she understood that the technique of referring to the audience is especially effective if it is complimentary, or involves an honest statement of praise. This is also what General Douglas MacArthur did in his famous "Old Soldiers Never Die" address, delivered before a joint session of Congress in 1951. He began his speech like this:

Mr. President, Mr. Speaker, and distinguished Members of the Congress, I stand on this rostrum with a sense of deep humility and great pride—humility in the wake of those great American architects of our history who have stood here before me, pride in the reflection that this forum of legislative debate represents human liberty in the purest form yet devised. Here are centered the hopes, and aspirations, and faith of the entire human race.[5]

***Refer to the Occasion***   A reference to the occasion could allude to the event of your speech:

> We are gathered here today, as we are on every Tuesday and Thursday at this time, to examine human communication  ..

It also might be a reference to the date:

> On this date, just five years ago, the campus computer center was established, dedicated to the proposition that all students should have access to state-of-the-art computers.

It could also be a reference to a particular holiday, anniversary, or commemoration:

> I know we're all looking forward to our Memorial Day holiday this weekend, the cookouts and family gatherings. But let's not forget why we observe this holiday . . .

The occasion doesn't have to be a particular holiday or anniversary. Sometimes you need to identify the occasion for your audience, to let them know that the times are significant in some way that they might not be familiar with.

***Refer to Something Familiar to the Audience***   There's an old rule about human interest: People are attracted to something that is different when it is surrounded by that which is familiar, and they are attracted to something familiar when it is surrounded by that which is different. The technique of referring to something familiar to the audience is especially effective if you are discussing a topic that might seem new or strange to them. This is the technique that Tiffany Meyer, a student at Oregon State University, used in her speech entitled "Damp Housing."

> Surrounded as we are by this beautiful architecture, and the luxurious comfort of this campus, it may be very difficult to imagine that six blocks away living conditions may rival those of some Third World countries.[6]

There are many other ways to take advantage of this technique. You can refer to a current event that would be prominent in audience consciousness; you can refer to a well-known historical event, a proverb, a work of literature, a poem, a story, a song lyric, a line from a recent or well-known television program or advertisement, or a famous movie line.

***Cite a Startling Fact or Opinion***   Jen Siebels, a student at Berry College in Georgia, used this technique in her speech entitled "AZT: The 'Magic Bullet' That Missed":

> It has claimed more lives than the Gulf, Korean, and Vietnam wars combined. According to a 1994 Centers for Disease Control report, AIDS has become the third leading cause of death for Americans between the ages of 25 and 44, and the sixth leading killer of 15- to 24-year-olds. But it seems that the treatment is worse than the disease. According to the April 18, 1994 *Newsweek,* a killer that is even more dangerous than the AIDS syndrome is the supposed "miracle drug" to treat it—AZT. *Newsweek* reports that the only long-term study conducted on AZT indicates that *patients who take it are more likely to die than if they take nothing at all.* With this in mind, it is important for us to realize that we don't have to be radical members of ACT UP in order to take reasonable action against a problem we all share.[7]

Another way to use this technique is to begin with a strongly worded opinion that you will then back up with evidence. Robert A. Plane, president of Wells College in Aurora, New York, began his address to the Women's Leadership Institute of Wells College this way:

> The real cause of many of today's social problems is a lack of shared values. We would not have lawlessness, corruption, violence, crime, child neglect, and many other maladies if we had a true sense of community. But we can't have a sense of community except by having a sense of shared values.[8]

This technique works best when your opinion concerns a profound thought or universal truth that you truly *can* back up.

***Ask a Question***   A rhetorical question is one that is designed to make the audience respond mentally, to think rather than to answer out loud. Eric Wolff of Concordia College in Minnesota asked three rhetorical questions in the introduction of his speech on flood insurance:

> If someone were to lose thousands of dollars gambling on horse races, would you want your tax dollars to bail them out? Probably not. What if they lost those thousands of dollars without having any knowledge they were even gambling? What if I told you sooner or later you might find yourself or someone you know in a similar predicament?[9]

Rhetorical questions can be easy to misuse. You should make sure, for example, that they are interesting and provocative. In the example above, the speaker didn't ask, "How many of you have thought about flood insurance?" because most of his audience probably hadn't, and didn't care to. Instead, he found a more interesting question that still related to his topic.

***Tell an Anecdote***   A personal story perks up audience interest because it shows the human side of what might otherwise be dry, boring information. Your opening anecdote doesn't have to be lighthearted. Avril Johnson, a student at Clackamas College in Oregon, began her speech on the dangers of air guns like this:

> I want to tell you a true story about two boys named Chris and Mike. Almost three years ago, when the boys were both ten, they were enjoying an ideal spring vacation. The weather was great and their days had been filled with activities that included catching frogs, building forts, and exploring the nearby woods. At night they traded off sleeping at each other's house. One morning, when they were both at Mike's, they got up early, got out some BB guns, and decided to do some target practicing. After shooting at some cans, Mike thought his gun was empty. So in jest, he pointed the gun at Chris and fired. The air-powered gun shot a BB with such force that it blew out Chris's cornea and left the BB embedded in the membrane between the eye and the brain. Chris was rushed to the emergency room. He had two surgeries in three days. He spent ten days in the hospital and two months recovering. He was then able to see only light and blur out of the injured eye. I know the details of this case because I am Chris's mother. I found out that his injury was not unusual.[10]

***Use a Quotation***   As we mentioned in the chapter on supporting material, quotations sometimes have a precise, memorable wording that would be difficult for you to say as well. Also, they allow you to borrow from the credibility of the quoted source.

Not all introductory quotations have to come from historic or literary figures. Sometimes you can use the words of a contemporary who is well known to your audience. This is what John J. McGrath, the director of communications for Argonne National Laboratory, did when he addressed a group of Chicago executives:

> "There are many excellent speakers in the United States. There also are many business executives. Apparently, the policy is not to intermingle the two."
>     Those are the words of Norman Augustine, chairman and CEO of Martin Marietta Corporation. I've known Norm Augustine for more than a decade. He is that rarest of creatures—an American chief executive who speaks common English, and speaks it well . . . even in public.[11]

***Tell a Joke***   If you happen to know or can find a joke that is appropriate to your subject and occasion, it can help you capture audience interest. President Clinton, speaking before the American Society of Newspaper Editors, used a joke as an introductory technique:

I was talking to a friend of mine the other day who said, "Well, in the '94 election we discovered the limits of liberalism, and now we're about to discover the limits of conservatism." And it put me in mind of a story I once heard about the late Huey Long, who, when he was governor and he was preaching his share-the-wealth plan, was out in the country one day at a little country crossroads. And he had all the people gathered up. And he was going on about how the people were being plundered by the organized wealthy interests in Louisiana.

And he saw a guy out in the crowd that he knew and he said, "Brother Jones, if you had three Cadillacs, wouldn't you give up one of them so we could gather up the kids and take them to school during the week and take them to church on the weekend?" Jones said, "Sure, I would." Huey Long said, "And if you had $3 million, wouldn't you give up just a million of it so we could put a roof over somebody's head and make sure everybody had food to eat?" Jones said, "Well, of course, I would." Long said, "And if you had three hogs—" Jones said, "Wait a minute, Governor, I've got three hogs."

Anyway, that's the limits of liberalism. Now we're about to discover the limits of conservatism.[12]

It is important to note that Clinton's joke was appropriate to the audience as well as to the topic, to the occasion, and to him as a speaker. If you use this device, remember that it's also important that the joke be funny and you know how to tell it; try it out with friends and family members before you use it on the audience. The hows and whys of humor will be dealt with in more depth in Chapter 15.

### Preview the Central Idea

After you capture the attention of the audience, an effective introduction will almost always state the speaker's central idea. As you will remember from Chapter 4, the central idea is a statement of the one idea that you want your audience to remember after they have forgotten everything else you had to say. Giving your audience a sense of the "big idea" gives them a cognitive framework to use as they organize your ideas in a way that will be comprehensible to them.

Sometimes the statement of your central idea will be straightforward:

▼ If you are going to buy a new computer this year, you should buy one that is capable of image scanning and digital photography.

▼ We live in an age in which federal government power threatens the rights of individuals.

▼ _____ is one of the most important issues facing us today.

Other times, your statement of your central idea might be more elaborate. Here's how Edwin Artzt, chairman of the board and chief executive of the Procter & Gamble Company, began his speech on the future of advertising before the American Association of Advertising Agencies:

> I'm honored to be here. My first job, before joining Procter & Gamble 41 years ago, was as an apprentice account manager in a Los Angeles advertising agency. If my first boss and mentor, Grace Glasser, were alive and here today, she would be as proud as I am—and she would probably be saying, "Get to the point, Ed. We have work to do."
>
> So, here's my point: The advertising business may be heading for trouble—or it may be heading for a new age of glory. Believe it or not, the direction—up or down—is in our hands.
>
> The reason: Our most important advertising medium—television—is about to change big time, and we have one whale of a stake in these changes.[13]

Although elaborate, Artzt's introduction made clear his central idea: that the direction advertising takes is in the hands of his listeners.

You might not want to refer directly to your central point in your introduction. Your reasons might be based on a plan calling for suspense, humorous effect, or stalling for time to win over a hostile audience. In that case, you might preview only your main points.

### Preview the Main Points

After the presentation of the central idea gives your audience a framework for your ideas, the preview of your main points begins to structure those ideas. Sometimes your preview of main points will be straightforward:

> I have three points to discuss: They are _____, _____, and _____.

Other times, your main points will be previewed more artistically. Amy Sjolander, a student at the University of Wisconsin–Eau Claire, previewed the main points of her speech on "The Disintegration of the American Jury System" this way:

> In order to understand the disintegration of this vital part of our legal system, we must initially explore the problems created by an increasing number of absent jurors. Next, we will uncover a variety of causes that perpetuate this legal dilemma. And finally, we'll outline specific steps we all must take to restore our jury system and protect our right to a fair trial.[14]

Molly Lovell, a student at the University of Florida, previewed her main points as follows when speaking on the issue of the abandonment of elderly people by their families:

> All too often caregivers, unable to cope with their situation any longer, abandon their loved ones for good. This is one of the nation's fastest

growing problems today. This is known as "granny-dumping." Today, we are going to discuss just what exactly granny-dumping is, its impact on our society, and finally, we will explore some possible solutions to help alleviate this quickly growing problem.[15]

## Set the Mood and Tone of the Speech

A speech could be said to have both atmosphere and attitude, and the introduction is the place to establish both these qualities. When Lukas Foss, composer-in-residence at Boston University School for the Arts, gave a lecture to the college community on the creative process, he wanted to establish a casual atmosphere for his remarks. He entitled his lecture "A Twentieth-Century Composer's Confessions," and began this way:

> What do I intend to confess? Sins, virtues? No, I will confess my fears—a composer's fears—and personal experiences. Since confessions are usually spontaneous, improvised, I do not feel obliged to organize my thoughts as neatly as I would had I decided on a more learned, more musicological title, like "studies" or "analysis" of the creative process.[16]

Katherine Graham, when she was the chairperson of the board of the Washington Post Company, addressed a group of businessmen and their wives in this way:

> I am delighted to be here. It is a privilege to address you. And I am especially glad the rules have been bent for tonight, allowing so many of you to bring along your husbands. I think it's nice for them to get out once in a while and see how the other half lives. Gentlemen, we welcome you.[17]

This was actually an inside joke. In spite of the fact that Graham was speaking that day on a serious topic, she began her speech this way because she was speaking before an all-male organization. The only women in the audience were the members' wives. Mrs. Graham felt it necessary to put her audience members at ease by joking with them about women's traditional role in society. By beginning in this manner, she assured the men that she would not berate them for the sexist bylaws of their organization (even though she didn't agree with them). She also showed them that she was going to approach her topic with wit and intelligence. Thus, she set the mood and tone for her entire speech. Imagine how different that mood and tone would have been if she had begun this way:

> Before I start today, I would just like to say that I would never have accepted your invitation to speak here had I known that your organization does not accept women as members. Just where do you Cro-Magnons get off, excluding more than half the human race from your little club?

## Establish Credibility and Goodwill

Closely related to the idea of establishing the mood and tone of the speech is the idea of establishing credibility and goodwill. Your introduction is your first chance both to demonstrate that you know what you are talking about, and to show the audience members that you have their best interests at heart.

To establish credibility, you tell about yourself, your qualifications, or your interest in the topic. You might tell about the research that you've done or some important experience that qualifies you to speak on your subject. Richard Lidstad, the vice-president of human resources for 3M Corporation, began his speech before the School of Management at the University of Minnesota like this:

> I was asked to talk to you today because I have always felt a strong, personal link to the University of Minnesota. My bachelor of science in business degree was from the University, more years ago than I'd like to remember. My relationship with the University has been strengthened over the last few years, partly because I have been a part of the Executive Mentoring Program for MBA students . . .[18]

Maureen Wilson, a student at Northern State University in South Dakota, found a way to establish her credibility and grab her audience's attention at the same time. This is the way she began her speech on virtual reality:

> I've seen Mel Gibson naked.
>     And not only did I see him in the raw, he also touched me. Impossible, you say. Not with virtual reality.[19]

To establish goodwill, you demonstrate that you appreciate the audience, that you have their best interests at heart. This is the way Steve Sax, the professional baseball player, established his goodwill when he spoke before the annual awards banquet of the Sacramento County Sheriff's Department:

> Thank you very much, Sheriff Craig, and good evening everyone. It's great to be here with you tonight to honor those who have brought honor to the uniform. I also appreciate the opportunity to speak with you, because I have some strong personal beliefs relating to crime that I'm sure many of you share with me.
>     I have a historical perspective on crime fighting; that is, I can remember when I was a kid, I wanted to be a cop when I grew up. Today, I realize that desire was rooted in more than just a career ambition; it reflected the values of that time as well.[20]

For an object lesson in establishing goodwill, listen to any successful politician. For example, here is the way Senator Bob Dole began his speech in Topeka, Kansas, in which he announced his 1995 candidacy for president:

Good morning, friends, and I thank you for that tremendous welcome. It's great to be in Kansas. Of course, I'm not the first Kansan to say, "There's no place like home." But for me, the words have special meaning. Wherever I have traveled in this life, I have never forgotten where I came from—or where I go home to.

Whatever lessons I have applied in public life were first learned here, in the capitol behind us. These days I spend much of my time in another capitol. You see many things from atop the hill in Washington where I work—but you can see America from here.[21]

### Demonstrate the Importance of Your Topic

Your introduction tells your audience why they should listen to the rest of your speech. An integral part of that introduction, therefore, is establishing the importance of the topic. For example, Amy Andrews-Hendrickson, a student at Eastern Michigan University, began her speech on Gulf War Syndrome this way:

Prior to serving his country during the Gulf War, Keith Payne was an average, healthy 22-year-old. The August 19 issue of the *Phoenix Gazette* reports that today he is essentially a prisoner in his own home. He suffers from a disorder called Chemical Hypersensitivity, which allows something as innocent as the smell of perfume to trigger violent reactions of vomiting, rashes, and memory loss. Keith is one of nearly 11,000 Persian Gulf War veterans who suffer from a strange variety of ailments collectively dubbed "Gulf War Syndrome."

This problem is of particular importance, as Steve Robertson, the legislative director of the American Legion, explains, because by denying these veterans access to appropriate medical care and disability pay, the government not only harms veterans, it undermines the military's ability to recruit and retain quality personnel.[22]

Your audience will listen to you more carefully if your

speech is important to them as individuals. That's one reason, as we mentioned earlier, that a direct reference to your audience is a great attention-getter. Based on your audience analysis, you should state directly *why* your topic is of importance to your audience. This importance should be related as closely as possible to their specific needs at that specific time. When Maria Ciach, a student at West Chester University in Pennsylvania, spoke about Hepatitis B, she related the importance of her topic directly to her college-student audience:

> The *Journal of the American Medical Association* reports that over 300,000 people between the ages of 18 and 39 will contract life-threatening cases of Hepatitis B each year. Even more frightening, the American College Health Association reveals that Hepatitis B has now reached near-epidemic proportions in colleges and universities across the country.
>
> Every college student in America is in the highest risk group in the nation and thousands of us will die each year.[23]

## Developing Introductions

### Plan the Introduction After the Body

There are many reasons to plan your introduction last, after the structure and content of the body of your speech have been well thought out. First, you have to know what your central idea is before you know how to introduce it, and you have to know what your main points are before you can preview them. But perhaps the main reason you will want to plan your introduction last is you will want to sift through all the supporting material you have uncovered to use your best attention-getting device in your introduction. Notice the device used by Laial Dahr, a student at Eastern Michigan University, in her speech entitled "Schools: Learning Zone or Battle Zone?" She had discovered a striking analogy in her research, and, in her opinion, it was her best attention-getting device. She began her speech like this:

> In 1940, some of the top-rated disciplinary problems faced by public school teachers were:

▼ talking out of turn,

▼ chewing gum in class, and

▼ running in the halls.

In 1990, this same question produced a different breed of problems:

▼ drug and alcohol abuse,

▼ suicide, and

▼ robbery.

If Laial had planned her introduction earlier, this striking piece of evidence might have wound up buried in the body of the speech, where it would have been less effective. You also might want to place some of your strongest ideas and research in your introduction. Laial continued her introduction like this:

> And as a result of these more violent problems, students have found more violent methods of solving them. In today's society it's become an all too common alternative to just aim and shoot. According to Senator Chris Dodd, as reported on February 3, 1994, by the Associated Press, almost three million crimes occur in or near U.S. schools each year—one every 10 seconds. "Each day more than 160,000 students skip school out of fear," notes the *USA Today* Weekend Edition, August 13–15, 1993.[24]

### Strive for Unity

Your introduction will probably comprise less than 25 percent of your speech, but that 25 percent is an integral part of the speech unit. Striving for unity means attempting, throughout your speech, to use only material that is directly related to your topic. Your instinct might be to use an unrelated attention-grabbing gimmick in your introduction, possibly because you are used to that technique in mediated messages. Media writing texts admit that television commercials use beautiful women and attractive men as well as "cute children, dogs, cats, and other intriguing animals" to catch our attention. These texts admit that these devices "sometimes seem to have little relevance to the product being advertised."[25]

Edgar Willis and Camille D'Arienzo, in their book *Writing Scripts for Television, Radio, and Film,* offer hope for the public speaker when they point out, "With so many special devices being used to gain attention these days, a single, unadorned voice may have the quality of unusualness that makes us listen."[26] In public speaking, that unadorned voice has to introduce the speech with information that is directly related to the rest of the speech. No matter which device you use to begin your speech, it must be an integral part—part of the "unit"—of your speech. It's bad form, and corny, to yell "SEX" and then say, "Now that I've got your attention . . ."

### ⬤ THE CONCLUSION

▼ All's well that ends well.

Shakespeare

The conclusion, like the introduction, is an especially important part of your speech. Your audience will have a tendency to listen carefully as your speech draws to a close; they will also have a tendency to consider what you say at the end of your speech as important. The conclusion has three primary functions: to review the central idea, to review the main points, and to provide a sense of closure.

## Review the Central Idea

You can review your central idea either through direct repetition or by paraphrasing it. Either way, your conclusion should include a short summary statement. Notice the way Professor D. Stanley Eitzen wrapped up a speech on the causes of violent crime:

> My premise is this: Everyone needs a dream. Without a dream, we become apathetic. Without a dream, we become fatalistic. Without a dream, and the hope of attaining it, society becomes our enemy. Many young people act in antisocial ways because they have lost their dream. These troubled and troublesome people are society's creations because we have not given them the opportunity to achieve their dreams—instead society has structured the situation so that they will fail. Until they feel that they have a stake in society, they will fail, and so will we.[27]

Professor Eitzen left no doubt about his central idea: that many young people act in antisocial ways because they have no dreams to aspire to. Newton Minow, speaking before a conference on improving the lives of children, spoke about how improving children's television would help. Some thirty years earlier, Minow had coined the phrase "vast wasteland" to describe television programming, and his central idea for his current speech was that we should begin to improve children's programming now, even though it's a huge job and will never be perfect. He ended his speech like this:

> President Kennedy told a story a week before he was killed, a story I have never forgotten. The story was about French Marshal Lyautey, who walked one morning through his garden with his gardener. He stopped at a certain point and asked the gardener to plant a tree there the next morning. The gardener said, "But the tree will not bloom for one hundred years." The marshal looked at the gardener and replied, "In that case, you had better plant it this afternoon."[28]

Minow had served on the Federal Communications Commission under President Kennedy, so his anecdote had a special resonance. It not only summarized his main idea, it helped the audience remember it. You can use any of the attention-getters suggested for the introduction to make the statement of your central idea memorable. In fact, one kind of effective closing is to refer to the attention-getter you used in your introduction and remind your audience how it applies to your central idea. Sonya Dehn, a student at South Dakota State University, began her speech on vaccine-preventable diseases with the story of Hector Lopez, a

▼ Some speakers need no introductions; what they need is conclusions.

Anonymous

little boy who had died of measles. In her conclusion, she referred to her introduction:

> In recent years, this nation has seen a resurgence of vaccine-preventable disease, as the measles epidemic demonstrates. Considering that we rank below Third World nations in the immunization of preschoolers, it is hardly surprising that children like Hector Lopez are dying. What is shocking, however, is the complacency with which we have accepted it.[29]

Like the introduction, you can use any type of effective supporting material in your conclusion to help your audience remember your central idea. Many speakers look for an effective quotation. U.S. Secretary of Defense William Perry, when he spoke to the students and faculty at Kansas State University about U.S. policy toward the war-torn nation of Bosnia, concluded his speech like this:

> I have shared with you today the consequences of alternative policy options in Bosnia. The truth, as I said, is unpalatable. It is, nonetheless, important to understand the truth. During the Second World War Winston Churchill once said, "Men occasionally stumble over the truth, but most pick themselves up and hurry away without being affected by it." I have tried today to make you stumble over the truth about Bosnia, and I hope that you will be affected by it. Thank you.[30]

Another device to assist the audience in remembering your central idea is to wind up with some type of memorable wording. This might be in the form of a carefully worded expression or a play on words. This was the device General Douglas MacArthur used when he said, "Old soldiers never die; they just fade away." Harold W. Stevenson, a professor of psychology at the University of Michigan, used memorable wording in the conclusion to his remarks on how self-esteem is over-stressed in American education. His final words were:

> Feeling good is fine; it is even better when we have something to feel good about.[31]

### Summarize the Main Points

▼ The first duty of a lecturer: to hand you after an hour's discourse a nugget of pure truth to wrap up between the pages of your notebooks and keep on your mantelpiece forever.

Virginia Woolf

Most speech teachers will ask their students to summarize their main points in their conclusion. Even when speaking outside the classroom, however, it is often appropriate to review your main points. This is especially true when a list of those points will help the audience remember your central idea, or their role in bringing a particular solution to fruition. Reviewing your main points can be done directly:

> I made three main points about _____ today. They are . . .

Sometimes, the points are summarized in a less obvious way. Katherine Graham, the publisher of the *Washington Post,* concluded her speech on press responsibilities like this:

So instead of seeking flat and absolute answers to the kinds of problems I have discussed tonight, what we should be trying to foster is respect for one another's conception of where duty lies, and understanding of the real worlds in which we try to do our best. And we should be hoping for the energy and sense to keep on arguing and questioning, because there is no better sign that our society is still healthy and strong.[32]

Mrs. Graham had posed three questions in her introduction. She dealt with those questions in her speech and reminded her audience, in her conclusion, that she had answered the questions.

| PREVIEW | REVIEW |
|---|---|
| 1. To whom is the press responsible? | 1. To its own conception of where its duty lies. |
| 2. What is the press responsible for? | 2. For doing its best in the "real world." |
| 3. How responsible has the press been? | 3. It has done its best. |

Most speech teachers want their students to summarize their main points in a direct, straightforward way. Jill Dineen, a student at Solano Community College in California, reviewed the main points of her speech on financial aid fraud this way:

> Today, we have taken a brief look at the complexities of financial aid fraud, and how it affects all of us as students, teachers, and taxpaying citizens, by first looking at the problems of financial aid fraud, and the two major drains on the system: that of trade schools, and then that of colleges and universities. Finally, we've examined the solutions to this problem, both through our legislature, as well as through personal protection . . .[33]

## Provide Closure

Another function of the conclusion is to provide closure for the audience—in other words, to signal that the speech is coming to an end. Closure is provided, in part, by signposts such as these:

| | |
|---|---|
| In summary, | To sum up, |
| In conclusion, | In the final analysis, |
| To wrap things up, | In closing, |

When you provide closure, you give your audience the sense that your speech is now a unit in itself, with a beginning, middle, and end. One effective way to provide closure, therefore, is to return to the theme of your introduction. To do so, you could use the same device to close the speech that was used to gain attention. If you asked a question, you could refer to that question again; if you told an anecdote, you could add to it; if you began with a quotation, you could remind your audience about it. Carrie

▼ Great is the art of beginning, but greater the art is of ending; Many a poem is marred by a superfluous verse.

Henry Wadsworth Longfellow

▼ There is endless merit in one's knowing when to have done.

Carlyle

Clarke, a student at Southern Utah University, began her speech on emergency room physicians with the following analogy:

> When I flip this coin, I have a 50-50 chance of getting heads. You have the same odds of getting a qualified physician in an emergency room.[34]

Carrie ended her speech with the same device:

> Don't risk your life to the same odds as a flip of a coin.[35]

You could also provide a sense of closure by ending with an appeal for action. This is what Adrienne Hallett, a student at the University of Iowa, did in the conclusion of her speech entitled "Dying in Your Sleep":

> Today we've explored the national epidemic of drowsy driving, the people killed because of our lack of awareness and what we can do to protect ourselves. Unlike many problems today, drowsy driving has no quick fix. We have the sole responsibility for this problem because the power lies in our hands to change it. You wouldn't knowingly climb into a car with a drunk driver. Don't make the same mistake with a drowsy one.[36]

Other speakers take their call for action a step further and end their speeches with a challenge. Scott Madison, a student at Morgan State University in Baltimore, did this in his speech on child labor:

> More than 20,000 children a year in America often work excessive hours, for less than minimum wage, in illegal and unsafe environments. How many more? We can only guess. We can continue to allow our children to be used for the sake of profit or we can speak up against these violations, no matter how small or inconsequential they may seem. No, America is not a Third World nation. So let's make sure that all of our children are treated like first-class citizens.[37]

We will have more to say about this type of conclusion in Chapter 13, on persuasion. We should add only one thought here: Remember that a polite "thank you" is an acceptable part of any conclusion. It should not, however, be a substitute for the entire conclusion.

## Developing Conclusions

### Plan Your Conclusion After the Body

▼ A speech is like a love affair. Any fool can start it, but to end it requires considerable skill.

Lord Mancroft

Like your introduction, you plan your conclusion after you have planned the body of your speech. You have to finish planning the body of your speech before you can summarize it, and you have to know what your "residual message" (the message you want your audience to remember) is before you can figure out how to help them remember it.

Planning your conclusion after the body of your speech will also enable you to find and use the best closing device. Whereas the opening device used in your introduction presents the possibilities of the main idea, a closing device summarizes that main idea. While an opening device assumes that more explanation is to follow, the closing idea assumes that no more will be said about it within the speech itself.

### General Guidelines

Your final remarks are important because they are the last words your audience will hear from you in the speech. You can make them most effective by avoiding the following mistakes:

*Don't End Abruptly or Ramble*   Make sure that your conclusion accomplishes everything it is supposed to accomplish. Your conclusion will be shorter than your introduction—perhaps only 10 percent of the content of your speech—but develop it fully. It's jarring to the audience to hear a sudden "Well, I guess that's about all I wanted to say . . ."

On the other hand, don't ramble either. Prepare a definite conclusion, one that covers all the functions discussed in this chapter, but make it as succinct as possible.

*Don't Introduce New Points*   The worst kind of rambling is "Oh, yes, and something I forgot to mention is . . ."

*Don't Apologize*   Don't say, "I'm sorry I couldn't tell you more about this" or "I'm sorry I didn't have more time to research this subject" or any of those sad songs. They will only highlight the possible weaknesses of your speech, and there's a good chance those weaknesses were far more apparent to you than to your audience. Instead, it is best to end strong.

▼ Remorse for what is done is useless.

Philo

##  SAMPLE SPEECH

The sample speech for this chapter was presented by Donald McPartland, a student at Emerson College in Boston.[38] The introduction comprises the first three paragraphs of Donald's speech. Notice how the first paragraph catches your attention. The second paragraph provides a statement of the central idea and establishes the importance of his topic. The third paragraph previews the main points of the speech. He then goes on to develop these points (paragraphs 4–25). His conclusion begins in paragraph 26, in which he reviews his main points. His device to aid audience memory is contained in paragraph 27.

## ⬤ FACELESS ENEMIES

Donald McPartland

Emerson College

1 They wait patiently beneath the surface of the earth, virtually unde-tectable. They sit motionless in utter silence for years at a time, yet in an instant can claim the life of any living being that crosses their path. They receive almost no media attention, and yet they number over 100 million and can be found in every corner of the globe.

2 They are the military land mines that lie scattered throughout a world plagued by war. Sadly, the United States is responsible for the production and distribution of a large number of these merciless killers. Unfortunately, we are just beginning to realize that these weapons often outlive the hostil-ities they are meant to serve. Unless the United States leads the effort to discover and disarm these abandoned explosives, and ultimately prohibit their very production, tens of thousands of innocent people will be killed or maimed within the next few years alone. Being the sole remaining super-power, the United States must set a precedent for other nations to follow.

3 To understand the severity of this dilemma, I will first explain how ex-traordinarily far-reaching the problem of land mines is, and which coun-tries suffer the greatest as a result. With this understanding, I will un-cover the constant fear and violence encountered by the innocent civilians who live in these regions. Finally, I will explain why we as a nation must help in the effort to remove these invisible weapons, and assure the world this threat will not arise again.

4 The devastation that lies in the wake of military land mines spans nu-merous countries. Land mines were introduced during World War II, in Europe and Africa. To this day many still remain. Combine any of the more than 60 countries including Cambodia, Afghanistan, Angola, Nicaragua, El Salvador, and Vietnam to the list, and the picture becomes frighteningly clear. Most of the wars that were fought in these nations have faded into history, but the mines have been left behind.

5 The United Nations estimates over 100 million mines are deployed throughout the world. Robert Muller, a Vietnam veteran, describes his awakening to the problem in the January 23, 1994, issue of the *New York Times Magazine,* when he explains after visiting Cambodia that: "One out of every 236 people living there was an amputee because of our mines." He concluded, "Land mines are the real weapons of mass destruction."

6 Thousands of mines are deployed each week in the former Yugoslavia. The toll they will take on future generations that had no part in this war will be a harsh reality. Nowhere is the magnitude of the problem more ev-ident than in Angola. The September 6, 1993, issue of *In These Times* re-ports: "There are two mines for every one of Angola's nine million people."

[7] Military leaders are attracted to mines for several reasons. They do not miss. They are unaffected by climate. They do not retreat, and they cost only a few dollars each. Most importantly, they often maim rather than kill their victim. A wounded victim drains resources, slows troops, and destroys morale.

[8] Land mines are divided into two groups—anti-tank mines and anti-personnel mines. Anti-tank mines measure approximately 12 inches in length, and weigh between 16 and 20 pounds. These mines tend to be strategically placed in areas that will disable heavily armored vehicles.

[9] The much more numerous anti-personnel mines may be only a few inches in diameter, and their purpose is to maim or kill the enemy. Oftentimes they are dropped from airplanes or deployed by rockets hundreds at a time. The random nature of their use only adds to the problem of locating and disarming them. Constructed almost entirely of plastic, they have nearly become undetectable to the most sophisticated metal seekers. The majority can be found deployed throughout forests, beaches, and rivers.

[10] Hundreds of ball-bearings and metal cubes make up the insides of a mine. Once detonation occurs from the slightest touch, these fragments shred limbs and take lives.

[11] Which brings me directly to the fear and violence encountered by the innocent civilians who live in these regions. The November 29, 1993, issue of the *New Yorker,* states, "Land mines cause one hundred and fifty casualties a week, most of them civilian."

[12] The vast majority of individuals affected by the use of these weapons are civilians. Farmers that attempt to harvest their crops come into contact with mines instead. Children that run and play anywhere other than beside their homes are often found wounded and bleeding in nearby fields.

[13] These faceless enemies offer a never-ending sense of fear. The January 23, 1994, issue of the *New York Times Magazine* acknowledges, "Anti-personnel mines are widely considered the cruelest and least discriminating weapon of war, maiming and killing up to 100,000 a year, 30 to 40 percent of whom are women and children."

[14] Mines cannot be aimed, nor can they cease fire if an innocent presence enters the battlefield. With just a few pounds of pressure, the mine will destroy anything that randomly steps within its territory.

[15] Land mines are not strewn about by the hand of some barbaric monster. All of the world's industrialized nations possess millions of them. Most of these nations have used their stockpiles as well. The United States is no exception. From Europe, to Cambodia, to Vietnam, to Nicaragua, the United States has left its deadly calling card for future generations to blindly encounter.

[16] Senator Patrick Leahy of Vermont states in the November 29, 1993, issue of the *New Yorker,* "I wonder how many people realize that all the deaths from chemical, biological, even nuclear weapons are only a

fraction of the number of people who have been killed or maimed by land mines."

[17] This disturbing yet undeniable fact leads me to why the United States has a moral obligation to aid in the removal of the leftover mines, and more importantly, to push for an international ban.

[18] Given the resources and manpower, any country would be able to slowly yet effectively rid its nation of land mines. Specially trained mine re-moval experts, armed with ultra-sensitive detectors, can clear any given field. Sadly, most of the countries riddled with mines cannot afford such expertise.

[19] Rae McGrath, a mine clearance expert, explains in the September 6, 1993, edition of *In These Times* that "most mined countries like Cambodia may require a decade of work to clear the most important areas—that is, if the funds were available to do it. It's basically funds that limit what we do." A mine that costs a few dollars to buy and bury may cost hundreds of dollars to remove.

[20] The United States and United Nations need to demonstrate to the international community that funds can and will be made available. The United States spends hundreds of billions of dollars each year ensuring its ability to take the greatest amount of lives in the quickest amount of time. If it took even a fraction of that amount, and spent it on saving these lives, the message would be clear: that we will stand responsible for the death and destruction we leave behind.

[21] The United States set a resounding precedent in 1993 when our nation passed a three-year moratorium on the sale, transfer, and export of personnel mines. Unfortunately, the moratorium does not include anti-tank mines, and it has no effect upon other nations. What is needed is an international ban.

[22] The February, 1993, edition of the *World Press Review* concludes, "What is required is an outright international prohibition on the use and manufacture of land mines, much like the measure that outlawed poison gas in 1925." It continues to state, "Although such a prohibition probably would not be completely effective, it would help to insure that any nation or guerrilla force that violated it would be stigmatized."

[23] One of the greatest obstacles preventing action is the lack of awareness within the American public. The United States has been blessed with a history untouched by land mines. Apparently, our cushion of safety has blinded us from seeing the destruction we have left for others.

[24] So we come to the ever-important question of what you and I can do about this tragedy. We can spread the word. Whether we choose to write an editorial to our local paper, or simply mention this situation at the family dinner table, the word needs to be spread. The more our nation becomes informed, the quicker this will move to the front of our agenda. That's the very least I ask of you.

[25] For those of us who wish to propel this issue with a little more force, however, we can contact any of the various groups that have joined forces

to see that our nation takes action. By supporting Human Rights Watch, Physicians for Human Rights in America, Handicapped International in France, and the Mines Advisory Group in England, we can strengthen the movement. These organizations are pitted against powerful industrial lobbyists, but if we help to uncover the saddening truth, the scales will be tipped in our favor.

[26] Understanding the facts surrounding this issue, I hope it is clear why I first explained how far-reaching the problem of land mines is. With that understanding I was able to uncover the constant fear and violence experienced by the innocent civilians who live in these regions. Finally, now that the saddening facts stand exposed, it should be clear why the United States has a responsibility to aid in the removal of these mines and lead the effort to prohibit their worldwide production.

[27] For now, however, many countries stand paralyzed. The people who walk their fields or step upon their beaches play a sickening game of unknowing roulette. Unfortunately, these people have no choice, and they face not one bullet, but millions.

 ## SUMMARY

The care that media professionals take when producing introductions and conclusions proves that they know how important are the beginning and ending of any message. What is true for media writers in this respect is equally true for public speakers: The introduction and conclusion help the rest of the speech make sense, and they help the speaker to have the desired effect. Listeners form their impressions of a speaker early, and they remember what they hear last.

> ▼ Begin in delight and end in wisdom.
>
> Robert Frost

The functions of the introduction include gaining the audience's attention, previewing the central idea of the speech, previewing the main points, setting the mood and tone of the speech, establishing the speaker's credibility and goodwill, and demonstrating the importance of the topic. Devices for capturing audience attention include referring to the audience, referring to the occasion, referring to something familiar to the audience, citing a startling fact or opinion, asking a rhetorical question, telling an anecdote, using a quotation, or using humor.

Previewing the central idea can be done either directly or in a less straightforward way, but it should leave no doubt in your audience's mind what your speech is all about.

The conclusion, like the introduction, is an especially important part of your speech. Your audience will have a tendency to listen carefully as your speech draws to a close; they will also have a tendency to consider as important what you say at the end of your speech. Because of this, the conclusion has three primary functions: to review the central idea, to review the main points, and to provide a sense of closure.

In the process of speech preparation, you should develop both the introduction and the conclusion after you have developed the body of your speech. Among other advantages, this will enable you to choose the best opening device for your introduction, and the best closing device for your conclusion. When delivering your conclusion, keep in mind the following important "don'ts": don't end abruptly (but don't ramble, either), don't introduce new points, and don't apologize.

You should strive for a sense of unity in your introduction, your conclusion, and your speech overall.

## ▼ EXERCISES

1. Choose a sample speech from *Vital Speeches of the Day* or some other source. With your classmates, form groups of four or five. Ignore the introduction and read about one minute of the speech to your group, starting with the first main point. Then ask the group members what questions and criticisms they have of the speech. Go back and read them the introduction. Analyze: Did the introduction take care of the questions?

2. The use of speech introductions is one thing that separates written from spoken style. To demonstrate this, take an essay from the editorial page of your local newspaper. Write a speech introduction for it.

3. Find a sample speech and analyze the conclusion. Check it against the list of functions discussed in this chapter. Does the conclusion fulfill all these functions? If it misses any, how would you correct it?

# NOTES:

1. The introductory teasers for news programs are also important. See, for example, Glen Cameron, Joan Schleuder, and Esther Thorson, "The Role of News Teasers in Processing TV News and Commercials," *Communication Research* 18 (1991), pp. 667–684. Special Issue: Cognitive Processing of Media.

2. Robert L. Hilliard, *Writing for Television and Radio,* 5th ed. (Belmont, Calif.: Wadsworth, 1991), p. 147.

3. See, for example, Daniel Garvey and William Rivers, *Broadcast Writing* (New York: Longman, 1982), p. 168.

4. Margaret Milner Richardson, "The Role of the Internal Revenue Service," *Vital Speeches of the Day,* March 15, 1995, p. 330.

5. Douglas MacArthur, "Old Soldiers Never Die," *Congressional Record, House,* April 19, 1951, pp. 4123–4125.

6. Tiffany A. Meyer, "Damp Housing," *Winning Orations, 1993* (Interstate Oratorical Association, 1993), p. 90. Tiffany was coached by Denise Krause-Yochum.

7. Jen Siebels, "AZT: The 'Magic Bullet' That Missed," *Winning Orations, 1994* (Interstate Oratorical Association, 1994), p. 20. Jen was coached by Randy Richardson.

8. Robert A. Plane, "The Quest for Shared Values: Higher Education Must Lead Society," *Vital Speeches of the Day,* February 1, 1995, p. 250.

9. Eric B. Wolff, Title Unknown, *Winning Orations, 1994* (Interstate Oratorical Association, 1994), p. 67. Eric was coached by Larry Schnoor and Jeff Hudson.

10. Avril Johnson, "Air Guns: Weapons or Toys," *Winning Orations, 1993* (Interstate Oratorical Association, 1993), p. 87. Avril was coached by Frank Harlow.

11. John J. McGrath, "Sell Your CEO! Winning the Corporate-Image Battle in the '90s," *Vital Speeches of the Day,* May 1, 1995, p. 444.

12. Bill Clinton, "We've Made Good Progress," *Vital Speeches of the Day,* May 1, 1995, p. 418.

13. Edwin Artzt, "The Future of Advertising," *Vital Speeches of the Day,* September 1, 1994, p. 684.

14. Amy Sjolander, "The Disintegration of the American Jury System," *Winning Orations, 1994* (Interstate Oratorical Association, 1994), p. 139. Amy was coached by Tom Glauner.

15. Molly Lovell, "The Dumping Ground for America's Elderly: The Growing Crisis of Elderly Abandonment," *Winning Orations, 1993* (Interstate Oratorical Association, 1993), p. 12. Molly was coached by Kellie Roberts.

16. Lukas Foss, "A Twentieth-Century Composer's Confessions: The Creative Process," *Vital Speeches of the Day,* December 15, 1994, pp. 144–145.

17. Katherine Graham, "The Press and Its Responsibilities," *Vital Speeches of the Day,* April 15, 1976.

18. Richard Lidstad, "The Qualities of Success: Leadership, Diversity, Community Service, and Career Development," *Vital Speeches of the Day,* July 1, 1995, pp. 559–561.

19. Maureen Wilson, "Say "AHA" to Virtual Reality," *Winning Orations, 1992* (Interstate Oratorical Association, 1992), p. 119. Maureen was coached by James Zeman.

20. Steve Sax, "Turning the Corner on Crime," *Vital Speeches of the Day,* April 15, 1995, p. 402.

21. Bob Dole, "Republican Candidate for President," *Vital Speeches of the Day,* May 15, 1995, p. 451.

22. Amy Andrews-Hendrickson, "Lessons Not Learned from History: Gulf War Syndrome," *Winning Orations, 1994* (Interstate Oratorical Association, 1994), p. 64. Amy was coached by Michael Tew.

23. Maria Ciach, "Hepatitis B—What Every College Student Doesn't Know," *Winning Orations, 1994* (Interstate Oratorical Association, 1994), p. 111. Maria was coached by Kevin W. Dean.

24. Laial Dahr, "Schools: Learning Zone or Battle Zone?" *Winning Orations, 1994* (Interstate Oratorical Association, 1994), pp. 61–62. Laial was coached by Michael Tew.

25. Edgar Willis and Camille D'Arienzo, *Writing Scripts for Television, Radio, and Film,* p. 21.

26. Ibid., p. 22.

27. D. Stanley Eitzen, "Violent Crime: Myths, Facts, and Solutions," *Vital Speeches of the Day,* May 15, 1995, p. 472.

28. Newton Minow, "The Communications Act: Our Children Are the Public Interest," *Vital Speeches of the Day,* April 15, 1995, p. 392.

29. Sonya Dehn, "An Ounce of Prevention," *Winning Orations, 1994* (Interstate Oratorical Association, 1994), p. 121. Sonya was coached by Joel Hefling.

30. William Perry, "Bosnia: We Must Stay the Course," *Vital Speeches of the Day,* April 15, 1995, p. 389. Perry delivered this speech as the 100th Landon Lecture at Kansas State University in Manhattan, Kansas, on March 9, 1995.

31. Harold W. Stevenson, "Oscars Made of Tin," *New York Times,* October 11, 1994, p. 21A.

32. Graham, "The Press and Its Responsibilities."

33. Jill Dineen, "The Fiasco of Financial Aid Fraud," *Winning Orations, 1994* (Interstate Oratorical Association, 1994), p. 12. Jill was coached by Gary Dreibelbis.

34. Carrie Clarke, Title Unknown, *Winning Orations, 1995* (Interstate Oratorical Association, 1995). Carrie was coached by Suzanne Larson.

35. Ibid.

36. Adrienne Hallett, "Dying in Your Sleep," *Winning Orations, 1995* (Interstate Oratorical Association, 1995). Adrienne was coached by Celeste DeVore.

37. Scott Madison, "Our First-Class Citizens," *Winning Orations, 1995* (Interstate Oratorical Association, 1995). Scott was coached by J. B. Bury.

38. Donald McPartland, "Faceless Enemies," *Winning Orations, 1994* (Interstate Oratorical Association, 1994), pp. 58–61. Donald was coached by Matt Sobnobsky.

▼ **CHAPTER 10**

# VISUAL AIDS

## ▼ CHAPTER 10 OBJECTIVES

**After reading this chapter, you should understand:**

**1.** The advantages of using visual aids in a speech.

**2.** The types of visual aids available to speakers.

**3.** The methods of displaying visual aids.

**You should be able to:**

**1.** Identify the points in a speech that could benefit from visual support.

**2.** Choose the type of visual aid that best illustrates a point.

**3.** Choose the presentational medium that best displays a visual in a given speaking situation.

## ⊙ VISUAL IMPACT IN THE MEDIA/INFORMATION AGE

The media/information age is a visual age. Television is a part of our lives. Magazines, newspapers, and books are filled with images that are often more powerful than printed words. Given the importance of visual imagery, it's no surprise that visual aids can make a speech more effective in several ways.

### Added Interest

Hearing a message can be interesting, but seeing it illustrated at the same time is even better. Talking about blues music isn't nearly as entertaining as hearing it played. Telling about how U.S. presidents age while in office won't drive the point home as well as comparing pictures of recent presidents at the beginning and end of their terms. Describing the Japanese art of origami may not impress some listeners, but creating beautiful sculptures out of paper probably will.

Besides being interesting in their own right, visuals stimulate an audience whose attention has wandered. Most listeners can follow a speech—even a good one—for only a short time before their thoughts begin to drift. You can prove this for yourself by noting your own level of attention during lectures by your instructors or speeches by fellow students. When the speaker does something besides talking, your interest probably picks up.

### Greater Clarity

Visuals clarify your ideas: In a speech about crime, a graph illustrating the rise in crime can drive the point home better than just talking about the statistics. Demonstrating how to save a choking victim is more helpful

# Calvin and Hobbes      by Bill Watterson

than just describing what to do. Showing the extent of destruction of the world's rain forests on a map is much more likely to get your point across than just describing the problem.

For example, in a speech about rhinoplasty, consider how the diagrams in Figure 10-1 clarify the points being made:[1]

### Increased Credibility

Well-conceived, well-designed visuals can make you more believable as a speaker. In one study, audiences rated speakers who used overhead transparencies during presentations as better prepared, more professional, more persuasive, and more believable than presenters who did not use visual aids.[2] It's easy to see why effective visuals can boost credibility. They show that you are familiar with your topic, and that you care about it.

### More Memorable Points

▼ To see sad sights moves more than hear them told.

Shakespeare

Good visuals help the audience remember important points. One report shows that visual aids are especially effective at helping listeners retain information after words alone have faded from their memory:[3]

| TYPE OF SUPPORTING MATERIAL | RECALL AFTER THREE HOURS | RECALL AFTER THREE DAYS |
| --- | --- | --- |
| Verbal only | 70% | 10% |
| Visual only | 72% | 20% |
| Verbal and visual combined | 85% | 65% |

**FIGURE 10–1 VISUAL CLARIFICATION:**     **POINTS BEING MADE**

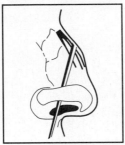

A large nose can be reshaped. The hump can be removed by means of an instrument inserted through the nostril. The excess bone is removed, leaving a more attractive profile.

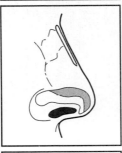

A broad or long nasal tip is narrowed and shortened by sculpting the cartilage around the tip of the nose, shown here by the shaded area. No external incision is needed.

The result is a more pleasant facial appearance. The nose is more attractive and has a natural look in proportion to the face.

Suppose, for example, that you decided to inform your listeners that the space surrounding earth is cluttered by some 7,000 pieces of space debris—including operating and dead satellites, explosion fragments from rocket engines, nuclear reactors, gar-bage bags, and frozen sewage dumped by astronauts. The statistics and examples you cite might be impressive, but actually *showing* your audience a visual representation of the space junk (see Figure 10-2) would drive the point home more clearly and dramatically.[4]

In some cases, visuals make a point memorable by adding human interest and drama that will stay with listeners after your words have faded from their minds. If you were trying to persuade an audience to spay or neuter their dogs and cats, you could hammer home the need by showing photos of adorable puppies and kittens from the local animal shelter, and sadly explain that all these animals had been put to death because no home could be found for them. If you really wanted to drive home the

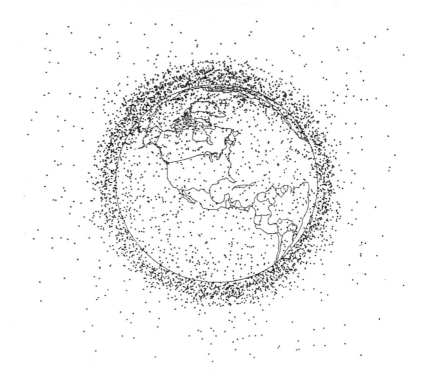

FIGURE 10–2 POINT MADE MEMORABLE: SPACE JUNK

point, you could even show them photos of the corpses of cats and dogs that had been "put to sleep." You might risk spoiling your listeners' day, but you can be sure they would remember your message.

### Help for the Speaker

Besides making the speech more interesting and memorable for your listeners, visuals can make *you,* as a speaker, feel more confident. Since you have created them in advance, there is little risk of surprise. If you know that a chart, model, or photograph will impress your listeners and keep your speech on target, you are likely to feel less nervous.

Visuals can also take away some of the pressure that comes when everyone's eyes are focused on you. One source of nervousness for many speakers is the feeling of standing all alone before an audience. When you display the visual, your listeners' attention is divided between you and the visual, leaving you less in the spotlight.

Visuals can also make it easier to deliver your remarks by serving as a form of speaker's notes, guiding you from point to point. In one respect, visuals are even better than written notes: You can follow them without shifting your attention away from the audience every time you glance at a set of cards or a piece of paper. Suppose, for example, that you wanted to show your classmates that making even small investments now can pay big dividends later. This topic would require explaining plenty of numbers, which could be hard to read from written notes. But by presenting your figures graphically on a series of charts or overhead transparencies, you can cover each point clearly and in the right order by using the visuals to keep you on track.

Of course, not all visual aids will have these benefits. In order to add interest and clarity, increase credibility, and make the speech more memorable, the visual aid has to be carefully prepared and well thought out. Visual aids that are not well conceived and designed can actually work to the detriment of a speech. Consider the visual in Figure 10-3.

You also need to determine which *type* of visual aid would be most beneficial for a particular use.

## ● TYPES OF VISUAL AIDS

The term *visual aid* covers a staggering array of support, including everything from a three-foot-long model of a cockroach to a chart of the Dow-Jones industrial averages since 1929. Choosing the right aid requires you to use critical thinking. You have to carefully consider the point you want to make and the audience to whom you are speaking.

**FIGURE 10–3 CONFUSING VISUAL AID**

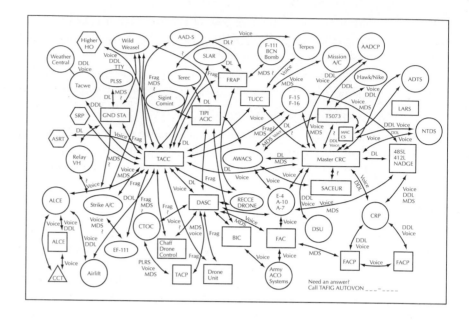

## Objects and Models

Sometimes the best way to explain an object is to show it to your audience. The clearest way to explain the difference between cross-country and downhill skis is to show each kind to your listeners. The best way to illustrate the art of floral arranging is to create arrangements with real flowers. If you want to demonstrate the benefits of a particular type of cellular telephone, the most effective way is to bring one into the classroom and show your audience how it works.

Not all objects are suitable for display in a speech. Some are too small, such as a computer microchip or a "killer bee." Others are too large, such as a nuclear power plant or a redwood tree. Some aren't available: You probably can't produce a medical victim with an unset broken arm to illustrate first aid, for instance. Many objects are downright dangerous or inappropriate for the classroom, such as a vial of crack cocaine or a letter bomb. Some objects haven't yet been created, such as a proposed building; others—a dinosaur, for example—no longer exist. In cases like these, you can still illustrate your point using a *model*—a scale replica of the object you are discussing.

In some cases, models are even better than the real thing, since they let you manipulate an object to make your point. With an anatomical dummy you can remove the heart or lift off the top of the skull—not too practical with a real person!

## Photographs

In many speeches, photographs are essential in illustrating a point. It's difficult to imagine how you could talk about the value of modern art without showing your audience pictures of important paintings. Likewise, if you are describing the impact of photojournalism on public attitudes, you have to show your audience examples of photos that have shaped history.

Even when they aren't absolutely necessary, photographs can make a speech more effective. For example, you could support the argument that beauty contests teach children the wrong values by showing photos of a lineup of six-year-old contestants trying to look provocative as a judge examines them in their skimpy bathing suits. Likewise, in an orientation speech to new freshmen on student services, you could show photographs of the building on campus where each service is located, and then display a picture of each staff member as you describe the person.

Despite their value, photographs need to be used with care. They must be large enough for all members of the audience to see them, and simple enough to show your point without containing too much clutter.

## Diagrams and Maps

*Diagrams* are drawings that show the most important properties of an object. Because they allow you to highlight just the information you are presenting and because they are easy to see, diagrams can often present material better than models or objects. Don't feel intimidated by the professionally drawn diagrams you see in newspapers and books. The ones you are likely to use in a speech can be quite simple   and well within your ability to create. See Figure 10-4 on page 254.

*Maps* are a useful type of diagram. They work most effectively when they are simplified to show only the features you are discussing (see Figure 10-5 on page 254). As with other diagrams, your maps should be simple enough to highlight the features you will discuss in your speech without distracting viewers with unrelated details.

## Word and Number Charts

When you want to emphasize certain ideas or statistics, a *word chart* or *number chart* will tell the story better than talk alone. Charts can also be useful for introducing steps in a process: preparing a recipe, performing first aid, operating a piece of equipment, and so on.

The kind of chart in Figure 10-6 might seem overly simple to a speaker who has spent hours researching and practicing a speech, but the

**FIGURE 10–4 DIAGRAM**

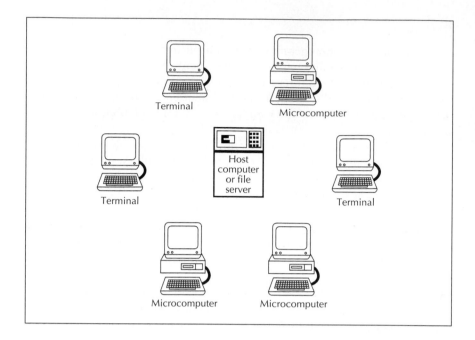

**FIGURE 10–5 MAP**

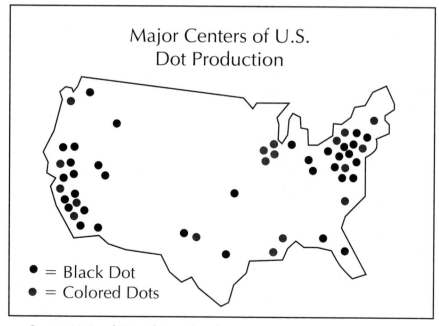

Source: National Dot Advisory Board

FIGURE 10–6 WORD AND
NUMBER CHART

Increasing Violence in Action Films

| | Deaths in Original | Deaths in Sequel |
|---|---|---|
| Die Hard | 15 | 162 |
| Robo Cop | 27 | 58 |
| 48 Hours | 9 | 20 |

information will be a real aid to listeners who aren't as familiar with the subject. It is easy to see how this sort of clarification can help in a speech. Remember that, unlike a book or magazine article, a speech gives listeners only one chance to understand information. They can't ask you to pause while they think about what was just said, and they can't replay a part of the speech they missed the first time around. If you present your ideas in a chart, there will be a better chance that your audience will understand and appreciate them. Another advantage of word and number charts is that they force you to spend more time discussing important material, which gives listeners a better chance to think about it before you move on to your next point.

## Graphs

*Graphs* paint a visual picture of statistical information. They work especially well when you want to explain numbers that are too large or complicated to appreciate when presented in words alone. For example, telling your listeners that tobacco use kills more than seven times as many people as the next greatest cause of death isn't nearly as effective as showing them a *bar graph* like the one in Figure 10-7. Other types of graphs shown in Figure 10-8 can be equally effective. *Column graphs* are similar to bar graphs, but the measures are aligned vertically instead of horizontally. *Pie graphs* (visualized as slices of a circle) show how various items relate to one another as percentages of a whole. *Line graphs* show how one or more items relate over time, and are especially good for showing trends.

## Demonstrations

People themselves can be interesting and effective visual aids. Sometimes a human model—either yourself or a volunteer recruited for that purpose—can illustrate a point better than any drawing or prop. For example,

**FIGURE 10–7 BAR GRAPH**

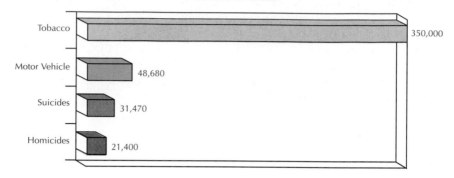

Causes of Death

Tobacco — 350,000
Motor Vehicle — 48,680
Suicides — 31,470
Homicides — 21,400

**FIGURE 10–8 TYPES OF GRAPHS**

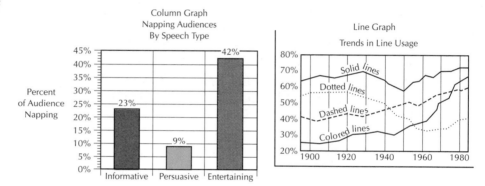

Column Graph
Napping Audiences
By Speech Type

Percent of Audience Napping

Informative — 23%
Persuasive — 9%
Entertaining — 42%

Line Graph
Trends in Line Usage

Solid lines
Dotted lines
Dashed lines
Colored lines

1900 1920 1940 1960 1980

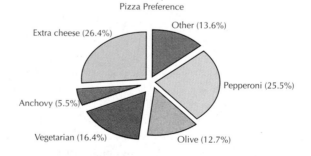

Pie Graph
Pizza Preference

Extra cheese (26.4%)
Other (13.6%)
Pepperoni (25.5%)
Olive (12.7%)
Vegetarian (16.4%)
Anchovy (5.5%)

demonstrations are probably the best way to teach an audience how to stretch before exercising or how to save a choking victim. Besides making a point more clearly, demonstrations can make a speech more interesting. You can be confident that your audience will pay close attention when they see you show how to ride out an earthquake or perform a magic stunt.

Along with the obvious advantages, there are risks involved in using other people as visual aids. The biggest one is choosing a subject whose nervousness or horseplay upstages you and your topic. A subject who giggles or fools around during your demonstration is more of a distraction than an asset. It's also important to be sure your helper can perform any requests you make of him or her. A demonstrator who can't juggle even two apples or who forgets the number of the playing card that is part of your trick can turn your speech into a fiasco. It's a good idea to line up and rehearse "volunteers" ahead of time.

## ▼ MEDIA FOR DISPLAYING VISUALS

After you have decided what kind of visual aids to use in your speech, you need to choose the best format to present them to your audience. One lesson we learn from an examination of the age of media is that different media are best for different messages. When presenting a visual aid there are many media at your disposal, and each has its advantages and drawbacks. The right medium can make the difference between success and failure: Even the most spectacular visuals won't impress an audience if they're too small to be seen or don't work in the room where you are speaking.

### Chalkboard

The *chalkboard* is the most familiar visual aid to students, who have seen it used and abused since kindergarten. The board does have its

advantages: You can develop ideas as you go along, adding ideas on the spot and removing them once they've served their purpose. This makes the chalkboard ideal for collecting ideas in a brainstorming session that involves audience responses.

There are other creative uses for chalkboards. Since audiences are used to chalkboards being used for impromptu scribblings, chalk diagrams or charts that have been carefully prepared in advance sometimes grab their interest. For example, you could prepare a blank graph beforehand, and then fill it in as you talk. This could be used to show the growth of a new virus over time, a development that might lose its impact if you showed it all at once on a posterboard.

Despite its advantages, the chalkboard has some serious drawbacks. First, it requires you to be a decent artist, or at least a decent printer. Writing or drawing neatly on the board takes more skill than some novices imagine. Just because your handwriting or sketches look good on paper doesn't guarantee you can recreate them in chalk. Writing words of consistent size in a straight line on a vertical surface—especially while speaking to an audience—takes practice. Also, writing *during* a speech is annoying to some audiences, since it takes time away from your talking and forces you to turn away from the audience.

If you do use the chalkboard despite its limitations, follow this advice:

▼ Whenever possible, sketch out a plan of your visual in advance and follow it as you create the drawing on the board. This will save you from unpleasant surprises like running out of space or hesitating to figure out the best way to present an idea.

▼ Use colored chalk to add interest and emphasize important points. Don't count on chalk being available in the room on your speaking day: Be sure to bring it with you.

▼ Erase chalkboard visuals after you have finished discussing them. Be sure the board is clean at the end of your speech out of courtesy to the next speaker.

## Flip Charts and Posterboards

*Flip charts* are large tablets, usually measuring roughly two by three feet. They mount on an easel so you can display them without using your hands. *Posterboards* are individual pieces of stiff paper stock, and come in a variety of sizes and colors.

A major advantage of both posterboards and flip charts is that you can prepare them in advance. They work well for diagrams, graphs, and charts listing words and numbers. You can spruce up their design by using marking pens in a variety of colors. Like the chalkboard, another advantage of flip charts and posterboards is that you can develop an idea as you go along in a speech by adding words and numbers with a marking pen.

Also like the chalkboard, flip charts and posterboards have drawbacks. Because of their size, they aren't easy to transport to and from a speech. They require some sort of easel or hanger to display. They can be clumsy to manipulate. Finally, they work well only for small and medium-sized audiences. When you are speaking to a group of 25 people or more, the image may be too small to see from the rear of the room.

The following suggestions will make your use of flip charts and posterboards most effective:

▼ Use at least two colors in your design to add interest. You might, for instance, write headings in black and key points in red, or list advantages in green and drawbacks in red.

▼ Use a thick marking pen and write in large characters. Use dark colors—yellows and some pastels are difficult to see.

▼ Use a blank sheet to cover your first visual until you introduce it, and separate each image by a blank sheet so listeners will see only one visual at a time, while you are discussing it.

## Overhead Transparencies

*Overhead transparencies* are acetate sheets, usually the size of a regular piece of typewriter paper, upon which a visual has been created. They are displayed on a screen by an overhead projector. They can be made either by drawing on a blank sheet with special marking pens or by running a pre-drawn image through a photocopy machine onto a transparency master.

Transparencies have many advantages. First, they are easy to make: You work with familiar materials on a regular size piece of paper or film. The finished product is easy to transport: A whole stack of transparencies will fit into a file folder. When projected, transparencies are quite large, making them ideal for larger audiences.

Transparencies give you a way to display images created by media professionals instead of starting from scratch. Books, newspapers, and magazines are full of professionally created images that would be ideal visual aids. You can transform this artwork into overhead transparency masters by following a few simple steps:

1. Cut out or photocopy a piece of artwork that will work as a visual.
2. Use correction tape or fluid to remove any distracting details.
3. Print or type any new information needed to explain the image. If you type, use a computer that can print in large sizes. You can also use rub-on letters available in most bookstores and art supply houses.

**4.** If necessary, use a photocopy machine to enlarge the image to roughly six by eight inches. Clean up any flaws on the enlarged version with tape or fluid.

**5.** Have your local copy shop transfer the image to an overhead transparency.

Like other media, overhead transparencies have their drawbacks. They require a projector, which may not always be available. You may have to turn the lights off, which makes *you* less visible and might give some audience members permission to nap. And sometimes the equipment is impolite enough to break down just when you need it. If you use an overhead projector to display your visuals, follow these guidelines:

▼ Point to the transparency when referring to the visual and not to the screen. This allows you to face the audience.

▼ Use a pencil or pen to point out parts of the transparency. This is less distracting than the shadow of your hand and finger, which can block out a large portion of the visual.

▼ Use a sheet of paper to cover up parts of the transparency you haven't discussed yet. Reveal each point as you come to it. This technique prevents the audience from getting ahead of you.

▼ If possible, turn off the projector light between visuals so the audience won't be distracted by the glare of a blank screen or the image you have finished discussing.

## Slides

When used skillfully, photographic *slides* can add tremendous interest to a presentation. No verbal description can match the impact of seeing the view from a hang glider or the visual pollution of billboards. Slides are easily seen by an entire audience, unlike photographic prints, which are almost always too small to show a group. Slides are also easy to create if you are a decent photographer: Your local photo lab can develop the film quickly, often in an hour. Slides are also easy to edit. You can add, delete, or rearrange them until they suit your needs.

Slides do have their drawbacks. Just like overhead projectors, slide projectors can break down: A burned-out bulb has broken the heart of many a speaker. The lights might have to be turned off, which creates the risk of losing the attention of some listeners who might find the darkness and whir of the projector's fan too lulling to resist.

When you do use slides to illustrate a speech, follow these guidelines for the best results:

▼ Run through your slide program before the speech to make sure the photos are in order and oriented correctly. Upside down, backward, or out-of-focus pictures distract the audience and make you look incompetent.

▼ Try to stand next to the screen while showing slides to keep the audience's attention. Whenever possible, use a remote control to change pictures. When this is not possible, have an assistant change slides for you.

▼ If possible, use a projector that shows a dark screen when no slide is in position. With this kind of equipment you can leave blank spaces in the tray for use when you are not showing pictures, allowing you to speak without competing with your own photos or having to turn the projector off and on. If your machine projects a bright light when a slide is not in place, insert thin cardboard squares the size of slide frames into the slide tray between segments of your show.

## Videotapes

With off-the-air taping and portable camcorders becoming more common, showing videos is an option that many speakers consider. *Videotapes* do have the advantage of showing real-life events in a way that other media can't match. The right videotape can add clarity and impact to a speech. One student dramatized the familiar warning about the possible consequences of not wearing seat belts by showing a videotape of a friend who suffered head injuries because he hadn't buckled up. The healthy, good-looking 20-year-old had suffered brain damage from the collision, and the tape showed him struggling in therapy to stack three simple blocks on top of one another. This real-life look at the consequences of failing to use seat belts startled the audience far more powerfully than any statistics or testimony by experts.

Camcorders can be used to document various events or personal observations and incorporate them into a speech. You could even use one to record a volunteer's demonstration (of a back exercise, for example) and then use it for a slow-motion analysis.[5]

When using videotapes, follow these principles:

▼ Remember that a videotaped message is a mediated message; it cuts down on the human contact that is the primary advantage of public speaking. Don't allow your tape to carry too much of the content of your speech. If you run a tape for more than a minute or so, stop it from time to time to interact with your audience.

▼ Find a television monitor with a screen large enough to be seen by the entire audience. For all but extremely small groups, a 25-inch screen is necessary. For larger audiences, it may be necessary to use two or more monitors.

▼ Make sure the tape is cued to the right spot and the monitor is warmed up and ready to go. Don't run the risk of an embarrassing delay while you figure out why there's no picture or sound.

## Handouts

*Handouts* work best when you want the audience to retain information after your speech is over. Your listeners can keep a copy of instructions, maps, addresses, and phone numbers for reference when the need arises. Handouts are also a good way to give your audience more details about a subject than you want to cover in your speech. For example, if you are describing the summer recreation program in your community, you might describe some of the activities during your speech and then give each person in the group a complete schedule later.

The biggest mistake speakers make with handouts is to circulate them before or during the speech. Giving the audience something to read while you are talking is an invitation to ignore you. A better approach is to promise your listeners that you will be giving them printed information later, and then to distribute the handouts at the end of your speech.

## High-Tech Options

The preceding media are the most commonly used for speech presentations. We should mention, however, at least two high-tech alternatives: computer projection and laser pointers. *Computer projectors* enable you to enlarge a graphic from a computer monitor onto a movie screen. If available, they can be effective for the discussion of any data that are stored in computer files or on the Internet. Computer data of this type can be manipulated during the course of a speech; graphs, for example, can be adapted to demonstrate information that comes from audience members during the speech. Computer projection screens are also the best medium for most discussions of computer hardware, software, services, and techniques. For example, it makes sense to try to obtain computer projection equipment if the topic of your speech is computer animation.

*Laser pointers* project a sharp, concentrated beam of light that can be seen within the image of a slide or any other type of projected image. Laser pointers are extremely effective in focusing the audience's attention where you want it, and they don't leave shadows like other types of pointers.[6]

## ▼ PRINCIPLES OF VISUAL DESIGN AND USE

We have discussed some of the guidelines for the design and use of specific visual aids. It is also useful to keep a few general principles in mind. These principles include purpose, visibility, quantity, quality, avoiding distractions, and integration with speech content.

## Advancing the Speech Purpose

In Chapter 4 and elsewhere, we have stressed the importance of a clear speech purpose. This is also the first principle in the design and use of visuals. You should always have a good reason for using a visual. Ask yourself whether each visual really improves the speech. Will it focus the audience's attention on your subject? Does it make your point more clearly than words alone? Is it more persuasive? Will it help your audience remember your message? If you can't answer "yes" to at least one of these questions, it may be best to skip using the visual.

Even outstanding visuals need to suit the topic of your speech or they shouldn't be used. One student spoke about the United States' proposed manned mission to Mars. Because a friend worked for NASA, the student was able to borrow several large models of satellites and spacecraft used in other space exploration projects. The models were very impressive, but they had nothing to do with the proposed journey to Mars. Their presence in the speech distracted her audience, who asked questions about the satellite models instead of focusing on the Mars expedition.

One final note on advancing the speech purpose: Always keep audience norms and expectations in mind. Do not allow your visual aid to offend your audience. In some cases guns or other weapons (presented as models), pornography, snakes, bloody images, or even illegal items such as alcohol or drugs can be offensive or frightening to audiences. These kinds of visual aids will not advance the speech purpose if they push the limits of audience acceptance.

## Visibility

When considering how large a visual to use, keep the back of your audience in mind. An object or chart that is easy to see at arm's length could be impossible to decipher from the middle or back of the room during your speech. Don't put yourself in the position of saying "I know this is hard to see, but . . ."

Don't be bashful about making words, numbers, and drawings large. If the object you want to show is too small, consider using a large diagram or model. Nobody will complain that your visuals are too easy to see! The best way to find out whether your visual is large enough is to prop it up and walk 20 or 25 feet away from it. If you have to squint or use your imagination to figure out what it says, make it larger.

Besides making the aid large enough to be seen by everyone in the room, be sure to position it so it will be easy to view. If you are displaying models, charts or posterboards, make sure they are placed high enough. Resting a chart in the chalkboard tray, for example, might make it too low.

If you are using an overhead projector, try to move around whenever you show a transparency so that your body won't block the view of some audience members.

## Quantity and Quality of Visuals

Along with the size of your visuals, the number you use is another important consideration. Some speakers make the mistake of assuming that, if a few images are effective, then more will be even better. In fact, several years ago, multimedia/multisensory presentations used slide shows, videos, films, and audio recordings all at once. These shows were sometimes impressive, but, generally, they left people confused. Once you have sketched out all the visuals you could possibly present, think about which ones are most useful and which ones aren't necessary. Then limit the number for greatest impact.

As you read earlier in the chapter, professional-looking visuals have several benefits, but the reverse is also true: Visuals that look like you threw them together on your way to class will lower the worth of your speech.

Computer software is making it easier for even amateurs to create high-quality visuals. With powerful, easy-to-use computers available almost everywhere, even novices can turn out professional-looking graphs and charts. Figure 10-9 illustrates a laboriously hand-drawn visual and two computer-generated alternatives.

Even though good-looking visuals are important, don't make the mistake of putting so much time into developing them that you ignore the other parts of your speech. You might discover effective visuals while you research your speech: a human skeleton from the chiropractor, a parachute from the local skydiving club, or a stuffed animal from a friendly taxidermist.

## Avoiding Distractions

Visuals can become your worst enemy when they draw the audience's attention away from what you are saying. One student chose to illustrate her speech about raising lop-eared rabbits by bringing in two of her own pets, which she left in a cage in front of her as she spoke. To her horror and the audience's amusement, in mid-speech the rabbits began mating. Needless to say, this distraction made it impossible for anyone to pay much attention to the remainder of her talk.

It doesn't take a catastrophe like this to distract listeners. Even exhibits that seem to illustrate a point perfectly can be distractions, sometimes because they are *too* powerful. For example, if the goal of your speech is to show that many scientific experiments torture laboratory

**FIGURE 10-9**

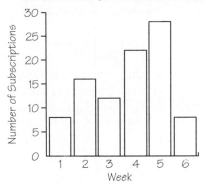

This hand-drawn graph displays information clearly. Visuals like this can be created easily with simple materials such as poster board, a ruler, and felt markers.

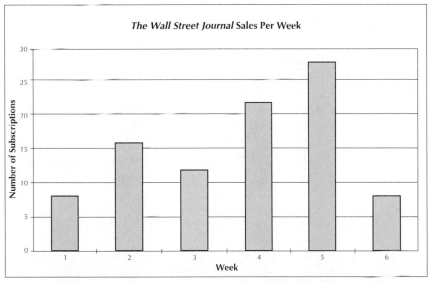

Many basic computer programs can produce charts like this one quickly and easily. This figure was created using a word processing program.

**FIGURE 10-9—CONTINUED**

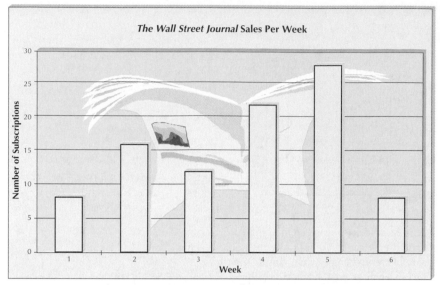

Many computer programs make it easy to produce even more sophisticated visuals. This figure was created using clip art from a desktop publishing program.

animals, you might consider showing graphic photos of electrocuted cats, eyeless rabbits, and baboons with smashed skulls. They *would* support your arguments. On the other hand, the images might be so disturbing that they could upset many of your listeners, or even drive some from the room.[7]

Another potential distraction is talking to your visual aid instead of the audience. Inexperienced speakers often turn their back to the audience and carry on an enthusiastic conversation with their chart or the projection screen. It's easy to understand why you might feel like spending more time talking to visuals than to listeners: They're familiar, they're not judgmental, and they don't stare back at you like a live audience!

Looking at visuals instead of the audience can also cause you to lose contact with your listeners, whose attention is likely to wander as a result. Even if the group wants to listen to you, your voice is likely to become muffled when it has to bounce off your visual or the wall of the room before reaching their ears.

Leaving a visual up after you have finished with it is another potential distraction. A photo, chart, graph, model, or other aid can draw the attention of your listeners away from what you are saying. Ironically, the more effective the aid, the greater the potential distraction. One student showed how state-of-the-art computer animation techniques could be put to an amazing array of uses. However, she made the mistake of leaving her display running after she had finished discussing it, and spent the rest of

▼ Out of sight, out of mind.

Barnabe Googe

her speech competing with a series of airplane crashes, blooming flowers, and other distractions.

Besides avoiding diversions, removing visuals will help keep your audience alert. After looking at an object, chart, or model for a while, audience members will be more willing to focus their attention back on you. Switching from visual to words alone and back again is a good way to add variety to your speech.

## Simplicity

Inexperienced speakers think that the same visual aid that works in a book, magazine, or newspaper can be used in a speech. This is rarely the case, since a visual illustrating the printed word can be read and studied until its meaning is clear. By contrast, visuals used in a speech need to be simple enough to be understood almost at a glance.

One way to keep a visual simple is to use relatively few words—probably no more than 25 letters per line of text. Ask yourself whether all the information is necessary and keep only the essential parts. Also, use a minimal number of lines. If you need more than eight lines of text, consider splitting the information into two or more separate exhibits. If you draw figures or graph lines, try to use straight lines and simple curves, which are easy to follow. Finally, use plenty of white space in your visual: Don't fill up a chart or graph with details.

## Integrating Visuals into the Speech

The final design/use principle involves integrating visuals smoothly into your speech. Your visuals should *add* to your speech, but they should also seem like a natural part of it. One technique that helps integrate a visual into a speech is to accompany it with a three-part verbal narration. This three-part structure has a function similar to that of the three-part structure (introduction, body, conclusion) of the speech itself. First, you should alert the audience that a visual is coming and introduce it:

> By now you can see that homelessness is a growing problem. You can appreciate how much the problem has grown by looking at this graph, which shows the increase in homeless people over the last ten years.

Then display the visual and explain its significance. Be sure to give the audience enough time to appreciate the message it communicates:

> You can see that there are four times as many homeless people now as there were ten years ago. It's even more disturbing to note the increase in homeless *families,* which are indicated by this blue line. They have grown at double the rate of single homeless.

Finally, relate the visual to the point you are making:

> These figures make it clear that the problem is getting worse, especially for children who aren't responsible for their situation. If we don't do something, the future appears grim—for the growing number of homeless people, and for the rest of the community, too.

### Practicing with Visuals

▼ Bruce Springsteen always did his own microphone checks and arrived hours early at the venue. Don't be a prima donna. Roll up your sleeves and check things out ahead of time.

Danielle Kennedy

Visual aids can illustrate Murphy's Law: Whatever can go wrong with them probably will. Posterboards teeter forward and fall off chalk trays, projector bulbs burn out, slides flash on the screen upside down and backwards, and models fail to work. The best way to minimize these catastrophes is to run through a full dress rehearsal of your speech, using all visuals exactly as you will present them to the group. If possible, do this rehearsal in the room where you will deliver the real speech. This will show you whether your extension cord is long enough, whether the room can be darkened enough to make your slides visible, and a host of other factors.

Despite your best efforts, some catastrophes are impossible to predict. The overhead projector you reserved from the media department may not show up as promised, or the "volunteer" who behaved perfectly in practice might become nervous during your speech and bungle his or her role. When the worst does happen, simply make the best of a bad situation by forging on with your speech. In other words, take advantage of the spontaneous, face-to-face nature of public speaking.

### ▼ SAMPLE SPEECH

The sample speech for this chapter was presented by Jeanne Klafin, a communications major at New York University.[8] Her visual aids consisted of charts and photographs, mounted on large pieces of one-quarter-inch-thick Styrofoam posterboard. This made them easy to handle; unlike those of some of her classmates, Jeanne's speech did not suffer from "flying charts."

### ▼ REASONS TO CONSIDER VEGETARIANISM

Jeanne Klafin

New York University

[1] Isaac Singer once said,

> People often say that humans have always eaten animals, as if this is a justification for continuing the practice. According to this logic,

we should not try to prevent people from murdering other people, since this has also been done since the earliest of times.

[2] Sometimes making your own choices and moving away from tradition can be the right thing. I am a vegetarian for two reasons. In the next few minutes I will tell you how a vegetarian diet can benefit your physical well-being. I will also make you aware of the cruel and harsh practice of factory farming, which is the modern way of raising animals for human consumption. [3] First, it is important to know that switching to a vegetarian diet can significantly improve your health. It is often incorrectly assumed that becoming a vegetarian will mean a sharp decrease in one's protein intake. However, the protein humans obtain from eating meat and animal products is filled with artery-clogging saturated fat and cholesterol. By switching to plant protein, which includes eating beans, legumes, and grains, many health problems can be avoided. The move to plant protein lowers LDL or "bad" cholesterol because soy protein has a different pattern of amino acids than animal protein, and it contains other constituents that lower cholesterol. If you will turn your attention to the first chart (Chart 1), you can see that heart disease is one of the leading causes of death in the United States.

A three-part verbal narration is needed here to introduce, explain, and relate the chart to speech content.

[4] According to nutritionist John Robbins, author of *Diet for a New America,* it is now confirmed beyond any doubt that heart disease has a direct link to the amount of meat consumed. As David Schardt reports in an article in *Nutrition Action,* studies have shown conclusively that populations eating more animal protein have higher rates of heart disease. Schardt

**CHART 1**

## The Ten Leading Causes of Death in the United States, 1990

The bars on this graph are easy to see, but the chart was only 8 by 11 inches, too small for the audience to read the print.

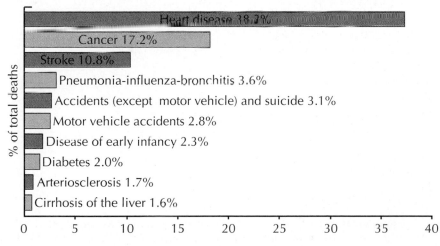

points out further that, by minimizing the intake of animal protein, not only does the chance of disease decrease, but the chances for cancer and osteoporosis are also lessened.

[5] Some people believe that there is a lack of vitamins, especially iron, in a vegetarian diet. In actuality, the best sources of iron are most vegetables, not meat. Furthermore, Vitamin C in fresh fruits and vegetables greatly increases the body's ability to absorb and use iron. In addition to this, milk and milk products not only provide no iron, but they also block its absorption. Often people tend to eat a food rich in iron, but then afterwards consume coffee, tea, or a calcium supplement that interferes with the body's ability to absorb the iron. The absence of this mineral in many of the regimens of Americans is usually attributed to the lack of meat in their diet, when in actuality the opposite is true. As you can see in the second chart, [Chart 2] vegetables such as spinach, cucumbers, and lettuce contain the most iron, while meat and dairy products are hardly even sufficient.

*Again, a three-part narration is needed.*

[6] Milk. We have all been brought up to believe that "milk does a body good." It is so ingrained in our minds that we hardly even question it. Not only can the vitamins, minerals, and protein contained in milk be consumed in several other ways, but it is actually healthier to do so. For example, the calcium content that milk is famous for is only good for the

*Once again, the basic design of this chart is good, but there are too many items listed, and the 8 by 11 chart was too small.*

**CHART 2**

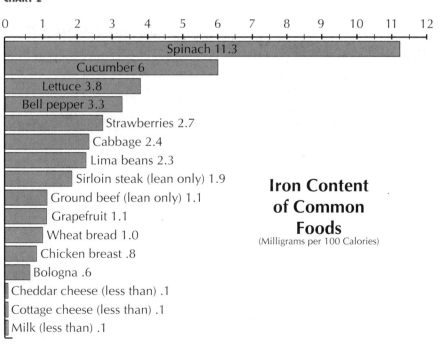

Spinach 11.3
Cucumber 6
Lettuce 3.8
Bell pepper 3.3
Strawberries 2.7
Cabbage 2.4
Lima beans 2.3
Sirloin steak (lean only) 1.9
Ground beef (lean only) 1.1
Grapefruit 1.1
Wheat bread 1.0
Chicken breast .8
Bologna .6
Cheddar cheese (less than) .1
Cottage cheese (less than) .1
Milk (less than) .1

**Iron Content of Common Foods**
(Milligrams per 100 Calories)

body when combined with an adequate amount of phosphorous, because the body can only utilize these two minerals together. The foods whose calcium is least available due to their low calcium/phosphorous ratio are chicken, beef, pork, and fish. The calcium in vegetables and fruits is much more available because of their high abundances of both calcium and phosphorous. Considering this, it is important to keep in mind the cows that allow us to have our glass of milk every day. If you will direct your attention to the last two charts (Charts 3 and 4), you can see that for the past fifty years, the United States' dairy cow population has drastically dropped, but the milk production per cow has radically increased. This is due in large part to the cruel treatment of dairy cows.

[7] This brings me to the second reason for adopting a vegetarian diet: It is more humane than consuming meat and animal products because animals bred for consumption are treated cruelly.

[8] The dairy industry looks at its cows as four-legged milk pumps. According to Robbins, they are bred, inadequately fed, and medicated for a single purpose—to maximize their milk production at a minimum cost. The average commercial cow now gives three or more times as much milk in a year as her ancestors. Today's dairy cows are injected with hormones to promote this ludicrous amount of milk production. Hormones, as you may

*More discussion of these charts is needed. For example, the audience should be told the source of the statistics.*

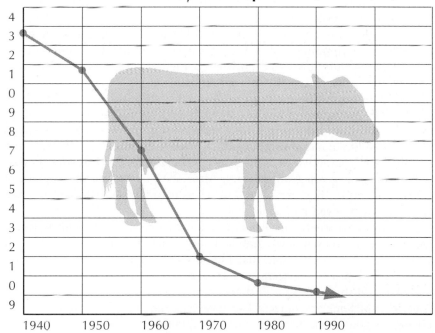

**Chart 3: U.S. Dairy Cow Population (in millions)**

*Line charts give striking evidence of these trends.*

## Chart 4: Average Annual Milk Production per Cow (in pounds)

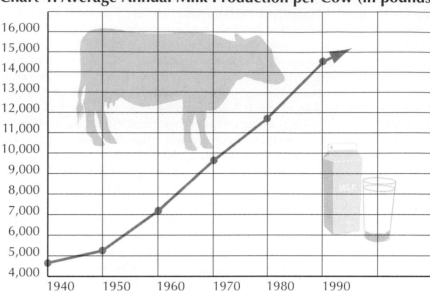

know, are incredibly potent substances that are naturally secreted by the bodies of animals, including humans. It takes extremely minuscule amounts of hormones to control our entire endocrine and reproductive systems. According to Robbins, if our taste buds were as sensitive to flavor as our target cells are to hormones, we would be able to detect a single grain of sugar in a swimming pool of water. Today's factory farmers implant the animals, especially cows, with such large amounts of hormones that their natural life cycles are completely set off balance.

[9] As you can see in these pictures (Photos 1 and 2), the cow's udder is so unnaturally large that her calves would have a hard time feeding from it, and might easily damage it if they were allowed to try. The cows spend their entire life in a constricting stall. They are pregnant at all times and are often so hyperactive from these ragged breeding practices that they often have to be given tranquilizers. After they have met their quota of calves and milk, they are often killed, reducing their average life span from twenty-five years to about four.

[10] The inhumane treatment is also true for chickens. It is difficult to forget the feeling of seeing a newly hatched baby chick. Chickens often flourish when treated with affection, just like any other animal. Yet, most of today's poultry producers seem unable to grasp the fact that chickens are animals, and this is proven in the way they are treated. At most farms in America, chickens are squeezed so close together that they can hardly lift a wing, as you can see in these pictures (Photos 3 and 4).

**PHOTO 1**

These were striking. Jeanne had them covered until she mentioned the inhumane treatment of dairy cows, and they were strong visual proof.

**PHOTO 2**

**PHOTO 3**

More visual proof, but less striking.

**PHOTO 4**

[11] The ceilings of their cages are so short that the chickens can barely stand upright. Because industrialists see chickens as profit per pound, the chickens are bred to be so fat that their skeletons can barely support their weight. The chickens brought up in these conditions are unable to run around and they never even see the light of day.

[12] Pork farmers have by and large followed the lead of the poultry industry in recent years. Instead of pig farms, today we have pig factories. If you will direct your attention to the pictures (Photos 5 and 6), the crowded and unbearable living conditions are visible.

[13] The sows are kept each in her own cramped stall with metal or concrete floors. Because a pig's hoof is designed for natural soft surfaces such as soil, the tissue in the foot develops lesions and sores which cripple the pig. Like the factory farm cows, hormones are given to these pigs so they can produce more than seven times the number of piglets nature designed them for. Pork breeders also constantly feel the need to develop fatter pigs. Unfortunately, the results of this obsession are sows so heavy that their bones and joints are literally crumbling beneath them. At each stage of the assembly line, especially the inhumane slaughtering of the animals, which is done indifferently, usually by machine, they are treated with complete disdain for the fact that they are our fellow creatures.

[14] In conclusion, I can't expect to change the thoughts and beliefs of all the men and women of this world, or even in this classroom. I fully respect the choices other people make, even if they are different from my own, but I

*Here, Jeanne's commentary helps integrate the visual aid into the speech.*

**PHOTO 5**

*Good pictures, but difficult for some members of the audience to see because the posterboard was not placed high enough.*

PHOTO 6

would at least like to open the eyes of those who may be misinformed about vegetarianism. Even though refraining from consuming meat goes against most traditional values, not to mention what we were taught most of our lives, it is important for all of us to evaluate our previous thoughts on the matter. It was when I became aware of the nutritional value of this diet and the cruel, inhumane treatment of the animals that I began to question my own thoughts and beliefs. Being a vegetarian for about three years, I can honestly say that I feel better about myself and the fellow creatures of this world.

## ⬤ SUMMARY

Our consideration of the media/information age is especially important when it comes to visuals. Just as in a mediated message, visuals can improve a speech in many ways. They can make it more interesting, clearer, and more memorable. They will boost the speaker's credibility. Finally, they help the speaker feel more confident, and they serve as speaking notes to keep the talk on track.

There are many varieties of visual aids. Some are three-dimensional, such as objects and models. Others are two-dimensional, such as photographs, diagrams, maps, charts, and graphs. Visuals can be presented in a variety of ways. Words, numbers, and diagrams can be sketched on a chalkboard during the speech or prepared in advance on flip charts, poster-boards, overhead transparencies, or handouts. Photographs can be shown with a slide projector and videotapes can be played for the audience. Each of these approaches has both advantages and drawbacks, which the speaker needs to consider before choosing the best one for a particular situation.

All visuals work best when they meet certain guidelines. Their type, number, and content should relate clearly to the content of the speech instead of distracting the audience. Their design should be simple, easy to view, and designed with enough polish to suit the occasion. The way visuals are presented is also important. The speaker should be sure they work smoothly, explain their meaning to the audience, and keep control of them. Each visual should be removed immediately after it has been displayed.

## ▼ EXERCISES

1. One of the most important lessons of the media/information age is that different types of messages require different media for maximum effectiveness. Use the advice in this chapter to explain which medium (chalkboard, flip chart, posterboard, overhead transparencies, slides, videotape, handouts) would be most effective in each of the following situations. You might use more than one medium in each situation.
   a. Demonstrating how to replace the battery in a digital watch.
   b. Illustrating cultural stereotypes in magazine ads.
   c. Showing the comparative costs of public and private colleges and universities.
   d. Explaining how using a computerized word processing program can produce better term papers.
   e. Developing a program to promote your college or university at local high schools.
   f. Teaching self-defense techniques for women.
   g. Persuading a skeptical audience that male ballet dancers can be considered athletes.

2. Analyze any sample speech for where visual aids might be effective. Describe the visual aids that you think will work best. Compare your ideas with those of your classmates.

## NOTES

1. From an ad placed by James J. Reardon, M.D., in the *New York Times Magazine,* May 21, 1995, p. 30.
2. "A Research Report on the Effects of the Use of Overhead Transparencies on Business Meetings" (St. Paul, Minn.: 3M Company, 1978).
3. Elena P. Zayas-Baya, "Instructional Media in the Total Language Picture," *International Journal of Instructional Media* 5 (1977–78), pp. 145–150.
4. This illustration was provided by Edward Tufte in his fascinating book *Envisioning Information* (Cheshire, Conn.: Graphics Press, 1990), p. 48.
5. Camcorders come highly recommended for educational purposes. See, for example, Carol Kellner Weaver, "Captivate the MTV Generation: Videos Motivate because Their Multisensory Format Brings a Subject Alive," *School Library Journal* 38 (April 1992), p. 50. See also Lori A. Forlizzi and Anne Mallery, "Video and Other Visuals Excite Adult Students about Literature," *Adult Learning* 6 (November–December 1994), p. 15.
6. When you use high-tech, watch out for the pitfalls. See Dick Schaaf, "Who's in Charge Here? Avoiding Technology's Traps," *Training* 29 (November 1992), p. S11. Schaaf points out five pitfalls: (1) Using too much glitz to attract attention, which inhibits comprehension, (2) using too many visuals, (3) using technology that you're not familiar with, (4) failing to prepare for the unexpected, and (5) being unwilling to explore the potential advantages of new presentation technologies. *Training* magazine presents a directory of audiovisual equipment and supplies each year in its November issue.
7. Classic experiments into the effectiveness of *fear appeals* have demonstrated this effect. Moderate fear appeals are more effective than those that cause the audience to feel *too much* emotion. See Shearon Lowery and Melvin DeFleur, *Milestones in Mass Communication Research* (New York: Longman, 1983), pp. 159–162.
8. Jeanne Klafin, "Reasons to Consider Vegetarianism," speech presented in Speech Communication class, Department of Culture & Communication, New York University, Fall, 1995.

# STYLE: DELIVERY AND LANGUAGE CHOICES

## ▼ CHAPTER 11 OBJECTIVES

**After reading this chapter, you should understand:**

**1.** The advantages of live delivery over mediated messages.

**2.** The differences among the various types of delivery.

**3.** The importance of careful language choices.

**4.** The visual and auditory aspects of delivery that help you make the best nonverbal choices during delivery.

**You should be able to:**

**1.** Choose the most effective type of delivery for a particular speech.

**2.** Follow the guidelines for effective extemporaneous, impromptu, manuscript, and memorized speeches.

**3.** Recognize the best remedy or therapy for speech anxiety, if necessary.

**4.** Improve your personal presentation style.

### ▼ DELIVERY, LANGUAGE, AND THE MEDIA/INFORMATION AGE

Media often brag of being "Live! Up Close and Personal!" but in fact that is the venue of the public speaker. The main advantage of face-to-face public speaking is the interaction the speaker enjoys with the audience. There's an excitement inherent within that interaction. When you combine that excitement with careful language choices, your personal style can have real impact. The goal of this chapter, therefore, is to help you refine your personal presentation style in terms of both its verbal and its nonverbal impact.

The term *personal style* is an important one. The object of training in public speaking is not to turn out legions of speakers with identical styles. Such a cookie-cutter approach would deny your individual identity, and it is that identity that will create your greatest audience attraction. You only need consider the most successful public speakers to realize how important personal style is. Roseanne is barely grammatical but self-assured; Woody Allen uses perfect English but stutters. Oprah Winfrey has a warm, personal style that is extremely self-disclosive, while David Letterman is far too ironic to project a feeling of closeness. Bill Clinton is known for his plain, straightforward language choices, while Jesse Jackson's are ornate and often rhyme. Nelson Mandela speaks with a formality that approaches stiffness; Julia Roberts seems shy and reticent. The only thing these speakers have in common, in fact, is that they are extremely successful.

The purpose of this chapter is to help you develop a *genuine* personal style. To do so, you have to be yourself, but be an intelligent, well-prepared, audience-centered version of yourself. The first thing to consider in this area is the style of delivery you choose.

> ▼ O the orator's joys!
> To inflate the chest, to roll the thunder of voice out from the ribs and throat,
> To make the people rage, weep, hate, desire with
> yourself.
>
> Walt Whitman

### ▼ TYPES OF DELIVERY

In choosing your style of delivery, your primary consideration should be to take advantage of the dynamic of the live public speaking event, that all-important interaction that gives public speaking its advantage over mediated messages.

The basic idea here is that you must take advantage of your medium. You cannot compete with the relative permanence of a printed message, or the high-interest visual/auditory nature of an electronic one. What you must do, therefore, is *connect* with your audience members and *interact* with them in a way that is impossible in any type of mediated communication. Otherwise, you might as well send them a fax.

> ▼ All styles are good except the tiresome kind.
>
> Voltaire

# Calvin and Hobbes

## by Bill Watterson

*Calvin and Hobbes* ©1997 Watterson. Distributed by Universal Press Syndicate. Reprinted with permission. All rights reserved.

There are four basic types of delivery—impromptu, extemporaneous, manuscript, and memorized. Each type creates a different impression and is appropriate under different conditions.

### Impromptu Speeches

An *impromptu speech* is given off the top of one's head, without preparation. This type of speech is given when a speaker doesn't know in advance that she will be called upon. An impromptu speech is often given in an emergency, such as when a scheduled speaker becomes ill and you are suddenly called upon:

> Moose Hakenson couldn't make it this evening, folks, but I notice in our audience another State U student leader who I am sure would be glad to say a few words . . .

▼ Wise people reflect before they speak; fools speak and then reflect on what they have uttered.

Jacque Delille

The big disadvantage of an impromptu speech is that it is given on the spur of the moment and, as more than one expert has pointed out, "Too often the 'moment' arrives without the necessary informed and inspired 'spur'"[1] Thinking of something worthwhile to say can be difficult, and mistakes can be made easily. In fact, this type of mistake has proven troublesome for many public figures because their words are so closely watched in the media/information age. Governor Christine Todd Whitman of New Jersey, in an impromptu speech about teenage pregnancy, made a comment about young black men playing a game called "jewels in the crown" that refers to the number of children they can father out of wedlock. She later had to apologize for the comment as insensitive and racially divisive.[2] The commander of the U.S. Forces in the Pacific, Admiral Richard C. Macke, was forced to resign when, in an impromptu speech about two

American sailors who had raped a 12-year-old girl in Okinawa, he mentioned that the incident could have been avoided if the sailors had simply paid for a prostitute.[3]

There are, however, advantages to impromptu speaking. For one thing, an impromptu speech is by definition spontaneous. It is the delivery style necessary for informal talks, group discussions, and comments on others' speeches. It also can be an effective training aid—it can teach you to think on your feet and organize your thoughts quickly.

To take full advantage of an impromptu speaking opportunity, remember the following points:

1. Keep a positive attitude. Remember that audience expectations are low. They know you haven't prepared in advance, and they don't expect you to be Patrick Henry.
2. Take advantage of the time between being called on to speak and actually speaking. Even if you have only a minute, you can still scribble a few brief notes to protect against mental blocks.
3. Don't be afraid to be original; you don't have to remember what every other expert says about your topic—what do *you* say about it? Review your personal experiences and use them.
4. Observe what is going on around you, and respond to it. If there were other speakers, you might agree or disagree with what they said. You can comment on the audience and the occasion, too, as well as on your topic.
5. Consider an all-purpose outline based on questions, such as the following:

   ▼ Who?
   ▼ What?
   ▼ When?
   ▼ Where?
   ▼ How?

   On your way to the front of the room you can formulate a plan to answer one or more of these questions. If you're called up at that sports banquet, you can speak on one of the following:

   ▼ *Who* was responsible for the winning season.
   ▼ *What* the team accomplished.
   ▼ *When* the "turning point" of the season occurred.
   ▼ *Where* the team is headed next season.
   ▼ *How* the coach's technique led to the championship season.

6. Finally, and perhaps most important, keep your impromptu comments brief. Especially, do not prolong your conclusion. If you have said everything you want to say or everything you can remember, wrap it up

▼ Speeches are like babies—easy to conceive, hard to deliver.

Pat O'Malley

▼ I had six honest serving men they taught me all I knew. Their names were what and where and when how and why and who.

Rudyard Kipling

as neatly as possible and sit down. If you forgot something, it probably wasn't important anyway. If it was, the audience will ask you about it afterward.

## Extemporaneous Speeches

An *extemporaneous speech* is planned in advance but presented in a direct, spontaneous manner. It is usually presented from brief notes or an outline. A speech presented extemporaneously will be researched, organized, and practiced in advance, but the exact wording of the entire speech will not be memorized or otherwise predetermined. Each time you present it, it will be a little different.

Extemporaneous speeches are conversational in tone, which means that they give the audience members the impression that you are talking to them, directly and honestly, without the artificiality that an obvious "prepared statement" has. Extemporaneous speeches *are* carefully prepared, but they are prepared in such a way that they create what actors call "the illusion of the first time"—in other words, the audience hears your remarks as though they were brand-new.

The extemporaneous style of speaking is generally accepted to be the most effective, especially for a college class. In a classroom you speak before a small audience (five to fifty people) made up of people with diverse backgrounds. Spontaneity is essential with this type of audience, but so is careful message planning. Extemporaneous speaking allows you to benefit from both careful planning and spontaneous delivery. Because you speak from only brief, unobtrusive notes, you are able to move and maintain eye contact with your audience.

Extemporaneous speaking is not only the most effective type of delivery for a classroom speech, it is also the most common type of delivery in the "outside" world. In spite of the glut of mediated messages, most people involved in communication-oriented careers find that the majority of their public speaking is done before audiences that, in terms of size and diversity of interests represented, resemble those found in a college classroom. Professional public speakers recognize the advisability of both careful planning and spontaneity with such an audience.

The extemporaneous speech does have some disadvantages. It is difficult to keep exact time limits, to be exact in wording, or to be grammatically perfect with an extemporaneous speech. Therefore, if you are speaking as part of a radio or television broadcast or if your speech will be reproduced "for the record," you might want to use a manuscript or to memorize your speech. Also, an extemporaneous speech requires time to prepare. If you don't have that time, an impromptu speech might be more appropriate.

## Manuscript Speeches

*Manuscript speeches* are read word for word from a prepared text. They are necessary when you are speaking for the record, as at legal proceedings or when presenting scientific findings. They are necessary for public figures, to avoid the kind of political mistakes that we mentioned in our discussion of impromptu speeches. The greatest disadvantage of a manuscript speech is the lack of spontaneity that may result. It is difficult for the audience to have a sense of dialog with the speaker; they tend to perceive the speaker as a performer with no particular audience in mind, and this invites them to tune out the speaker because they know they are essentially irrelevant to the message.

Manuscript readers have even been known, to their extreme embarrassment, to read their directions by mistake: "And so, let me say in conclusion, look at the audience with great sincerity . . ."

Manuscript speeches are difficult and cumbersome, but they are sometimes necessary. If you find occasion to use one, here are some guidelines:

1. *Use Large Type.* Print out the manuscript triple-spaced, in capital letters, with a dark ribbon (or high-quality printer setting). Underline the words you want to emphasize.
2. *Use Short Paragraphs.* They are easier to return to after establishing eye contact with your audience.
3. *Use Stiff Paper.* That way, it won't fold up or fly away during the speech. Type on only one side, and number the pages by hand with large, circled numbers.
4. *Rehearse.* You need to be able to "read" whole lines without looking at the manuscript.
5. *Be Conversational.* Take your time, vary your speed, and try to concentrate on ideas rather than words.
6. *Write a Speech, Not an Essay.* It is important to recognize the differences between written essays and speeches. As one expert has pointed out, "Speeches use more words per square thought than well-written essays or reports."[4] We'll have more to say about the differences between written and spoken style in a moment.

## Memorized Speeches

*Memorized speeches*—those learned by heart—are the most difficult and often the least effective. They often seem excessively formal. However, like manuscript speeches, they are sometimes necessary. They are used in oratory contests and on very formal occasions, such as eulogies or church

▼ Good results are seldom led to. When people feel they're being read to.

Charles Osgood

rituals. They are used as training devices for memory. They are also used in some political situations. For example, in presidential debates, the candidates are usually allowed to make prepared speeches, but they are not allowed to use notes. Thus, they have to memorize precise, for-the-record wording, and make it sound natural.

In fact, because of the hazards of politics in the media age (an earlier speech might be played back to you, on prime-time TV), a large number of professional speeches are memorized. This is true for corporate leaders and entertainment celebrities as well as politicians. Everyone, it seems, tries to control his or her image in the media/information age. Memorized messages are one way to do that, and yet we stress extemporaneous speaking on the college campus and recommend it throughout life. It's all part of the liberal arts campaign to encourage people to *be* ethical rather than to just maintain an ethical image.

There is only one guideline for a memorized speech: Practice. The speech won't be effective until you have practiced it so you can present it with that "illusion of the first time" that was mentioned earlier.

One final note on delivery styles: Any speech might incorporate more than one type of delivery. For example, a speech could be mostly extemporaneous, but an important quotation could be read from notes or memorized.

## ▼ WRITTEN AND SPOKEN STYLE

There are significant differences between written essays and speeches.[5] As we mentioned before, this is an important consideration in manuscript speeches. It is also a general consideration in speech style.

▼ The very weakness of writing, which is adjectives, is the strength of speaking.

Shana Alexander

Spoken language is generally less formal than written language.[6] It contains more sentence fragments, more colloquial language, more contractions, and more interjections, such as "well," "oh," and "now," than written language. Spoken language is generally more personal, too. More references are made to yourself ("I," "me," "mine") and to your specific audience. There are subtle stylistic differences, too. Speeches use more adverbs and adjectives.

They also tend to be more redundant. The structured introduction, body, and conclusion of a speech might seem unnecessarily repetitive if the same message were written out. You are required to repeat yourself in a speech, because your audience cannot go back to look over your words. Therefore *restatement* and *paraphrasing* are valuable tools for a speaker.

## ⬤ LANGUAGE CHOICES

No matter what type of delivery you are using, you should take the time to consider the best way to put your ideas into words. Even in the most spur-of-the-moment statement, you have time to consider more than one way of expressing your ideas. Language choices can be made even more carefully while preparing a planned speech. You make them while determining your main points, while roughing out the speech, and while practicing the speech. You need not memorize exact wording: Simply making your language choices in advance will lead to a clearer presentation.

As you make your language choices, it is important to remember the difference between connotation and denotation. *Denotation* is the literal meaning of the word (the meaning found in the dictionary), and *connotation* is what the word suggests to the listener. The terms "cruel," "ruthless," and "inhuman" all denote an insensitivity to the suffering of others, yet the connotations of these words differ markedly. A "cruel" person, for most audiences, would be one who enjoys the suffering of others. A "ruthless" person would probably be one who is insensitive *while in pursuit of a goal.* An "inhuman" person would be one totally lacking in the compassion expected of a civilized human being. The difference between connotation and denotation makes it necessary to plan the words you use in a speech as carefully as possible. There are three basic guidelines for effective vocabulary: *clarity, vividness,* and *appropriateness.*

▼ Language is the dress of thought.

Samuel Johnson

### Clarity

*Clarity* is saying what you mean in such a way that it will have the best chance of being understood. Saying what you mean requires careful word

DILBERT

by Scott Adams

*Dilbert* reprinted by permission of United Feature Syndicate, Inc.

choice. When planning a speech you have to become a wordsmith, an artisan like a silversmith or a watchsmith. Just like any other person involved in a craft, as a wordsmith you have to use the tools that are available to you. If you are the type of wordsmith who likes simple, all-purpose tools, you might like to use a good standard dictionary—preferably a full-sized, current college edition. Dictionaries can be used for more than spelling and denotative meaning; they also supply word derivations, pronunciation guides, synonyms, antonyms, and word variations. All these things help you determine nuances of meaning.

If you are the type of wordsmith who likes specialized tools, you might like to use a thesaurus, a dictionary of synonyms and antonyms. If you were planning a speech on some aspect of education, you might find yourself repeating the word "teaching" without any variation in nuance. You might look up "teaching" in *Roget's Thesaurus* and find the following:

> teaching, pedagogics, pedagogy, instruction, edification, education, tuition, tutorship, tutelage, direction, guidance.

If those are not enough for you, the thesaurus will list alternatives for "preparation, lesson, teach, expound, train," and "educational" in the same section.[7] Each of the terms listed will have a fine shade of connotation.

A word of warning is appropriate here: Some students tend to go "thesaurus crazy," and try to use as many different words for the same thing as they can. They especially like relatively obscure words like "pedagogics" and "tutelage." Fanciness is definitely the *wrong* use for a thesaurus, and you should guard against it.

Whether you are using a thesaurus or a standard dictionary, there are two characteristics of clarity that, if you recognize them, will help you make the best word choice. These characteristics are *specificity* and *concreteness*.

### Specificity

A specific word is one that restricts the meaning that can be assigned to it. General words name groups of things; specific words name the individual things that make up that group. The term "transportation" is general. "Automobile," "sports car," and "1968 Corvette Mako Shark 427" are increasingly specific terms. Someone who says, "I had an automobile accident the other day" is likely to evoke less sympathy from a sports car enthusiast than one who says, "I demolished my 1968 Corvette Mako Shark 427 the other day."

One of the reasons some people distrust politicians is that politicians often do not speak in specifics. On one hand, this is understandable: Politicians have to please a broad audience, and the more specific they become, the more chances they have to say something that some voters don't want to hear. Still, their affinity for general terms makes careful listeners wary. Candidate X favors "getting tough on crime." But what does that mean? Does the candidate favor the suspension of the defendant's constitutional rights, or the suspension of the Fourteenth Amendment? (That is the one that guarantees "due process of law.")

## Concreteness

Concrete words refer to things in actual physical reality, things that we can perceive with our senses. Abstract words refer to concepts that we cannot see, hear, taste, touch, or feel. "Freedom," "democracy," "capitalism," and "communism" are typical abstract concepts, whereas "hot fudge sundaes," "skinny bodies," and "the smell of rotten garbage" are more concrete.

Concrete words help us visualize abstract concepts. Farah Walters, a hospital executive, was speaking about discrimination in America. Rather than just saying "minorities faced discrimination," she said,

> Let us go back 100 or 150 years. . . .
> It was a time in which, throughout this great land, they literally hung signs that said "Irish Need Not Apply" or "Italians Need Not Apply" or "Catholics Need Not Apply" or "Jews Need Not Apply."[8]

### Vividness

*Vivid* comes from the Latin term meaning "to live." Vivid language is lively because of the images the words evoke. In the media/information age, images have become extremely important. We are used to having our attention captured by new, original, novel images. In the glut of messages, these striking images are, in fact, in constant competition for our attention. As a public speaker, it is important to remember that images can appear in the human mind from two routes: Either they can be presented visually, as they are through television, movies, and full-color magazine spreads (and, for that matter, through certain types of visual aids), or they can be presented through words that evoke images. Sometimes the symbols—the words—are actually more effective, because they allow the listeners' imaginations to do the work.

Vivid language *evokes the senses* by using words that refer to things we can see, hear, smell, touch, or taste. Objects have size, color, shape, and position that can be seen. The size has dimension, the color has brightness, the shape has contours, and the position has some relationship in space to other objects. These qualities evoke images based on the sense of sight. You can evoke images based on hearing by telling of the tone, rhythm, and melody of a sound. Sounds *do* things. They chime, chatter, clang, clatter, clink, crackle, crash, and creak. We can use words to duplicate sounds by using onomatopoeia. For example, you can describe the "blip" of a radar screen or the "hiss" of a distant waterfall. Words that evoke images of smell will tell us about the sharpness or intensity of an odor. Odors can be "moldy" or "musky." They can also be "balmy" or "woodsy." Words that evoke images of taste could describe the sweetness, sourness, bitterness, or saltiness of a flavor. Words that evoke images of touch could refer to pressure, texture, or warmth of contact. A touch could be "slimy" or "stinging." It could also be "satiny" or "smooth."

A speech on women's gymnastics, for example, could begin like this:

> When Mary Lou Retton took a deep breath at the head of the runway leading to the vaulting horse, all America seemed to inhale with her. The tiny 16-year-old dynamo charged down that runway, little legs pumping like pistons, hit that springboard, rocketed above that horse, flipped, twisted, landed . . . yes! Ramrod straight, no stumble: A perfect 10! A gold medal![9]

Vivid language tends to avoid clichés. In fact, clichés are the opposite of vivid language; they are expressions that are "dead" from overuse. Some expressions are clichés because they have been around for so long:

▼ never ceases to amaze me     ▼ better late than never

▼ a lame excuse     ▼ in no uncertain terms

▼ avoid it like the plague     ▼ in this day and age

- ▼ last but not least
- ▼ too good to be true
- ▼ fighting city hall
- ▼ sad but true

Other clichés are of a more recent vintage, but are still clichés because they are both overused and vague:

- ▼ cool
- ▼ neat
- ▼ dude
- ▼ awesome
- ▼ totally (as in, "totally awesome, dude")
- ▼ for sure (especially when pronounced, "fer shure")

Rather than relying on clichés, you should try to put your own words together in an interesting, original manner. You do not need the vocabulary of a genius to do so. You just have to be honest. You have to conjure up the image that *you* want to relate, and use *your own words* to describe that image.

Vivid language can be achieved through *syntax* (the way you put your words together) as well as vocabulary. One method, for example, is *parallel sentence structure*. Parallel sentence structure allows one idea to balance with another, such as John F. Kennedy's "Ask not what your country can do for you, ask what you can do for your country."[10]

Of course, some expressions are vivid not because of a device like parallelism, but because the speaker has experimented with different ways of saying something and then said it the way it sounded best. Consider how the first sentence of Lincoln's Gettysburg Address might have sounded if someone else had written it:

Eighty-seven years ago, the founders of this country established a system of government based on the idea that everyone should be free and equal.

Lincoln, on the other hand, wrote:

Fourscore and seven years ago our fathers brought forth on this continent a new nation, conceived in liberty, and dedicated to the proposition that all men are created equal.

The first version is not terrible; it is merely adequate. Lincoln's version, on the other hand, has an almost biblical sound, as illustrated by both "fourscore and seven" and "fathers" rather than "founders."

Of course, by today's standards Lincoln's sentence might sound old-fashioned—especially the near-sexist "fathers." If Lincoln were enrolled in a public speaking class today, he'd have to worry about our third language principle: appropriateness.

## Appropriateness

The words you use should be appropriate to you, to your audience, and to your message. Four types of words are infamous for their frequent inappropriateness: *obscenity, slang, jargon,* and *bigotry.*

## Obscenity

Obscenity offends and, because of that, obscene language is almost never appropriate in public speaking.[11] Even when a juicy expletive would seem to match the intensity of the speaker's emotions, and the audience members seem like the type of people who would sit still for it, there is still a chance that the language would offend at least some members of your audience. Every culture has words that are not taboo in very small groups of individuals but are very much taboo when used in larger groups. Even if your audience members don't get up and walk out in protest, chances are that the obscenity will distract them from the ideas you are trying to get across. Because of this, when it comes to obscenity in public speaking, the rule is: Don't use it.

## Slang

Slang words are those that are not yet an accepted part of the language. "Bus," "cab," "hoax," and "mob" were all slang terms at one time, but they later became standard. "Ripped off" (meaning "stolen" or "victimized"), "uptight" (meaning "anxious"), and "laid back" (meaning "calm") are slang terms of a recent generation. "Nerd," "dweeb," and "spazz" are current slang terms.[12]

Slang terms often enter the popular culture directly from the mass media: When Mike Meyers did his "Wayne's World" skit on *Saturday Night Live*," the next day kids across America were saying "schwang!" and "babadocious." Or when he did a "Coffee Talk" segment, the next day we heard a dozen people saying, "I'm all verklempt." A few years ago, when the Big Three networks garnered more than 90 percent of the prime-time audience, it was relatively easy to assume that people were familiar with slang from the most popular shows and commercials. Today, there are so many media channels, it is impossible to be sure that all members of an audience are familiar with a term.

Slang is more appropriate in a spoken message than in a written message, but it is troublesome even when spoken. Slang should not be used unless all members of the audience would understand it. Otherwise, it should be replaced with a more standard usage. You could say "They were very conceited" instead of "They were on a real ego trip," and "It was boring" instead of "It was a drag."

## Jargon

Jargon includes words of a specialized nature that are used only by specific groups of people. Educators, for example, talk of "empirically validated learning" and "multimode curricula," and, rather than saying that a child needs improvement, they say that "academic achievement is not commensurate with abilities." Doctors and military strategists are famous for their use of jargon, also. A heart attack is a "cardiovascular accident" for doctors, while air raids are "routine limited duration protective reactions" to the military. Computer hackers, businesspeople, religious groups, sports enthusiasts, lawyers, and many other groups have semiprivate vocabularies. Words from these vocabularies are appropriate only when they are addressed to those who use them regularly.

The rule works in reverse, too. If you can use a limited amount of an audience's jargon to communicate ideas they are not familiar with, you could be one step ahead in the make-yourself-clear game. You could explain gourmet cooking to a group of computer experts by referring to the input-output of recipe ingredients or by stressing the GIGO principle (garbage in, garbage out) in selecting ingredients.

## Bigotry

Bigotry is the language of prejudice and intolerance. It includes the "isms" of sexism, racism, antisemitism, jingoism (language that reflects a mindless patriotism toward your own country and disparages people of other countries or geographic regions), and ethnocentrism (language that suggests that other ethnic groups are inferior to your own).

Sexist language is made up of terms that stereotype people according to their sex. There are three types of sexist language to watch out for. The first is derogatory slang, such as "doll," "gal," "broad," and "chick" as substitutes for "woman." That these words *sound* old-fashioned is a good sign that sexist language styles are changing. The second type of sexist language is the use of occupational terms that include the word "man" when a woman also might have the job. Such terms include "salesman," "spokesman," "congressman," "sanitation man." These terms can easily be changed to "sales representative," "spokesperson," "congressional representative," and "sanitation worker." This type of sexist language also works in reverse, such as the use of "cleaning lady" instead of "office cleaner" and "lady lawyer" instead of "lawyer." The third type of sexist language is the use of "he" as an indefinite pronoun. This is the most difficult type of sexist language to work with because it is, by tradition, grammatically correct. In spite of its grammatical correctness, however, this usage should be avoided when it perpetuates a sexual stereotype. It is usually awkward to attempt to say "he or she" wherever one of these phrases occurs. When possible, therefore, it is advisable to use the plural form:

▼ Instead of saying, "A child who excels should be told *he* has done well," say, "Children who excel should be told *they* have done well."

▼ Instead of saying, "A secretary has to be careful of the way *she* dresses," say, "Secretaries have to be careful of the way *they* dress."

▼ Instead of saying, "A doctor should be proud of *his* accomplishments," say, "Doctors should be proud of *their* accomplishments."

Another type of bigotry involves racial and ethnic stereotyping. We live in an age in which people are extremely sensitive to any language usage that can be taken as a racial or ethnic slur. *Epithets,* which are derogatory slang terms for any race, color, or creed, should be avoided. Furthermore, when referring to racial or ethnic background for any reason, try to use the term that is most acceptable to your audience. It makes sense, for example, to refer to blacks as "African Americans," which coincides nicely with "European Americans" instead of "whites." "Asian American" is generally preferred to "Oriental," and "Latin American," "Latina," and "Latino" are sometimes preferred to "Hispanic."

## ▼ NONVERBAL ASPECTS OF DELIVERY

Clarity, vividness, and appropriateness are important guidelines for the *verbal* aspects of your personal presentational style. You also need to consider the *nonverbal* messages you send as a speaker. Nonverbal messages (those that don't use words) can change the meaning assigned to the spoken word and, in some cases, can contradict that meaning entirely.[13] In fact, if the audience wants to interpret how you *feel* about something, they are likely to trust your nonverbal communication more than the words you speak. If you tell an audience, "It's good to be here today," but you stand before them slouched over with your hands in your pockets and an expression on your face that says "Just kill me, all right?", they are likely to discount what you say. This might cause your audience to react negatively to your speech, and their negative reaction might increase your negative feelings. This cycle of speaker and audience reinforcing each other's feelings can work *for* you, though, if you approach a subject with genuine enthusiasm—the kind of enthusiam that is shown through the nonverbal aspects of your delivery.

### Visual Nonverbal Aspects of Delivery

The nonverbal aspects of delivery are of two types: visual and auditory. Visual aspects of delivery include such things as appearance, movement, posture, facial expressions, and eye contact.

▼ An honest good look covereth many faults.

Thomas Fuller

### Appearance

Appearance is not a presentation variable as much as a preparation variable. Some communication consultants suggest new clothes, new glasses, and new hairstyles for their clients. In case you consider any of these, be forewarned that you should be attractive to your audience but not flashy. Clothing, jewelry, and hair should not distract from your speech. Research suggests that audiences like speakers who are similar to them, but they prefer the similarity to be shown conservatively.[14] This means that even though you might be addressing an audience dressed primarily in ripped jeans, the audience would probably rate you higher if *your* jeans were in one piece.

## Movement

Movement is an important visual aspect of delivery. The way you walk to the front of your audience, for example, will express your confidence and enthusiasm. And once you begin speaking, nervous energy can cause your body to shake and twitch, and that can be distressing to both you and to your audience. One way to control *involuntary* movement is to move voluntarily when you feel the need to move. Don't feel that you have to stand in one spot or that all your gestures need to be carefully planned. Simply get involved in your message, and let your involvement create the motivation for your movement. That way, when you move, you will emphasize what you are saying in the same way you would emphasize it if you were talking to a group of friends.

Movement can help you maintain contact with *all* members of your audience, in a way that no mediated message could. Those closest to you will feel the greatest contact with you whereas the people who are less interested will have a tendency to sit farther away to begin with. This creates what is known as the "action zone" of audience members sitting in front and center of the room. Movement enables you to extend this action zone, to include in it people who would otherwise remain uninvolved.

Without overdoing it, you should feel free to step forward, back, or from side to side in front of your audience. Of course, your movement should be natural to you—some people like to move more than others. If you feel unnatural moving your entire body, you can move just your hands or arms by gesturing. Whichever type of movement you choose, move with the understanding that it will add to the meaning of the words you use. It is difficult to bang your fist on a podium or to take a step without conveying emphasis. Make the emphasis natural by allowing your message to create your motivation to move.

## Posture

Generally speaking, good posture means standing with your spine relatively straight, your shoulders relatively squared off, and your feet angled out to keep your body from falling over sideways. In other words, rather than standing at military attention, you should be comfortably erect.

> They don't care how much you know, until they know how much you care.
>
> Cavett Robert

> ▼ Gesture, but do not *make* gestures. Let your gestures spring from the impulse common to all expression through action.
>
> James Winans

Of course, you shouldn't get *too* comfortable. There are speakers who are effective in spite of the fact that they sprawl on tabletops and slouch against blackboards, but their effectiveness is usually in spite of their posture rather than because of it. Sometimes speakers are so awesome in stature or reputation that they need an informal posture to encourage their audience to relax. In that case, sloppy posture is more or less justified. But because awesomeness is not usually a problem for beginning speakers, good posture should be the rule.

Good posture can help you control nervousness by allowing your breathing apparatus to work properly; when your brain receives enough oxygen, it's easier for you to think clearly. Good posture increases your audience contact because the audience members will feel that you are interested enough in them to stand formally, yet relaxed enough to be at ease with them.

### Facial Expression

▼ There's no art
To find the mind's construction in the face.

Shakespeare

The expression on your face can be more meaningful to an audience than the words you say. Try it yourself with a mirror. Without varying your voice, say "College is excellent" with a smirk, with a warm smile, deadpan, and then with a scowl. It just doesn't mean the same thing.

It is just about impossible to control facial expressions from the outside. Like your movement, your facial expressions will reflect your involvement with your message. Don't try to fake it. Just get involved in your message, and your face will take care of itself.

### Eye Contact

Eye contact is essential to the conversational quality of public speaking. When you speak to others, you look them in the eyes, at least occasionally. If you don't, they won't feel that you're talking *with* them or even treating them as people. They might even resent you for "objectifying" them.

Mass media professionals know the importance of eye contact. Consider, if you will, the extremes to which the television industry goes to make sure that their newscasters *appear* to be making eye contact with their television audience. The main device they use is a teleprompter, which is essentially a high-tech electronic mirror trick. The teleprompter is a closed-circuit television monitor that is scrolling the script of the news report. It is placed under the lens of the camera shooting the newscaster, pointing up to a mirror above the lens. That mirror points down onto a piece of glass *in front of* the camera lens. The script reflects on this glass so the newscasters can read the script while looking straight into the camera's eye, and therefore straight into the eye of the hypothetical viewer. The most experienced newscasters don't even move their eyes as they read the script from left to right.

Eye contact is perhaps the most important nonverbal facet of delivery. It not only increases your interaction with your audience; it also should increase their interest in you by making you more attractive. Eyes are beautiful things; much more beautiful than eyelids, foreheads, or scalps. Eye contact is also a form of reality testing. The most frightening aspect of speaking is the unknown. How will the audience react? What will they think? Direct eye contact allows you to test your perception of your audience as you speak. Usually, especially in a college class, you will find that your audience is more "with" you than you think.

## Time Usage

There is one other source of nonverbal messages that you should keep in mind: How you use time. Showing up on time, making good use of your speaking time, and staying within time limits send a range of messages dealing with your respect for your audience, your preparation, and your commitment to your message.

▼ To make a speech immortal you don't have to make it everlasting.

Lord Leslie Hore-Belisha

## Auditory Nonverbal Aspects of Delivery

The voice, like the visual aspects of delivery, is also a form of nonverbal communication. Researchers use the term *paralanguage* to describe messages that use the voice without using words. These researchers have identified the communicative value of paralanguage through the use of "content-free speech"—ordinary speech that has been electronically manipulated so that the words are unintelligible, but the paralanguage remains unaffected. (Hearing a foreign language that you do not understand has the same effect.) Subjects who hear content-free speech can consistently recognize the emotion being expressed as well as identify its strength.[15]

The impact of paralinguistic cues is strong. In fact, research shows that listeners pay more attention to the vocal messages than to the words that are spoken when asked to determine a speaker's attitudes.[16] Furthermore, when vocal factors contradict a verbal message, listeners judge the speaker's intention from the paralanguage, not from the words themselves.[17]

Vocal changes that contradict spoken words are not easy to conceal. If the speaker is trying to conceal fear or anger, the voice will probably sound higher and louder, and the rate of talk may be faster than normal. Sadness produces the opposite vocal pattern: quieter, lower-pitched speech delivered at a slower rate.[18]

In public speaking, your paralanguage says a great deal about you—most notably about your sincerity and enthusiasm. In addition, using your voice well can help you control your nervousness. It's another cycle:

▼ There is no less eloquence in the tone of the voice, in the eyes and in the air of the speaker, than in his choice of words.

La Rochefoucauld

Controlling your vocal characteristics will decrease your nervousness, which will enable you to control your voice even more. But this cycle can also work in the opposite direction. If your voice is out of control, your nerves will probably be in the same state. Controlling your voice is mostly a matter of recognizing and using appropriate *volume, rate, pitch,* and *articulation.*

## Volume

▼ The trumpet does not more stun you by its loudness, than a whisper teases you by its provoking inaudibility.

Charles Lamb

Volume—the loudness of your voice—is determined by the amount of air you push past the vocal folds in your throat. The key to controlling volume, then, is controlling the amount of air you use. The key to determining the *right* volume is audience contact. Your delivery should be loud enough so that your audience can hear everything you say but not so loud that they feel you are talking to someone in the next room. Too much volume is seldom the problem for beginning speakers. Usually, they either are not loud enough or have a tendency to fade off at the end of a thought. Sometimes, when they lose faith in an idea in midsentence, they compromise by mumbling the end of the sentence so that it isn't quite coherent. That's an unfortunate compromise, like changing your mind in the middle of a broad jump.

One contemporary speaker who has been criticized for inappropriate volume is Senator Ted Kennedy. One researcher pointed out that "Kennedy tended to shout when an audience was small or uninterested or when he sensed he was losing them. Thus, his volume was often inappropriate to the time and place."[19] *Newsweek*'s John Walcott observed, "When he had an unresponsive-audience—300 Iowa farmers who were not jumping up on their chairs—he tended to shout more and it became more and more incongruous."[20]

## Rate

▼ Many a pair of curious ears had been lured by that well-timed pause.

Li Ang

Rate is your speed in speaking. There is a range of personal differences in speaking rate. Daniel Webster, for example, is said to have spoken at around 90 words per minute, which would be considered slow even by nineteenth-century standards. On the other hand, an actor who is known for his fast-talking commercials speaks at about 250 words per minute. Normal speaking speed, however, is between 120 and 150 words per minute. If you talk much more slowly than that, you may tend to lull your audience to sleep. Faster speaking rates are stereotypically associated with speaker competence,[21] but if you talk too rapidly, you will tend to be unintelligible. Once again, your involvement in your message is the key to achieving an effective rate.

Nervousness plays a factor in speech rate. It is important in the first few minutes of a speech, when speech anxiety tends to be the worst, to speak slowly enough to be understood. If this tends to be a problem for you, make a conscious effort to slow down, even if it feels like you are going at a snail's pace.

## Pitch

Pitch—the highness or lowness of your voice—is controlled by the frequency at which your vocal folds vibrate as you push air through them. Because taut vocal folds vibrate at a greater frequency, pitch is influenced by muscular tension. This explains why nervous speakers have a tendency occasionally to "squeak" whereas relaxed speakers seem to be more in control. Pitch will tend to follow rate and volume. As you speed up or become louder, your pitch will have a tendency to rise. If your range in pitch is too narrow, your voice will have a singsong quality. If it is too wide, you may sound overly dramatic. You should control your pitch so that your listeners believe you are talking *with* them rather than performing in front of them. Once again, your involvement in your message should take care of this naturally for you.

When considering volume, rate, and pitch, keep *emphasis* in mind. You have to use a variety of vocal characteristics to maintain audience interest, but remember that a change in volume, pitch, or rate will result in emphasis. If you pause or speed up, your rate will suggest emphasis. Words you whisper or scream will be emphasized by their volume. One student provided an example of how volume can be used to emphasize an idea. He was speaking on how possessions like cars communicate things about their owners. "For example," he said, with normal volume, "a Cadillac says, 'I've got money!' But a Rolls-Royce says, 'I'VE GOT MONEY!' " He blared out those last three words with such force that the podium shook.

## Articulation

For our purposes here, *articulation* means pronouncing all the parts of all the necessary words and nothing else. It is not our purpose to condemn regional or ethnic dialects within this discussion. The purpose of this discussion is to suggest *careful,* not standardized, articulation. Incorrect articulation is nothing more than careless articulation. It usually results in (1) leaving off parts of words (deletion), (2) replacing part of a word (substitution), (3) adding parts to words (addition), or (4) overlapping two or more words (slurring).

***Deletion*** The most common mistake in articulation is *deletion,* or leaving off part of a word. The most common deletions occur at the end of words, especially *-ing* words. *Going, doing,* and *stopping* become *goin', doin',* and *stoppin'.* Parts of words can be left off in the middle, too, as in *natully* for *naturally* and *reg'lar* for *regular.*

***Substitution*** *Substitution* takes place when you replace part of a word with an incorrect sound. The ending *-th* is often replaced at the end of a word with a single *t,* as when *with* becomes *wit.* (This tendency is especially prevalent in many parts of the northeastern United States.) The *th-* sound is also a problem at the beginning of words, as *this, that,* and *those* have a tendency to become *dis, dat,* and *dose.*

***Addition***   The articulation problem of *addition* is caused by adding extra parts to words that are already perfectly adequate, such as *incentative* for *incentive, athalete* instead of *athlete,* and *orientated* instead of *oriented.* Sometimes this type of addition is caused by incorrect word choice, such as when *irregardless* (which is not a word) is used for *regardless.*

Another type of addition is whole words—"like," "you   know," dropped randomly into sentences:

> My speech today was, like, different for me to, you know, put together . . .

Sometimes these additions occur as "tag questions" at the end of sentences, such as "you see?" or "right?" To have every other sentence punctuated with one of these barely audible, superfluous phrases can be maddening.

Probably the worst type of addition, or at least the most common, is the use of *uh* and *anda* between words. *Anda* is often stuck between two words when *and* isn't even needed. If you find yourself doing that, you might want to just pause or swallow instead. At first the "dead space" might make you uncomfortable, but it's bound to be less noticeable to your audience than the self-interruption of *anda.*[22]

***Slurring***   *Slurring* is caused, in effect, by trying to say two or more words at once—or at least overlapping the end of one word with the beginning of the next. Word pairs ending with *of* are the worst offenders in this category. *Sort of* becomes *sorta, kind of* becomes *kinda,* and *because of* becomes *becausa.* Word combinations ending with *to* are often slurred, as when *want to* becomes *wanna.* Sometimes even more than two words are blended together, as when "that is the way" becomes "thasaway." Careful articulation means using your lips, teeth, tongue, and jaw to bite off your words, cleanly and separately, one at a time.

The rule for articulation in extemporaneous speaking is to be both natural and clear. Like all matters of personal style, the rule is to be yourself, but be an understandable, intelligent-sounding version of yourself.

There are several techniques for practicing articulation. One is to tape-record your voice. When you play back the tape, listen carefully to your articulation, paying special attention to the articulation problems mentioned earlier. Compare your articulation with that of your favorite television news anchor, and make an effort to emulate it.

Another technique for practicing articulation is to ask your instructor for an evaluation. Once you recognize whether you add, substitute, drop, or slur word sounds, you can make a special effort to avoid those problems.

One cause of poor articulation is speech anxiety, a topic we will now attack in some detail.

## ▼ SPEAKING WITH CONFIDENCE

We discussed the idea of debilitative speech anxiety in Chapter 1. It's time to take another look, from the vantage point of personal style. In Chapter 1 we defined *facilitative* speech anxiety as the speech anxiety that enables the speaker to perform better. *Debilitative* speech anxiety was that which inhibited effective self-expression.

We suggested four ways to overcome debilitative speech anxiety:

**1.** Be rational
**2.** Be receiver-oriented
**3.** Be positive
**4.** Be prepared

These four guidelines will enable most speakers to control their speech anxiety to the point where it will be facilitative rather than debilitative.[23] Here, we will expand upon the idea of how "being rational" can help you overcome speech anxiety. Of course, two guidelines for speech anxiety are the height of rationality. They are:

**1.** For most novice speakers, rehearsal, practice, and experience lead to increasing confidence.
**2.** Remember that you don't *look* as nervous as you feel.

At another level, "being rational" means recognizing sources of debilitative speech anxiety.

### Recognizing Sources of Speech Anxiety

When we suggest "being rational," we mean using critical thinking to talk yourself out of any irrational beliefs that get in the way of speech confidence. People often feel apprehensive about speaking because of unpleasant past experiences.[24] Most of us are uncomfortable doing *anything* in public, especially if it is a form of performance. A performance, after all, puts our talents and abilities on the line. An unpleasant experience in one type of performance can cause you to expect that a future similar situation will also be unpleasant. These expectations can be realized through a *self-fulfilling prophecy,* which occurs when a person's expectation of an event

▼ Courage is resistance to fear, mastery of fear—not absence of fear.

Mark Twain

makes the outcome more likely to occur than would otherwise have been true. A traumatic failure at an earlier speech or low self-esteem from critical parents during childhood are common examples of experiences that can cause later speech anxiety.[25]

You might object to the idea that past experiences cause speech anxiety. After all, not everyone who has bungled a speech or had critical parents is debilitated in the future. To understand why some people are affected more strongly than others by past experiences, we need to understand irrational thinking. Cognitive psychologists argue that it is not events that cause people to feel nervous but rather the beliefs they have about those events.[26] Certain irrational beliefs leave people feeling unnecessarily apprehensive. Psychologist Albert Ellis lists several such beliefs, or examples of *irrational thinking,* which we will call "fallacies" because of their illogical nature.[27]

1. Catastrophic Failure. People who succumb to the *fallacy of catastrophic failure* operate on the assumption that if something bad can happen, it probably will. Their thoughts before and during a speech resemble these:

   ▼ "As soon as I stand up to speak, I'll forget everything I wanted to say."

   ▼ "Everyone will think my ideas are stupid."

   ▼ "Somebody will probably laugh at me."

Although it is naive to imagine that all your speeches will be totally successful, it is equally wrong to assume they will all fail miserably. One way to escape from the fallacy of catastrophic failure is to take a more realistic look at the situation. Ask yourself: Would the audience really hoot me off the stage? Will they really think my ideas are stupid? Even if I do forget my remarks for a moment, would the results be a genuine disaster? It helps to remember that nervousness is more apparent to the speaker than to the audience.[28]

2. **Approval.** The mistaken belief called the *fallacy of approval* is based on the idea that it is vital—not just desirable—to gain the approval of everyone in the audience. It is rare that even the best speakers please everyone, especially on the topics that are at all controversial. To paraphrase Abraham Lincoln, you can't please all the people all the time . . . and it is irrational to expect you will.

▼ I don't know the key to success, but the key to failure is trying to please everybody.

Bill Cosby

3. **Overgeneralization.** The *fallacy of overgeneralization* might also be labeled the fallacy of exaggeration, because it occurs when a person blows one poor experience out of proportion. Consider these examples:

   ▼ "I'm so stupid! I mispronounced that word."

   ▼ "I completely blew it—I forgot one of my supporting points."

   ▼ "My hands were shaking. The audience must have thought I was a complete idiot."

   A second type of exaggeration occurs when a speaker treats occasional lapses as if they were the rule rather than the exception. This sort of mistake usually involves extreme labels, such as "always" and "never."

   ▼ "I *always* forget what I want to say."

   ▼ "I can *never* come up with a good topic."

   ▼ "I can't do *anything* right."

4. **Perfection.** Speakers who succumb to the *fallacy of perfection* expect themselves to behave flawlessly. Whereas such a standard of perfection might serve as a target and a source of inspiration (rather like making a hole-in-one for a golfer), it is totally unrealistic to expect that you will write and deliver a perfect speech—especially as a beginner. It helps to remember that audiences don't expect you to be perfect.[29]

   In fact, many professional communicators are loved by their fans *because of,* rather than in spite of, their imperfections.

▼ Nobody roots for Goliath.

Wilt Chamberlain

 **SAMPLE SPEECH**

The sample speech for this chapter was delivered by Amy Wong, a student at Carrol College in Montana.[30] The speech was delivered from memory.

Amy later pointed out,

> When delivering a speech that has been memorized, it is easy to get into a real pattern of delivery. The challenge was in making each delivery genuine and unique. Eye contact is the key in this sense. I was coached to deliver an entire sentence or even thought, depending on the size of the audience, to an individual. This made the delivery more personal, creating a relationship between the audience and the speaker.[31]

Words that are italicized in this transcript were emphasized in Amy's delivery, usually by changes in volume, rate, and pitch. Pauses longer than a normal "comma" length are represented with ellipses (. . .) and paragraph separations, to demonstrate the pacing of the speech.

The movements mentioned were for *one* presentation of this speech. They weren't choreographed, and would be different were Amy to give the speech again, for another audience.

## ◉ EMS FOR KIDS

### Amy Wong
#### Carrol College

She begins by standing comfortably erect beside a three foot stand with some visual aids on it. She starts off with a serious facial expression. Notice the simple, direct language that is used.

She has picked up her pace at this point, from 125 to 145 words per minute. She articulates carefully to make sure that the increased speed doesn't decrease audience comprehension.

She continues to pick up the pace . . .

. . . and then slows down here, as she takes two steps closer to her audience.

Language choices include those within the quota-

1 In August, three-year-old Joshua Jordan developed a runny nose, coughed persistently, and lost his appetite. Joshua's mother sought *emergency medical attention* for her son. The local Atlanta doctor made a diagnosis which *probably* would have been accurate for an adult, but which was *fatal* for Joshua, a child. Discovering "normal" blood pressure, the doctor ruled out heart failure. What this doctor *forgot* was that in children blood pressure can remain high, *even as they approach death.* A *simple* chest x-ray would have shown an enlarged heart. Joshua *died* before a *common life-saving surgical procedure* could be performed. Cause of death, the National Association of Emergency Medical Services for Children would say: . . . *neglect.*

2 *Today,* we'll examine this *unnecessary neglect* which is claiming the *lives* of our children *by the thousands. First,* we'll survey what is, or more accurately, *isn't* going on in the world of *emergency services for children.* We'll see just how the *system* has failed.

3 *Next,* we'll take inventory of *emergency rooms* and *ambulances* to find out *why* we have a *crisis.*

4 *Finally,* we'll seek ways to better *protect* our children from this fate.

5 Let's begin by taking a *closer* look at the problem.

6 "Even in the *best* hospital systems, kids are *dying,* and being maimed, *unnecessarily,*" says Dr. J. Alex Haller, head children's surgeon at Johns

Hopkins Hospital in Baltimore. "Imagine when there is *no* system, which is the case in *most* of the country."

[7] According to the January 27, 1992 issue of *U.S. News & World Report, six times* more children died from *accidents* as from *cancer,* which is the second-leading cause of *death* for children.

[8] The National Safety Council reports that *each year* 600,000 children are hospitalized because of injuries, and almost 16 million *more* are treated in emergency rooms. Approximately *25,000* of these children . . . *die.*

[9] The startling fact is that, *unless* these children are taken to a *sophisticated* children's hospital, they may well receive care that is *insufficient, inappropriate,* or, in far too many cases, *injurious.* . . .

The *tragedy* is that, for far too many children who die accidental deaths, the worst part of the accident occurs *after* the ambulance arrives.

[10] Dr. Frank Castello, director of pediatric care at Children's Hospital of New Jersey, is *convinced* that far too many doctors, nurses, paramedics, and emergency medical technicians continue to treat *children* as *miniature adults.* Dr. Susan D. McHenry, in a July 1993 report from the Virginia Health Department, agreed. "Training for emergency service personnel places only a *small* emphasis on children," wrote McHenry, "and *many* emergency service care providers have had little experience with *young* patients."

[11] The fact that *children* die more quickly than *adults* in a traumatic situation *compounds* the problem. For *adults* who have suffered trauma, getting treatment within one hour is crucial. For *children,* the critical time is only one-*half* hour. The younger the child, the *shorter* the opportunity to *save his or her life.*

[12] "Just because there's a sign on the building that says EMERGENCY ROOM doesn't mean the people inside have the *tools* or the *knowledge* to treat *kids,*" says Harvard researcher Richard Flyer. "The *worst* thing is after it's all over, the child is dead . . . and parents come up and say, 'We know you did everything you could.' . . . My head is exploding because *I* know, too often . . . it's not true."

[13] Now that we've glimpsed the *magnitude* of the problem involving emergency medical services for children, we can identify *two main causes* which are combining to create an emergency care *crisis* for *children.*

[14] Those two causes are *inadequate training* of health care providers and *inappropriate* or *insufficient equipment.*

[15] Care providers are clearly *not* being trained to treat *children.* They are trained to treat *adults.* Hence, *children* are often being treated as though they were *miniature adults.*

[16] The 110-hour course required to become an emergency medical technician devotes only *two hours* to the pre-hospital *emergency* care of *infants* and *children.*

---

tions you use. Here Amy quotes a doctor's jargon-free statement. Notice also how crisply she identifies the source of the quotation.

Careful word choice makes this idea clear.

Making purposeful eye contact with each member of her audience, she uses specific, concrete terms and statistics.

Notice the carefully constructed syntax of "the worst part of the accident occurs *after* the ambulance arrives."

A slight modulation of her voice signifies the direct quotation.

Here she chooses to use the nonsexist "his or her." Because each of our children is precious to us, regardless of sex, "his" as an indefinite pronoun would be inappropriate here.

She moves now to the right of her audience when she feels the impulse to move. As she moves, she especially seeks out the eyes of those audience members who *don't* seem interested.

She gestures by raising two fingers.

The first finger remains up for a moment as she starts this point.

She again changes pitch
slightly to show that she is
quoting.

She moves now to the left
and returns to the front of
the room.

She picks up one mask in
each hand from the stand
and then replaces them before she picks up one tube
in each hand. Exhibiting
these devices increases
clarity and creates move-
ment that is interesting to
the audience.

She replaces the child's
tube on the podium and
holds the adult tube in
front of her own chest, jab-
bing the tube outward to
demonstrate the disastrous
effects of using the wrong-
sized tube.

She chooses a vivid quotation.

"Cynical forensicators"
happens to be a current
slang/jargon term being
used among her audience.
It's appropriate here. At
the end of this statement
she pauses and reestab-
lishes eye contact with all
members of her audience
by sweeping the room with
her gaze.

¹⁷ Dr. Stephen Ludwig, chairman of the American Academy of Pediatrics,
explains, "Most pediatric residency programs devote three *months* to
emergency care during three *years* of instruction. Critics say this is *insufficient.*" Many nurses who evaluate emergency cases also are *not* prepared
to handle pediatric emergencies. One nurse at Philadelphia's Children's
Hospital stated, "It is an open secret in many hospitals that nurses are
*very* wary of having to care for such children."

¹⁸ But even with proper training, medical personnel need *the right equipment* to treat *kids.* The August 25, 1993 *Journal of the American Medical
Association* pinpoints part of the blame on a lack of *pediatrically equipped
facilities.*

¹⁹ Only *43 percent* of the pediatricians surveyed by Johns Hopkins Medical School in 1993 said their offices contained *all* the equipment and drugs
on a list of *commonly* used pediatric emergency equipment. For example,
children need *smaller* oxygen masks. This is quite apparent when we look
at this child-sized mask and this adult-sized mask. [HOLD UP MASKS]
The *larger* mask may not seal around a child's mouth, thus preventing the
child from receiving *oxygen.* Because children have *smaller* lungs and air-
ways, they need plastic airway tubes which are less than *half* the width of
those made for adults. [HOLD UP TUBES]

²⁰ Despite this knowledge, a 1993 study by the American College of Emergency Physicians found that *79 percent* of hospitals in the United States
do not even have the *right sized tubes* and often resort to rigging *adult*
tubes in frantic attempts to force air into a *child's* lungs, posing a risk that
air could be forced *through* the lung walls *into* the chest cavity outside the
lungs, a potentially fatal condition.

²¹ If *emergency care facilities, hospitals,* and *ambulances* were equipped
with the necessary equipment, *lives* would be *saved.* As Dr. Michael Mat-
lak, a pediatric surgeon in Salt Lake City, bluntly states, "*Speed* saves; delays *kill.*" . . . Dr. Ann DiMaio, director of the Pediatric Emergency Room
at New York Hospital–Cornell Medical Center, believes that if emergency
medical personnel *knew* what to do at an emergency scene, they could
"give us the extra five minutes we *need* to save a life."

²² Saving the *lives of children*—a cause that even cynical forensicators
can't argue with. [PAUSE]

²³ So what can we *do* to *solve* the problem which is plaguing our nation
and stealing the lives of the innocent? The *Harvard Medical Journal* reports that the *best* approach lies in *education* and *enforcement.*

24 The *first* step is becoming *educated.* If you've remained relatively coherent for this speech, you've already begun to accomplish that. The Emergency Medical Services for Children National Resource Center publishes a newsletter and can help you to organize a coalition for support within your state. Their phone number is (202) 884-4297. In response to my request for information, the center sent me this packet [SHOW PACKET] which includes a *list* of each state's Emergency Medical Services for Children contacts, *samples* of grants written by several states currently seeking federal funding, and a *"media kit,"* equipped with camera-ready public service announcements, radio-ready announcements, and a press release, [SHOW ITEMS] *all* geared to excite local support.

The volume of her voice has risen with her increased speed. Here she lowers it a notch as she slows down.

"Remained relatively coherent" is a carefully chosen phrase, designed to provide comic relief without losing the seriousness of the topic. Does it work? She places "EMSC: (202) 884-4297" on the chalkboard behind her and picks up the various items from the visual aid stand.

25 Education includes more than knowledge. To be *meaningful,* education must end with *action.* Unlike *some* social problems, like the energy shortage or the housing crisis, *this* crisis responds directly to grassroots efforts. Educated parents have *already* made a *difference* in communities *throughout* the U.S.

26 *What* are they doing? *Determining* local needs, *informing* the community, and *raising money.*

She moves now to the right of her audience, reestablishing eye contact.

27 The *final* step is enforcement of *existing* laws and passage of *new* laws to protect children.

28 Gratefully, some efforts are currently being made by the American College of Emergency Physicians to create new standards of curriculum for emergency pediatric care. In fact, *Texas* passed an Emergency Medical Services for Children Law on June 3rd. Other states are trying to produce legislation, but, of course, they face the usual roadblocks of *time* and *money.*

As the speech winds down she makes a special effort to maintain careful articulation. She knows that this can sometimes be lost in the relief of hitting the "home stretch."

29 The National Association for Child Advocates has provided me with a *list* of *individual state contacts* working toward sufficient emergency medical services for children. The state lobbyists have outlined *a plan* for their own regions and there is a role for each of us. Usually, speeches ask you to write your representative who lives in Washington, D.C., and visits home for elections. *I'm* asking you to make contact with one of your *neighbors.* A parent who is already working to save lives needs your help.

30 And a *small* fund-raising campaign goes a *long* way. With a mere $1,100 you could *fully* equip a local ambulance for coping with pediatric emergencies. Remember the equipment I referred to earlier? The oxygen mask and the airway tubes? I purchased *all* of it at my local community oxygen bank for $10. Federal grants for local efforts *are available.* The House Appropriations Committee has provided *$7.5 million* for the Emergency Medical Services for Children Program for *this year.*

31 As in all areas of life, *private* action is likely to be *cheaper* and *more effective* than bureaucratic efforts.

She points back to the equipment on the stand.

³² Improving the system and protecting our children will take *intensive* efforts on the part of government, physicians, and parents, but the *means* for employing the solutions *aren't* complicated. By better educating our emergency care providers to *recognize* the differences in treating *adults* and *children,* by improving the *pediatric support equipment* in hospitals and ambulances, by heightening national awareness of the *special needs of children,* and by *enforcing legislation* . . . we *can save our children.*

She returns to the front of the room for her conclusion, providing a type of nonverbal closure.

³³ When it comes to health care for *children,* we have to remember that *one* size *won't* fit all.

## ▼ SUMMARY

▼ There are always *three* speeches, for every *one* you actually gave: The one practiced … the one you gave … the one you wish you gave!

Dale Carnegie

One important lesson we learn from the media is this: Take advantage of your medium. Taking advantage of the medium of public speaking means maximizing audience contact. You do that by developing a personal style that is most effective for you. To develop a genuine personal style you should be yourself, but you should be an intelligent, well-prepared, audience-centered version of yourself.

There are four basic types of delivery—impromptu, extemporaneous, manuscript, and memorized. An *impromptu speech* is given without preparation. It is the delivery style necessary for informal talks, group discussions, and comments on others' speeches. An *extemporaneous speech* is planned in advance but presented spontaneously, usually from brief notes or an outline. A speech presented extemporaneously will be researched, organized, and practiced in advance, but the exact wording will not be memorized or otherwise predetermined. Extemporaneous speaking is the most effective type of delivery for a classroom speech as well as most speeches in the outside world. *Manuscript speeches* are read word for word from a prepared text. They tend to make it difficult to be spontaneous with the audience. *Memorized speeches*—those learned by heart—are increasingly common in the media/information age, in which so many people are concerned with image. Memorized speeches also tend to suffer from a lack of spontaneity.

In all types of delivery, it pays to recognize the difference between spoken and written style. Effective spoken language is generally less formal, more personal, and more redundant, and uses more modifiers than written language.

Part of your personal style will depend on your language choices. These should be made carefully, with due consideration of the difference between *denotation* (the literal meaning of words) and *connotation* (what words suggest to the listener). There are three basic guidelines for effective word choice. *Clarity* involves the use of specific, concrete language. *Vividness* is the liveliness that derives from evoking images within the listener's imagination. *Appropriateness* involves avoiding obscenity and bigotry, and using slang and jargon only when they would be understandable and unobjectionable to the audience.

The nonverbal aspects of speech delivery include appearance, movement, posture, facial expressions, and eye contact (the visual aspects), and volume, rate, pitch, and articulation (the auditory aspects).

One final consideration for developing personal style involves developing confidence. You can work on this by recognizing the root causes of speech anxiety (unpleasant prior experiences, self-fulfilling prophecies, believing in irrational fallacies). In this and in all ways, your personal style should enhance the main advantage of face-to-face public speaking over mediated communication: that is, the interaction the speaker enjoys with the audience.

## ▼ EXERCISES

1. Analyze your personal style in terms of language and delivery choices, as discussed in this chapter. What are your strengths as a speaker? What are your weaknesses?

2. Here's an exercise to increase eye contact skills. As you begin your next speech in class, have each member of your audience raise a hand. Each member of the group keeps his or her hand raised until you maintain eye contact with that person for three to five seconds. It is the speaker's job to continue talking until all members of the audience have felt sufficient eye contact, and therefore lower their hands.

## NOTES

1. A. H. Monroe and D. Ehninger, *Principles and Types of Speech Communication,* 7th ed. (Glenview, Ill.: Scott, Foresman, 1974), p. 142.

2. Joseph F. Sullivan, "Whitman Apologizes for Remark on Blacks," *New York Times,* April 14, 1995, p. B6.

3. Irvin Molotsky, "Admiral Has to Quit Over His Comments on Okinawa Rape," *New York Times,* November 18, 1995, p. 1.

4. J. Tarver, "Can't Nobody Here Use This Language? Function and Quality in Choosing Words," *Vital Speeches of the Day,* May 1, 1979, pp. 420–423.

5. An interesting study in this area is D. P. Hayes, "Speaking and Writing: Distinct Patterns of Word Choice," *Journal of Memory and Language* 27 (October 1988): 572–585. Earlier studies pertaining to the differences between written and spoken language are reviewed in J. F. Wilson and C. C. Arnold, *Dimensions of Public Communication* (Boston: Allyn & Bacon, 1976), pp. 195–198.

6. When we refer to "written language," in this sense, we mean nonfiction, essay, and journalistic writing. Fiction, of course, can be anything it wants to be.

7. *Roget's Pocket Thesaurus* (New York: Pocket Books, 1977), item 537.

8. Farah M. Walters, "Successfully Managing Diversity," *Vital Speeches of the Day,* June 1, 1995 p. 497.

9. Lawrie Mifflin, "Very Little Women," *New York Times Book Review,* June 11, 1995, p. 37.

10. From John F. Kennedy's Inaugural Address, delivered January 20, 1961.

11. The exceptions might include when the topic of the speech is obscene language.

12. The author of this text would not even attempt to define, much less distinguish among, such terms as "nerd," "dweeb," and "spazz."

13. See, for example, E. Hall, *The Hidden Dimension* (Garden City, N.Y.: Anchor Books, 1969). See also Chapter 5 of Ron Adler and George Rodman, *Understanding Human Communication 5th ed.* (Fort Worth: Harcourt Brace, 1994).

14. For example, studies run in 1972, when long hair on males was becoming popular, showed that even long-haired listeners considered long-haired speakers less credible than shorter-haired speakers.

These studies are reviewed in L. R. Rosenfeld and J. M. Civikly, *With Words Unspoken* (New York: Holt, Rinehart and Winston, 1976), p. 62. Also see S. Chaiken, "Communicator Physical Attractiveness and Persuasion," *Journal of Personality and Social Psychology* 37 (1979), pp. 1387–1397.

15. J. A. Starkweather, "Vocal Communication of Personality and Human Feeling," *Journal of Communication* 11 (1961), pp. 69; and K. R. Scherer, J. Koiwunaki, and R. Rosenthal, "Minimal Cues in the Vocal Communication of Affect: Judging Emotions from Content-Masked Speech," *Journal of Psycholinguistic Speech* 1 (1972), pp. 269–285.

16. K. L. Burns and E. G. Beir, "Significance of Vocal and Visual Channels for the Decoding of Emotional Meaning," *The Journal of Communication* 23 (1973), pp. 118–130. See also Timothy G. Hegstrom, "Message Impact: What Percentage Is Nonverbal?" *Western Journal of Speech Communication* 43 (1979), pp. 134–143; and E. M. McMahan, "Nonverbal Communication as a Function of Attribution in Impression Formation," *Communication Monographs* 43 (1976), pp. 287–294.

17. A. Mehrabian and M. Weiner, "Decoding of Inconsistent Communication," *Journal of Personality and Social Psychology* 6 (1967), pp. 109–114.

18. P. Ekman, *Telling Lies: Clues to Deceit in the Marketplace, Politics, and Marriage* (New York: Norton, 1985), p. 93.

19. L. P. Devlin, "An Analysis of Kennedy's Communication in the 1980 Campaign," *Quarterly Journal of Speech* 68 (November 1982), pp. 397–417.

20. Ibid.

21. A study demonstrating this stereotype is R. L. Street, Jr., and R. M. Brady, "Speech Rate Acceptance Ranges as a Function of Evaluative Domain, Listener Speech Rate, and Communication Context," *Speech Monographs* 49 (December 1982), pp. 290–308.

22. One study that looked at the effect of additions such as "uh" and "anda" was L. A. Hosman and J. W. Wright II, "The Effects of Hedges and Hesitations on Impression Formation in a Simulated Courtroom Context," *Western Journal of Speech Communication* 51 (Spring 1987), pp. 173–188.

They found that hedges and hesitations produce low perceptions of authoritativeness and attractiveness, and also make the speaker look guilty.

23. A substantial body of research literature on communication apprehension and anxiety has accumulated. See J. C. McCroskey, "Oral Communication Apprehension: A Summary of Recent Theory and Research," *Human Communication Research* 4 (1977), pp. 78–96. Or see J. C. McCroskey, "Oral Communication Apprehension: A Reconceptualization," in *Communication Yearbook* 6, M. Burgoon, ed. (Beverly Hills, Calif.: Sage, 1982), pp. 136–170.

24. In fact, most recent research suggests that this type of "trait" anxiety operates more powerfully than the "state" anxiety of the public speaking situation. See, for example, M. J. Beatty and M. H. Friedland, "Public Speaking State Anxiety as a Function of Selected Situational and Predispositional Variables," *Communication Education* 38, (April 1990), p. 142.

25. Expectations are a significant predictor of communication apprehension. See, for example, J. O. Greene and G. G. Sparks, "The Role of Outcome Expectations in the Experience of a State of Communication Apprehension," *Communication Quarterly* 31 (Summer 1983), pp. 212–219.

26. See J. O. Greene and G. G. Sparks, "Explication and Test of a Cognitive Model of Communication Apprehension: A New Look at an Old Construct," *Human Communication Research* 9 (Summer 1983), pp. 349–366. See also R. R. Behnke and M. J. Beatty, "A Cognitive-Physiological Model of Speech Anxiety," *Communication Monographs* 48 (June 1981), pp. 158–163.

27. Adapted from A. Ellis, *A New Guide to Rational Living* (North Hollywood, Calif.: Wilshire Books, 1977).

28. R. R. Behnke, C. R. Sawyer, and P. E. King, "The Communication of Public Speaking Anxiety," *Communication Education* 36 (April 1987), pp. 138–141. Indicates that audiences perceive speaker anxiety levels to be lower during performance than the speakers themselves report.

29. J. Ayres, "Perception of Speaking Ability: An Explanation for Stage Fright," *Communication Education* 35 (July 1986), pp. 275–287. Argues that stage fright is a function of the speaker's mistaken perception that ability falls short of audience expectation.

30. Amy Wong, Title Unknown, *Winning Orations, 1994* (Interstate Oratorical Association, 1994), pp. 80–83. Amy was coached by Brent Northup.

31. Letter from Amy K. Wong Little, May 2, 1996.

# CHAPTER 12

# INFORMATIVE SPEAKING

**After reading this chapter, you should understand:**

**1.** The types of informative speeches you are likely to deliver and hear.

**2.** Why informative speeches are an important type of public communication.

**3.** The techniques of effective informative speaking.

**You should be able to:**

**1.** Use the principles in this chapter to make an informative speech interesting.

**2.** Use the principles in this chapter to make an informative speech clear.

## ⬤ INFORMATIVE SPEAKING IN THE INFORMATION AGE

▼ The best way to send information is to wrap it up in a person.

J. Robert Openheimer

The "information" part of the media/information age means that we are living—some might say drowning—in a sea of information. The number of words and images we face every day is staggering. A single edition of the *New York Times* contains more information than the average person living in the seventeenth century was likely to read in a lifetime.[1] In 1994 alone, over 11,000 books and 16,000 magazines were published.[2] Virtually every home has a telephone, and cellular technology is making car phones and pocket phones commonplace. The average American household's television set is turned on for over seven hours per day, flooding viewers with more than 2,500 programming hours per year.[3] The U.S. Postal Service deluges households with 153 billion pieces of mail every year.[4] On top of all this, more than 30 million people use the almost unlimited information stream of the Internet, the global computer network.[5] More than 2.5 million "host computers" feed interactive information onto the Internet every day.[6] Computer information services are growing, making it possible for users to gain quick access to everything from airline schedules to the archives of the U.S. Department of Health to soap opera summaries.

Humans still need food, air, and shelter to survive and prosper. But today, more than ever, they also depend on information. Sometimes they look for answers to questions about personal, practical needs:

▼ Which brands of cars are the most reliable?

▼ What careers will have the most growth in the next ten years?

▼ What makes some marriages succeed and others fail?

Information also can provide insights about broader social questions:

▼ Are children treated better or worse today than in the past?

▼ What parts of the country have the highest quality of life?

▼ Exactly what is acid rain, and what are its effects?

Sometimes we welcome information just because it is interesting:

▼ How good are "experts" at predicting the future?

▼ Why are some people right-handed and others lefties?

▼ How do products like Grape Nuts and Kleenex get their names?

Because the range of information that people want and need is so great, it's no surprise that informative communication plays an important part in most public speaking courses and in the world beyond the classroom.

## Informative vs. Persuasive Topics

Sometimes the line between informative and persuasive speeches is fuzzy. In fact, some rhetoricians argue that *all* speeches are persuasive, since they contain the implied message "this topic is important." It is easy to see how a persuasive message can creep into some ostensibly informative talks. For example, a speech describing the lies and distortions that often appear in tabloid newspapers like the *National Enquirer* and the *Star* could easily become an indictment of cheap journalism. Likewise, a description of how the North American prairie is being bulldozed out of existence could turn into an argument for its preservation.

There is a fine line between the speaker's purpose in an informative and a persuasive speech. In an informative speech, for example, you are constantly trying to "convince" your audience to listen, understand, and remember. In a persuasive speech, you "inform" your audience about your arguments, your evidence, and so on.[7]

There are, however, two basic characteristics that differentiate an informative topic from a persuasive topic.

### An Informative Topic Tends to Be Noncontroversial

In an informative speech, you generally do not present information with which your audience is likely to disagree. Once again, this is a matter of degree. For example, you might want to give a purely informative talk on chiropractic medicine—the treatment of general health through adjustments of the spine. However, if any members of your audience are also members of the American Medical Association, giving a purely informative speech might be difficult, since the medical establishment generally does not accept chiropractic adjustments as a form of medical treatment.

The noncontroversial nature of informative speaking does not mean that your speech topic should be uninteresting to your audience, simply that your approach should not generate conflict. You could speak about the animal rights movement, for example, and explain the points of view of both sides in an interesting but objective manner.

### An Informative Speaker Does Not Intend to Change Audience Attitudes

The informative speaker does seek a response (attention and interest) from the listener and does try to make the topic important to the audience. But the speaker's primary goal is not to change attitudes or to make the audience members *feel* differently about the topic. For example, an informative speaker might explain how a microwave oven works, but she will not try to "sell" a specific brand of oven to her audience.

Recognizing these differences, it is easy to see that there are plenty of purely informative topics. Consider a few examples from one public speaking class:

▼ All information is imperfect. We have to treat it with humility.

Jacob Bronowski

▼ I was brought up to believe that the only thing worth doing was to add to the sum of accurate information in the world.

Margaret Mead

▼ The discoveries of the *Voyager* space probe

▼ How professional sports schedules are created

▼ The true story of Johnny Appleseed

▼ The odds of asteroids and other heavenly bodies striking earth

▼ The history of the Jeep

▼ How new words enter the English language ("hacker," "yuppie," "gridlock," "condo")

Probably the best way to judge whether you have taken a purely informative approach is to ask yourself whether you have an axe to grind about the subject. If your only goal is to share some interesting or useful information with your audience, you are on the right track. If you want to motivate your listeners—to change their thoughts or behaviors from what they would otherwise be—then you may be better off saving the topic for a persuasive speech.

## ⬤ TYPES OF INFORMATIVE SPEECHES

No matter who you are, you can expect to do your share of informative speaking, both in and outside school. A look at the various settings for informative speeches shows their widespread nature.

### Outside the Speech Classroom

Most students take only one public speaking class, but after that course is over they still are likely to give plenty of informative speeches—although the communication may go by other names.

#### In Other Classes

You have probably been giving oral reports since the first grade, and you can expect to keep giving them as long as you are a student. Professors like to assign oral reports for many reasons. Perhaps the strongest one is that students who have to explain a subject to others are likely to understand it better than they would by taking an exam or writing a paper. Knowing that you have to share your knowledge (or your ignorance) with an audience is a strong motivation to prepare. Another advantage of oral reports is that students can learn from one another. Hearing material from a classmate gives students a nice break from hearing the same instructor week after week—and it gives the professor a break, too!

Earning a respectable grade on most oral reports depends not only on how well you understand the material. Your success will also depend on your ability to communicate that knowledge to your classmates and the instructor. In other words, the skills you learn in this chapter will help you do better in other courses as well as your public speaking class.

## On the Job

You will probably never hear the words "informative speech" on the job, but you can count on doing plenty of informative speaking in the course of your work: to your boss, peers, subordinates, and members of the public.[8] In the business world, common informative presentations go by several names. *Reports* describe the condition of an operation. Status reports, progress reports, sales reports, and dozens of similar presentations keep others you work with posted about what is going on in your area of responsibility. *Briefings* are talks that help others perform their job. Briefings are often given at the beginning of a work shift, or at the start of a project. *Training* sessions help an audience learn how to do something: operate a piece of equipment, deal with customers, follow company policy, and so on.

## In the Community

Sooner or later you can expect to inform listeners in your community, probably as a teacher of one sort or another. Perhaps you will coach a Little League team. You may teach a Sunday school class. You could volunteer to report on crime statistics or zoning changes to your neighbors. You might report on the cost of awards or an end-of-season party to the members of your softball team. In one way or another, sooner or later, you can count on sharing your knowledge with others.

▼ An individual without information cannot take responsibility.

Jan Carlzon

## In the Speech Classroom

Even if you never deliver a speech outside of school, you can count on giving at least one informative speech in your class. There are several reasons instructors assign informative speeches. First, they are relatively straightforward. Although the idea of speaking informatively may seem challenging now, this sort of speech is easier to give than the persuasive talks that usually come later in the course. They offer a good chance to practice the basic principles of effective public communication: choosing and researching a topic, adapting your material to the speaking situation, organizing ideas, and supporting your points verbally and visually. Finally, informative talks—at least good ones—are good for the audience: They are interesting and useful. Among other things, they help audience members hone their skills in recognizing the difference between information and persuasion—a useful skill in the media/information age.

Most of the informative speeches assigned in communication classes fit into a specific type or category, although the categories can overlap.

## Introductions

In the first chapter we discussed one type of informative speech: introducing yourself to the audience. But there are many more types of introductory speeches. You can introduce your audience to objects (image scanners), processes (learning to ride a unicycle), events (the *Apollo 13* flight), and concepts (nihilism, pragmatism, or any other "ism") with which they are unfamiliar.

## Instructions

If you introduced your audience to a new product—say, an image scanner—and then taught them how to operate it, you would be using instructions as part of an introductory speech. But instructions can be a type of speech in themselves when your main purpose is to teach an audience how to do something. The "something" may be practical: how to read the nutrition ratings on a cereal box, negotiate the best price when buying a used car, argue a case in small claims court, lose weight, prevent sports injuries, or play a better game of tennis. Still others can be relatively frivolous: how to perform a foolproof card trick or play the harmonica. Whatever the topic, the goal of every instructional speech is to have the audience learn how to do something new or better.

## Demonstrations

Demonstration speeches could be one type of instruction, or they could be a separate type of speech. Whereas instructions teach listeners how to do something, demonstrations show how something works. The goal of a demonstration is not always to teach—sometimes you aim only to increase their understanding, appreciation, or enthusiasm for your topic.[9] For example, consider the topic of CPR (cardiopulmonary resuscitation). You might start out with the idea of instructing your audience how to use CPR in an emergency, but soon realize that this goal isn't realistic in the short time you have to speak. After all, it takes six hours to complete a Red Cross CPR course, and you have less than ten minutes. You could still use the topic by demonstrating how CPR works, hoping that an appreciation for its value might encourage your listeners to take a course in the future.

Some demonstrations describe processes and procedures: how pickpockets operate, or ten ways to make conversation with a stranger. Other demonstrations illustrate objects or equipment: how firefighters use heat sensors to save lives, or the features of a computer word processing program.

## Explanations

Once again, explanations can be part of the other types of informative speeches, or they can be types by themselves. Whereas demonstrations show how something works, explanations tell *why* something works as

it does. Some explanations describe physical substances or actions: the physiological effects of cocaine, or how medical science saves the lives of premature infants. Other explanatory speeches clarify ideas or concepts: everything from existentialism to the Treaty of Versailles. Some explanations describe procedures, like the steps necessary to challenge a rent increase or what it takes to become a saint in the Roman Catholic church. Finally, some explanations are simple descriptions: of how corporate headhunters perform their trade, the history of nursery rhymes, or the attractions of a vacation in rural New Jersey.

You should feel free to combine these types of informative speeches. An explanation of the game of lacrosse might also involve a demonstration of stick technique, and an introduction to the World Wide Web might include instructions on how to sign on to the Internet. No matter what the subject or type, though, every informative speech needs to be *interesting* and *clear*. The remainder of this chapter will help you plan and deliver speeches that meet these two criteria.

## ▼ MAKING THE INFORMATIVE SPEECH INTERESTING

Whatever other virtues an informative speech (or any speech) has, it must be interesting. If you bore your audience into a stupor, they won't appreciate even the most important material. You might assume that the key to an interesting speech is to pick an interesting topic, but in truth most topics aren't inherently interesting or boring in themselves. The way you present the information will either turn your listeners on or off. We might go so far as to say that there are no such things as interesting or boring speeches—just interesting or boring approaches.

You can see the truth of this principle by considering how to plan a speech on the polka. It's hard to imagine a topic less likely to excite most classroom audiences. Despite this challenge, suppose you defined your goal as getting your listeners to see that the polka is an exciting dance with an interesting history. There certainly are boring ways to approach this topic. For instance, you could say:

▼ The polka was an expression of Czech nationalism against the absolutist Germanic Hapsburg rule. The name of the dance refers to the Czech word for "half," referring to the abortive revolution of 1830–1831.

▼ Like many other dances, polka music is in 2-4 time; but unlike others, the emphasis is on the first beat. This rhythm encourages dancers to slide on the second beat and precede it with a hop. This hop-slide movement gives the dance its energetic tone.

▼ There are two styles of polkas today. The Eastern style is fast, with complex musical arrangements and complex orchestration. The Chicago style is slower paced and less sophisticated, and is performed with fewer instruments.

After hearing a few minutes of this sort of material, most of your classmates would probably lapse into a coma. But with the right approach, the same topic can grab and hold the attention of an audience. The key to success is to focus on information that will interest the audience and at the same time achieve your goal of offering new information:

▼ Today the polka has a bad image. Unfortunately, as one writer put it, the dance conjures stereotypical images of "men in bowling shirts married to women who cook greasy sausage and dance with each other." Some New Age bands have made their reputation putting down the polka: Polkacide, whose image is a skull and crossbones with the crossbones replaced by sausages; the Polish Muslims, whose signature tune is "Love Polka Number Nine"; and Rotondi, whose big hit is "Polka Till You Puke."

▼ Today the polka may seem old-fashioned and dull, but when the dance was new it was viewed as outrageous and scandalous. Unlike other dances of its day, men and women clung together with their arms around each other's waists, bodies brushing, completely independent of other dancers. An English polka manual recommended that dancers carry needle and thread to fix the rips in clothing that almost always were caused by the wild dancing. It also advised men to "stop when you hear your partner sobbing very painfully or when you observe her gown is coming off."

▼ At its height of popularity, the polka was a worldwide craze—more popular than any dance today. It spread from the United States south through Mexico and all the way to South America, where it became Paraguay's national dance. It was a hit in Italy, Spain, and Portugal, where there were proposals to name a "polka legislator." It entered North Africa with French soldiers. It was danced in Finland and Russia, in India and Indonesia. Even Queen Victoria and her guests danced the polka at Buckingham Palace.[10]

From this example you can see that, with the right approach and enough research, you can make almost any informative topic interesting and make your listeners glad to learn what you tell them. And you don't have to guess at the most effective material: Use one or more of the research techniques discussed in Chapter 6 to determine the approach and the information that your audience will find interesting. You can use a survey to find out how much your audience knows about your topic; you can use an interview or a focus group to find out which aspects of the new information they find most interesting.

Some speakers have an instinctive sense of how to make an informative topic grab and hold the attention of an audience. But you don't have to be a born speaker to make your material interesting. The following approaches are almost certain to work.[11] Not every topic lends itself to all of them, and you don't need to use every one to interest your listeners. But no matter what your informative topic, you can use several of these strategies to capture and hold the attention of an audience.

## Novelty

Interesting speeches satisfy the "new news" requirement. They present information that is fresh enough to give the audience a reason to listen. Don't make the mistake of many amateur speakers and pick a topic or approach that your listeners will find utterly familiar. Everyone knows fatty foods are unhealthy, that stretching is good for you, and that the world is choking in pollution; so you are making it hard on yourself by choosing to talk about this sort of familiar topic.

Of course, you won't always want or need to speak about fresh topics. In class you might be assigned to discuss a familiar subject—perhaps a local political issue or an upcoming holiday. On the job, you might have to cover potentially dull, familiar material: how to fill out company paperwork or the proper way to dispose of waste. At times like these you can

▼ There are three things which the public will always clamour for, sooner or later: Namely, novelty, novelty, novelty.

Thomas Hood

▼ I will capture your minds with sweet novelty.

Ovid

keep your audience interested by finding a new angle. If you are explaining college registration procedures to a group of new students, you could capture their interest by telling a series of horror stories about people who didn't follow the program correctly and ended up taking difficult classes from terrible instructors at horrible times. You could then introduce your theme as "how to get an awful schedule," knowing that this approach will show people what to do to get the courses they are seeking.

## Variety

▼ Variety's the very spice of life,
That gives it all its flavour.

Cowper

The early days of television programming were filled with hours of "talking heads"—uninterrupted images of speakers droning on at length. This approach to presenting material gave educational television a reputation for being boring. In recent years, TV programmers have learned that most viewers will stay tuned only when material is presented in more varied, interesting ways. From the time they watch *Sesame Street* as toddlers through the hours they spend enjoying MTV as young adults, television viewers have grown accustomed to fast-paced programming. The same variety is present in more serious shows. A documentary on teenage gang violence is sprinkled with scenes of police skirmishes and interviews of gang members and their victims, probably accompanied at times by a musical soundtrack. A report on refugees around the world shows footage of squalid refugee camps and fancy computer graphics to illustrate the problem. Your own "educational programming" needs to follow the same principle. If you present your material in a variety of ways, your listeners are more likely to stay mentally tuned. For instance, if you were inspired by this chapter to actually give a speech on polkas, you could add variety and activity by playing a bit of polka music, showing album covers from the New Age bands that lampoon the dance, or even demonstrating the dance with a companion or a volunteer from the audience.

## Drama

▼ Information's pretty thin stuff, unless mixed with experience.

Clarence Day

Another way to make an informative speech interesting is to make it dramatic. Instead of merely presenting information factually, consider telling it in the context of a story that will interest or perhaps even excite your listeners. One student took this approach when she explained the importance of an archaeological project in northern Florida:

> What happened that day, over 10,000 years ago? The fossil record of a stone spearpoint buried in a bison's skull makes us wonder. Did a brave hunter drive his weapon into the head of a charging animal in a last-ditch act of desperation? Was it an act of compassion, ending the suffering of an injured animal whose spirit the

hunter respected? Or was the spear thrust a cruel prank, a last insult to an animal that was already dead?

It's questions like these that make the job of an archaeologist so challenging and exciting. Archaeologists are like detectives, piecing together the past from shreds of evidence.

With a little imagination you can probably find ways to dramatize even seemingly dry topics. You could compare your traffic-choked community to a potential heart attack victim with blocked arteries. You could use the metaphor of a ticking time bomb to introduce the certainty that a devastating earthquake will strike your community sooner or later. You could use colorful language to describe the utter cold of interstellar space or the unimaginable heat of nuclear fusion. Listeners love drama, so use your imagination to make your information interesting as well as informative.

## Immediacy

Immediacy is defined as the quality of having direct relevance to the present time, place, purpose, or audience. Immediacy is the general principle behind an idea introduced in Chapter 9: "Establish the importance of the topic to your audience."

One of the best ways to establish this importance is to show your audience members how the information in your speech affects their lives. Sometimes the personal connection is easy to make. If you are speaking about inflation, you can show how its growth affects your listeners' spending power and the value of their savings. If your topic is the danger of radon gas, you can talk about how much of that toxic substance your listeners are breathing at home—or even in the classroom as you speak.

Linking some topics to your listeners requires more creativity, but the results are worth the effort. You could connect a topic such as "How immigration patterns shaped North American society" to your classmates by asking:

> How many people here are at least part Irish or Italian? Polish or Russian? How about Chinese, Korean, or Japanese? Anyone here have family from Mexico or Central America? If you raised your hand, then you are probably here because your ancestors were among the millions of immigrants who came to the United States in the past few hundred years. Today I'd like to tell you what they went through so that their descendants—that's us— could be here now.

No matter what your topic, it probably has some connection to the lives of your audience and to their present situation. If you can find that linkage, you are giving them a reason to listen to your speech.

## Specificity

It's hard to get excited about generalities. Your listeners will tune in more willingly and listen more carefully when your remarks are specific. Using the kinds of supporting material described in Chapter 7 will add interesting details. Notice how much more interesting general points become when specifics are added in a speech about the jury system:

| GENERAL | SPECIFIC |
|---|---|
| Jury duty may seem like a burden today, but it used to be much tougher. | In colonial days, jurors were locked up without food or water to encourage quick verdicts. If they brought back the "wrong" verdict, they could be arrested and tried themselves. |
| Despite the attempts of attorneys to screen out biased jurors, personal attachments do occasionally occur. | In a recent Southern California trial, a juror voted to spare a murderer from the gas chamber and then married him. |
| The jury system is stronger in America than anywhere else in the world. | Americans use four times more juries than the rest of the world combined. |
| Your odds of serving as a juror in this community are small. | Using last year's statistics as a guide, the odds against your being seated as a juror are about thirty to one. |

## ● MAKING THE INFORMATIVE SPEECH CLEAR

▼ Everything that can be thought at all can be thought clearly. Everything that can be said can be said clearly.

Ludwig Wittgenstein

Capturing and holding the attention of your audience is certainly important, but it takes more than interesting material to make an informative speech effective: You also have to present your information in a way that your audience will understand. This can be especially challenging with complicated or specialized subjects. Because of specialized training or experience you might understand the biochemistry of addiction or the intricacies of fly fishing, but it will take some effort to get information like this across to listeners who don't have your background. The following techniques can help make your ideas clear.

### Define Key Terms

Definitions are especially necessary if the term you're using qualifies as jargon, or might be misunderstood in the context in which you are using it.

A good definition is simple and concise and is stated in such a way that no other terms within the definition need to be defined. Dictionary definitions are a handy way of determining the most acceptable meaning for a word, but you should be careful about using them to define terms in your speech. Your own carefully chosen words are usually more interesting and clearer than a dictionary definition. For example, if you were speaking on an area of American politics, you might want to define "statesman." The dictionary would give you "one engaged in the business of government," while your own definition might be "a statesman is a public official who expects to be judged by history, not by an opinion poll."

There are two types of definitions: traditional and operational. A *traditional definition* places something in a class and tells how it is different from other things in that class. If you needed to define *pancreas* for a speech on the digestive system, you could tell your audience that it is the gland that secretes digestive juices into the small intestine. Thus the pancreas is placed in a class (glands) and distinguished from other members of that class (it is the one that . . .).

*Operational definitions* tell you what you would have to do to experience the thing being described. Usually this is done by giving a short, observable example. Operational definitions for the term *man* might sound something like this:

> You want to know what a man is? Go down to the graduation ceremonies for Marine boot camp. Now *those* are men.

or,

> You want to know what a man is? Go to the Special Olympics, and watch the men who work with those kids every day with compassion and unfailing patience. Those are men.

In many cases it might be best to combine traditional and operational definitions, such as:

> A man might be the male half of the human species, but for my money a man is a male person who is secure enough in his sexuality to be able to care for children.

Some speakers use a string of short examples as an operational definition. One speaker wanted to define what he called a "culture of lying." He did so as follows:

> We encounter the culture of lying in the contrived statements of government and corporate officials trying to look good on the nightly news. We encounter it in a union leader's complacent advocacy of an action that will benefit his members in the short term but endanger their jobs and harm the U.S. economy in the long term. We see it in phony claims of danger to national security

▼ A definition is the enclosing of the wilderness of an idea within a wall of words.

Samuel Butler

made by businesses seeking protection from foreign firms making better products at lower prices. We encounter it in the TV anchorman's unctuous pretensions to an authoritativeness no human being could possibly possess. We see its reflection in polls showing that the American people don't trust their leaders to tell the truth.[12]

Defining your key terms in this way will help you follow our next principle.

## Speak at the Level of Your Audience

▼ Eloquence is the power to translate a truth into language perfectly intelligible to the person to whom you speak.

Ralph Waldo Emerson

One of the biggest mistakes an informative speaker can make is to talk over the heads of an audience. This is easy to do: You are familiar with the topic, and it may be hard to realize how confusing it can be to the uninitiated. One student, a physics major, made this mistake when he was planning a speech describing how light is affected by gravity. He explained this phenomenon according to Einstein's general theory of relativity—admittedly a tough subject for a general audience. Unfortunately, his explanation didn't make the idea very clear:

Before Einstein, people viewed light as a force that wasn't affected by gravity. But Einstein showed that gravity is a property of space itself, including the dimension of time. Physical matter warps space/time, including the behavior of light.

By this time, the speaker's audience was glassy-eyed. His ideas were just too complicated to follow—at least in the way he presented them. Most of his listeners weren't familiar with the concept of gravity beyond knowing that what goes up must come down; and the concept of space/time was too difficult to comprehend without more explanation. If this speaker had translated his material into simpler concepts, it would have been easier to understand:

> You can understand the effect of gravity on light by imagining that the entire universe is fitted onto a two-dimensional rubber sheet. Suppose that Earth is near one side of the sheet, and that a star is on the other.
>
> According to Einstein, objects—matter, that is—make dimples on that sheet. Those dimples are what we call gravity. The heavier the object, the deeper the dimple.
>
> Now let's represent light from that distant star as a marble, rolling across the sheet towards us on Earth. As the light passes near other stars—which are very heavy, of course—it passes across their "gravity dimples" and is bent. That's why the light from stars we see in the night sky doesn't come to us in a straight line.

Making your material too obscure is certainly a problem, but it can be just as bad to oversimplify your material. One mistake is to choose too simple a subject. Unless you have something new to say to your audience, it would be a bad idea to talk about how a child develops from conception to birth or Darwin's theory of evolution. Even with new topics, be careful not to present information at a level that's *below* your audience's ability. Oversimplification can insult your listeners, who are likely to resent you for treating them like simpletons.

## Cover a Manageable Amount of Material

Don't make the mistake of trying to cover more information than you can comfortably fit into the available time. Classroom speeches are rarely more than ten minutes in length, and they are often much shorter. This limited amount of time just isn't enough to cover many complicated topics. Rather than biting off more than you can chew, consider ways to narrow down a promising topic until you can do it justice. Notice how each of the following broad topics can be focused into good topics for brief informative speeches:

▼ A great many people think that polysyllables are a sign of intelligence.

Barbara Walters

▼ We know more than we can tell.

Michael Polanyi

| TOO BROAD | MORE MANAGEABLE |
|---|---|
| The physiology of sleep | Effects of sleep deprivation |
| African-American cultural contributions | African-American contributions to jazz |
| The Middle Ages | The black plague |
| Modern police techniques | A day in the life of a police officer |
| How to get a job | How to succeed in an employment interview |

▼ Speak properly, and in as few words as you can, but always *plainly;* for the end of speech is not ostentation, but to be understood.

William Penn

## Use a Simple Organizational Plan

Like all speeches, an informative talk should preview your ideas in an introduction, develop them in the body, and review them in your conclusion. This three-part format is especially useful when you are educating listeners. The introduction provides an overview that helps listeners understand where you are headed, the body unfolds the material, and the conclusion drives home the highlights.

Within the body of an informative speech, the simplest forms of organization described in Chapter 8 are usually the best: for example, a spatial plan works well for geographic topics (the spread of Islam) or discussions of physical objects (the distribution of fat and muscle in men and women) while chronological plans are the logical choice for any topic that develops over time (a history of the moustache).

## Emphasize Important Points

There are several ways to separate those statements that are especially important—those that you want to be sure your audience understands and remembers—from the rest of your speech.

Signposts, for example, can be used to announce where you are in the development of an idea. They are especially useful when you are orienting listeners to steps in a process or stages in your explanation:

▸ We've looked at what a dollar used to buy. *Now let's see* what it will get you today . . .

▸ *A second reason* given by couples for their divorce is . . .

▸ *Now let's look at* another way landlords can cheat renters . . .

In order to make your information clear, you should make a conscious effort to use more signposts than you would in your writing or in everyday conversation. Remember that your audience is listening to several uninterrupted minutes of new information. The chance of their losing track of your line of thought is dangerously high, and signposting can lessen the risk.

Interjections can be used as a type of signpost. Interjections are words or phrases thrown into a commentary to highlight the importance or placement of an idea. They serve as a kind of verbal underlining that makes key points stand out:

▼ By now you can see—*and this is important*—that labels don't tell everything you need to know to see if food is healthy.

▼ How important is appearance? *Think about this:* Researchers have found that the impression you make on an employment interviewer in the first minute can overpower anything that happens in the remainder of the session. And what makes the first impression? The way you dress and groom yourself.

Redundancy is also an effective way to hammer home a point.[13] Sometimes you can restate the same point more than once, but paraphrase it by using different words each time:

The disease and violence are so great in Mozambique that over 35 percent of Mozambican children die in their first two years. That means one out of every three doesn't live to see her third birthday.

## Involve the Audience

One of the best ways to help your listeners understand you is to get them personally involved with the material. There are several ways to involve listeners.

### Overt Responses

An overt response gets your audience to act in some observable way. You might have listeners test their body flexibility by trying a few exercises, or you could have them learn relaxation techniques by trying them during your speech.

Having the audience get physically active isn't the only way to generate involvement. A less disruptive and often more practical way to get overt responses is to ask questions of your listeners. You might ask for a show of hands: "Let's see how much we depend on government aid," you might ask. "Raise your hand if you are getting through school with the help of a student loan. What about college work study? How many of you drive on the interstate highway?"

### Use Volunteers

Involving the entire audience isn't always practical. Getting people involved may take more time than you can afford in a brief speech. For instance, you would never have the time to read the palm of every person in your audience or let each one practice CPR on the dummy you borrowed from the Red Cross. Audience involvement can often get your listeners *too* excited, making it hard to settle them down for the rest of your speech. Giving them a chance to yodel or try a judo throw would probably result in chaos.

Despite these drawbacks, you can still involve listeners by asking one or two members of the audience to serve as volunteers: performing exercises, answering questions, and so on. With this approach, the non-volunteers will identify with the people who do not participate and learn from their experience. A big advantage of this approach is that you can choose and rehearse the "volunteers" ahead of time to make sure they will be cooperative and skillful enough to help you make your point. The last thing you need during your speech is an assistant who has the giggles or one who botches your demonstration.

### Question-and-Answer Periods

If the time and structure of the speech permit, you can also invite questions from the floor. Answering questions either during or after a speech turns a potential monologue by the speaker into more of a two-way conversation. Question-and-answer sessions do have their drawbacks: They can cause a speech to run over time and possibly get off the original track. But in many situations the benefits of greater involvement outweigh the risks.

### Silent Responses

Sometimes asking for any sort of overt reaction can risk embarrassing your audience. For example, you probably wouldn't ask listeners to publicly declare if they had flunked a course or if they had been sexually abused. And even for less personal topics, you may have a reticent audience in which no one is willing to volunteer *anything*. In situations like these you can invite the audience to give silent responses.

*Rhetorical questions* are one way to invite silent responses. A rhetorical question doesn't call for an overt response: It is clearly an invitation for each listener to respond privately. Some examples show how rhetorical questions can get listeners involved in your topic:

▼ Are you a cheater? Have you ever taken a peek at a neighbor's test? Copied a friend's term paper? I won't ask you to answer publicly, but let me tell you what some research on this campus has found out about the characteristics of students who cheat at school compared to those who don't.

▼ Have you ever thought about suicide? Has life seemed so bad that just ending it all seemed like the best alternative? What kinds of pressures make some people face this decision and start to live while others surrender to the pain? In the next few minutes, I'll talk about what psychologists have learned.

When you do use rhetorical questions, make sure your listeners know that you aren't expecting an overt answer. Sometimes the nature of your question will make this clear; but if there is any doubt, save your listeners embarrassment by telling them early that you only want them to answer privately.

*Hypothetical examples* are another way to generate involvement through silent responses. They allow you to put each of your listeners into a situation that fits them personally:

▼ Suppose that while you're sitting here in class a burglar decides to support his drug habit by breaking into homes in your neighborhood. Does your place have anything worth stealing? A television? A stereo? Maybe a computer or some jewelry? How easy would it be to rob?

▼ What's it like to be homeless? Imagine that you had no place to sleep, no place to keep your things, no place to take a shower. That would be bad enough now, but think about how much worse it would be in the middle of winter, or if you were sick. Imagine that you had no address where you could receive mail, and no phone where people could count on reaching you. You'd want to get a job, but how would you clean up for an interview? Where would you tell the boss to reach you?

As you can see, there is a wide variety of techniques for making informative speeches interesting and clear. See if these techniques are being used to good effect in the following sample speech.

## ▼ SAMPLE SPEECH

The following is an "explanatory" type of informative speech. It was presented by Diane Johnson Handloser, Professor of Art History at Santa Barbara (California) City College, as the Annual Faculty Lecture, in which a distinguished faculty member is chosen by colleagues to deliver an address on a scholarly subject of general interest.[14]

We've had to compress the original one-hour lecture considerably, but the flavor of the informative speech is here. If Professor Handloser were to write out a purpose statement for this speech, it might read as follows:

> After listening to my speech, my audience will understand that the myth of the artistic personality does not always conform to reality.

And her central idea might sound like this:

> Artistic myths are stereotypes that conceal some truths and reveal others.

The body of the speech conforms to a three-point topical organization:

I. The myth of the artist is made up of three ideas:
   A. The artist as hero with divine powers.
   B. The artist as bohemian who never conforms to the norms of society.
   C. The artist as commercial superstar.
II. The myth of the artist obscures certain truths.
   A. Many artists lead quiet domestic lives.
   B. Artists come from both sexes and from all races and socioeconomic groups.
III. The myth also reveals certain truths.
   A. The myth mirrors the culture of the times.
      1. In the Renaissance, mental powers were appreciated.
      2. In the Romantic period, feeling and sensation were appreciated.
      3. In the Modern era, commodities are appreciated.
   B. The myth reveals that artists *are* different.

Notice the striking variety of images as the various artists' work is projected from slides. Comments on other informative techniques are listed alongside the speech.

## ⦿ MYTHS ABOUT ARTISTS AND THEIR WORK

Diane Johnson Handloser

Santa Barbara Community College

After a few remarks customized for her audience and occasion (which we have cut for purposes of brevity), Professor Handloser begins with an introduction that involves her audience. A specific, well-known example, using the technique of interesting the audience with something that is familiar to them, but making it "new news."

The new news is that the stereotypical view of Van Gogh as a "typical" artist is probably wrong. Language is carefully chosen for clarity. Questions help involve the audience.

1 I have always been interested in the public perception of the personality and character of artists. This subject has intrigued the public at large throughout history, and continues to do so today. I find that people often know far more about the details of an artist's life than they know about that artist's work. For example, students just beginning to study the history of art always know that Vincent Van Gogh *(Figure 1)* is the one who cut off his ear. In fact for many, Van Gogh is a kind of archetype of what the artist is, embodying many of the stereotypes of the creative individual.

2 It is often assumed that artists are eccentric, disorganized, temperamental and difficult to get along with, egocentric, obsessed with their work, crazy, alienated from society and different from "normal" people. I think most people recognize these as stereotypes, but still this image of the artist persists. I have wondered about the roots of these stereotypes. How was this image born? Why are we so ready to accept such images as *typical* of the artistic temperament?

3 What follows are the results of my investigation into these questions. We will first examine the myth, and then look at how the myth relates to reality, to the truth about artists. To clarify the intriguing, complex, and

at times contradictory stereotypes I have uncovered, I will focus on three aspects of the myth of the artist: We will look at the myth of the artist as hero, the artist as bohemian, and the artist as superstar.

⁴ The earliest Renaissance biographies begin in the fifteenth century to treat the artist as somehow larger than life, a hero, a chosen one of blessed birth and blessed life, linked to God by his gifts.

⁵ Alberti, the great architect and theorist, called artists "a second

god." Michelangelo *(Figure 2)* himself often compared his power as a sculptor to the power of God to make man. And he said that as a sculptor he was merely unlocking the figure encased in the stone, as the soul was incarcerated in the body. Michelangelo and Raphael were both called "il divino" by their contemporaries, and references were made to the divine paintbrush of Titian.

⁶ Another recurring theme has God working through artists in a miraculous way. According to legend, El Greco *(Figure 3)* broke off an arm of Christ from a sculptured crucifix and proceeded to paint with it. I find it hard to imagine the artist painting with this sculptured arm, but in the myth, the emotional power of El Greco's compositions is said to have come from divine intervention through this arm.

⁷ The next phase of our inquiry explores the myth of the artist as bohemian: one who refuses to conform to society's accepted norms. The greatest contribution to the myth of the artist as bohemian comes of course from the Romantic period, the early nineteenth century. The Romantic philosophy preached the necessity of experiencing all of life, especially life at its most extreme, so that the artist would have the emotional information available to him to describe life at its most powerful and sublime. In Géricault's *Portrait of an Artist in His Studio (Figure 4),* we have the Romantic ideal of the artist, whose creativity stems from his sensitive and intuitive nature. Exploring his own genius, the Romantic artist learned to trust the primacy of his emotions, and attempted to work

**FIGURE 2**
Michelangelo, *St. Matthew (Detail),* c. 1504.
Photo courtesy of Diane Handloser, Santa Barbara City College.

Paraphrasing helps define *bohemian* as "one who refuses to conform to society's accepted norms." Romantic period defined and the Romantic artist described.

Vivid language and narration used to describe this example dramatically.

Dramatic narration.

Careful, specific word choice makes this idea vivid and interesting.

with absolute spontaneity in response to his sensations. From this philosophy sprang many examples of nonconformist behavior.

8 The nineteenth-century French painter, Eugene Delacroix, is an embodiment of the Romantic myth of the artist. In his *Death of Sardanapalus (Figure 5),* Delacroix, only 28 years old at the time he painted it, gives us the perfect Romantic picture, filled with lush color, organized and energized by a powerful diagonal which cuts across the composition. In it he tells the story of Lord Byron's play of the same name, in which an Assyrian general, facing certain defeat in battle, has all his most valued possessions, his concubines, his eunuchs, his finest horses, his jewels, brought to his tent. There, presiding over it all, he has the tent set ablaze, choosing death over defeat.

9 Delacroix's paintings suggest, by their subject matter and style, a full involvement with the Romantic philosophy of a celebration of the senses. And yet, it is interesting to note that Delacroix, after a brief foray into bohemian behavior in his youth, spent most of his life living in his own aristocratic circle. He never married, but devoted his life to his work, producing an astounding output of more than 850 oils and thousands of drawings and watercolors, confounding another aspect of the bohemian myth, that artists don't work.

10 The Romantic ideal of the artist's genius lived on into the late nineteenth century and early twentieth century. Paul Gauguin represents the bohemian image most vividly because he chose to abandon "this filthy Europe," as he called it, in an effort to find humanity in a purer state, in the South Seas. The Gauguin myth tells of a middle-class stockbroker who suddenly abandoned his wife and three children in order to paint, eventually retiring to Tahiti, where, in the words of the painter's son, Emil Gauguin, "he lived and loved and painted and died like a savage." Emil Gauguin contradicts the legend, affirming that his father had been interested in painting for years, and that his mother had agreed to let Gauguin go off to the South Seas, "not because she had faith in his genius, but because she respected his passion for art."

11 In an 1889 self-portrait, *(Figure 6)* Gauguin was thinking of himself in mythic terms, depicting himself as an icon. This may have been painted tongue in cheek. He never explained what he meant. Nonetheless,

Gauguin portrays himself as a saint, a prophet, a magician, and, at the very least, as a hero of the new order of painting. What Gauguin found when he arrived in Tahiti was a people who had been Christianized for over a generation, who wore clothes, and had already been subject to strong Euro-

**FIGURE 5**
Delacroix, *Death of Sardanapalus*, 1827.
Photo courtesy of Diane Handloser, Santa Barbara City College.

pean influences. What Gauguin created in his work was a version of truth that was closer to what he anticipated finding in Tahiti, than to actual reality. Disappointed by what he found, he created his own Romantic myth about his life and art. Nonetheless, Gauguin makes us taste the mangoes and smell the sweet scent of abundance.

**FIGURE 6**
Gauguin, *Self Portrait with Halo,* 1889.
Photo courtesy of Diane Handloser, Santa Barbara City College.

12 The myth of the artist as genius is still shaped by the Romantic ideal. In the twentieth century, however, there are other elements which begin to influence the myth of the artist, the most important of which are the mass media and the marketplace.

A perfect example of this idea . . .

. . . and a perfect quotation.

13 Andy Warhol best exemplifies the image of the twentieth-century artist as commercial success and gallery superstar.

14 By celebrating money, in his art and his lifestyle, he reversed the bohemian myth. The artist, according to Warhol, must be a good businessman. He said, "Being good in business is the most fascinating kind of art. Making money is art and working is art and good business is the best art . . . I like money on the wall. Say you were going to buy a $200,000 painting. I think you should take that money, tie it up, and hang it on the wall. Then, when someone visited you, the first thing they would see is the money on the wall." All of this was delivered with deadpan seriousness. He left us wondering whether this was a magnificent put-on or simply the honest recognition of the reality of the influence of big money on the art world. As Suzi Gablic points out in her book, *Has Modernism Failed?,* Warhol's power lay in the myth he created, in his enigmatic personality, in the moral ambiguity of his statements.

15 All of these tales are amusing and entertaining, but what interests me is how the myth relates to reality, to the truth about artists. The myth often blurs and conceals the truth; it just as often reveals something essential about the nature of artists and the society in which they live.

Transition to final point.

16 Let's look at the truths. The first truth that the myth conceals is that there is no such thing as the stereotypical artist. Yes, there have always been artists to illustrate the myth, but, by far, the great majority of artists

Development of final point begins.

in the history of art have lived outside the myth, not fulfilling the stereotypes of behavior expected of them. Great art has been created by artists who exhibit all types of behavior, reflecting the range of behavior found in the rest of society.

[17] An example of a great artist whose life did not conform to the myth was John Constable, the nineteenth-century English painter. He lived a quiet domestic life, focused on his family and his painting. Essentially a self-taught artist, he produced marvelous depictions of the English countryside *(Figure 7)*. He made great art out of his own experience, just as Jane Austen, living a narrow life surrounded by nieces and nephews, produced great literature about that life. Constable said, "My limited and restricted art may be found under every hedge." And he once wrote in a letter to a friend, "The sound of water escaping from mill dams . . . willows, old rotten banks, slimy posts, and brickwork. I love such things. They made me a painter (and I am grateful)." We should be grateful as well, for his fresh views of the English countryside cause us to breathe deeper, and remember our connection to the earth.

[18] The myth also conceals the truth about who becomes an artist. Artists come from both sexes, from all races and socioeconomic groups. As interpreters of experience, artists are found in all segments of society. Last spring, a contemporary woman artist, Carmen Lomas Garza, visited this campus. She spoke eloquently of the experience of growing up a Chicana near the Mexican border, in Texas, and the difficulty of living in two cultures. Her narrative art, in all its directness and simplicity, interprets her

*Quotation used to good effect. Note the careful wording of the final sentence in this paragraph.*

*Example from her own campus lends immediacy.*

**FIGURE 7**
Constable, *Wivenhoe Park,* 1816.
Photo courtesy of Diane Handloser, Santa Barbara City College.

life in a way which makes it accessible to those of us who have not shared that life experience. In her work, she deals with specific events of her own childhood, and, through those specific events, she also deals with values which are universal and which cross cultural lines.

19 The mythology of artists also *reveals* certain truths about artists. The myth, no matter how far-fetched it may appear, mirrors the culture of the time. In other words, the myth is ultimately grounded in the attitude of the time toward artists. Thus, in the Renaissance, when creative power was thought to arise from the intellect and the rational mind, there was an appreciation of the mental powers required to make a work of art. When, in the nineteenth century, feeling and sensation were viewed as the source of creativity, artists were expected to, and often did, sate their senses in nonconformist behavior in order to inform their art. Lastly, the commercialism of late-twentieth-century Western society has produced a myth which represents the unfortunate devaluation of art as a locus of spiritual value, and the appreciation of art as one more commodity in a secularized and commercial world.

Notice the paraphrase that begins "In other words . . .", followed by an internal review that begins the third and final main point.

20 Finally, the fact that a mythology of artists exists at all is recognition of another truth in which the myths are all grounded: that when all is said and done, there *is* an "otherness" about artists. The very existence of the myth confirms that artists, at their best, hold a certain power over us, a power which at times may touch us deeply and personally. Artists offer us, in the words of Lewis Hyde, "images by which to imagine our lives." They offer us a way of understanding our past, sorting out the present and foreseeing our future.

Conclusion begins.

21 Artists, by maintaining a connection to the child within them, awaken in us a sense of play and wonder. Their vision makes us more keenly aware of our own. By presenting us with evidence of their gifts, the fruits of their own rich inner life, they remind us of our own potential, encouraging us to nurture our own creative selves.

Careful, memorable word choice helps her main ideas stay with us.

22 This lecture has been my homage to artists, artists of the past, and those I work with every day. We should value them. We should support their work. For in nourishing their own imaginations, they feed our spirits.

## ▼ SUMMARY

The ability to speak informatively is important and necessary, both in school, in the community, and on the job. In a public speaking class, informative speeches usually fall into four categories: introductions, instructions, demonstrations, and explanations.

No matter what the topic or setting, an informative speech has to be interesting to hold the attention of an audience. This chapter described a number of ways to build interest. Choosing an unusual topic or developing a familiar one in a unique way were recommended. Using a variety of presentation methods keeps listeners' interest high. Presenting a topic in dramatic terms by playing to emotions like suspense, humor, or fear can be effective. Showing how a topic affects the lives of the audience is likely to keep them listening. Finally, addressing a topic specifically instead of in generalities makes a speech more interesting.

In addition to being interesting, a speech must be clear in order to inform an audience. Defining key terms and speaking at the level of the audience are probably the most important ingredients in clarity. Other elements include covering a manageable amount of material, organizing it simply and logically, and emphasizing important points. Involving the audience either overtly or covertly is another way to help them understand the information being explained.

### ⬢ EXERCISES

1. Select an informative speech from *Vital Speeches of the Day, Representative American Speeches,* a newspaper, or any other source. Analyze this speech in terms of its effectiveness as an informative message. Point out where the speaker used effective techniques, using this chapter as a guide. If necessary, point out places where effective techniques are still needed, making specific suggestions for improvement.

2. Select an informative piece of writing that is only moderately interesting. This might be an essay, an editorial, or any type of article. Now propose how the topic of the article might be made more interesting as an informative speech through the use of one of these devices:
   a. Novelty
   b. Variety
   c. Drama
   d. Immediacy
   e. Specificity

3. Find any sort of message, spoken or written, that seems to you to be less than clear. This might come from a scientific or technical journal,

or even one of your textbooks. Now discuss ways the message could be made clearer through the use of one of the following:

**a.** Defining key terms
**b.** Speaking at the level of the audience
**c.** Covering less material
**d.** Simplifying the organizational plan
**e.** Emphasizing important points
**f.** Involving the audience

## NOTES

1. H. Evans, "The Facts of Life," *U.S. News & World Report,* February 27, 1989, p. 79.

2. Ibid.

3. F. Williams, *The New Communications,* 2d ed. (Belmont, Calif.: Wadsworth, 1989), p. 269.

4. U.S. Bureau of the Census, *Statistical Abstract of the United States, 1989,* p. 543.

5. This is an estimate based on a survey of e-mail users in October 1994. See Peter H. Lewis, "Technology: On the Net," *New York Times,* May 29, 1995, p. 39.

6. Ibid.

7. Research stresses that the clear comprehension of information affects the audience's perception of the speaker's credibility and the persuasibility of the information. See, for example, S. Ratneshwar and Shelly Chaiken, "Comprehension's Role in Persuasion: The Case of Its Moderating Effect on the Persuasive Impact of Source Cues," *Journal of Consumer Research* 18 (June 1991), pp. 52–63. See also Vicki L. Smith, "Impact of Pretrial Instruction on Jurors' Information Processing and Decision Making," *Journal of Applied Psychology* 76 (April 1991), pp. 220–230.

8. For a discussion of presentational speaking on the job, see R. B. Adler, *Communicating at Work: Principles and Practices for Business and the Professions,* 3d ed. (New York: McGraw-Hill, 1989); and F. E. X. Dance, "What Do You Mean Presentational Speaking?" *Management Communication Quarterly* 1, no. 2 (November 1987), pp. 260–271.

9. B. D. Peterson, N. D. White, and E. G. Stephan, *Speak Easy,* 2d ed. (St. Paul, Minn.: West, 1984), p. 176.

10. R. P. Crease, "In Praise of the Polka," *Harper's,* August 1989, pp. 78–83.

11. See B. Goss, *Processing Communication* (Belmont, Calif.: Wadsworth, 1982); and K. D. Fransden and D. A. Clement, "The Functions of Human Communication in Informing: Communicating and Processing Information," in *Handbook of Rhetorical and Communication Theory,* C. C. Arnold and J. W. Bowers, eds. (Boston: Allyn & Bacon, 1984), pp. 338–399.

12. Paul H. Weaver, *News and the Culture of Lying: How Journalism Really Works* (New York: The Free Press, 1994), pp. 13–14.

13. J. T. Cacioppo and R. E. Petty, "Effects of Message Repetition and Position on Cognitive Responses, Recall, and Persuasion," *Journal of Personality and Social Psychology* 37 (1979), pp. 97–109.

14. The following is a selected bibliography for this speech:

    Clark, Kenneth. *The Romantic Rebellion.* New York: Harper & Row, 1973.

    Feldman, Edmund B. *The Artist.* Englewood Cliffs, N.J. Prentice-Hall, 1982.

    Gablik, Suzi. *Has Modernism Failed?.* New York: Thames and Hudson, 1984.

    Gaertner, Johannes A. "Myth and Pattern in the Lives of Artists." *Art Journal,* Fall 1970, XXX/I, pp. 27–30.

    Gauguin, Paul. *Paul Gauguin's Intimate Journals,* translated by Van Wyck Brooks. New York: Liveright, 1921.

    Hall, Donald and Wykes, Pat Corrington. *Anecdotes of Modern Art.* New York: Oxford University Press, 1990.

    Harris, Ann Sutherland and Nochlin, Linda. *Women Artists: 1550-1950.* New York: Alfred A. Knopf, 1976.

    Hyde, Lewis. *The Gift.* New York: Vintage Books, 1983.

    Kris, Ernst and Kurz, Otto, *Legend, Myth, and Magic in the Image of the Artist.* New Haven: Yale University Press, 1979.

    Landau, Ellen G. *Jackson Pollock.* New York: Harry N. Abrams, Inc., 1989.

    McShine, Kynaston (ed.). *Andy Warhol. A Retrospective.* New York: The Museum of Modern Art, 1989.

    Rosenthal, Michael. *Constable.* London: Thames and Hudson, 1987.

    Wittkower, Rudolf and Margot. *Born Under Saturn, The Character and Conduct of Artists.* New York, W. W. Norton & Co., 1963.

# PERSUASION I: PERSUASIVE STRATEGY

## ▼ CHAPTER 13 OBJECTIVES

**After reading this chapter, you should understand:**

**1.** What is involved in a persuasive strategy.

**2.** How various theories of persuasion relate to public speaking.

**3.** The importance of analyzing and adapting to your audience.

**You should be able to:**

**1.** Formulate an effective persuasive strategy to convince or actuate an audience.

**2.** Bolster your creditibility as a speaker by enhancing your competence, character, and charisma.

**3.** Organize a persuasive speech for greatest audience effect.

This is the first of two chapters on persuasion. This chapter is an introduction to general strategies for persuasive speeches. The next chapter deals strictly with logical argumentation. The strategies dealt with in this chapter are neither logical nor illogical in nature. They are, as you will see, *psychological* in nature.

## ◉ PERSUASION IN THE MEDIA/INFORMATION AGE

*Persuasion* is the process of motivating someone, through communication, to change a particular belief, attitude, or behavior.

One characteristic of the media/information age is that people are constantly surrounded by persuasive messages. Advertising, public relations, politics, religion, and education are all institutions bent on persuasion. Advertising, of course, is the most pervasive of these. U.S. advertising is a $180-billion-a-year business.[1] Advertisers spend more than a million dollars for a single 30-second ad on a top-rated television program, such as the Superbowl. Leslie Savan, a columnist who writes about the effects of advertising in American life, summarizes the prevalence of advertising messages this way:

> Television-watching Americans—that is, just about *all* Americans— see approximately 100 TV commercials a day. In that same 24 hours they also see a host of print ads, billboard signs, and other corporate messages slapped onto every available surface, from the fuselages of NASA rockets right down to the bottom of golf holes and the inside doors of restroom stalls. Studies estimate that, counting all the logos, labels, and announcements, some 16,000 ads flicker across an individual's consciousness daily.[2]

*DILBERT*                                                                      by Scott Adams

*Dilbert* reprinted by permission of United Features Syndicate.

Many of the persuasive messages that you are subjected to are not beneficial for you. Persuasion, as practiced in public speaking, is an antidote for these messages. Just as parents correct media perceptions for their children on a one-to-one basis, public speakers do the same thing for groups of people. The media might teach young girls that thin is beautiful, but their health teachers can explain the benefits of a balanced diet. Young boys might think chewing tobacco is a manly right of passage, but their Little League coach can explain the dangers of mouth cancer. And this media correction goes on throughout life. Your favorite sitcom might suggest that hanging around the water cooler is great for business, but your boss might correct that perception at the next staff meeting.

## The Ethics of Persuasion

▼ The persuasion of a friend is a strong thing.

Homer
*Iliad*

Even if you are comfortable with the importance of persuasion in today's world, *ethical* persuasion tends to be confusing. In Chapter 3 we defined ethical communication as communication in the best interest of the audience that does not depend on false or misleading information. We need only modify this definition slightly to define *ethical persuasion*.[3] For our purpose, we will consider it as *communication in the best interest of the audience that does not depend on false or misleading information to change an audience's attitude or behavior.*[4] The best way to appreciate the value of this simple definition is to consider the many strategies listed in Chapter 3 that do not fit it:

Unethical Persuasion
A. Dishonesty
    1. Deliberate Lying
    2. Withholding Information
    3. Pandering
    4. Feigning Enthusiasm
B. Inaccuracy
    1. Ignorant Misstatement
    2. Reporting Opinions as Truth
    3. Reporting Rumors as Truth
C. Strategies Not in the Audience Interest

You might also keep in mind the three specific guidelines from Chapter 3, which advised you to avoid the following:

**1.** Plagiarism
**2.** Statistical Manipulation
**3.** Irrationality

Besides being wrong on moral grounds, unethical attempts at persuasion have a major practical disadvantage: If your deception is uncovered, your credibility will suffer. If, for example, prospective buyers uncover your attempt to withhold a mechanical flaw in the used car you are trying to sell, they will probably suspect that the car has other hidden problems. Likewise, if your speech instructor suspects you are lifting material from other sources without giving credit, your entire presentation will be suspect. One unethical act can cast doubt on future truthful statements. Thus, for pragmatic as well as moral reasons, honesty really *is* the best policy. Senator Joseph Biden found this out in his 1988 presidential campaign. He plagiarized parts of an English politician's speech and the resulting publicity forced him to drop out of the race.[5]

It is through ethical persuasion that you fight national, and even global, media appeals that might not be beneficial to your community. When you do this, you influence others' lives in worthwhile ways. Look at the good you can accomplish through persuasion: You can convince a loved one to give up smoking or to give up some other destructive habit; you can get members of your community to conserve energy or to cooperate in some other beneficial action; you can persuade an employer to hire you for a job where your own talents, interests, and abilities will be put to their best use.

We begin our examination of persuasive strategy with an analysis of its types.

## ⬙ CATEGORIZING TYPES OF PERSUASION

There are several ways to categorize the kinds of persuasive attempts you will make as a speaker. Two major questions arise: What results will you be seeking? How will you go about getting those results? To answer these questions, we look at desired outcome, directness of approach, and logic of approach.

### Desired Outcome

We can divide persuasion according to two major outcomes: *convincing* and *actuating*.

### Convincing

When you set about to convince an audience, you want to change the way they think. When we say that convincing an audience changes the way they think, we do not mean that you have to swing them from one belief or attitude to a completely different one. Sometimes an audience will already think the way you want them to, but they will not be firmly enough committed to that way of thinking. When that is the case, you *reinforce,* or strengthen, their opinions. For example, if your audience already believed that the federal budget should be balanced but did not consider that idea important, your job would be to reinforce their current beliefs. Reinforcing is still a type of change, however, because you are causing an audience to adhere more strongly to a belief or attitude. In other cases, convincing might *begin* to shift attitudes without bringing about a total change of thinking. For example, an effective speech to convince might get a group of skeptics to consider the possibility that bilingual education is (or isn't) a good idea.

### Actuating

When you set about to actuate an audience, you want to move them to a specific behavior. Whereas a speech to convince might move an audience to action based on the ideas you've convinced them about, it won't be any specific action that you've recommended. In a speech to actuate, you do recommend that specific action.

There are two types of action you can ask for—adoption or discontinuance.[6] The former asks an audience to engage in a new behavior; the latter asks them to stop behaving in an established way. If you gave a speech for a political candidate and then asked for contributions to that candidate's campaign, you would be asking your audience to adopt a new behavior. If you gave a speech against smoking and then asked your audience to sign a pledge to quit, you would be asking them to discontinue an established behavior.

## Directness of Approach

We can also categorize persuasion according to the directness of approach employed by the speaker.

### Direct Persuasion

Direct persuasion is that which does not disguise the speaker's persuasive purpose in any way. In direct persuasion you will make your purpose clear, usually by stating it outright early in the speech (in the statement of your central idea). This is the best strategy to use with a friendly audience, especially when you are asking for a response that the audience is reasonably likely to give you:

▼ I'm here today to let you know why you should take part in the Red Cross blood drive . . .

▼ Have you ever wished that students had more rights and power? They can, if they organize effectively. I'm here today to show you how to do just that . . .

▼ I'm going to ask for your vote today . . .

Direct persuasion is the kind we hear in most academic situations. Laura Oster, a student at North Dakota State University, announced her intention to persuade in her speech about the destruction of tropical rain forests:

> Deforestation has been the focus of nearly every popular magazine in the past few months. We've all read about it, we've all heard about it, but what have we done about it? At this very moment hundreds of acres of rain forest are being demolished. Time is running out. In order to enact solutions, however, we need to have an understanding of the magnitude of this problem. We can then examine the causes of the destruction; and finally, armed with understanding and knowledge, each of us can take action to halt this continuing holocaust.[7]

### Indirect Persuasion

Indirect persuasion disguises or deemphasizes the speaker's persuasive purpose in some way. The question "Is a season ticket to the symphony worth the money?" (when you intend to prove that it is) is based on indirect persuasion, as is any strategy that does not express the speaker's purpose at the outset.

Indirect persuasion is sometimes easy to spot. A television commercial that shows us a handsome young man and a beautiful young woman romping in the surf on a beautiful day and then flashes the product name on the screen is pretty indisputably indirect persuasion. Political oratory sometimes uses indirect persuasion, also, and it is sometimes more difficult to identify as such. A political hopeful might be ostensibly speaking on some great social issue when the real persuasive message is "Please—remember my name, and vote for me in the next election."

In public speaking, indirect persuasion is usually disguised as informative speech. For example, a supposedly informative speech on AIDS could actually have the intent of persuading audience members to remain celibate before marriage and monogamous after marriage. Persuasive intent has also been known to appear in the guise of special occasion speaking. This is best exemplified in Shakespeare's version of Marc Antony's funeral oration for Julius Caesar.[8] Brutus, one of Caesar's assassins, has just finished convincing the crowd that Caesar's murder was just and honorable. Antony has to appear cordial toward the assassins so they will allow him to speak over Caesar's body in the forum. Antony begins by saying that he has "come to bury Caesar, not to praise him," but he slowly works his crowd back to an appreciation of their murdered leader and rage against those who killed him.

Indirect persuasion is the approach to use when your audience is hostile to either you or your topic. It is also often necessary to use the indirect approach to get a hearing from listeners who would tune you out if you took a more direct approach. Under such circumstances, you might want to ease into your speech slowly.[9] You might take some time to make your audience feel good about you or the social action you are advocating. If you are speaking in favor of your candidacy for city council, but you are in favor of a tax increase and your audience is not, you might talk for a while about programs that could solve community problems. You might even want to change your desired audience response. Rather than trying to get them to rush out to vote for you, you might want them simply to read a policy statement that you have written or become more informed on a particular issue. The one thing you cannot do in this instance is to begin by saying, "My appearance here today has nothing to do with my candidacy for city council." That would be a false statement. It is more than indirect; it is unethical.

Indirect persuasion *can* be ethical, however. The test of the ethicality of an indirect approach would be whether you *would* express your persuasive purpose directly if asked to do so. In other words, if someone in the audience stopped you and asked, "Don't you want us to vote for you for city council?", if you were ethical, you would admit to it rather than deny your true purpose.

## Emotion vs. Logic

Finally, we can categorize persuasion according to the logic of the approach. The logical approach, which we will deal with in depth in the next chapter, relies on reasoning rather than emotion. Although logical argu-

▼ Would you persuade, speak of interest, not of reason.

Ben Franklin
*Poor Richard's Almanack*

ment has the better reputation, do not discount the power of emotional appeals. We have known since the ancient Greeks that human beings are not strictly logical.[10] They are instead *psychological,* which means that they respond strongly to emotional proofs.

The use of emotion is one of the major lessons of the media age, in which emotional evidence is often the only evidence given. Television advertising goes to great extremes just to set a mood, or to create a feeling, while giving little if any information about the product. The guideline media advertisers adhere to is, "Sell the sizzle, not the steak." Through your study of public speaking, especially these two chapters on persuasion, we hope you'll become proficient in selling both the sizzle *and* the steak. Emotional appeals are appropriate with a topic that might otherwise be boring to an audience, but such appeals are inappropriate when they are used to mislead or to cloud the audience's mind on a question of fact. And they are unethical when they are based on false or misleading information.

## ⊙ THEORIES OF PERSUASION

Persuasion is a popular topic of research. Aristotle started it more than 2,000 years ago, and modern research into persuasion has been particularly robust since World War II, when enemy propaganda and the advent of the media age made it alluring. There are hundreds of theories about how and why people are persuaded. Three that have attracted a significant amount of research (and are useful to public speakers) are balance theory, social judgment theory, and inoculation theory.

▼ You don't have to give reasons to a jury. Make them *want* to acquit your client, and they'll find their own reasons.

Clarence Darrow

### Balance Theory

The basic idea behind balance theory is that people like to feel psychological consistency.[11] They like to feel that their ideas are in a balanced state. If they like or respect someone, they like to feel that they think the same way that person thinks. If they have a particular image of themselves (I'm a generous person), they like to think that their behavior is consistent with that image (I give to the United Way). Frederick Williams, in his book *The New Communications,* explains the power of psychological balance this way:

▼ All personal breakthroughs begin with a change in beliefs.

Anthony Robbins

> If there is a general motive in human behavior, it is that we wish to live among our satisfactions rather than our dissatisfactions— among what is agreeable to us rather than disagreeable. Balance seems to be one of our major sources of satisfaction.[12]

We strive to maintain psychological balance, but without imbalance we would feel no pressure to change. That might sound all right to you—

perhaps you don't care much for change—but it is important to remember that life involves constant change. Without change, you would accomplish nothing. Think about it this way: Without change, you would simply stay in bed in the morning, theoretically until you starved to death. The fact is, you did find a reason to move (to "motivate") out of bed this morning. That reason was based on an imbalance that is otherwise known as *motivation*—what "moves" you. To understand this type of psychological imbalance, think back to this morning. You were probably happy and comfortable in your bed when the alarm rang. What motivated you to get up? Thinking about that question leads you to a list of audience motivators:

| MOTIVATOR | HOW IT GETS YOU OUT OF BED |
|---|---|
| Fear: | If you don't get up you'll lose your job/fail a class/anger a significant other. |
| Guilt: | You have obligations and responsibilities to meet. A good person would get out of bed and meet them. |
| Health: | You need to work out, or you'll gain weight. |
| Comfort: | You need to eat breakfast, or use the bathroom. |
| Loyalty: | You promised your boss/professor/ teammates that you would show up, and they depend on you. |
| Competition: | Other people are getting up, and if you don't, they might get the job/grade/object of affection that you want. |
| Curiosity: | You wonder what surprises the day has for you. |

The list goes on: There's the desire for wealth, love, sympathy, respect, safety, enjoyment, conformity, and a hundred other motivators you could list. The fact is, the same motivators that get you out of bed in the morning are the motivators that you can use to change your audience's attitudes, and each of these motivators works because it sets up a psychological imbalance in the mind of the audience member.

Consider the way the typical advertisement sets up imbalance. First, it asks you a question: Do you feel tired and run-down? Is your car giving you trouble? Do your kids disrespect you? Does your spouse ignore you? Is your body/face/hair an embarrassment? Do people look at your clothes with disdain? The imbalance is enhanced by your lack of the product that is being sold. That imbalance is designed to motivate you to buy the product.

Balance theory is helpful to keep in mind because it reminds you that you have to knock the audience off balance somewhat. In persuasion, as the old saying goes, "You can't make an omelet without breaking eggs."

Sometimes you have to confront an audience with information that they might have otherwise avoided: the idea that a current audience behavior will lead to hardships in the future, the fact that children are starving in Africa, the reality that your government's involvement in a far-off civil war is being fueled by selfish political motives.

Balance theory also suggests why you should build and maintain your credibility as a speaker (a topic we'll expand on in a moment). We like to feel in agreement with those around us. If we don't, we generally seek other companions. By the same token, if audience members trust you but are made uncomfortable by what you tell them, you've created the psychological imbalance that will enable persuasion to take place. In short, balance theory gives you a question to ask: Will this information put my audience into a state of psychological imbalance? If not, persuasion will probably not occur.

## Social Judgment Theory

Social judgment theory begins where balance theory leaves off.[13] Like balance theory, social judgment theory suggests that persuasion occurs when people feel a lack of psychological balance, but it goes on to explain *how much* imbalance is optimal. Social judgment theory tells us that when members of an audience hear a persuasive appeal, they compare it with opinions that they already hold. The preexisting opinion is called an *anchor,* but around this anchor there exist what are called *latitudes of acceptance, latitudes of rejection,* and *latitudes of noncommitment.* A diagram of any opinion, therefore, might look something like Figure 13-1.

Each latitude is not always the same "width." The latitude of rejection is often largest and the latitude of noncommitment is often smallest. In fact, people who care very strongly about a particular point of view (called "highly ego-involved" by communication researchers) will have a very small latitude of noncommitment. People who care less strongly will have a larger latitude of noncommitment. The idea is to try to change an audience's attitudes as much as possible *within their latitude of noncommitment.* Research suggests that audience members simply will not respond to appeals that fall within their latitude of rejection. In fact, they *reject* positions in this area and cling more strongly to their initial position.

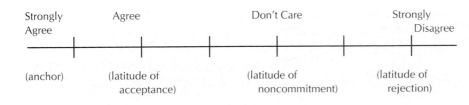

**FIGURE 13–1 LATITUDES OF ACCEPTANCE, REJECTION, AND NONCOMMITMENT**

Social judgment theory reminds us that persuasion in the real world takes place in a series of small movements. It is not a one-shot affair. One persuasive speech may be but a single step in an overall persuasive campaign. The best example of this is the various communications that take place during the months of a political campaign. Candidates watch the opinion polls carefully, adjusting their appeals to the latitudes of acceptance and noncommitment of the uncommitted voters. In fact, social judgment theory goes a long way toward explaining why campaign messages sound the way they do.

Public speakers who heed the principle of social judgment theory tend to seek realistic, if modest, goals in their speeches. For example, if they were speaking on the pro-life/pro-choice question, they would consider a range of central ideas, such as these:

▼ Abortion should be considered simply a form of birth control.

▼ Abortion should be available anytime to anyone.

▼ Abortion should be discouraged but legal.

▼ Abortion is a woman's personal decision.

▼ Abortion should be allowed only during the first three months of pregnancy.

▼ A girl under the age of eighteen should be required to have a parent's permission before she has an abortion.

▼ A woman should be required to have her husband's permission to have an abortion.

▼ Abortion should be allowed only in cases of rape and incest.

▼ Abortion should be absolutely illegal.

▼ Abortion is a sin.

The speaker could estimate the audience's potential latitudes of acceptance, rejection, and noncommitment by imagining how the audience would arrange this list from most acceptable to least acceptable point of view. The statement that best represented the audience's point of view would be their "anchor." Other items that might also seem reasonable to them would make up their latitude of acceptance. Opinions that they could not accept would make up their latitude of rejection. Those statements that are left would be their latitude of noncommitment. The speaker would therefore advance a proposition that fell within this latitude of noncommitment in an attempt to move the audience *toward* the ultimately desired position. The speaker would not try to move an audience from "abortion is a sin" to "abortion should be considered simply a form of birth control."

Social judgment theory therefore gives you a question to ask: Will my claims/arguments/evidence hit this audience in their appropriate latitude?

## Inoculation Theory

Inoculation theory deals with the audience's resistance to subsequent persuasion. The theory works on a medical analogy. When you are inoculated against a specific disease, you are injected with a small dose of that disease. Your body then develops natural antibodies that make you immune to the disease. In inoculation theory, you present your audience with the arguments of the opposing point of view, so that when they subsequently hear those arguments from the other side, they will be less effective. For the speaker, this means that you don't pretend that the opponents' side doesn't exist; you admit to the opposing arguments, and refute them.

Inoculation is effective not only for those audience members who are so gullible that they are at the mercy of the last argument they heard. Research suggests that even highly intelligent audience members are persuaded better through two-sided arguments.[14] Inoculation is also valuable because it enables you to show an understanding of the other side's arguments. One educator who believed strongly that condoms should not be distributed in public schools used inoculation in this way:

> The reply of condom distribution advocates to my reasoning is predictable. Sexual activity among the young is inevitable, they will say, even natural, and for reasons of birth control, avoidance of unwanted teenage pregnancies, and protection from sexually transmitted diseases, including AIDS, it is better that students should use condoms than not. They will insist that the availability of condoms does not increase the likelihood of sexual activity and that, in any case, many students who use the condoms will be selectively active rather than promiscuous.
>
> The counterarguments are equally straightforward. If we teach the young that sexual activity is what we expect of them, at least some of them will come to expect it of themselves. We have no right to exhibit, or to have, such low expectations—especially toward those whose decisions about whether to become sexually active remain in the balance or who hope to live in an environment where restraint is not only respected but genuinely admired.[15]

In this way, this speaker showed an understanding for (although not agreement with) his opponent's arguments.

The question that inoculation theory leads you to ask is: Have I taken the opposing arguments into consideration? At the very least, this will enable you to provide enough information for your audience to answer those arguments for themselves.

### ▼ PLANNING YOUR PERSUASIVE STRATEGY

In a way, persuasive strategy is a culmination of everything discussed in this book. Four attributes of your planning, however, take on prime importance. These attributes include purpose, structure, audience adaptation, and speaker credibility.

#### Persuasive Purpose

Remember that your objective in a persuasive speech is to move the audience to a specific, attainable attitude or behavior. As we explained in Chapter 4, your purpose statement should always be specific, attainable, and worded from the audience's point of view. "The purpose of my speech is to save the whales" is not a purpose statement that has been carefully thought out. In a speech to convince, the purpose statement will probably stress an attitude:

> After listening to my speech, my audience members will agree that steps should be taken to save whales from extinction.

In a speech to actuate, the purpose statement will stress a behavior:

> After listening to my speech, the audience members will sign my petition to the United Nations.

A clear, specific purpose statement will help you stay on track throughout all the stages of speech preparation. Because the main purpose of your speech is to have an effect on your audience, you have a continual test that you can use for every idea, every piece of evidence, and every organizational structure that you think of using. The question you ask is: Will this help me to get the audience members to think/feel/behave

**FIGURE 13–2 MODEL OF A PERSUASIVE SPEECH**

Speech to Convince

Speech to Actuate

**A.** Describe the problem
  **1.** Discuss the nature of the problem.
  **2.** Show how the problem affects your audience.

**B.** Describe the solution
  **1.** Show that the plan will work.
  **2.** Discuss the advantages of the plan.

**C.** Describe the desired audience action
  **1.** Explain exactly what the audience should do.
  **2.** Describe the benefits of the response you are seeking.

in the manner I have described in my purpose statement? If the answer is yes, you forge ahead.

## Persuasive Structure

Of all the organizational patterns discussed in Chapter 4, the one that is most useful for the *analysis* of strategy in a persuasive speech is the problem-solution pattern. All persuasive speeches, no matter how elaborate their structure, are at heart problem-solution speeches.

The model of a simplified persuasive speech is outlined in Figure 13-2. With this model, a speech to *convince* concentrates on the first two components: establishing the problem and describing the solution. For a speech to *actuate,* the model suggests that you add the third component, describing the desired audience reaction.

### The Problem

In order to convince an audience that something needs to be changed, you have to show them that a problem exists. After all, if your listeners don't recognize the problem, they won't experience the psychological imbalance that will enable persuasion to take place. An effective description of the problem will answer two questions, either directly or indirectly.

***What Is the Nature of the Problem?*** Your audience might not recognize that the topic you are discussing is a problem at all, so your first task is to convince them that there is something wrong with the present state of affairs. For example, if your thesis is "This town needs a shelter for homeless families," you might need to show that there are, indeed, homeless families in their community and that the plight of these homeless families is serious.

***How Does the Problem Affect Your Audience?*** It's not enough to prove that a problem exists. Your next challenge is to show your listeners that the problem affects them in some way. This is relatively easy in some cases: the high cost of tuition, the lack of convenient parking near campus, and so on. In other cases, you will need to spell out the impact to your listeners more clearly.

### The Solution

Your next step in persuading your audience is to convince them that there is an answer to the problem you have just introduced. In describing your solution, you should answer three questions:

***Will the Plan Work?*** A skeptical audience might agree with the desirability of your solution but still not believe that it has a chance of succeeding. In the homeless speech example, you would need to prove that establishment of a shelter can help unlucky families get back on their feet—especially if your audience analysis shows that some listeners might view such a shelter as a way of coddling people who are too lazy to work.

***What Advantages Will Result from Your Plan?*** You need to describe in specific terms how your plan will lead to desired changes. This is the step where you will paint a vivid picture of the benefits of your proposal. In the speech proposing a shelter for homeless families, the benefits you describe would probably include these:

1. Families will have a safe place to stay, free of the dangers of living on the street.
2. Parents will have the resources that will help them find jobs: an address, a telephone, washing machines, and showers.
3. The police won't have to apply antivagrancy laws (such as prohibitions against sleeping in cars) to people who aren't the intended target of those laws.
4. The community (including your listeners) won't need to feel guilty about ignoring the plight of unfortunate citizens.

***Is Your Plan Superior to Alternatives?*** This final question might require you to look at opposing plans for the same problem. For our homeless shelter example, there might be proponents for plans to arrest the homeless, to put them on buses out of town, or to enroll them in expensive rehabilitation programs. To prove that your solution is the best choice, you might have to discuss and compare these other plans.

### The Desired Audience Response

When you want to go beyond a strategy to convince your audience and use a strategy to actuate them to follow your plan, you need to describe exactly what you want them to do. This is the way Kathleen Tracy, a student at St. Joseph's University in Pennsylvania, described the desired audience responses in her speech about Romania's "forgotten children," orphans who desperately need care:

> The picture I present may appear hopeless; the reality is, much can be done to rescue these innocent victims. That is why we as individuals must realize there are many things we can do to help these suffering children. Among them are traveling on a relief mission, giving a monetary donation, or even adopting a Romanian child.
>
> Several organizations have been established that sponsor relief missions to these Romanian institutions. Those who journey to Romania do it strictly on a voluntary basis, providing medical care,

food, clothing, and much needed love to these children. Obviously, these missions take 100 percent time and commitment. If you think you have the time and ability to dedicate to one of these missions, the sponsors would be more than happy to hear from you. At the conclusion of my speech I will distribute a handout with the names and addresses of four such organizations.

However, if journeying on a mission is not an option for you, certainly giving donations is a viable alternative, for these organizations simply cannot function without funds.

Finally, the most difficult and yet rewarding action we can take is adoption. Already, hundreds of Western couples have traveled to Romania and returned with a son or daughter from an AIDS-free designated institution, yet thousands upon tens of thousands of children remain institutionalized. It takes a special person, couple, or family willing to adopt, so if you feel you have the capability and more importantly the desire to adopt, many children await you in Romania. At the bottom of the handout is a number at the U.S. Department of State. The officials there will readily answer any procedural questions you might have relating to adopting a Romanian child.[16]

Like Kathleen, you should answer two questions in developing your desired audience response:

***What Can the Audience Do to Put Your Plan into Action?*** Make the behavior you ask your audience to adopt as clear and simple as possible for them. If you want them to vote in a referendum, tell them when and where to go to vote and how to go about registering, if necessary. (Some activists even provide transportation.) If you're asking them to support a legislative change, don't expect them to write their congressional representative. *You* write the letter or draft a petition, and ask them to sign it. If you're asking for donations, pass the hat at the conclusion of your speech, or give each audience member a stamped, addressed envelope and simple forms that they can return easily.

***What Are the Direct Rewards of This Response?*** Your solution might be important to society, but your audience will be most likely to adopt it if you can show that they will get a personal payoff. For example, you can show that supporting legislation to reduce acid rain will produce a wide range of benefits from reduced lung damage to healthier forests to longer life for their cars' paint. Explain that saying no to a second drink before driving will not only save lives but also help your listeners avoid expensive court costs, keep their insurance rates low, and prevent personal humiliation. Show how helping to establish and staff a homeless shelter can lead to personal feelings of satisfaction and provide an impressive demonstration of community service on a job-seeking resume.

### Adapting the Basic Model

Describing the problem and the solution make up the basic structure for any persuasive speech. However, you don't have to analyze too many successful persuasive speeches to realize that the best of them do far more than the basic minimum. One way to augment the basic structure of a speech to actuate is to use the organization suggested by Alan Monroe in his Motivated Sequence, which suggests that a successful persuasive speech should contain the following steps:[17]

1. **The Attention Step.** As you would expect, Monroe suggests that the introduction of the persuasive speech should grab the audience's attention and make them aware of the problem. This is the way Brent Wainscott, a student at Northwest Missouri State University, caught his audience's attention in his speech on the medical benefits of humor:[18]

> Are you . . . tired? Maybe even bored? . . . Come on, you can admit it. Maybe you just feel bad. Maybe? OK, try this . . . look at someone next to you, and frown at them real hard. Go ahead, you can do it. Give them the look of death. Now laugh at how ugly they look. That's it, now you've got it. Smile at them real big. Good. Now look at me with those big smiles.
>
> I don't know if you feel better or not, but I sure feel more comfortable standing up here now that you're smiling.

2. **The Need Step.** This is Monroe's term for establishing the problem. Calling it the "need" step helps us remember that the problem isn't really a problem unless it relates to audience needs in some way. Here's how this step began in Brent's speech:

> The need for smiles and laughter become obvious if you just realize what they can do for you. We all feel gloom or depression sometimes in our life. Sometimes things happen beyond our control to make us feel bad, like tornados, floods, AIDS, heart disease, cancer, death in the family . . . or waking up in the morning with drool hanging out of the corner of your mouth, and then realizing that you're still in class.

Brent then backed up this problem with research he had uncovered about how people who don't have a sense of humor tend to become sick and depressed more often than people who do.

3. **The Satisfaction Step.** This is Monroe's term for establishing the solution. Once again, the title helps remind us that the solution will only work for the audience if it supplies them with a feeling of satisfaction. Here's how this step began in Brent's speech:

Smiles, Laughter, Humor. They can do many things for us. They make us feel more comfortable, more safe, more welcome. A simple smile can better your outlook, and a laugh or two can cure depression, or even sickness.

Brent then backed up his proposed solution with scientific studies proving that humor and a positive outlook can help cure disease.

4. **The Visualization Step.** This part of Monroe's paradigm describes the results of the solution in a way that allows the audience to "see" it. Again, in Brent's speech:

> You can use smiles and laughter to help yourself anytime you need it. Like a self-induced happy drug a simple smile can raise your spirits and give you the better outlook you need. Those common colds that all of us get can be cured through the timeless remedy of laughter. Think about it: What would you rather take? Tylenol, Advil, Contac, and NyQuil, or Eddie Murphy, Bill Cosby, and the Stooges? I know I'd much rather watch Robin Williams than take a swig of Pepto Bismol.

5. **The Action Step.** This is Monroe's term for the desired audience behavior. In Brent's speech, part of the action step sounded like this:

> By this point in my speech, you may begin wondering, "My God, what does he want me to do now?" I'm not asking you to boycott

any products, sign any petitions, or write your congressman. I am asking you to do something that I sincerely hope you practice when you leave this room today, that you do next week, next month, and next year. All I'm asking is this: Say cheese. Just smile at people more often. Laugh a little bit more. Make it easier to show your pearly whites.

You probably noticed that Brent's casual approach and use of language would be effective mostly with a younger, hipper audience. Like Brent, once you have your persuasive purpose and structure clear in your mind, your next strategic consideration is audience adaptation.

## Audience Adaptation

It is important to know as much as possible about your audience for a persuasive speech. To do so, you can use all the demographic, psychographic, and situational forms of analysis that were discussed in Chapter 5. For one thing, you should appeal to the values of your audience whenever possible even if they are not *your* strongest values. This advice does not mean you should pretend to believe in something. According to our definition of ethical persuasion, pretense is against the rules. It does mean, however, that you have to stress those values that are felt most forcefully by the members of your audience. For example, you could well find yourself speaking to a faculty group about letting a production company shoot a movie on your campus. You might have uncovered, from your audience analysis, that the majority of the faculty are against the idea, because they feel the filming would be disruptive of both classes and campus atmosphere. You would therefore stress the increased publicity that the movie will bring to your campus, which will in turn lead to the best possible student applicants. That might not be your primary motive to allow the production company on campus, but you'd use it to be effective.

Also, you should analyze your audience carefully to predict the type of response you will get. Sometimes you have to pick out a *target audience*—that subgroup you *must* persuade to reach your goal—and aim your speech mostly at them. Some of your audience members might be so opposed to what you are advocating that you have no hope of reaching them. (To borrow from a theory discussed earlier, their "latitude of rejection" would be too large.) Still others might already agree with you, so they do not need to be persuaded. A middle portion of your audience might be undecided or uncommitted, and they would be the most productive target for your appeals. To return to our campus filming example, you might not target the most hardline professors, and you certainly wouldn't waste your breath "persuading" those who already agree with you. You might instead aim your remarks at those professors who are flexible enough to see your point of view.

Of course, you need not ignore that portion of your audience that does not fit your target. For example, if you were giving a speech against smoking, your target audience might be the smokers in your class. Your main purpose would be to get them to quit, but at the same time, you could convince the nonsmokers not to start or to persuade smokers they know to quit.

## Establish Common Ground

It helps to stress as many similarities as possible between yourself and your audience. This technique helps prove that you understand them: If not, why should they listen to you? Also, if you share a lot of common ground, it shows you agree on many things; therefore, it should be easy to settle one disagreement—the one related to the attitude or behavior you would like them to change.

Even if your audience is strikingly different from you, don't assume that you have nothing in common. Use your audience investigation, be it questionnaires, interviews, or focus groups, to determine the attitudes held by your audience. If there are real differences, deal with them directly. Steve Allen, a well-known entertainer, suggests that you simply say something like:

> I know a number of you here this evening differ with me on this particular point, but I very much appreciate your having invited me to speak to you about the matter, because it gives me the opportunity to explain why I feel as I do.[19]

The manager of public affairs for *Playboy* magazine gave a good demonstration of establishing common ground when he reminded a group of Southern Baptists that they shared some important values with him:

> I am sure we are all aware of the seeming incongruity of a representative of *Playboy* magazine speaking to an assemblage of representatives of the Southern Baptist Convention. I was intrigued by the invitation when it came last fall, though I was not surprised. I am grateful for your genuine and warm hospitality, and I am flattered (although again not surprised) by the implication that I would have something to say that could have meaning to you people. Both *Playboy* and the Baptists have indeed been considering many of the same issues and ethical problems; and even if we have not arrived at the same conclusions, I am impressed and gratified by your openness and willingness to listen to our views.[20]

## Organize According to the Expected Response

One role of audience adaptation is to use your knowledge of your audience to arrange your points so you develop a "yes" response. In effect, you get your audience into the habit of agreeing with you. It is much easier to get an audience to agree with you if they have already agreed with you on a previous point. For example, if you were giving a speech on the donation of body organs, you might begin by asking the audience if they would like to be able to get a kidney if they needed one. Then you might ask them if they would like to have a major role in curbing tragic and needless dying. The presumed answer to both questions is yes. It is only when you have built a pattern of "yes" responses that you would ask the audience to sign organ donor cards.

An example of a speaker who was careful to organize material according to expected audience response was Robert Kennedy. Kennedy, when speaking on civil rights before a group of white South Africans who believed in racial discrimination, arranged his ideas so that he spoke first on values that he and his audience shared.[21] First, he spoke about the importance of independence for the South African people. Then, he spoke about the value of freedom, and how economic stability contributed to both independence and freedom. With his audience in agreement with all these values, he then went on to relate them all to the idea of civil rights for minority groups.

If an audience is already basically in agreement with you, you can organize your material to reinforce their attitudes quickly and then spend most of your time convincing them to take a specific course of action. If, on the other hand, they are hostile to your ideas, you have to spend more time getting the first "yes" out of them.

### Adapt to a Hostile Audience

▼ Speech is power; speech is to persuade, to convert, to compel. It is to bring another out of his bad sense into your good sense.

Ralph Waldo Emerson

One of the trickier problems in audience adaptation occurs when you face an audience that is hostile to you or to your ideas. Hostile audiences are those that have a significant number of members who feel adversely about you, your topic, or the speech situation. Members of a hostile audience could range from unfriendly to violent. Two effective guidelines for handling this type of audience are (1) show that you understand their point of view, and (2) if possible, use appropriate humor. A good example of a speaker who observed these guidelines was Barbara Bush, when she was invited to speak at the commencement exercises at Wellesley College in 1990. After the invitation was announced, 150 graduating seniors signed a petition in protest. They wrote, in part:

> We are outraged by this choice and feel it is important to make ourselves heard immediately. Wellesley teaches us that we will be rewarded on the basis of our own work, not on that of a spouse. To honor Barbara Bush as a commencement speaker is to honor a woman who has gained recognition through the achievements of her husband.[22]

Mrs. Bush knew that these 150 students, and others who shared their view, would be in the audience. Mrs. Bush diffused most of this hostility by presenting a speech that stressed that everyone should follow her personal dream, and be tolerant of the dreams of others.

> For over fifty years, it was said that the winner of Wellesley's annual hoop race would be the first to get married. Now they say the winner will be the first to become a C.E.O. Both of these stereotypes show too little tolerance. . . . So I offer you today a new legend: The winner of the hoop race will be the first to realize her dream, not society's dream, her own personal dream.[23]

Thus, Mrs. Bush first demonstrated that she understood the hostility that had been expressed, and then gave her opposing point of view. She deflected the rest of the hostility through humor by adding, at one point in her speech,

> And who knows, somewhere out in this audience may even be someone who will one day follow in my footsteps, and preside over the White House as the president's spouse. I wish him well.[24]

It is important that Mrs. Bush's joke was appropriate and made fun mostly of herself. To make the audience the butt of the joke might have provoked more hostility.

▼ Opposition always inflames the enthusiast, never converts him.

Friedrich von Schiller

## Building Credibility as a Speaker

*Credibility* refers to the believability of a speaker. Credibility isn't an objective quality; rather, it is a *perception* in the minds of the audience. In a class such as the one you're taking now, students often wonder how they can build their credibility. After all, the members of the class tend to know each other pretty well by the time the speech assignments roll around. This familiarity illustrates why it's important to earn a good reputation *before* you speak, through your class comments and the general attitude you've shown.

It is also possible for credibility to change during a speaking event. In fact, researchers speak in terms of *initial credibility* (what you have when you first get up to speak), *derived credibility* (what you acquire while speaking), and *terminal credibility* (what you have after you finish speaking). It is not uncommon for a student with low initial credibility to earn increased credibility while speaking, and finish with much higher terminal credibility.

Without credibility you won't be able to convince your listeners that your ideas are worth accepting even if your material is outstanding. On the other hand, if you can develop a high degree of credibility in the eyes of your listeners, they will be likely to open up to ideas they wouldn't otherwise accept. An audience forms judgments about the credibility of a speaker based on their perception of many characteristics, the most important of which might be called the "Three C's" of credibility: competence, character, and charisma.[25]

### Competence

Competence refers to the speaker's expertise on the topic. Sometimes this competence can come from personal experience that will lead your audience to regard you as an authority on the topic you are discussing. If everyone in the audience knows you've earned big profits in the stock market, they'll probably take your investment advice seriously. If you tell them you lost 25 pounds from a diet-and-exercise program, they'll almost certainly respect your opinions on weight loss.

The other way to be seen as competent is to be well prepared for speaking. A speech that is well researched, organized, and presented will greatly increase the audience's perception of the speaker's competence. Your personal credibility will therefore be enhanced by the credibility of your evidence, including the sources you cite, the examples you choose, the way you present statistics, the quality of your visual aids, and the precision of your language.

### Character

Competence is the first component of being believed by an audience; the second is being trusted, which is a matter of character. *Character* involves the audience's perception of at least two ingredients: honesty and impartiality. You should try to find ways to talk about yourself (without boasting, of course) that demonstrate your integrity. You might describe how much time you spent researching the subject or demonstrate your open-mindedness by telling your audience that you changed your mind after your investigation. For example, if you were giving a speech arguing against a proposed tax cut in your community, you might begin this way:

> You might say I'm an expert in the municipal services of this town. As a lifelong resident, I owe a debt to its schools and recreation programs. I've been protected by its police and firefighters and served by its hospitals, roads, and sanitation crews.
>
> I'm also a taxpayer who's on a tight budget. When I first heard about the tax cut that's been proposed, I liked the idea. But then I did some in-depth investigation into the possible effects, not just to my tax bill but to the quality of life of our entire community. I looked into our municipal expenses and into the expenses of similar communities where tax cuts have been mandated by law . . .

### Charisma

Charisma is spoken about in the popular press as an almost indefinable, mystical quality. Even the dictionary defines it as "a special quality of leadership that captures the popular imagination and inspires unswerving allegiance and devotion." Luckily, communication scholars favor a more down-to-earth definition. For them, *charisma* is the audience's perception of two factors: the speaker's enthusiasm and likability. Whatever the definition, history and research have both shown us that audiences are more likely to be persuaded by a charismatic speaker than by a less charismatic one who delivers the same information.

Enthusiasm is sometimes termed *dynamism* by communication scholars. Your enthusiasm will mostly be perceived from *how* you deliver your remarks, not from *what* you say. The nonverbal parts of your speech will show far better than your words that you believe in what you are saying. Is your voice animated and sincere? Do your gestures reflect your enthusiasm? Do your facial expression and eye contact show you care about your audience?

You can boost your likability by showing that you like and respect your audience. Insincere flattery will probably boomerang, of course, but if you can find a way to give your listeners a genuine compliment, they'll be more receptive to your ideas.

Building your personal credibility through a recognition of the roles of competence, character, and charisma is an important component of your persuasive strategy. When combined with a careful consideration of audience adaptation, persuasive structure, and persuasive purpose, it will enable you to formulate the most effective strategy possible. The other major component of persuasion, logical argument, will be dealt with in the next chapter.

## ● SAMPLE SPEECH

The sample speech for this chapter was presented by Bond Benton, a student at Wichita State University in Kansas.[26] He presented it at the Annual Contest of the Interstate Oratorical Association at Arizona State University during the spring of 1995. He won first prize.

The purpose statement for this speech would be:

After listening to my speech, my audience members will carefully monitor the use of private police in their communities.

The central idea might be:

You should monitor your local private police, who are often untrained and unqualified.

The outline of the speech (with corresponding paragraph numbers in parentheses) looks like this:

INTRODUCTION
 I. Preview of Central Idea (1)
    Example: John Padilla (1)
    Statistics: *Los Angeles Times* (2)
II. Preview of Main Points (3)
BODY
 I. *The Problem:* There are serious dangers associated with private police. (4)
    A. They are often unqualified. (4)
       1. They are often untrained.
       Stats: *New York Times*
       2. Their backgrounds are not checked adequately.
       Example: Michael Huston (5)
       Stats: *Los Angeles Times* (5, 6)
    B. They are often culturally insensitive. (7)
       Stats: *Journal of Social Problems*
       Example: *Chicago Tribune*
    C. They are widely used. (8)
       Interview: Frank Jones
       Stats: *New York Magazine*
       Quotation: Luis Lopez
II. *The Solution* includes both long-term and short-term plans.
    A. Private police can play a helpful role, but: (11)
       1. They must be screened.
       2. They must be trained.
    B. There are long-term alternatives. (12, 13)
       1. Community programs (12)
       2. Education (13)

C. There are short-term solutions. (14)
    1. Be aware of private police in your community.
    2. Inform authorities of any irregularities.
CONCLUSION
 I. Review of main points and central idea
II. Final remarks

As this outline suggests, Bond adapted the basic model of persuasive structure by devoting the greater part of his speech to convincing the audience that this is a serious problem. Also, he structured his speech so the solution and the desired audience response are blended.

## ▼ VERY FAKE BADGES—VERY REAL GUNS

### Bond Benton

Wichita State University, Wichita, KS

¹ What's a guy to do? You steal a car, assault two minors, carry an automatic submachine gun, and get arrested on charges of cocaine possession. What can you do for an encore? Well, if you're John Padilla of Long Island, New York, you get hired by the city as a privately employed police officer. Still on probation for a narcotics conviction, Mr. Padilla attended the obligatory two-week training session, then took to the street. While on duty, Padilla fired sixteen shots at a car parked in front of a local high school, killing two young men and critically wounding three others. Commenting on the incident, Padilla's mother stated that he may in fact . . . be mentally unstable.

² Well, putting Mrs. Padilla's brilliant detective work aside, our society faces a new dilemma. More and more, cities are employing private police, who are roughly the equivalent of security guards, to perform functions previously performed by fully accredited state officers. According to the *Los Angeles Times* of September 4, 1994, the current demand for crime prevention, coupled with the era of shrinking budgets, has created a situation in which by the end of the century, state-employed private police officers will outnumber their traditional counterparts, 3 to 1. Already, these officers do $4.6 billion in damages each year, killing over 300 people. Very soon, this nation may become inundated with people who carry very fake badges and very real guns. And in examining all this we must ask ourselves the question: Should our public safety be sold to the lowest bidder? With careful examination of the costly dangers of employing state-sponsored private police, we can indeed see that the answer is no.

The introduction is designed to set up psychological imbalance in the minds of the audience.

Sarcasm directed toward *anyone*'s mother isn't usually the best strategy, but Bond seems to get away with it here.

The importance of the topic is established well. The use of statistics helps establish Bond's credibility, just as careful citation helps establish the credibility of those statistics.

Preview of main points, showing the problem/solution structure of the speech. The "solution at the personal level" will be the desired audience response.

Here he begins to establish the nature of the problem.

An example that is wild but true is backed up with statistics . . .

. . . and more statistics.

Pounding a few last nails into the establishment of this problem.

Internal review; the problem is brought home to the audience.

[3] To better understand this dilemma, we will begin by taking aim at the problem of private policing by looking at the system's inherent harms and how those harms have become so widespread. We'll then try to arrest a few solutions at both the governmental, but most importantly, at the personal level, as well.

[4] But initially, we will examine some of the dangers associated with private police. To understand these negative effects, you only need examine the minuscule amount of training the officers receive. According to the *New York Times* of July 13, 1993, the average training period of a private police officer is only fifteen days. Additionally, any background check of an applicant is haphazard at best. While this may be adequate for the crack security force that eyes the customers at a shopping mall, the article notes that such training can't even begin to cover all the basic knowledge a traditional police officer uses every day.

[5] Take, for example, Michael Huston, a Vietnam veteran whose family claimed he was mentally disabled. Hired as a private police officer in 1992, Huston patrolled the Hollywood area of Los Angeles. After witnessing a burglary at Universal Studios, Huston decided that his best course of action was to burn down the portion of the studios in which the burglary occurred, since he was unable to track down the suspects. After doing $25 million in damage to several movie sets, Mr. Huston then reported the incident to a superior, hoping to earn praise. Later at a trial, Huston claimed that another person who lived inside him had caused the damage. And incidents such as this are not isolated. The *Los Angeles Times* of November 28, 1993, states that private police officers, while numbering fewer than their traditional counterparts, do 74 percent more property damage each year when figured on the national average.

[6] And these numbers shouldn't be that surprising as the article cites a recent survey that indicated that when it comes to using firearms 40 percent of all private police officers are self-taught.

[7] But as if poor training coupled with high liability isn't enough, private security officers would also probably not fit the classification of being exceedingly culturally sensitive. In fact, according to the *Journal of Social Problems,* August 1992, private officers are 20 times more likely to commit an act of police brutality against an African American suspect than their white counterparts. According to the *Chicago Tribune,* March 28, 1993, racism in the private police that patrolled the predominantly black South Side was so pervasive, the community actually celebrated when the department disbanded. Commenting on the city's move away from private police, Ray Collin, a lifelong South Side resident, stated, "I think we'll have more security, now that we got rid of those damn security guards."

[8] Well, now that we have examined the risks of the state using private police officers, it would seem that only a few misguided, penny-pinching areas would use such an incredibly flawed system on a mass scale.

However, the *Journal of Criminal Justice,* June 1994, states that virtually every community in America utilizes private police officers. In fact, in a telephone interview that I conducted with Frank Jones of the Tempe police department, I was told that the city we are in right now employs private police officers in a patrolling and investigative capacity, particularly in the area on and around this campus. And the reason actions like this have been necessitated is simple: Cities right now are experiencing a dramatic rise in crime, while in turn they are receiving less money to run their police forces. And although private police represent a big risk, they are very cheap. According to the *New York Magazine* of March 13, 1995, private police officers earn as little as one-tenth the salary of traditional police. As former state trooper and current New York City councilman Luis Lopez stated, "When issues like this come up, I usually abstain from voting. I have big doubts about these guys, but there's no way I can vote against them."

[9] Lopez's doubts are echoed in the minds of many politicians, yet as long as America demands a greater police presence on the streets, while continuing to feel apprehension about any tax increases, hiring private officers will remain a politically viable solution to this dilemma.

[10] At this point, we have observed some of the harms inherent in private policing by first looking at the dangerously low quality of service that the officers provide, and secondly, understanding how this problem has become so widespread in our society. With this new understanding, we can now go about looking at some pragmatic solutions to this difficult dilemma.

*Internal review.*

[11] Now it would be unwise to imply that all of these officers are corrupt and incompetent, or that there is no role for private police in our society. In fact, Les Johnson, in his 1993 book *The Rebirth of Private Policing,* states that well-trained private police officers are integral to private industry and that they may play a very helpful role in helping the public in areas such as clerical work and traffic duty. Yet before this can occur, Johnson contends that steps need to be taken to clean up the process by which the applicants are both screened and trained. Determining little things, like is the potential officer a rapist or murderer, would be a beneficial start in this direction. As the *Los Angeles Times* of January 28, 1995, explains, the current situation dictates that cities can't do the job alone, but at the very least, private police must be checked by a policy that dictates they are part of the solution, rather than part of the problem.

*Counterarguments are given as a form of inoculation.*

[12] The government would also do well to examine other options in the area of crime control before they put all their eggs in the private policing basket. The *Journal of Planning,* June 1994, states that community-based crime prevention programs may actually be preferable to private police in terms of cost, effectiveness, and long-term support. Simple measures, such as setting up neighborhood watch programs, give citizens advocacy in

owning their own self-protection. Yet, perhaps the greatest advantage to such programs is that they rely on internal solutions to solving crime, rather than counting on the visibly inefficent help that outside forces attempt to provide.

<sup>13</sup> Yet all these measures are invalid unless individuals take action on them. And amazingly enough, you don't even have to write your congressman. In hearings on private security held before the U.S. House of Representatives, Dr. John Chavela, professor of Law Enforcement Administration at Western Illinois University, stated that this is a battle that will be decided largely at the local level. Essentially this means that simply educating yourself to actions occurring in your community is a crucial first step. By making a phone call to your mayor regarding these concerns about private policing or even joining your local neighborhood watch program, you can have an immeasurable impact.

<sup>14</sup> Now such measures may be well and good in the long run, but there are basic steps that need to be remembered when dealing with the problems that this issue presents in the meantime. First of all, by law, all privately employed state police officers must wear uniforms and badges designating them as such. If you are ever a victim of a crime and aren't comfortable talking with one of these officers, simply request to see a fully accredited police official. But most importantly, if you ever witness any suspicious-looking action on the part of a private officer, inform the local authorities immediately. As the *New York Times,* November 4, 1993, states, public scrutiny is the only way the actions of these individuals can be monitored and effectively dealt with.

<sup>15</sup> Today we have examined the problems of private policing by first examining how these officers are unequipped for their roles as police and how this problem has become so widespread in society. We then examined some simple and pragmatic solutions to this problem at both the societal and, finally, at the personal level.

<sup>16</sup> Thomas Jefferson once stated that one corrupt officer of the law is more deplorable than a thousand thieves. If we as individuals and as a society don't take action against the problems that private policing has created, we stand on the verge of proving this old adage true.

The left margin annotations read:

*Desired audience responses are made as simple . . .*

*. . . and as specific as possible.*

*Review of main points.*

*Conclusion includes an effective paraphrase.*

## ▼ SUMMARY

Persuasion—the act of moving someone, through communication, toward a belief, attitude or behavior—is an inherent part of the media/information age. With so much persuasion around us, it is important to understand how it works.

Persuasion can be both worthwhile and ethical. Ethical persuasion requires that the speaker be sincere and honest and avoid such behaviors as poor preparation and plagiarism. It also requires that the persuasion be in the best interest of the audience.

Persuasion can be categorized according to its intended outcome (convincing or actuating), its approach (direct or indirect), or its logic (rational or emotional), although any persuasive speech might have characteristics of all three categories.

Three theories of persuasion—balance theory, social judgment theory, and inoculation theory—provide insight into effective persuasion. Balance theory reminds us of the need to create psychological discomfort in the minds of our audience members. Social judgment theory reminds us to target our appeals to an idea that the audience can potentially accept, and inoculation theory reminds us to take opposing arguments into consideration.

Planning your persuasive strategy involves setting a clear persuasive purpose, as well as careful structure. A typical structure for a speech to convince requires you to explain what the problem is and then propose a solution. For a speech to actuate, you also have to ask for a desired audience response. This basic three-pronged structure can be adapted to more elaborate persuasive plans, but the basic components will remain a part of any persuasive strategy. For each of these components, you need to analyze the arguments your audience will have against accepting what you say and then answer those arguments.

Audience adaptation is an integral part of persuasive speaking. Adaptation techniques include establishing common ground, organizing in such a way that you can expect a "yes" response along each step of your persuasive plan, and adapting to a hostile audience.

The final component of persuasive strategy dealt with in this chapter was building credibility as a speaker. Credibility is made up of three components: competence (how much you know), character (how much you can be trusted), and charisma (your enthusiasm and likability).

Many of the persuasive strategies dealt with in this chapter are nonlogical in nature. The next chapter will deal with developing logical arguments.

## ⬙ EXERCISES

1. What specific behaviors could you request from an audience, in a strategy to actuate, for each of the following speech topics:

   ▼ Discrimination against gays in the military should (should not) be banned.

▼ Censorship of school materials by religious and political groups should not (should) be allowed.

▼ Teenage pregnancy is (is not) a serious problem.

▼ Telemarketing is (is not) an invasion of privacy.

**2.** To better understand the concept of latitudes of acceptance, rejection, and noncommitment, formulate a list of perspectives on a topic of your choice. This list should contain eight to ten statements that represent a variety of attitudes, such as the list pertaining to the pro-life/pro-choice issue on page 352. Arrange this list, from your own point of view, from most acceptable to least acceptable. Then circle the single statement that best represents your own point of view. This will be your "anchor." Underline those items that also seem reasonable. These make up your latitude of acceptance on this issue. Then cross out the numbers in front of any items that express opinions that you cannot accept. These make up your latitude of rejection. Those statements that are left would be your latitude of noncommitment. Do you agree that someone seeking to persuade you on this issue would do best by advancing propositions that fall within this latitude of non-commitment?

**3.** Identify someone who tries to persuade *you* via public speaking or mass communication. This person might be a politician, a teacher, a member of the clergy, a coach, a boss, or anyone else. Analyze this person's credibility in terms of the three dimensions discussed in this chapter. Which factor is most important in terms of the effectiveness of this person's persuasiveness on you?

# NOTES

1. Stuart Elliott, "Advertising: A Sunny Forecast for Ad Spending Grows Even Brighter," *New York Times,* June 14, 1995, p. D9.

2. Leslie Savan, *The Sponsored Life: Ads, TV, and American Culture* (Philadelphia: Temple University Press, 1994), p. 1.

3. For a research perspective on ethical guidelines, see R. Arnett, "The Status of Communication Ethics Scholarship in Speech Communication Journals from 1915 to 1985," *Central States Speech Journal* 38, no. 1 (Spring 1987), pp. 44–61. See also J. A. Jaska and M. S. Pritchard, *Communication Ethics: Methods of Analysis* (Belmont, Calif.: Wadsworth, 1988).

4. R. L. Frank, "The Abuse of Evidence in Persuasive Speaking," *National Forensic Journal* 1 (Fall 1983), pp. 97–107. Discusses three ethical problems with the use of evidence by student finalists in the Persuasion Section of the 1981 National Forensic Association's Individual Events National Tournament: (1) fabrication of sources and data, (2) source deception, and (3) plagiarism.

5. "Biden Drops Out of Race for Democratic Presidential Nomination," *New York Times,* September 24, 1987, p. 1, col. 1.

6. For our purposes here, a third type of action, *continuance,* or reinforcement, is categorized as a type of "convincing."

7. Laura K. Oster, "Deforestation: A Time for Action," *Winning Orations, 1990* (Interstate Oratorical Association, 1990), pp. 79–80. Laura was coached by Theresa Krier.

8. W. Shakespeare, *Julius Caesar,* Act III, Scene ii.

9. Some research findings suggest that audiences may perceive a direct strategy as a threat to their "freedom" to form their own opinions. This perception hampers persuasion. See J. W. Brehm, *A Theory of Psychological Reactance* (New York: Academic Press, 1966). There also exists considerable evidence to suggest that announcing an intent to persuade in the introduction can reduce a message's effectiveness. Sample studies on this matter include J. Allyn and L. Festinger, "The Effectiveness of Unanticipated Persuasive Communications," *Journal of Abnormal and Social Psychology* 62 (1961), pp. 35–40; and C. A. Kiesler and S. B. Kiesler, "Role Forewarning in Persuasive Communications," *Journal of Abnormal and Social Psychology* 18 (1971), pp. 210–221.

10. An overview of the functions of emotional appeals is provided in Peter Jorgensen, "Capturing the Mind and the Heart: An Exploration of the Function and Role of Emotional Appeals in the Persuasion Process," paper presented at the Speech Communication Association annual convention, New Orleans, November 1994.

11. There are actually several balance theories, including Consistency Theory, Congruency Theory, and Cognitive Dissonance Theory. The distinctions among these aren't important to us here, but those who are curious should see Charles Larson, *Persuasion: Reception and Responsibility,* 6th ed. (Belmont, Calif.: Wadsworth, 1992), p. 78.

12. Frederick Williams, *The New Communications,* 3d ed. (Belmont, Calif.: Wadsworth, 1992), p. 98.

13. Social Judgment Theory, also known as Social Judgment-Involvement Theory, was first advanced in the work of Muzafer Sherif. See Carolyn Sherif, Muzafer Sherif, and Roger Nebergall, *Attitude and Attitude Change: The Social Judgment-Involvement Approach* (Philadelphia: W. B. Saunders, 1965). For a current summary of this theory see Kim Griffin, *A First Look at Communication Theory* (New York: McGraw-Hill, 1991), pp. 178–185, or Sarah Trenholm, *Human Communication Theory,* 2d ed. (Englewood Cliffs, N.J.: Prentice-Hall, 1991), pp. 232–235.

14. See, for example, Lowry and DeFleur, *Milestones in Mass Communication Research,* p. 132.

15. Edwin J. Delattre, "Condoms and Coercion: The Maturity of Self-Determination," speech delivered by the Dean Ad Interim of the Boston University School of Education to the Chelsea Management Team and the Public, January 14, 1992. Reprinted in *Vital Speeches of the Day,* April 15, 1992, p. 412.

16. Kathleen Tracey, "The Forgotten Children," *Winning Orations, 1991* (Interstate Oratorical Association, 1991), p. 99. Kathleen was coached by Robert G. Del Casale.

17. A. Monroe, *Principles and Types of Speech* (Glenview, Ill.: Scott, Foresman, 1935).

18. Brent Wainscott, Title Unknown, *Winning Orations, 1990* (Interstate Oratorical Association, 1990), pp. 70–73. Brent was coached by William Laubert.

19. Steve Allen, *How to Make a Speech* (New York: McGraw-Hill, 1986), p. 118.

20. A. Mount, speech before Southern Baptist Convention, in *Contemporary American Speeches,* 3d ed., W. A. Linkugel, R. R. Allen, and R. Johannessen, eds. (Belmont, Calif.: Wadsworth, 1973).

21. H. J. Rudolf, "Robert F. Kennedy at Stellenbosch University," *Communication Quarterly* 31 (Summer 1983), pp. 205–211.

22. Introduction to Barbara Bush's speech, "Choices and Change," in *Representative American Speeches, 1990-1991,* Owen Peterson, ed. (New York: H. W. Wilson Co., 1991), p. 162.

23. Barbara Bush, "Choices and Change," speech presented to the graduating class of Wellesley College in Wellesley, Massachusetts, on June 1, 1990, before an audience of approximately 5,500. Reprinted in Peterson, *Representative American Speeches, 1990-1991,* p. 166.

24. Ibid.

25. J. A. DeVito, *The Communication Handbook: A Dictionary* (New York: Harper & Row, 1986), pp. 84–86.

26. Bond Benton, "Very Fake Badges—Very Real Guns," *Winning Orations, 1995* (Interstate Oratorical Association, 1995). Bond was coached by Chris Leland.

# PERSUASION II: LOGICAL ARGUMENT

## ▼ CHAPTER 14 OBJECTIVES

**After reading this chapter, you should understand:**

1. How a logical argument is structured.

2. How propositions, claims, subclaims, and evidence can be examined for validity.

**You should be able to:**

1. Improve your persuasive speeches by using the guidelines provided in this chapter.

2. Formulate a logical argument that is free of fallacies.

3. Recognize fallacies in others' arguments.

##  ARGUMENTATION IN THE MEDIA/INFORMATION AGE

You don't have to listen to the television talk shows for long to wonder what's become of logic. On a program about the dangers of tobacco, a teenager says he smokes because "I heard they have a cure for cancer now." On a program about alcoholism, another teen says, "These days, they just give you a new liver." On the dangers of red meat, an obese man says. "If you gave up everything those scientists say is bad for you, you'd starve to death." On the dangers of suntanning, a successful model opines, "At least I'll leave a great-looking corpse."

There is perhaps no area in which the effects of the media/information age have been so acute. Looking at the current state of reasoning, historians are concerned. One of them asserts, "We are in a race between the rational, disciplined, cooperative potentialities of mankind, and the urge to destroy, which also lurks in every human psyche."[1] Scientists, too, are concerned about the apparent lack of modern-day reasoning. They see faith healing, astrology, pseudoscience (including the fascination with near-death experiences and alien abductions), and paranormal charlatanism as symptomatic of a general flight from reason.[2] Paul Kurtz, a professor of philosophy at the State University of New York at Buffalo, has gone on record as saying that the widespread lack of reasoning power is an "erosion of the cognitive process which may undermine democracy."[3]

Whether or not reasoning is in eclipse in the media/information age, the study of reasoning and argumentation has become increasingly important. The study of argumentation supplies you with important tools to analyze the glut of persuasive messages that you encounter, as well as the ability to build your own.[4]

*Dilbert*                                                                  by Scott Adams

*Dilbert,* reprinted by permission of United Features Syndicate, Inc.

## ◉ THE STRUCTURE OF ARGUMENT α

⟶▷ Argumentation is defined as *the process of making claims and backing them up, logically and rationally.* In its purest form, *argumentation provides an audience with a series of statements, backed up with support, that lead to the conclusion the speaker is trying to establish.*

The various components of an argument are organized in the same way that speech material is organized (according to the rules of outlining). The primary components of arguments are claims, propositions, subclaims, evidence, and reasoning.

### ⋊ Claims

▼ The best argument is that which seems merely an explanation.

Dale Carnegie

As we have mentioned in previous discussions,[5] *a claim is an expressed opinion that the speaker would like the audience to accept.* Although claims are most important in persuasive speeches, you make claims in any kind of speech. A proposition is one type of claim.

### ⋊ The Proposition

As we first mentioned in Chapter 4, the central idea of any speech tells you the one idea that you want your audience to remember after they have forgotten everything else you had to say. It is the one idea to which everything in your speech relates. In a persuasive speech, the central idea is called the *proposition*. The proposition is *the primary claim of a persuasive speech*. In fact, an argument is sometimes defined as a set of statements that attack or defend a proposition.

The place to begin analyzing the validity of an argument is with the proposition. If you start off with an invalid proposition, it doesn't matter how brilliant your argument is from that point forward. For example, a school board member in Half Moon Bay, California, caused a nationwide furor when he proposed banning homework.[6] His supporting claims sound reasonable:

▼ Most homework is busy work that can turn students sour on learning and rob them of valuable family time.

▼ It is unfair to grade students on homework when some have a computer and helpful parents, while others go home to an environment that is less conducive to learning.

The problem with this argument is the basic proposition, which suggests that individual homework is not an essential ingredient in the process of public education. Common sense tells us that it is, and our observations of the performance of students in countries where homework is rigorous confirms that common sense.

This does not mean that a proposition cannot be controversial. In fact, some controversial propositions make for speech topics that are interesting, provocative, and profound:

▼ Speed limits appear to have little or no effect on highway safety.[7]

▼ With the exception of a few of the largest metropolitan centers, American cities no longer truly exist.[8]

Most persuasive speeches fall into one of three categories, depending upon the type of proposition, or overall claim, that you are advancing. The three categories are propositions of fact, propositions of value, and propositions of policy.

## Propositions of Fact

Some persuasive messages focus on *propositions of fact:* issues in which there are two or more sides with conflicting evidence, where listeners are required to choose the truth for themselves:

▼ Canada's nationalized health care is (is not) more efficient than our system of providing health services.

▼ O. J. Simpson was (was not) telling the truth during his murder trial.

▼ The Los Angeles riots of 1992 were (were not) caused by failed liberal programs of 20 years ago.

These examples show that many questions of fact can't be settled with a simple yes or no or with an objective piece of information. Rather, they are open to debate, and answering them requires careful examination and interpretation of evidence, usually collected from a variety of sources. That's why it is possible to debate questions of fact, and that's why these propositions form the basis of persuasive speeches, and not of informative ones.

### Propositions of Value

*Propositions of value* go beyond issues of truth or falsity and explore the worth of some idea, person, or object. Propositions of value include the following:

▼ Cosmetic surgery is (is not) a waste of medical facilities.

▼ The use of laboratory animals for many scientific experiments is (is not) cruel and immoral.

▼ Magazines such as *Playboy* and *Cosmopolitan* are (are not) sexist.

In order to deal with most propositions of value, you will have to explore certain propositions of fact. For example, you won't be able to debate whether the experimental use of animals in research is immoral—a proposition of value—until you have dealt with propositions of fact, such as whether lab animals suffer during experiments and whether such experiments are necessary.

▼ It is better to debate a question without settling it than to settle it without debate.

Joseph Joubert

### Propositions of Policy

*Propositions of policy* go one step beyond questions of fact or value; they recommend a specific course of action (a "policy") for the audience. Some questions of policy are these:

▼ Condoms should (should not) be distributed in high schools.

▼ Genetic engineering of plants and livestock is (is not) an appropriate way to increase the food supply.

▼ The United States should (should not) intervene to prevent human rights abuses in other countries.

Looking at persuasion according to "type of proposition" is a convenient way to generate topics for a persuasive speech. Remember, however, that a fully developed persuasive speech is likely to include all three types of propositions. If you were preparing a speech advocating that college athletes should be paid in cash for their talents (a proposition of policy), you might want to first prove that the practice is already widespread (proposition of fact) and that it is unfair to athletes from other schools (value).

## Subclaims

Within a proposition several claims and subsidiary claims, or subclaims, are usually advanced. These are organized according to the rules of outlining discussed in Chapter 6:

I. Proposition
  A. Claim
    1. Subclaim
    2. Subclaim
  B. Claim
    1. Subclaim
    2. Subclaim
  C. Claim
    1. Subclaim
    2. Subclaim

The basic structure of an argument, therefore, is the arrangement of the claims that back up the proposition and the subclaims that back up the claims. In a speech on the health hazards of fast food, one claim might be backed up as follows:

  A. Soft drinks are bad for you.
    1. They contain empty calories, which are stored within the body as fat.
    2. The sugar rots your teeth.
    3. They actually make you thirstier than you were.

Some subclaims will need further subclaims to back them up:

    3. Soft drinks make you thirstier than you were.[9]
      a. Sugared drinks are absorbed more slowly than water.
      b. You need fluid to digest the sugar. So sugar actually causes you to lose fluid.
      c. Caffeine is a mild diuretic, so it increases water loss.

The structure of every argument is different. Even the *same* argument might be structured differently for different audiences. A claim that will be accepted at face value by one audience will need a number of subclaims with another audience.

Take the following proposition:

We should do away with the tolls on our local bridge.

If you were speaking to an audience of residents of your town who were uniformly fed up with the inconvenience of those tollbooths, you might be able to advance the following claim without subclaims backing it up:

A. The traffic delays caused by the tollbooths are bad for the community.

However, were you to advance the same argument to a group of state legislators, some of whom had no experience with the tollbooths or the delays they cause, you might have to back up your claim with sub-claims:

A. The traffic delays caused by the tollbooths are bad for the community.
   1. The delays harm local businesses.
   2. The delays cause a waste of fuel.
   3. The delays increase air pollution.

For the same proposition with a third audience—one concerned about the income produced by the tolls—you might have to add a second claim:

B. The same revenue could be generated through taxes.

For yet another audience, you might have to back up that claim with subclaims:

B. The same revenue could be generated through taxes.
   1. Only a slight increase in real estate taxes would be necessary.
   2. Residents would be willing to pass such a tax proposal, because they hate the traffic tie-ups.

### Evidence

*Evidence* is *supporting material that the speaker uses to prove any type of claim.* All the forms of support discussed in Chapter 7 can be used to back up your persuasive arguments.[10]

Your objective in finding evidence is not to find supporting material that just clarifies your ideas, but to find the perfect example, description, analogy, anecdote, statistic, or quotation to establish the truth of your claim in the minds of this specific audience.

### The Toulmin Model

In its most basic form, a model of argument proposed by philosopher Stephen Toulmin calls for every claim to be supported not only with evidence but with a *warrant* that ties the claim and evidence together.[11] A warrant, in this sense, is a statement that justifies the use of evidence for a particular claim. The Toulmin model is demonstrated in Figure 14-1.

The point of the Toulmin model is that *every claim you make has to be examined to see if it needs evidence to back it up, and all the evidence you use needs to be examined to see if it needs a warrant to justify*

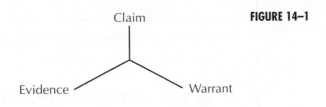

**FIGURE 14–1**

**FIGURE 14–2**

*it in light of the claim.* Sometimes neither the evidence nor the warrant needs to be stated out loud. For example, a typical college audience would accept the following claim today:

> Cigarette smoking is dangerous to your health.

After all, such an audience would be familiar with the research linking smoking to respiratory and heart diseases. However, if you were speaking to a group of tobacco company executives, you might need evidence to back up that claim, and a warrant to prove that the evidence is justified in light of the claim (Figure 14-2).

Christy Kennedy, a student at Hastings College in Nebraska, advanced the following claim in her speech about infant formula addiction:

> Using infant baby formula could be causing American babies to die.[12]

She backed up her claim with the following evidence:

> According to the U.N. World Health Organization, one million children die from diseases such as diarrhea, sudden infant death syndrome, and pneumonia.

She tied her evidence into her claim with this warrant:

> These deaths could have been avoided if the mothers had used breast milk instead.

There could be many different types of evidence and warrants for any given claim. If you check your arguments by applying the Toulmin model to each claim you make, you reduce the chances that your audience will discount what you say because of a weak link between claim and evidence. You can further strengthen your argument by following a few simple rules for evaluating evidence.

## ⬤ RULES FOR EVALUATING EVIDENCE

▼ I shall adopt new views as fast as they shall appear to be true views.

Abraham Lincoln

The guidelines for evaluating evidence are similar to the guidelines for evaluating supporting material in general. Those guidelines were discussed in Chapter 7. Here is the way they relate to evidence.

### Currency

To verify currency, ask "Is this evidence as recent as it needs to be?" Some evidence is timeless. When you are speaking before a group of believers, a quotation from one of the ancient religious books would be as persuasive today as it was a few thousand years ago. But sometimes a piece of evidence loses validity with age. In some cases, the validity of evidence might change by the minute. Take, for example, the situation that President George Bush faced when the riots broke out in Los Angeles. When Bush made his televised address before a worried nation, he made sure his information was up to date:

> Fifteen minutes ago I talked to California's Governor Pete Wilson and Los Angeles Mayor Tom Bradley. They told me that last night was better than the night before; today, calmer than yesterday.[13]

The necessity for Bush to have up-to-the-minute evidence to prove that the situation was improving was caused by one facet of the media/information age: So much information is available, there is a good chance that, if his information wasn't absolutely current, the audience would know. The audience's predictable impression would be that, if they knew about some piece of information, then someone presenting himself as the voice of authority should certainly know about it also. Out-of-date evidence would have cost Bush credibility.

### Relevancy

Another question that must be answered is, "How relevant is this evidence to the argument at hand?" Again, when President Bush addressed the nation about the riots in Los Angeles, he had to deal with the fact that at least part of the cause of these riots was racial hatred. He chose to make the point that the racial hatred seen in the riots was not a general characteristic of the people of Los Angeles. In order to calm his audience, he had to back up this claim with evidence that was relevant to this point:

Among the many stories I've seen and heard about these past few days, one sticks in my mind—the story of one savagely beaten white truck driver—alive tonight because four strangers, four black strangers, came to his aid. Two were men who had been watching television and saw the beating as it was happening, and came out into the street to help. Another was a woman on her way home from work—and the fourth, a young man whose name we may never know. The injured driver was able to get behind the wheel of his truck and tried to drive away. But his eyes were swollen shut. The woman asked him if he could see. He answered, no. She said, "Well, then I will be your eyes."

Together, those four people braved the mob and drove that truck driver to the hospital. He's alive today—only because they stepped in to help.[14]

If Bush had used this piece of evidence to try to prove a different point—say, that racial tensions are lessening in the United States today—it would have been clearly irrelevant. One act of tolerance cannot be used to prove a general trend. But because this evidence clearly proved Bush's specific point—that not *everyone* in Los Angeles hates those of other races—it was clearly relevant.

## Credibility

Another question to test the quality of your evidence is, "How believable is it to this audience?" Were your quotations and testimony obtained from unbiased sources? Were your statistics and examples presented in a straightforward way, or were they "cooked" (made to look better) for the occasion?

To return to our example of President Bush's address to the nation: On one hand, Bush approached his audience from a position of great credibility. He was, after all, President of the United States. On the other hand, he had to concern himself with the lack of credibility inherent in being a professional politician, as well as the defender of a criminal justice system that had apparently broken down in the police brutality case that precipitated the riots. President Bush had to choose credible evidence to prove the point that the system could and would still work: He stated that he, like most people who had seen the videotaped evidence against the Los Angeles police, was shocked at the outcome of the trial. He then continued,

But the verdict Wednesday was not the end of the process. The Department of Justice had started its own investigation immediately after the Rodney King incident and was monitoring the state investigation and trial. And so let me tell you what actions we are taking on the federal level to ensure that justice is served.

Within one hour of the verdict, I directed the Justice Department to move into high gear on its own independent criminal investigation into the case. And next, on Thursday, five federal prosecutors were on their way to Los Angeles. Our Justice Department has consistently demonstrated its ability to investigate fully a matter like this.

Since 1988, the Justice Department has successfully prosecuted over 100 law enforcement officials for excessive violence. I am confident that in this case, the Department of Justice will act as it should. Federal grand jury action is underway today in Los Angeles. Subpoenas are being issued. Evidence is being reviewed. The federal effort in this case will be expeditious and it will be fair. It will not be driven by mob violence, but by respect for due process and the rule of law.[15]

In order for Bush's evidence to be credible, it had to come from a competent, honest source, one without bias. Bush took pains to present the Department of Justice as just such a source. To be credible, Bush's evidence also had to be *verifiable*. In Bush's case, this was extremely important, because every fact he uttered would be checked and double-checked by the national press. If any of his statements failed the verification process, he would be crucified in the news media. For the beginning speaker, establishing the credibility of your evidence is pretty much a one-shot deal. Your audience has to accept it on the spot. It is important, therefore, for you to cite your sources carefully. Don't feel that your audience won't have the patience to hear the full background of your evidence. For example:

If you are quoting the source of an interview, give a full statement of that source's credentials:

> According to Sean Wilentz, professor of history and director of the Program in American Studies at Princeton University, and the author of several books on this topic . . .

If the currency of the interview is important, you might add, "I spoke to Professor Wilentz just last week . . . "

If you are quoting an article, give a quick statement of the author's credentials, and the full date and title of the magazine:

> According to Professor Sean Wilentz of Princeton University, in an article in the June 25, 1995, *New York Times Magazine* . . . .

You do not need to give the title of the article (although you may, if it helps in any way), or the page number.

If you are quoting from a book, you also include a quick statement of the author's credentials:

> According to Professor Sean Wilentz of Princeton University, in his book *The Kingdom of Matthias* . . .

You don't need to include the copyright date unless it's important to authenticate the currency of the quotation, and you don't have to mention the publisher or city of publication unless it's relevant to your topic.

Generally, if you're unsure about how much information to include in a citation, you should err in the direction of *too much* rather than *too little*. This leads us to the question of *sufficiency*.

## Sufficiency

Your final questions concerning evidence deal with the quantity as well as the quality of that evidence: Is there enough to carry the point? Is there enough to be clear to this audience? Is there enough to be consistent with what they probably already know? Reasonable people will disagree on what is sufficient in a given argument. It is best to err on the side of "too much" but not "way too much." It is best to be prepared with enough evidence to prove each point according to your perception of the audience member who is least inclined to agree with you. During your speech, if your observation of the audience suggests you are overdoing it, you can always adjust your level of proof at that point.

Currency, relevancy, credibility, and sufficiency are powerful tests of evidence, especially when they are combined with your analysis of your proposition, claims, and subclaims. Another level of analysis is reached when you analyze the quality of the basic reasoning that ties these components together.

##   TESTS OF SOUND ARGUMENT

Some arguments can be analyzed according to their type. The most common types of arguments involve reasoning by deduction, induction, analogy, sign, and cause-effect.

▼ The aim of argument should not be victory, but progress.

Joseph Joubert

### Deduction

Deduction is reasoning from a general rule to a specific conclusion. In its purest form, you start with a claim that includes all members of a group:

Harvard University accepts only excellent students.

You then add a second claim that refers to a member of that group:

Dean Taylor went to Harvard.

You then reach a conclusion:

Dean Taylor must have been an excellent student.

We analyze the soundness of a deductive argument through the use of syllogisms, which reduce these arguments to two claims called premises. The first claim, the one which identifies all members of a group as having some characteristic, is called a major premise. The second claim, the one that asserts that someone or something is a member of that group, is called a minor premise. The third claim, which derives from the combination of the first two, is called a conclusion. The classic syllogism is:

> All men are mortal. (major premise)
> Socrates is a man. (minor premise)
> Therefore, Socrates is mortal. (conclusion)

If all logical appeals were expressed as complete syllogisms, people could examine the major and minor premises and decide if the conclusions drawn from those premises were valid. This method would make most arguments cumbersome, however, so we generally use enthymemes for logical appeals.[16] An *enthymeme* is a compressed version of a syllogism in which the underlying premises are concealed, as in:

> Because Socrates is a man, he is mortal.

Enthymemes become dangerous when they disguise faulty premises. Some of the best examples of faulty premises are provided in the form of arbitrary rules. For example, take the rule enforced by some college-town landlords: "Because this applicant is a college student, he will have to pay an extra damage deposit before he can rent an apartment." This rule is based on an enthymeme that is based on the following syllogism:

> All college students wreck apartments.
> This applicant is a college student.
> Therefore, this applicant will wreck this apartment.

The conclusion—"This applicant will wreck this apartment"—is based on an untrue, unstated premise: "All college students wreck apartments."

The frustration you feel when you are subjected to illogical rules ("There's no sense arguing. We don't need to give you a *reason*. It's a rule.") is the same frustration that an audience feels when it is subjected to an argument that does not supply valid reasons. That is why we take this close look at deductive reasoning: To make sure that the reasons we use in deduction are valid, we examine the underlying premises of our argument. For example, in deductive reasoning you have to be careful of the "allness" fallacy. Very few statements are true in all possible cases. To paraphrase an earlier example, consider the following syllogism:

> Harvard University accepts only excellent students.
> Ted Kennedy went to Harvard.
> Ted Kennedy must have been an excellent student.

The problem here is evident. Although Senator Edward (Ted) Kennedy has had a distinguished career as a U.S. Senator from Massachusetts, the record shows that he wasn't a particularly good student at any point in his life. It might also be true that some people were excellent students in high school, but once they got into Harvard they fell apart. The best deductive arguments, therefore, deal in probabilities:

> Those who go to Harvard are probably excellent students.

It is a good idea to carefully analyze any deductive reasoning that is based on an "allness" premise.

## INDUCTION

*Induction, or inductive reasoning, is reasoning from specific evidence to a general conclusion.* In induction we observe that something is true for a specific sample or several examples. From this evidence we reason that it is *generally* true.

One educator who was opposed to condoms being distributed in his local high school used induction to prove that such distribution was unnecessary:

Free condoms are available for distribution from the Chelsea Health Clinic at 100 Bellingham Street; from ROCA at 184 Washington Avenue; from Choice Thru Education at 160 Pearl St.; from Centro Hispano at 5 Everett Avenue; from the Chelsea Substance Abuse Clinic at 100 Everett Avenue; from Concilio Hispano at 380 Broadway; from Washington Cove Variety Store at 181 Washington Avenue; and from Magic Shears Hair Salon at 1346 Washington Avenue. Surely, no one can reasonably suppose that any adolescent in Chelsea would have difficulty getting free condoms if he or she wanted them.[17]

Induction might be the appropriate type of reasoning to use with a skeptical or hostile audience where you do not want to state an unpopular claim right away. If you are seeking to prove that your local government is generally corrupt, for example, you might build your case with specific examples: The mayor has been convicted of accepting bribes, the building inspector has resigned after being charged with extortion, the fire chief has been indicted for running the station's Dalmatian at the track, and the chief of police has admitted to keeping his infant nephew on the police department's payroll. If you used these specific instances to conclude that most of your local officials are corrupt, you would be using induction.

To check for the validity of induction, ask yourself three questions:

1. Are the examples true? As we pointed out in Chapter 3, advocates who are otherwise perfectly ethical sometimes exaggerate, out of enthusiasm for their cause. Could this be such a case?
2. Are the examples representative? Did the examples really relate to the claim being put forward? If you gave three examples of murders that occurred in one weekend in your town, you might then reason, "This proves that our town is unsafe." But was that weekend representative of the typical weekend in your town? If they were the only murders all year, or in a decade, then your examples would *not* be representative.
3. Are the examples relevant? Sometimes examples are so striking or shocking that a speaker may fail to see that they don't really prove the point. If you said, "There were over 150 murders in this town last year; therefore, the town is unsafe for tourists," the examples would be irrelevant if the murders were mostly of the domestic variety, in which the victims knew their murderers.

Although induction and deduction are the most common types of logical reasoning, there are other forms. These forms include reasoning by sign, reasoning by analogy, and causal reasoning. Often these forms are combined with induction and deduction, but each has its own tests of validity.

## Reasoning by Sign

*Sign reasoning* is reasoning from specific evidence to a specific conclusion without explaining how the evidence and conclusion are related. The classic example of sign reasoning is, "It is snowing outside; therefore, it must be winter." The test for the validity of sign reasoning is in the relationship between the evidence and the conclusion: Is it a valid relationship, or does it just *sound* valid? For example, one teenager says he smokes because, "if cigarettes were so bad for you, they wouldn't be so easy to buy." For this teen, the fact that cigarettes are available in every convenience store and in many vending machines is a sign that they are safe. The more rational explanation is that this is a sign that they are profitable, or that we live in a society in which people are free to do things that are bad for them, if they choose to.

You can use your understanding of sign reasoning to spot invalid arguments. If you are part of a hiring committee and someone says of a candidate, "She was very outspoken. I don't like that in a woman," you could point out that outspokenness is often taken as a sign of aggressiveness in women, while it is accepted and even approved of in men.[18] The argument breaks down when you recognize that it does not obtain equally for men and women.

Sign reasoning is used when the argument will be easily accepted by the audience. For example, an audience would probably accept the claim that an increase in bank robberies is a sign that a community is becoming more dangerous to live in. You would not need to go into a long, logical explanation of your reasoning in that case, and the time you save could be used to develop more important aspects of the argument. For example, you might want to go on to claim that another community's solution to the bank robbery problem would work in your community. That would require reasoning by analogy.

## Reasoning by Analogy

*Reasoning by analogy is reasoning from specific evidence to a specific conclusion by claiming that something is like something else.* This type of reasoning could not be used for legal proof. You could not argue, for example, that a suspect was guilty because this crime was *like* other crimes of which he or she had been convicted. Still, a well-chosen analogy can help prove a point to an audience. For example, if you were arguing that the methods of law enforcement that curbed bank robbery in a nearby city would also work in your city, you would have to argue that your city is similar to that nearby city in all the respects that are important to your argument—number of banks, size of banks, size of police department, and so on. Thus, if you could argue that the two cities are alike except in one respect—the size of their police forces—you could argue that this is what makes the difference in the incidence of bank robbery. If you did so, you would be arguing by analogy.

As with sign reasoning, the problem with reasoning by analogy is that some comparisons *sound* reasonable when they really aren't. The problem usually involves two incomparables:

> Why should we give him a trial? He didn't give his victim one.

This statement, a favorite of the victim's family on the evening news, at first sounds not only like an apt analogy, but also a statement of almost biblical justice: "An eye for an eye, a tooth for a tooth." But a criminal's actions cannot be compared with the actions of a just state. To do so implies that the just state should become more criminal-like.

## Causal Reasoning

*Causal reasoning,* like sign reasoning, is reasoning from one specific to another specific. However, in causal reasoning you go on to prove that something happened or will happen *because* of something else. If you claimed that the increase in bank robberies in your community was caused by a decrease in police personnel, you would be involved in causal reasoning. In fact, you would be using effect-to-cause reasoning, which is based on the organizational pattern of the same name discussed in Chapter 8. Effect-to-cause reasoning is used when you are talking about something that has already happened. If you were arguing about something that *will* happen (for example, the probability of future bank robberies because the police have cut the size of their force or the hours they patrol), you would be using cause-to-effect reasoning.

Problems in causal reasoning are created by *ignored causes* or *ignored effects*. Examples of *ignored causes* run rampant through everyday conversations. Take a typical discussion about college sports:

> State U. beat State Tech.
> State Tech creamed State Teachers.
> Therefore, State U. will murder State Teachers.

This argument might ignore previously injured players who are now back in action, stars who are now injured, or a host of other variables. Problems based on ignored effects can be even worse:

> If too much of our state budget is committed to paying our state debt, we should simply cancel the debt.

The fact is, a state does have the right to cancel a debt; but that argument ignores the undesirable effects of that action, such as the inability of the state to borrow money for future projects.

## ⬤ LOGICAL FALLACIES

A *fallacy* (from the Latin word meaning "false") is an error in logic. Although the original meaning of the term implied a purposeful deception, most logical fallacies are not recognized by those who use them. Scholars have devoted lives and volumes to the description of various types of logical fallacies.[19] The three most common types are fallacies of *non sequitur, evasion,* and *language.* Most fallacies can be included in one of these categories.[20]

### ⋏ Fallacies of Non Sequitur

*Non sequitur* fallacies are those in which the conclusion does not relate to (literally, "does not follow from") the evidence.

#### Post Hoc

Take, for example, the non sequitur fallacy known as *post hoc,* which is short for *post hoc, ergo propter hoc.* Translated from the Latin, that phrase means "after this, therefore because of this." This fallacy occurs when it is assumed that an action was caused by something that happened before it. Post hoc arguments are often applied to politics:

> Bill Clinton's policies caused the bombing of the Federal Building in Oklahoma City. It happened, after all, during his administration.

Just because the bombing happened after Clinton was elected does not necessarily mean his policies somehow "caused" the bombing.

Another post hoc political argument was advanced when a young woman named Susan Smith killed her two young sons in South Carolina. The nation was shocked. But some were even more shocked when Congressman Newt Gingrich of Georgia said that the case "vividly reminds every American how sick the society is getting," and that "the only way you get change is to vote Republican."[21] The full irony of Gingrich's statement was revealed later when it came to light that Susan Smith's psychological state was partially caused by her stepfather molesting her when she was 15. Her stepfather served on the executive committee of the state Republican Party.

Spurious research is often post hoc:

> Nearly all heroin users started with marijuana. Marijuana obviously leads to the use of harder drugs.

> Nearly all marijuana users started with aspirin, too, but aspirin does not necessarily lead to the abuse of drugs.

#### Unwarranted Extrapolation

A second type of non sequitur is an *unwarranted extrapolation,* which is a statement that suggests that, because something happened before, it will happen again, or that because something is true for a part, it is true for a whole.

▼ State U. has massacred State Teachers every year for the past five years. They'll do it again this year.

▼ Jack Nicholson and Michelle Pfeiffer are great actors. *Wolf* must be a great movie.

One type of unwarranted extrapolation is the "slippery slope" argument, which states that, if one first step is taken, you will fall down a slippery slope to disaster:

▼ If we do it for you, we'll have to do it for everyone.

▼ A student who will smoke will drink, and a student who will drink, God knows what she'll do.

▼ If we let our children wear makeup, the next thing you know they'll want to stay out all night.

Slippery slope reasoning is quite common in the rationalizations of authoritarian bureaucracies and inexperienced parents, both of which seek to control their constituencies with warnings of dire consequences.[22]

### Evasion of Argument

In this type of fallacy the speaker dodges the question at hand by arguing over some other, unrelated point. These are sometimes referred to as "fallacies of misdirection" and sometimes as "begging the question."

#### Red Herring

One such evasion is the *red herring*. This fallacy, which derives its name from the practice of dragging an odoriferous fish across a trail when running away from bloodhounds, consists of evading an issue by concentrating on another, more volatile one:

> Should the tollbooths be removed? The real question is, "Who would like to see us remove those tollbooths?" And the obvious answer to that question is, the Devil Worshippers. And believe me, folks, the threat of Satanism is as real today as it was . . .

Granted, that example is extreme. Less farfetched red herrings are often introduced by a designation of "the real problem":

> The real problem is not the lack of motorcycle helmets. It's that too many bikers don't ride well and too many automobile drivers don't look out for motorcycles.

There might well be more than one problem when it comes to motorcycle safety. But that doesn't help us analyze the question of whether helmets should be required. Consider another red herring:

Guns don't kill people. People kill people.

There may be sound reasons not to ban handguns, but this argument isn't one of them. In this classic slogan the argument that handgun ownership should be controlled is sidetracked by the much larger problem of man's inhumanity to man. The fallacy here is satirized in the alternative slogan, "Guns don't kill people, people with guns kill people."

## Ad Hominem

A second type of evasion of argument is the *ad hominem* ("to the person") argument, which is the fallacy of attacking the person who brought up the issue rather than the issue itself:

> Of course, Louie thinks marijuana should be legalized. Louie is a college dropout who hasn't held a job in over a year.

## Ad Populum

Another evasion of argument is known as *ad populum,* which means, literally, "to the people." An ad populum argument asserts that popular opinion is a justification of the claim.

▼ Motorcyclists should not be required to wear helmets. In a survey of 2,500 bikers, 98 percent of the respondents said they opposed such laws.

▼ Most people believe we have too much freedom of speech. It is time to consider revoking the First Amendment.

▼ The president's position in the polls proves he is doing a bad job.

▼ More than half of the people polled believe electric power lines cause cancer.

The fact is, just because a majority of people believe something, doesn't make it true. Popular belief, in fact, often runs counter to objective reality. If you ask an average group of senior citizens, for example, if the government spends more on foreign aid or social security, the vast majority will say foreign aid. In reality, the government spends on foreign aid only a small fraction of what it spends on social security.

## Appeal to Tradition

Another type of evasion of argument is known as the *appeal to tradition*. The appeal to tradition says, "We've always done it this way, so it must be right." A clumsy example of this fallacy was heard from a tobacco grower when President Clinton announced his fight against teenage smoking. The grower stated:

> The U.S. government is trying to wreck the tobacco industry. Don't they know that the tobacco industry is older than the government?[23]

Thus, tobacco was presented as a tradition that should be venerated. The fallacy here is easily seen when one realizes that slavery, religious persecution, and the plague are also older than the U.S. government. That alone, however, is no reason to preserve them. Religious arguments often contain interesting appeals to tradition. On one talk show, an audience member argued against plastic surgery:

That's the body God gave you; you should leave it alone.

The much-enhanced subject of the show was quick to respond with her own appeal to tradition:

If God didn't want us to use plastic surgery, he wouldn't have created plastic surgeons.

### Straw Argument

Another evasion of argument is known as the *straw argument*. The straw argument attacks a weakened form of an opponent's argument or an argument the opponent did not advance. The name is a metaphor for building an argument out of straw, which is then easy to knock down. This is a common fallacy found in public speaking classes, in which students often react to (and refute) ideas that they haven't investigated thoroughly. (You can make sure you don't do that by investigating the other side's argument.)

The straw argument fallacy occurs when you state only part of an opponent's argument, or you pervert it in some way:

▼ Clinton's plan for medical care would take away free choice.

▼ Freud believed that women are inferior.

▼ Professor Murray's bell curve claims that some races are inferior to others.

Straw arguments are often used to refute solid scientific studies by oversimplifying them to the point where they seem to reflect something that defies common sense.

### Fallacies of Language Use

Fallacies of language use occur when wording is used to make it appear as if a logical argument is being advanced when it isn't. For example, a fallacy of language use can occur when a speaker uses a word with more than one meaning:

We shouldn't study argumentation in public speaking class. The members of this class argue too much already.

## Weasel Words

Fallacies of language use also occur when language is carefully structured to seem to say something that it actually doesn't. This occurs with the advertising technique of *weasel words* (also known as "equivocation"), such as "virtually."

> Acnaway will give you virtually clear skin in 90 days.

The weasel word in that claim is "virtually." As it's used there, it means "almost," but the advertisers wouldn't sell as much acne cream if they only promised "almost clear" skin.

## Parity Statements

Another form of weasel wording is the *parity statement,* in which the product appears to be claiming superiority to the competition, but in fact is only claiming to be as good as (have parity with) the competition:

▼ No product has been proven to last longer than Advil.

▼ No car has been proven to give you more value than a Buick.

## Reasoning by Slogan

*Reasoning by slogan* is another form of language fallacy. Reasoning by slogan occurs when we use a catchy expression as "proof":

▼ When guns are outlawed, only outlaws will have guns.

▼ Abortion is murder.

> Folksy, familiar expressions are sometimes used to reason by slogan:

▼ You can't teach an old dog new tricks.

▼ You're damned if you do and damned if you don't.

The fact is, sometimes you *can* teach an old dog new tricks, and sometimes you *aren't* damned if you do and damned if you don't. The philosopher Max Black provides two more examples of folksy fallacies:

> We hear all too often that "the exception proves the rule." Probably not one person in a thousand who dishes up this ancient morsel of wisdom realizes that "prove" is here used in its older sense of "probe" or "test." What was originally intended was that the exception tests the rule—shows whether the rule is correct or not. The contemporary interpretation, that a rule is confirmed by having an exception, is absurd. This formula has the advantage of allowing a person to glory in the fact that a general principle does *not* square with the facts.
>
> "It's all right in theory, but it won't do in practice," is another popular way of reveling in logical absurdity. The philosopher Schopenhauer said all that needs to be said about this

sophism: "The assertion is based upon an impossibility: what is right in theory *must* work in practice, and if it does not, there is a mistake in theory; something has been overlooked and not allowed for; and consequently, what is wrong in practice is wrong in theory too."[24]

It's all right to use slogans to make an idea memorable, to summarize a point, or state a proposition—just don't use them as a form of proof or reasoning.

## ▼ SAMPLE SPEECH

The sample speech for this chapter was presented by Tai Du, a student at the University of Oklahoma.[25] Tai does a relatively good job of arguing for regulatory reform within the Food and Drug Administration. His argument, however, is not perfect. In fact, as some of the accompanying comments suggest, in many places the argument could have been improved by the judicious application of some of the principles explained in this chapter.

Tai's proposition might be expressed this way:

The FDA's overregulation of medical devices costs lives and jobs, and should be corrected.

Some of the claims advanced in support of this proposition are as follows (the numbers in parentheses are the paragraphs in which these claims are stated):

I. The FDA is a power-hungry monster whose overregulation drives small businesses into oblivion and keeps life-saving medical products from dying patients. (2)

    A. The road to approval is filled with almost impossible and costly detours. (2)

    B. The FDA affects nearly all aspects of our lives. (4)

II. The FDA approval process takes too long. (5)

    A. The initial application is supposed to be processed within 90 days. (5)

    B. The initial application for Wright's Sensor Pad, however, dragged on for over a year. (5)

    C. The approval procedure has gone on for 9 years, and cost over two million dollars. (5)

III. Other countries approve devices more quickly. (5)

    A. The Sensor Pad is actively in use in most of Europe, Japan, Singapore, Korea, Thailand, and Canada. (5)

B. Canada approved the Sensor Pad within 60 days. (5)

C. The heart pump, another device that the FDA has failed to approve, is required in all Austrian ambulances. (6)

D. The heart pump has been approved for use in many other countries. (6)

IV. The impact of the problem includes loss of life and economic loss. (9)

A. The FDA's actions kill people. (10)

1. Lives could have been saved through the use of the Sensor Pad. (9)

2. Lives could have been saved through the use of the heart pump. (9)

3. Lives could have been saved through the use of the defibrillator. (9)

B. The FDA's actions cause inventors to relocate to other countries. (11)

V. We can and we must take action. (18)

A. You should support congressional action toward deregulation. (14)

B. You should support the industry movement to privatize some FDA procedures. (15)

C. You should sign our petition to end "regulation run amok." (16)

## ⬤ DEATH BY FEDERAL MANDATE

Tai Du

University of Oklahoma

[1] In the sleepy town of Decatur, Illinois, controversy is almost unheard of. Decatur, however, does lay claim to a very industrious inventor, Earl Wright. Throughout the years Earl has invented everything from Corn Silk makeup, for women, to tricolored Jello, especially for Bill Cosby. It wasn't until recently, though, that Earl was ecstatic about another invention. Earl invented a lifesaving device known as the Sensor Pad. The device helps women detect lumps during self-examination for breast cancer. The pad, composed only of two soft sheets of plastic with silicon inside, helped Mary Gorman of Chevy Chase, Maryland, discover a pea-sized lump in her breast. A mammogram had missed it. Where can you get this miraculous device? Nowhere. That is, nowhere in the United States. Why? According to *The Wall Street Journal* of April 12, 1994, after 9 years and 2 million dollars of research, our federal Food and Drug Administration— the FDA—has yet to approve it.

Earl Wright is being presented as an example leading to the proposition; an inductive argument is under way.

[2] *USA Today* of March 7, 1995, suggests that the FDA is a power-hungry monster whose overregulation drives small businesses into oblivion and

This statement of the general conclusion will now

lead to a deductive argument, as Tai backs it up with evidence.

The preview of main points helps us follow the lines of the argument.

The term "therefore" tips you off that a syllogism is being advanced here.

Argument by analogy, comparing the United States to other areas of the world.

A logical fallacy is pointed out to show the error of the opposing (FDA) view. The device saves unconscious patients, but the FDA won't allow the device to be tested because the patients are unconscious.

There are claims being advanced here. Are they supported?

The next two claims are previewed.

keeps lifesaving medical products from dying patients. For lifesaving devices such as the Sensor Pad, the road to approval is filled with almost impossible and costly detours.

³ In order to understand the seriousness of the FDA's unwillingness to approve lifesaving devices, we must first examine the inadequate treatment given to these products. Next, we will focus on the ramifications of this disapproval, and finally we must look at some viable solutions which will enable us to wake up from this bureaucratic nightmare.

⁴ According to the *Library Journal,* March 1, 1994, the FDA is authorized to inspect, test, approve, and set safety standards for foods, drugs, chemicals, cosmetics, and most medical devices. Therefore, this agency affects nearly all aspects of our lives.

⁵ However, the FDA application process often seems daunting to those without the time or money to withstand the bureaucratic red tape. According to Herbert Burkholz's 1994 book, *FDA Follies,* the initial application is supposed to be processed within 90 days. The initial application for Wright's Sensor Pad, however, dragged on for over a year. Nine years later, the FDA proceedings have consumed over 1,200 pages of paperwork, and the Sensor Pad still lacks the FDA's go-ahead. Although it is illegal for use in the United States, the *New York Times* of September 4, 1994, reports that the Sensor Pad is actively in use in most of Europe, Japan, Singapore, Korea, Thailand, and Canada. In fact, the Canadian regulatory agency approved the Sensor Pad within 60 days and consumed less than 50 pages of paperwork.

⁶ But Wright's device is not alone in FDA limbo. Another medical lifesaver known as the heart pump, which assists in performing CPR on heart attack victims, has also run into a brick wall. An initial study at the University of Minnesota in the fall of 1993 found that the heart pump enables paramedics to resuscitate more victims than do traditional CPR methods. The heart pump is required in all Austrian ambulances, and has been approved for use in many other countries. But *Nursing Magazine* of September 1994 reveals that "the FDA shut down tests on the heart pump at the University of Minnesota because patients were not (for obvious reasons) giving informed consent ahead of time."

⁷ So what's the problem? Why are such simple yet lifesaving devices being withheld from the market and denied for our use? Well, *Fortune Magazine* of April 4, 1994, reports that "the real cause of ineptitude at the FDA is a deadening bureaucracy and a lack of leadership, coupled with a workload that has expanded geometrically." Because of this, the developers of these devices and many others lack the resources necessary to complete the FDA's exacting and often impossible standards for approval.

⁸ Now that we've seen the nature of the problem, it is important that we focus on the implications that the FDA's shortcomings have on the medical community and the general public. The impact is twofold: loss of life and a burden to our economy.

[9] The worst danger is the loss of life. The best protection against breast cancer is prevention. As an *Associated Press Newswire* dated September 1, 1994, reports, "Breast cancer strikes 180,000 American women every year and kills 46,000 annually." Furthermore, *The Wall Street Journal* of January 13, 1995, states that 14,000 heart attack victims have died, so far, during the two years the FDA has delayed approval of the heart pump.

[10] *Business Week* of January 30, 1995, reports that the FDA can also take away approved products—often with devastating results. For instance, a medical device known as the defibrillator is used on victims of cardiac arrest. Laerdal, a defibrillator manufacturer, was recently prohibited from distributing its product because the FDA found clerical paperwork violations. Laerdal eventually fought the FDA successfully in court. Due to this delay, though, Dr. Richard Cummings of the American Heart Association estimates in *Consumer's Research Magazine* of December 1994 that 1,000 lives were lost unnecessarily to cardiac arrest. So, apparently, as Sam Kasban, chair of the Free Market Advocate group, stated on ABC's "20/20" of August 12, 1994, "The FDA kills people and it should acknowledge this."

*Causal reasoning. The conclusion of this syllogism—"the sensor pad might have saved some of these lives"—goes unstated. The impact might have been stronger if the conclusion were stated explicitly. The second claim also has an unstated conclusion. The audience might ask, "How many of these deaths might have been prevented by the use of the heart pump?"*

[11] On an individual level this strict regulation affects all of our lives; on a global level, however, this unwillingness to promote and approve lifesaving devices is hindering our economy. In the January 1995 issue of *The American Spectator,* 45 percent of our medical device inventors state that they intend to relocate to other countries. The reason: The FDA makes it impossible to invent and survive in America. Because of this, *The Wall Street Journal* of April 12, 1994, states that the U.S. trade deficit will increase 18 billion dollars a year, and 112,000 American jobs will vanish. Dr. Joel Noble, of the Emergency Control Research Institute, explained to me in a telephone interview on September 22, 1994, "We are virtually the laughingstock of the international medical device auxiliary industry." Dr. Noble insists that, "We are killing our own industry."

*Good job of backing up this claim.*

[12] So the ramifications of the FDA's actions on our health and economy are astounding. We must now focus on some viable solutions to this foreboding problem through government reform, industry strength, and individual effort.

*Transition: review and preview.*

[13] First and foremost, we as the general public must be aware of the problem. We must realize that, indeed, the FDA does play an appropriate role in safety, but this should not include powers to remove or deny devices from the market unless there is a clear and present danger to substantial segments of the population.

*Solution*

*A quick bit of inoculation.*

[14] Secondly, since the only body regulating the FDA is Congress, it is imperative that we support the current wave in Congress toward regulatory reform. The House Commerce Committee is currently holding hearings on overregulation. The hearings are championed by Representative Thomas J. Bliley of Virginia. Bliley states in *The National Journal* of February 18, 1995, "My goal is to speed up approval of devices for the American people."

*Solution.*

*Solution.*

This move is supported by a vast majority of Congress, including Speaker of the House Newt Gingrich, who explained on the "McNeil-Lehrer News Hour," March 28, 1995, "The problem with health care, and the leading job killer in America, is the FDA."

*Solution.*

[15] Industry groups such as the Health Industry Manufacturers Association, or HIMA, report in the *Washington Post* of February 22, 1995, that they want to contract out some of the FDA's review procedures and functions to private firms. There would be a message or label on these new devices that shows clearly that it has not met FDA approval—allowing you, the consumer, and your physician, the expert, to make educated decisions. Because as *Consumer's Research Magazine* of February 1994 explains, "People should have the ability to make informed judgments and not rely on an overburdened and understaffed agency to make decisions for them."

[16] Now, if you want to take a more active role in the solution process, you may fill out the petition to end "regulations run amok." Working in conjunction with HIMA, we will forward your concerns to the Subcommittee on Regulatory Relief—chaired by Representative David McIntosh of Indiana—and to your respective congresspersons. It is only through grassroots efforts such as these that a moratorium will be declared on FDA overregulation.

*The desired audience response is made as simple— and effective—as possible.*

[17] Today, we examined the problem of FDA stagnation by first looking at the inadequate treatment given to lifesaving devices. Secondly, we focused on the astonishing impact of the disapproval of these devices on our health and our economy. Finally, we developed some vital solutions to this growing problem.

*Review of main points.*

[18] The problem could be stated simply: The FDA has lost its common sense. Products designed to better our health or save our lives should not be bound by bureaucratic overkill. Mr. Earl Wright, the inventor of the Sensor Pad, told me in a recent telephone conversation, "I tried my whole life to invent something that could save lives and help humanity in America, and I finally accomplished that. But the FDA does not allow my vision to become reality." The simple fact of the matter is that people are dying and our economy is needlessly suffering; we can and we must take action. For if we don't act NOW, when any one of us needs a medical lifesaving device, there may be no place to get it.

## ▼ SUMMARY

This chapter dealt with the structure and validity of logical arguments. This topic is increasingly crucial in the media/information age, in which the crush of information and emotion-based images seems to be interfering with the ability to create and evaluate logical messages.

Argumentation is defined as the process of making claims and backing them up, logically and rationally. In its purest form, argumentation provides an audience with a series of statements, all of which are true, that lead to the conclusion the speaker is trying to establish. The primary components of arguments are propositions, claims, subclaims, evidence, and reasoning.

A claim is any opinion that the speaker would like the audience to accept. The primary claim of a persuasive speech is the proposition. Within a proposition, several claims and subsidiary claims, or subclaims, are usually advanced. These are organized according to the rules of outlining. The structure of every argument is different, depending on the audience; a claim that will be accepted at face value by one audience will need a number of subclaims with another.

Evidence is supporting material used to back up your claims. Your objective in finding evidence is to find the best piece of supporting material to establish the truth of your claim in the mind of a specific audience. Evidence is evaluated according to its currency, relevancy, credibility, and sufficiency.

The reasoning within your argument can be analyzed according to its type. The most common types of argument involve reasoning by deduction, induction, analogy, sign, and cause-effect. Each type has its own tests of validity. You can also analyze the validity of your arguments by watching for logical fallacies. Three types of fallacies were discussed in this chapter: Fallacies of non sequitur, which include post hoc and unwarranted extrapolation; evasion of argument, which includes red herring, ad hominem, ad populum, appeal to tradition, and straw arguments; and fallacies of language use, which include weasel words, parity statements, and reasoning by slogan.

## ▼ EXERCISES

1. Videotape approximately five minutes of formal argument from television. This might be a congressional hearing broadcast over PBS, or one of the trials broadcast over *Court TV* or one of the major networks. View the tape two or three times. Within that five minutes, what form of argument is the speaker using? Do you think the argument is effective? Can you spot any potential fallacies?

2. For each of the following points, devise one argument based on induction and one based on deduction. Using the same points, try to come up with an argument based on reasoning by sign, causal reasoning,

and reasoning by analogy. In a small group, discuss your arguments with your classmates. Do they find your arguments valid?

▼ Your school is storing the last of the smallpox virus. It should (should not) be saved for research.

▼ We should (should not) ban capital punishment.

▼ The way juries are selected in this country, in high-profile cases especially, is (is not) damaging to respect for law.

▼ Bilingual education should (should not) be offered in all schools in which students speak English as a second language.

# NOTES

1. William H. McNeill, *A World History* (New York: Oxford University Press, 1979), p. 537.
2. Malcolm W. Browne, "Scientists Deplore Flight from Reason," *New York Times,* June 6, 1995, p. C1.
3. Ibid.
4. It is difficult to examine the process of public speaking without discussing the many facets of argumentation. Since Chapter 1, we have been bouncing up against related ideas: the importance of research and support, audience analysis, ethics, language choices, and clarity all are concepts essential to the understanding of argumentation.
5. Specifically, in Chapter 1 in our discussion of supporting material, and in Chapter 7 in our discussion of the "proving" function of support.
6. This claim was put forth by Garrett Redmond, a school board member in Half Moon Bay, California. It made his community, previously known only for its annual pumpkin festival, the brief focal point of the national media. The school board president accused Redmond of "trying to become the patron saint of all high school students." See "Ban Homework in Half Moon Bay? Pupils See a Half-Baked Idea," *New York Times,* October 29, 1994, p. 7.
7. Brock Yates, "Speed Doesn't Kill. Bad Drivers Do." *New York Times,* July 24, 1995, p. A13.
8. Peter Shaw, "Let a Hundred Cities Bloom," *National Review,* July 11, 1994, p. 50. Shaw adds, "Maps still locate them, airports take their names from them, some people even venture into them during daylight hours. But they have declined to the point where they represent little more than focal points around which suburbs are organized."
9. Karen Baar, "You May Be Thirstier Than You Feel," *New York Times,* August 2, 1995, p. C8.
10. For an excellent review of the effects of evidence, see John Reinard, "The Empirical Study of the Persuasive Effects of Evidence: The Status after Fifty Years of Research," *Human Communication Research,* Fall 1988, pp. 3–59.
11. S. E. Toulmin, *The Uses of Argument* (New York: Cambridge University Press, 1964).
12. This paraphrase is adapted from Christy Kennedy, Title Unknown, *Winning Orations, 1995* (Interstate Oratorical Association, 1995). Christy was coached by Kevin Heineman and Bill Cue.
13. George Bush, "Civil Disorder in Los Angeles," televised speech delivered to the nation from Washington, D.C., May 1, 1992. Reprinted in *Vital Speeches of the Day,* June 1, 1992, p. 482.
14. Ibid., p. 483.
15. Ibid.
16. Aristotle once stated, "Everyone who persuades by proof in fact uses either enthymemes or examples. There is no other way." *The Rhetoric,* 1, 2, 7. A modern look at the enthymeme and the nature of argument is T. M. Conley's "The Enthymeme in Perspective," *Quarterly Journal of Speech* 70 (May 1984), p. 168.
17. Edwin J. Delattre, "Condoms and Coercion: The Maturity of Self-Determination," speech delivered by the Dean Ad Interim of the Boston University School of Education to the Chelsea Management Team and the public, January 14, 1992. Reprinted in *Vital Speeches of the Day,* April 15, 1992, p. 412.
18. Bonnie Erbe, "In My Opinion . . .," *Ladies Home Journal,* November 1994, p. 288.
19. See, for example, Vincent E. Barry, *Practical Logic* (New York: Holt, Rinehart and Winston, 1976).
20. There are, of course, other classifications of logical fallacies. See, for example, Barbara Warnick and Edward Inch, *Critical Thinking and Communication: The Use of Reason in Argument,* 2d ed. (New York: Macmillan, 1994), pp. 137–161.
21. See, for example, Frank Rich, "Beverly Russell's Prayers," *New York Times,* August 2, 1995, p. A19.
22. See James F. Keenan, "What's Your Worst Moral Argument?" *America,* October 2, 1993, p. 17.
23. Anonymous grower interviewed on *ABC World News with Peter Jennings,* August 10, 1995.
24. Max Black, "Fallacies," in *Readings in Argumentation,* Jerry M. Anderson and Paul J. Dovre, eds. (Boston: Allyn & Bacon, 1968), pp. 301–311.
25. Tai Du, "Death by Federal Mandate," *Winning Orations, 1995* (Interstate Oratorical Association, 1995). Tai was coached by Jerry L. Miller, John R. Nash and Karla Larson.

▼ **CHAPTER 15**

# SPEAKING ON SPECIAL OCCASIONS

## ▼ CHAPTER 15 OBJECTIVES

**After reading this chapter, you should understand:**

1. The types of special occasion speaking.

2. The requirements and some techniques of humor.

**You should be able to:**

1. Plan an effective special occasion speech.

2. Use appropriate humor in a speech.

### ⬤ SPECIAL OCCASION SPEAKING IN THE MEDIA/INFORMATION AGE

▼ The occasion is piled high with difficulty, and we must rise with the occasion.

Abraham Lincoln

The term *special occasion speaking* is reserved for speeches that are not primarily informative or persuasive in nature, and are not presented as part of our jobs or everyday routine. This type of speaking is done at a special event, such as a wedding, a memorial service, an awards presentation, a retirement, or a banquet.

Special occasion speaking provides a special contrast to mediated communication because it exemplifies the public speech as human contact. Toasting your best friends at their wedding or saying your final goodbye to a loved one, presenting an award or accepting one, introducing another speaker or being the master of ceremonies at a banquet, are all types of

THE FAR SIDE, by Gary Larson

"Today, our guest lecturer is Dr. Clarence Tibbs, whose 20-year career has culminated in his recent autobiography, *Zoo Vet—I Quit!*"

communication in which human contact is important. However, this type of speech is very often presented over the media for the appreciation of a larger audience; for that reason, there are a wealth of media models we can draw on to improve these events.

Obviously, there are more "special events" than we could hope to cover in depth in one chapter. There are a few events that happen so often, however, that it is worth our while to discuss them here. They include introductions, awards, acceptances, speeches of commemoration, and after-dinner speeches.

## ▼ TYPES OF SPECIAL OCCASION SPEAKING

### Introductions

A common type of special occasion speaking involves the introduction of another speaker. When you are called upon to introduce a speaker, there are certain rules to keep in mind. The most important rule is that the speaker being introduced is the star, not the introducer. This rule underlies all the others, which include these:

*Be brief.* The audience, no matter how enthusiastic, has a limited store of patience, and that patience should be primarily reserved for the speaker. The speaker has a right to feel shortchanged if you use up too much of the audience's listening energy. The British statesman Arthur Balfour once demonstrated the consequences of an overly long introduction. After a 45-minute introduction he got up and said,

> I'm supposed to give my address in the brief time remaining. Here it is: 10 Carleton Gardens, London, England.[1]

*Show appropriate respect.* You should demonstrate an appreciation of the speaker, without going overboard. It is all right to list the speaker's major accomplishments, but do not gush. It would only embarrass a speaker to be introduced as "the world's greatest authority on . . ." if that is an obvious exaggeration.

*Set up the topic.* Find out the speaker's topic in advance, and try to pique audience interest in it. If you were introducing someone who was speaking on the topic of organized crime, you would not be laying it on too thickly if you said:

> Our speaker tonight, [speaker's name], will discuss a subject that affects all of us every day, even though it stays generally hidden from public view. It causes our taxes to go up. It adds to the cost of what we buy. Worst of all, it threatens our personal safety and

▼ The relationship of the toast-master to the speaker should be the same as that of the fan to the fan dancer. It should call attention to the subject without making any particular effort to cover it.

Adlai Stevenson

that of our families—indeed, our very freedom. It causes untold damage to human lives and human health, yet its revenues are estimated to exceed the net profit of all the *Fortune* 500 corporations combined. Our speaker will tell us about organized crime in America.[2]

*Adapt your remarks for the audience and the occasion.* Years ago, when the humorist Will Rogers introduced the presidential candidate Franklin Roosevelt at the Hollywood Bowl, he said:

> Governor Roosevelt, you are here tonight the guest of people who spend their lives trying to entertain. This great gathering is neither creed nor politics, Jew nor Gentile, Democrat nor Republican. Whether they vote for you or not—and thousands of them won't, never mind what they tell you—every one of them admires you as a man. Your platform, your policies, your plans may not meet with their approval, but your high type of manhood gains the admiration of every person in this audience.[3]

Thus Rogers acknowledged both his audience and the political occasion of the speech.

Above all, *make sure that what you say is entirely accurate.* The most embarrassing type of introduction is one in which the speaker's name is mispronounced or some piece of information is incorrect. Whenever possible, it is a good idea to read your introduction, in advance, to the person being introduced.

## Awards

One common type of introduction introduces the speaker as the winner of an award. In an awards presentation, many of the preceding guidelines still apply, plus you have to explain briefly the significance of the award. Here's how actor Jack Nicholson presented a special Academy Award to the Italian director Michelangelo Antonioni:

> This year the Academy board of directors has voted to present the Honorary Oscar to one of the movies' great visionaries: Michelangelo Antonioni.
> Most movies celebrate the ways we connect with each other. The films of this master mourn the failures to connect. In the empty silent spaces of the world he has found metaphors that illuminate the silent places of our hearts and found in them too a strange and terrible beauty; austere, elegant, enigmatic, and haunting.[4]

An award differs from a speaker's introduction in that it need not be quite as brief. The presenter should still be to the point, without rambling, but because the winner of the award will probably be modestly brief, the awarder can afford to be a little more expansive.

## Acceptances

An acceptance speech is twofold: You show your appreciation for the award and you thank the people who made it possible. With an acceptance speech you walk a fine line between self-aggrandizement ("This illustrious honor is the pinnacle of my glorious career") and humility ("Aw, shucks, folks. I don't deserve this award").

It is important to adapt your acceptance to the occasion. It is extremely important, for example, to know how many other speakers there will be and how long you will be expected to speak.

There are often many people to thank in an acceptance speech; for example, consider the long list that most winners of Oscars and Emmys reel off. To keep the list from being boring to all except those who are mentioned in it, find a meaningful way to thank each individual. Rather than just saying, "I want to thank _____, _____, and _____," tell something about each person, like Jamie Lee Curtis did when she accepted her American Comedy Award:

> I truly feel that this was a big team effort and I should take this home and jackhammer it into hundreds of pieces and send it to every member of the crew and cast, but I won't. I'll just invite them over and they can take a Polaroid with it.
>
> I'd like to thank Jim Cameron—and who would have ever thought that Jim could direct a comedy? I mean, have you ever met him?
>
> I'd like to thank all the actors I've worked with, especially Arnold Schwarzenegger—and by the way, his skin is very soft! You wouldn't think it, but it's lovely.
>
> I would like to thank my husband, Christopher Guest, who is the funniest of funnymen, who makes me laugh even when I'm trying desperately not to. . . . And my daughter Annie Guest, who makes me laugh when I least expect to. And I would like to thank one person who's made me laugh all my life, a great comic actor who makes it look so easy [mimicking a line from one of her father's early movies], "I love you Spartacus, like the father I never had," my father, Tony Curtis, who is here with me tonight.[5]

## Speeches of Commemoration

Speeches of commemoration honor the memory of a person or event. Their purpose is to keep a memory alive, so the choice of language is extremely important. One of the most famous commemorative speeches is Lincoln's Gettysburg Address. This speech's language is so inspiring that schoolchildren are still required to memorize it.

One common type of speech of commemoration is the eulogy, which honors a person who is recently deceased.

▼ We are united by our difficulty in finding a language for mourning

Frederick Busch

Honest emotion is especially important in a eulogy; trite, oversentimental, or clichéd language will rob the occasion of its dignity. Speak honestly even when the person being eulogized is in some way controversial, as in the case of "Baby Fae," the infant who died three weeks after receiving the world's first animal-human heart transplant. In her short life this infant had touched many hearts, as her struggle for survival was captured nightly on the television news. Marie Whisman, the head nurse of the hospital unit where Baby Fae lived and died, had this to say at the infant's memorial service:

> We wish you could have seen our smiles, but they were hidden by those green masks that you by now had become so accustomed to. You brought joy to so many. The video you starred in won you worldwide popularity. A casual stretch and a yawn will never be

forgotten. While the press was printing that you were grasping at lines and tubings, we knew you were also grasping and holding our fingers. Through this touching we tried hard to convey to you the love and caring of the many letters and gifts that were arriving from all over the nation. You were really a sweet-dispositioned baby. . . . It was impossible not to love you.[6]

If a commemoration is the most serious type of special occasion speaking, our final category is the least.

## After-Dinner Speeches

After-dinner speeches are given at social and business events, such as parties, club meetings, and banquets, with the main purpose of entertaining the audience. There will probably be some sentiment or idea underlying the entertainment, but it is important to keep it light. No one is eager for great profundity on a full stomach—especially a stomach full of the food and drink that is offered at the typical banquet. An after-dinner speech is usually expected to be humorous, but you do not *have* to be humorous to be entertaining. The word *entertain* derives from the Latin word *tenere,* meaning "to hold." Entertainment is anything that holds your audience's attention by making your message interesting and pleasant for them. An assortment of stories and anecdotes about your audience, for example, will suffice as long as they are presented genially, in a manner that suggests that you yourself are having a good time.

Still, humor remains one of the hallmarks of special occasion speaking. Because it is often a component of many other types of speeches as well, we'll take a look at it now.

## 🔻 HUMOROUS SPEAKING

We study humor within the realm of public speaking for two reasons. First, humor is the main component of many after-dinner speeches. Second, humor can be injected into a wide variety of informative and persuasive speeches. According to the experts, "Humor can show that you have a complete mastery of your subject."[7] It can also make a dull message more interesting, and therefore more effective.[8] Of course, humor is not appropriate for all speeches. Appropriateness, in fact, is one of the three requirements that you have to consider before using humor in a speech.

### Requirements for Humor

It is easiest to discuss humor by borrowing examples from professional comedians and professional speakers. A word of caution is appropriate: The goal of this discussion is not to make you a professional entertainer. We take professionals as examples only because it pays to learn from the best. The requirements for humor include levity, originality, and appropriateness.

### Levity

Levity is the quality of being light. When coming up with humor for a speech, "funny" is not necessarily the key word. The handier word is "light." A speech to entertain does not take itself altogether seriously. It deals with the serious in an absurd manner or with the absurd in a serious manner.

For example, the health hazards of tobacco and sugary snack foods are serious topics, but when Kevin Nealon of *Saturday Night Live* dealt with them, seriousness took a back seat to absurdity. In one episode of Nealon's "Weekend Update," his send-up of television news reporting, he began this way:[9]

| | |
|---|---|
| Visual: A table full of tobacco company executives, right hands raised, being sworn in before a congressional committee | "This week seven top tobacco company CEOs testified before a congressional health committee." |
| Visual: Newspaper clipping, headlined "Seven Tobacco Executives Deny Cigarettes Are Addictive" | "The executives said that they believed that nicotine is not addictive. They also testified that asbestos is a good source of fiber." |

Visual: Another newspaper clipping, headlined "Cigs Bigs Try Twinkie Defense"

"The president of the American Tobacco Company said cigarettes were no more dangerous than Twinkies. He later clarified his statement, saying what he meant was Twinkies have a longer shelf life than most cigarette smokers."

Visual: Pack of Twinkies

"In a related story, this week marked the 64th anniversary of the Twinkie. To commemorate the occasion, Hostess proudly displayed the very first Twinkie, which is expected to reach its expiration date sometime next year."

## Originality

Routines such as Nealon's "Weekend Update" have become classics. Classic routines, however, are usually not the most effective tactics for an amateur speaker. For example, take the old-time comic Henny Youngman—please.[10] Most people think it's funny when he says, "My grandson complains about headaches all the time. I tell him, Larry, when you get out of bed, *feet first* . . ."[11] The same line might not be funny if you said it.

Anecdotes of your own about strange experiences, strange people, or unique insights into everyday occurrences are the best ingredients for a speech to entertain. *Original* in this sense does not mean "brand-new." It means "firsthand" or "derived from the source." Take Ellen Degeneris's observations about air travel:

> The only bad thing about being a comedian is that I have to fly these little commuter airlines to obscure places, little eight-seater planes with an open cockpit, where you can see the pilot reading a manual called "So You Want to Fly a Plane."
>
> The seats recline about an inch, all except for the guy in front of me, whose seat comes back so far I could do dental work on him.
>
> I'm scared of flying. First of all, I don't think we have to go that high in the air. I think they're showing off, those pilots.
>
> And the food is the tiniest little food I've ever seen. I guess they figure everything's relative: You get that high up, you look out the window and then back at your food and you say, "Well, it's as big as that house down there."
>
> Salads are always two pieces of dead lettuce. Salad dressing comes in that astronaut package, so as soon as you open it, it goes on your neighbor's lap. "Could I just dip my lettuce in that? That's a lovely skirt—what is that, silk?"[12]

Somewhere beneath the surface there are two lessons here: (1) Original anecdotes don't have to be on original topics. Stories on the frustrations of air travel are as common as news stories about crime, but Degeneris manages to put her own stamp on her observations. (2) Original anecdotes are not original in the sense of being "brand-new." They are tested, tried, and true. A comedian who does a "bit" knows it is funny. Comedians test their humor in all their interactions, and they do not get up in front of an audience with an unproved product. This second lesson is probably the more important one. Test out your humorous anecdotes first.

### Appropriateness

Humor must be appropriate to the audience, the speaker, and the occasion. Be careful telling Polish jokes to the Kasimir Pulaski Social Group, or drunk jokes at an Alcoholics Anonymous meeting. Joan Rivers's comments on a well-known actress who is having a weight problem might not be appropriate for an audience of the actress's fans, or anyone who is weight conscious:

> Is she fat? Oh, grow up! She has a walk-in belly button. She got stuck between the arches trying to get into McDonald's![13]

To be fair, we should add that Joan Rivers also makes potentially inappropriate comments about svelte starlets ("She's so dumb she studies for her pap test") and herself ("My body is falling so fast my gynecologist wears a hard hat").

Sometimes humor can be derived from making an inappropriate observation more appropriate, through the use of a euphemism. David Letterman provided an example:

> One of the reservoirs that supplies about 20 percent of the drinking water here in New York City is going to be closed for a couple of weeks because they found traces of "organic matter" in it. Man, I'll be honest with you, when I read this, it scared the organic matter out of me.[14]

The Japanese ambassador to the United States knew he faced a tough audience when he spoke at George Washington University in Washington, D.C. It was the spring of 1994, and U.S./Japanese trade talks had recently broken down. Relations between the two countries were at a low point. After the ambassador was introduced, he said,

> Thank you. I'm delighted to be part of your Ambassador Lecture Series. I think it's very brave of you to invite ambassadors to speak. We're not especially known for our oratory or clarity.
>
> Someone once noted that a diplomat is a person who thinks twice before saying nothing.
>
> Someone else said that if a diplomat says yes, he means perhaps; if he says perhaps he means no; and if he says no, he's no diplomat.

So traditionally when ambassadors give speeches we try to put everything on a positive, upbeat note of cooperation and progress. Sometimes we're a little like spin doctors—to use a phrase that's popular in this town—putting the best face on whatever problems arise. But in this spring of 1994, it would be less than honest of me to spin a speech that ignores the current problems between our two countries.[15]

## Some Techniques of Humor

There are many techniques of humor. Physical humor, for example, includes pratfalls, pies in the face, dressing in outlandish outfits, and walking into walls. The beginning of the media/information age produced a number of comedians whose specialty was physical humor: Lucille Ball, Red Buttons, and Tim Conway, to name a few. Today, a little bit of physical humor seems to be part of every comic's act, but, perhaps fortunately, physical humor is not of much use to the average public speaker. There are several more cerebral techniques that can make your own experiences or insights entertaining, including the following:

### Humorous Description

Humorists have to be sensitive to the scenes in life that sound funny when they are recounted later. They look at life more observantly than everyone else, and point out things that are, upon examination, a little out of whack. Tim Muehlhoff, when he was a student at Eastern Michigan University, told how he expected a traditional welcome on his first visit home from college. Instead, he said he found this scene:

> There was my mother wearing Jordache jeans, with blue streaks in her hair, and a button that said "Nuke the Whales." My dad was wearing a sequined Sergeant Pepper uniform, sunglasses, and one black glove. They were both dancing to Michael Jackson's "Thriller."[16]

Of course, humor in that passage does not just rely on description—there is also a suggestion of exaggeration, our second technique.

### Exaggeration

Exaggeration—magnifying description beyond the truth—is one of the most effective humorous techniques. The humorist Dave Barry provides an example:

> I keep seeing young teenage males wearing *enormous* pants; pants that two or three teenagers could occupy simultaneously and still have room in there for a picnic basket; pants that a clown would refuse to wear on the grounds that they were too undignified. The

young men wear these pants really low, so that the waist is about knee level and the pants butt drags on the ground.

I asked my son about these pants, and he told me that mainly "bassers" wear them. "Bassers" are people who like a lot of bass in their music. They drive around in cars with four-trillion-watt sound systems playing recordings of what sound like aboveground nuclear tests, but with less of an emphasis on melody.[17]

You could begin a speech with this exaggeration:

In order to prepare today's speech I read 27 books, interviewed 36 experts, ran 14 carefully controlled experiments, and surveyed the entire population of Tanzania. I worked on the speech for over a year, taking only short breaks for sustenance and catnaps. During that time I have lost considerable weight as well as my entire life's savings, and my wife has run off with a stevedore from San Diego. I am proud to tell you, though, that it was all worth it, for today I am fully prepared to explain to you *Why Ice Floats* . . .

Representing something as *less* than what it is (understatement) is another form of exaggeration:

I had a difficult time investigating this topic. I tried researching it at our library, but it was closed. Someone had checked out the book.

### Incongruity

Incongruities (statements that are out of place or inconsistent) can also inject humor into a speech. Jerry Seinfeld used this type of humor in his observations about leather jackets:

I once had a leather jacket that got ruined in the rain. Now why does moisture ruin leather? Aren't cows outside a lot of the time? When it's raining, do cows go up to the farmhouse, "Let us in! We're all wearing leather! Open the door! We're going to ruin the whole outfit here!"

"Is it suede?"

"I *am* suede! The whole thing is suede! I can't have this cleaned. . . . It's all I've got!"[18]

Elreta Alexander, a district court judge, used an incongruity in her address at a high school commencement. After thanking her audience for a warm welcome, she said:

Viewing you in your radiance, I am impelled to respond as did a witness in court after I repeatedly admonished him to look at the jury as he testified. I finally ordered, "Mr. Witness, will you please address the jury!" He nodded, turned to the jury, and said, "Howdy."

Howdy, all you beautiful people. Your presence is encouraging.[19]

## Play on Words

A play on words allows you to create humor by manipulating language. One way is to place an unexpected ending on a familiar expression:

Where there's a will, there's a lawsuit.

Another way is to change a word or two in a familiar expression:

You can lead a man to college, but you can't make him think.

You can also rearrange words in some nonsensical way:

I showed that wiseguy. I hit him right in the fist with my eye.

Or just use a common word or expression in an unexpected way:

I get so tired of putting my cat out at night. I wish he would stop playing with matches.

Gary Shandling provides a play on words when he discusses how he has risen above his obsession with his hair:

I don't talk about my hair anymore because I've matured and I realize now that looks aren't important, it's what kind of hair you have inside that counts.[20]

Steve Martin uses a play on words this way:

I like a woman with a head on her shoulders. I hate necks.[21]

A *pun* is a special type of play on words. It uses a word or expression to emphasize different meanings (such as when you introduce a dentist as a person who looks down in the mouth) or uses a word that sounds like another word (a girl's best friend is her mutter).

Puns should be handled carefully in a speech. They are usually clever rather than funny. They "fool" people rather than entertain. They make people groan, rather than laugh. Therefore, they are a high risk.

People have a tendency to think that puns are the lowest form of humor, unless they think of them first. Still, puns can be used sparingly for humorous effect as long as they do not interfere with your message.

## Satire

Satire (humor based on an exposé of human vice or folly) is considered a much higher form of humor than puns.[22]

When Jay Leno learned that the French government, in an attempt to keep the French language "pure," had banned American English words that had worked their way into the French language (words such as *le cheeseburger, le bulldozer,* and *le chewing gum*), he announced that we would henceforth exclude the following French words from American English:[23]

| FRENCH WORD | WILL NOW BE CALLED: |
|---|---|
| Bidet | Doggy drinking fountain |
| Hors d'oeuvres | Greasy overpriced Ritz crackers |
| Maitre'd | Dork in the bad tux |
| Résumé | Falsified job history |
| Paté | Gag! What the hell is this? |

Satire, as much as any other type of humor, has to be handled carefully. It has to be appropriate to the speaker, the audience, and the occasion.

No matter what type of humor you use, you should follow three rules during your presentation:

1. Do not, under any circumstances, *try* to be funny. Be light, be original, and be appropriate, but let the funny take care of itself.
2. If you do get a laugh, do not step on it. Wait until the laughter has hit its peak and is beginning to subside before you resume speaking.
3. If you do not get a laugh, keep going as though nothing happened.

## ▼ SAMPLE SPEECHES

The sample speeches for this chapter are Bill Cosby's presentation of the 1995 *Essence* Award to General Colin Powell, and General Powell's acceptance of that award.[24] The award is given annually by *Essence* magazine.

Along with being a model special occasion speech, Cosby's is a good example of how video clips can be used as audiovisual aids. It also exemplifies many of the techniques of informative speaking discussed in Chapter 12, such as novelty, variety, and drama.

## ▼ BILL COSBY'S PRESENTATION

His first line leaves no doubt that, Powell is the star of the evening.

Clip I: [News footage of Powell, in uniform, presenting a speech. Montage of photos and film clips of African American servicemen.]

[1] General Colin L. Powell is an American Hero. A career soldier, devoted husband and father, he has captured the national imagination in a way that transcends political partisanship and may yet transcend race. His triumph signals hope for us all.

*Clip I: [Powell:] From the earliest days of our nation African Americans answered the call to arms in defense of America. Whenever that call came, black men and women on the battlefield were crucial to victory. Yet the fame and fortune that were their just due never came. I am deeply mindful of the debt I owe to those who went before me. I climbed on their backs. I will never forget their service and their sacrifice. I know where I came from. All of us need to know where we came from.*

² On October 1, 1989, General Colin L. Powell was named chairman of the Joint Chiefs of Staff. He was the first African American ever appointed to head the combined U.S. Armed Forces. Born in Harlem and raised in the South Bronx, Colin Powell resisted the temptations of the street.

> *Clip II: [Powell:] People ask me, "Did you have a strong family life?" I say, "Yeah, it was a powerful family." But we didn't sit around at night like the Brady Bunch, talking about values. I just watched how my parents lived. And that's how values are passed on.*

³ Colin Powell graduated from the ROTC program at City College in New York and entered the Army as a 2nd lieutenant. Later, as a young captain in Vietnam he earned a Purple Heart, a Bronze Star, and the Soldier's Medal for Valor after going back into a burning helicopter to pull his fellow servicemen to safety. Rising through the ranks, Powell became military aide to Secretary of Defense Caspar Weinberger, and it was Weinberger who recommended him four years later to become the first African American National Security Advisor.

> *Clip III: [Weinberger:] He's advanced because of his enormous innate ability. He's never let any handicap of any kind that might arise from color stand in his way.*
>
> *Clip IV: [Powell:] I have been thrown out of hot dog stands in Georgia when I was a young captain just coming home from a year in Vietnam. And the way I deal with it is, "I'm gonna beat you."*

⁴ In 1989 General Powell received his fourth star and was appointed chairman of the Joint Chiefs by President Bush later that year. General Powell was present at the dawn of *glasnost* and *perestroika* in the former Soviet Union. He led the nation's young men and women in Operation Desert Storm. And General Powell was the first chairman of the Joint Chiefs to deploy American troops on a humanitarian mission.

> *Clip V: [Jimmy Carter:] On the Haitian trip I saw him in the role of a peacemaker. Colin Powell was startlingly effective in describing to the generals . . . the overwhelming military force that was poised to destroy them. In fact he said later, somewhat jokingly, that he described weapons that didn't even exist. [laughing] But his presentation was very sobering to the generals.*

⁵ Colin Powell has yet to be all he can be. But he continues to be a beacon of hope for the nation, and an inspiration to many, from present policymakers to future world leaders.

> *Clip VI: [Powell:] Don't let anyone ever tell you that you are limited, because you came from the inner city, because you're black, because*

---

The video clip continues: Powell being sworn in by President Bush, photos of Powell as a child.

Clip II: [News interview footage with Colin Powell; montage of family photos.]

Clip: Montage of Powell as a soldier in these various stages.

Clip III: [Interview with Caspar Weinberger.]

Clip IV: [Powell, speaking to high school students.]

Clip: Montage of ceremonies celebrating Powell's accomplishments.

Clip V: [Interview with former President Jimmy Carter; montage of Powell and Carter working together in Haiti.]

Clip: Powell in a parade.

Clip VI: [Powell, speaking to school children.]

*you didn't go to the right schools. The only thing that should ever be a limitation is your own dream.*

No visuals in the conclusion, to allow the audience to focus on these important words.

[6] For his courage, for the image of pride and strength he's provided, for his vision of an America that could be and should be, it gives me great pleasure to present the 1995 *Essence* Award to General Colin L. Powell.

## ▼ GENERAL POWELL'S ACCEPTANCE

Cosby handed Powell the award, and they shared a private word and laughed. Powell showed his great speaker's instinct by making that private exchange public.
Powell focuses his remarks on the larger meaning of the award: the recognition of African-American contributors to society.

[1] Thank you so very, very much, ladies and gentlemen. Dr. Cosby said to me, as he was handing me this award, that I could only speak for about thirty seconds. And I told him, "I'm a general and you aren't." [audience laughter]

[2] I want to express my appreciation to *Essence* and also offer my congratulations on their 25 years of service to the nation. I'm deeply touched by this and I'm touched by the fact that you would give it to a soldier—a professional soldier. But I can't accept it in my own name. I've got to accept it in the names of all the wonderful young men and women in uniform who you saw on the screen before you.

[3] This sacrifice of African Americans was not made for me to get where I am or to win this award tonight. They did it to make this a better country. They did it to let this country live up to its dream.

He concludes his brief acceptance with a call for his audience to accomplish even more.

[4] And so let's all here tonight dedicate ourselves to that proposition, to an America that is great and to an America that will be better still with our sacrifices, with our hard work, and with our dreams.

[5] Thank you very much.

## ▼ SUMMARY

Special occasion speaking is the type done at special events, such as weddings, memorial services, or banquets. This type of speaking includes introductions of other speakers, awards presentations, acceptances of awards, speeches of commemoration (such as eulogies), and after-dinner speeches.

Humor, one of the mainstays of after-dinner speaking, has three requirements: levity (dealing with the serious in an absurd way and the absurd in a serious way), originality (derived from your own experience), and appropriateness (to the audience, the occasion, and the speaker). Techniques of humor include humorous description, exaggeration, incongruities, plays on words, and satire.

**EXERCISES**

**1.** Interview a class member about his or her life. Assuming that everyone deserves an award for *something,* what kind of an award would you present to your interviewee? Write a brief presentation.

**2.** Tape a few minutes of humorous speaking. This might be a monologue from one of the late-night comedy shows, or almost anything from The Comedy Channel. Analyze the presentation in terms of the requirements of humor (levity, originality, and appropriateness) and the techniques used.

# NOTES

1. James C. Humes, *Roles Speakers Play* (New York: Harper & Row, 1976), p. 8.

2. Adapted from introduction to William French Smith, "Combating Organized Crime," *Vital Speeches of the Day,* February 1, 1984, pp. 229–231.

3. From *The Autobiography of Will Rogers,* Donald Day, ed. (Boston: Houghton Mifflin, 1977).

4. Jack Nicholson, Presentation of Honorary Academy Award to Michelangelo Antonioni, Academy Awards, March 27, 1995.

5. Jamie Lee Curtis, acceptance of American Comedy Award for "Funniest Female: Motion Pictures," March 6, 1995.

6. Marie Whisman, quoted in *New York Daily News,* November 18, 1984, p. 2.

7. Donald H. Dunn, "The Serious Business of Using Jokes in Public Speaking," *Business Week,* September 5, 1983, p. 93.

8. See Dorothy Markiewicz, "Effects of Humor on Persuasion," *Sociometry* 37 (September 1974), pp. 407–422.

9. Kevin Nealon, "Weekend Update," "*Saturday Night Live,*" NBC Television Network, April 16, 1994.

10. For those born too late, this clever phrase refers to Youngman's most classic line: "Take my wife— please." Like most humor, if you have to explain it, it's not funny.

11. "Take My Wife—Please," *Newsweek,* February 2, 1976, p. 75.

12. Ellen Degeneris, HBO *Comedy Showcase,* shown in its syndicated version over WNBC-TV, July 17, 1994.

13. Rivers was famous for these comments as guest host of the *Tonight Show* during the 1980s. See "Joan Rivers," *Newsweek,* October 10, 1983, pp. 58–60.

14. *The Late Show with David Letterman,* CBS Television Network, Friday, September 7, 1994.

15. T. Kuriyama, "U.S. and Japan Trade Relations," *Vital Speeches of the Day,* May 1, 1994, pp. 421–422.

16. Tim Muehlhoff, "The Best Is Yet to Be," after-dinner speech presented at the 1984 National Forensics Association National Tournament.

17. Dave Barry, *Dave Barry Is Not Making This Up* (New York: Crown, 1994), pp. 243–244.

18. Jerry Seinfeld, *Seinlanguage* (New York: Bantam, 1993), p. 41.

19. Elreta Alexander, "Reflections for a Graduate," *Vital Speeches of the Day* 42, August 1, 1976.

20. Gary Shandling, as seen on the Emmy Awards broadcast, September 9, 1994, from a stand-up appearance taped earlier.

21. Steve Martin, comment at the 1995 Academy Awards presentations.

22. Experimental evidence into the effects of satire is somewhat inconsistent. There is some evidence to suggest that, if an audience is initially favorable to a speaker's position, both the message and speaker will be evaluated more favorably when satire is employed. See L. Powell, "Satire and Speech Trait Evaluation," *Western Journal of Speech Communication* 41 (Spring 1977), pp. 117–125. However, if listeners tend to be neutral or in opposition, satire is either at best ineffective or at worst counterproductive. See N. Vidmar and M. Rokeach, "Archie Bunker's Bigotry: A Study in Selective Perception and Exposure," *Journal of Communication* 24 (1974), pp. 36–47.

23. *The Tonight Show with Jay Leno,* NBC Television Network, July 11, 1994.

24. *Essence* Awards, Spring 1995.

# GROUP PRESENTATIONS

## ▼ CHAPTER 16 OBJECTIVES

**After reading this chapter, you should understand:**

**1.** The components of group process.

**2.** The types of group presentations.

**You should be able to:**

**1.** Organize an effective group.

**2.** Organize an effective group presentation.

##  GROUPS IN THE MEDIA/INFORMATION AGE

One problem of the media/information age is that there is often too much information, and too many perspectives on that information, for one person to handle. Because of this, group work is becoming increasingly common in school, at work, and in social activities. When people get together in a group, they are able to share knowledge and perspectives, to combine their samplings of the information stream so together, as a group, they miss as little of it as possible. Group work is useful in the media/information age, both for planning and presenting information. Groups combine resources in planning; in presenting, each group member is able to concentrate on and become expert in a specialized area, while the other group members back up that speaker with their various specialties and perceptions.

▼ There are many objects of great value which cannot be attained by unconnected individuals, but must be attained if at all, by association.

Daniel Webster

THE FAR SIDE, by Gary Larson

"Well, time for our weekly brain-stem-storming session."

When time permits, a group presentation is often assigned in a public speaking class. This assignment is designed to promote an understanding of group process during the meetings to plan the presentations, as well as to introduce students to an important type of speech format in the presentation itself. We'll begin with the planning process.

## ▼ PLANNING THE GROUP PRESENTATION

▼ Before everything else, getting ready is the secret of success.

Henry Ford

Let's say you're given a group speaking assignment. Your own assignment might differ, but for our purposes here, let's say your group is asked to make a presentation in which each member gives a formal presentation of 3-5 minutes on some aspect of a group topic. Your first task would be to plan the presentation with your group. This will probably require at least three group sessions. First, you have to meet to get acquainted (if necessary), to get organized as a group, to decide on a topic, and to divide the research tasks. On your second meeting you might go over the results of your research and organize the individual presentations. On the third meeting you might rehearse those presentations as a group.

You might need more meetings than that (for example, a second or third research or organization session), but you probably won't need less. As you work in your group, you'll be most effective if you understand group process.

In group process the accomplishments of the group tend to be more, in both quantity and quality, than the output the same people would have working separately. There are at least three reasons for this beneficial aspect of group work. The first is the idea of division of labor. Individual members can do the work they are best suited for, and that work can be coordinated, so there is a minimal duplication of effort.

The second benefit of group work is that, when it works correctly, it increases individual energy. It has this effect because there is often a social, fun dimension to group work. After all, getting together with other people is what most people like to do for recreation. Also, some members will pick up others when their energy flags. This is one of the secrets of most successful sports teams: Everyone tires at a different point, so when you're still high in energy you help out others who are low.

The third reason groups provide an extra bonus is group work tends to increase individual creativity. This occurs because group members can build on each other's ideas, combining and adapting ideas that have already been expressed. This advantage of group work is enhanced through the technique of brainstorming. *Brainstorming,* which involves the spontaneous contribution of ideas from each member of a group, can be done formally or informally. "Brainstorming informally" is done in everyday conversations, with no stated rules. This is the type of brainstorming that you do with friends over coffee, telling them about your speech assignment and using the conversation to generate ideas rather than just to kill time. Informal brainstorming might, for example, lead to the discovery of new and different materials, including films, television programs, popular books, magazines, or newspaper articles that might relate to your topic. *Formal brainstorming* involves five stated rules, all of which are designed to facilitate the free flow of ideas:

1. No criticism of ideas—just get them out, record them, and go on to the next idea.
2. The wilder the idea, the better.
3. Quantity, rather than quality, of ideas is stressed.
4. Adaptation, improvement, and combination of ideas are encouraged.
5. No ownership of ideas. No one takes personal credit, so there's no "ego involvement" in the idea.

After the brainstorming session is completed and you have the chance to cool down, you review the ideas for quality and winnow out the ones that don't work.

To understand group process further, you should understand some of its primary components, including group goals, roles, norms, rules, and leadership.

## Group Goals

The first step in understanding group process is to recognize the goals of the group. This might sound obvious, since in a group assignment the "goal"—to prepare that presentation—will be assigned by the instructor. But in fact there are different types of goals. There is the explicitly stated goal (prepare the presentation) but there might also be implicit goals (get a great grade on this assignment, impress the instructor with your individual effort, meet an attractive potential object of affection). As these examples suggest, there is a potential conflict between *individual goals* (the motives of individual members) and *group goals* (the outcome the group seeks to accomplish).

There is also a potential conflict between *task-oriented* goals (such as dividing the research tasks) and *socially oriented* goals (making that aforementioned social contact). In analyzing the task-oriented goals, you should recognize that some goals are appropriate for groups and some are more appropriate for individuals. A group task is a large one, beyond the capacity of one person. It is usually a task that requires the individual group members to be committed to the solution. In our example, individual group members need to feel good about their participation in the various decisions of the group (what research to do, how to organize the ideas) in order to do a good job on the presentation.

In analyzing the socially oriented goals, you should beware of *hidden agendas* (social goals that are kept secret, such as a desire for revenge against another group member). The best blend is a balance in which social goals help energize the group but do not get in the way of getting the work done.

## Group Roles

*Group roles* refer to *the different types of behavior performed by individual group members.* There are *formal roles* and *informal roles.* The formal roles might assign general responsibilities, such as group leader, moderator, or recording secretary; or specific responsibilities, such as the interviewer, current periodicals researcher, or visual aids artist.

There are also informal roles, which are often unstated but are still valuable in terms of moving the group forward and helping it complete its tasks. Informal roles are based on the idea that everyone has different strengths, the combination of which results in maximum productivity. Consider the following informal roles:[1]

| | |
|---|---|
| ▼ Initiator | Proposes new ideas |
| ▼ Clarifier | Finds ways of expressing ideas that lead to groupunderstanding |
| ▼ Coordinator | Smooths the relationship among ideas, or among group members |
| ▼ Diagnostician | Indicates what the problems are |
| ▼ Summarizer | Briefly condenses what has been accomplished |
| ▼ Energizer | Prods the group to action |
| ▼ Evaluator | Analyzes group accomplishments according to agreed upon criteria |
| ▼ Harmonizer | Reconciles disagreements and helps group members get along |

It is important to recognize these unstated roles to keep them functional. There are also dysfunctional roles, such as "idea blocker" or "recognition seeker,"[2] that should be avoided. Once they are knowledgeable about these roles, all group members can encourage functional roles and discourage the dysfunctional ones.

## Group Norms and Rules

Norms and rules are both limitations on acceptable behavior within the group. The difference is that norms are unstated, while rules are stated. Rules might sound like this:

1. We will meet every Tuesday and Thursday after class.
2. Meetings will last no longer than one hour.
3. Group members will choose the designated leader by vote.
4. Group decisions will be determined by majority vote.

Group norms, on the other hand, might sound like this:

1. You can cut up and tell jokes during the first few minutes of the meeting, but after the group work gets started in earnest, jokes will be kept to a minimum.
2. It's all right to express opinions, but back them up with facts.
3. It's all right to be occasionally critical of group progress, but maintain a positive attitude overall.

Like group roles, it is important for group members to recognize group norms so they can use them to encourage productivity in the group.

## Group Leadership

To understand how group leadership works and how to make it effective, we begin by looking at *types of leadership* and the *functions of leaders.*

### Types of Leadership

Many task-oriented groups have designated leaders, chosen by the group or by an outside authority. Other groups have no particular leader, and still others have *emergent* leaders, who take over leadership roles informally as the group progresses. No matter which type, it is a good idea to examine traditional styles of group leadership. Traditionally, three leadership styles are identified.

*Authoritarian Leadership* The first leadership style is *authoritarian leadership,* in which the leader seeks a maximum amount of control. The authoritarian leader is concerned mostly with efficiency—getting the job done as quickly and easily as possible—and therefore seeks compliance rather than commitment from the other group members.

*Laissez-Faire Leadership* The second leadership style is the *permissive* or *laissez-faire* style of leadership. This type of leader does not guide the group in any way. The laissez-faire leader sometimes relinquishes leadership responsibility in favor of being "just another member" or, even more passively, just an observer of the group. This style encourages spontaneity among group members, but often leads to disorganized discussions.

▼ Leadership is the art of changing a group from what it is to what it should be.

Anonymous

***Democratic Leadership*** The third style is democratic leadership. The *democratic leader* encourages all members to contribute and interact, while at the same time keeping them on the topic.

At its best, democratic leadership will be just as efficient as authoritarian leadership and will stimulate spontaneity just as well as laissez-faire leadership. For this reason, it is the preferred type of leadership in most discussion groups. Still, you should recognize that the other styles have their place. Military units are still most comfortable with authoritarian leadership, and therapy groups that attempt to encourage reticent members to express their feelings are most effective when handled by a laissez-faire leader.

### Shared Leadership

▼ A community is like a ship; everybody ought to be prepared to take the helm.

Henrik Ibsen

Group leaders are well advised to share leadership responsibility with the group. *Shared leadership* increases member commitment and satisfaction in group discussion. In some cases, it increases group output. There are two ways to share leadership. One is to have no designated leader, and the other is to have a designated leader who is willing to share responsibility.

When you have a formal leader (or "moderator" or "coordinator"), that leader takes on the responsibility of making sure that certain things get done. In a leaderless group, these functions still need to be met, so they are distributed among group members. These things include matters that have to be handled *before* the group meets, such as securing a room, making sure the lights and temperature controls work, and notifying all the group members. The traditional leadership functions also include responsibilities *during* the group discussion: controlling the amount of interaction and conflicts, reviewing progress, and maintaining an agenda.

*Traffic Control*  Traditionally, the group leader takes on the responsibility of regulating *who* talks, *when,* and for *how long.* Part of traffic control is encouraging discussion from all members; therefore, if one member tends to monopolize the group's time, the leader is expected to inhibit that member in some way. (The leader might say, "That's a good idea, Fred, and your anecdote about summer camp certainly proves it. But let's see what some of the others think.") If a member does not contribute in any way, the leader is expected to draw that member out. Sometimes this work requires a sensitivity to nonverbal cues. Members who want to speak might not say so. They might just look puzzled or exasperated. At such times those members should be specifically invited to speak. ("Did you have a question, George?" or "Martha, did you want to add something?")

Sometimes traffic control is enhanced by the physical arrangement of the group. People sitting across from each other, for example, tend to interact more. People physically isolated from the group—such as two members in the back of the room, alone—will tend to form a clique and interact with themselves rather than with the rest of the group. A circle is considered the ideal physical arrangement for most group interaction.

*Conflict Control*  Some conflicts are functional; arguments over ideas and opinions that are leading to increased understanding, for example, tend to energize the group and increase creativity. Most important, functional conflicts tend to keep *groupthink* to a minimum. Groupthink is a form of dysfunctional conformity; it occurs when there is a collective striving for unanimity that discourages realistic appraisals of alternatives. The worst examples of groupthink take place in cults, in which the unspoken norm is "no dissent, show only enthusiasm." With no dissent, the group begins to take on a feeling of invulnerability; it acquires an unquestioning belief that its ideas are correct, and even morally right.

There are times, however, when conflict becomes *dysfunctional,* such as when members begin to personally attack each other, or fight over matters that are unrelated to the group's work. At such times, the leader is expected to control the conflict and help the group move beyond it. For example, if two group members begin arguing over who did the most work

▼ People are never so likely to settle a question rightly as when they discuss it freely.

Macaulay

▼ A leader is best when people barely know that he exists ... They will say, "We did it ourselves."

Lao-tzu

in the last group they both belonged to, the leader might have to step in and say, "Let's not dwell on past history. This is a new group, and a new opportunity for success. Now, which one of us would be best to conduct a telephone survey?"

***Agenda Control*** The discussion leader organizes an agenda, which is a plan of group activities. For example, if you have an assignment to give a group presentation, your agenda for your first group discussion might look like this outline:

    I. Introduce group members
        A. Areas of interest
        B. Areas of expertise
   II. Establish group goals
        A. Requirements for the assignment
        B. Rules for the group
            1. How often to meet
            2. When and where to meet
            3. Time limits for meetings
            4. Attendance requirements for members
            5. Other
  III. Choose topic for presentation
        A. Discussion
        B. Brainstorming
        C. Evaluation
  IV. Discuss topic
        A. Analysis of topic
        B. Division of labor among group members
   V. Explore avenues of research
        A. Library research
        B. Interviews
        C. Surveys/experimentation

Subsequent meetings would include agenda items for evaluating research and planning the presentation. Whatever the agenda items, they will be organized in outline form, according to the principles of outlining presented in Chapter 8.

One of the leader's responsibilities in terms of maintaining the agenda is to periodically review the group's progress on that agenda. ("So far we've accomplished _____, _____, and _____. According to the agenda we've agreed upon, we still have to accomplish _____.")

This brief look at group process should help you prepare for your group presentation, which might be one of three types.

##  TYPES OF GROUP PRESENTATIONS

A specific format is helpful in a group presentation. The most common formats are symposia, panel discussions, and forums, all of which have variations.

### The Symposium

In a symposium each participant gives a prepared presentation on a specific part of the topic. The suggested procedure for a symposium is as follows:

1. The moderator introduces the topic and the panel members in the order in which they will speak.
2. The members then make their formal presentations. Although they may refer to each other, they do not interact during the presentations.
3. The moderator generally supplies transitions from one participant to the next. However, in one variation the members supply the transitions themselves as part of their conclusions.
4. The chairperson, or the final speaker, summarizes the discussion. If scheduled, an audience forum begins.

### The Panel Discussion

In a panel discussion, the participants do not make individual formal presentations. The suggested procedure for a panel discussion is as follows:

1. The moderator introduces the topic and the panel members.
2. The moderator then poses a question to one of the panel members.
3. All members discuss the question informally.
4. The moderator controls traffic, making sure that each panelist is given a chance to complete a thought before the next panelist begins speaking, and asking specific questions when the interaction seems to falter.
5. The moderator clarifies, summarizes, restates, or paraphrases ideas if necessary.
6. At the end of the allotted time, the moderator summarizes the discussion.
7. The audience might be invited to ask questions or comment. The moderator controls the audience "traffic," also.

The atmosphere of a panel discussion encourages interaction and spontaneity; participants often interrupt each other and exchange comments. In spite of the informality, panel members should be well prepared for this type of presentation.

If audience members are invited to ask questions and make comments to the panelists, the panel discussion becomes a forum.

### The Forum

The forum is primarily an interaction between panel members and the audience. Generally the moderator announces the topic of the forum and the rules for interaction: how audience members are chosen to speak, how long they can speak, and so on. Then the panel members are introduced and audience members are encouraged to participate, perhaps with well-chosen questions. In a forum, as in any other type of group presentation, the panel members should be well prepared in advance.

## ▼ SAMPLE GROUP PRESENTATION

Our sample group presentation is a classroom symposium given by four students in an Introduction to Speech Communication class at New York University. Notice the way the topic of finding a job is divided among the panel members. Notice also the way the group organizes their presentations as a whole, with an overall introduction, transitions, and conclusion. Each individual's presentation is organized in the same way.

## ▼ How to Find the Job of Your Dreams
## Introduction

Kristin Liguori

[1] The topic for our group presentation today will impact all of our lives in the near future. All of us in this room have a common goal to make something of our lives, and to be productive, prosperous, and happy. College will prepare us for a career in the real world, but how we go about finding a job will determine what kind of life we will lead and where the future will take us. [2] If there's a secret to finding the job of your dreams, it consists in these four techniques [Chart 1]. For our presentation, each of us will discuss one of these techniques. I will begin by discussing the importance of preparing an effective résumé. Norman will then explain the advantages of networking. Irving will speak on the valuable information you can gain from researching your prospective company. Finally, Kathy will conclude our presentation with some tips for a successful interview.

Introduction seeks to interest audience in overall topic of group.

**Chart 1**

> 1. **Résumé**
> 2. **Networking**
> 3. **Researching**
> 4. **Interview**

Main points of group previewed.

## ▼ Designing the Résumé

Kristin Liguori

[1] The first step in your job hunt is the preparation of your résumé. According to résumé experts Ronald Krannich and William Banis, authors of *High Impact Résumés and Letters: How to Communicate Your Qualifications to Employers,* "The résumé will become the single most important piece of paper you will need for getting jobs in the 21st century." It may sound strange, but this single sheet of paper tells your prospective employer more about you than you know. According to Tom Jackson, author of *The Perfect Résumé,* your résumé makes an indelible impression in twenty to thirty seconds.

[2] You should choose the best format for your résumé, one that will accentuate your best qualities. [Chart 2] Some examples of typical subsets that appear on résumés include:

Kristin now elaborates on her own topic.

**Chart 2**

> * **Objective**
> * **Work Experience**
> * **Education**
> * **Achievements**
> * **Capabilities**
> * **Special Projects**

▼ *Objective,* stating what position you are seeking and what you hope to accomplish there. This is a good opportunity to personalize your résumé for a particular job opportunity.

▼ *Work Experience,* related or unrelated to the career you are seeking, depending on the format you choose.

▼ *Education,* at the top of the résumé if you are recently out of school and at the bottom if not.

▼ *Achievements,* that you are especially proud of and that will prove that you are able to handle the job.

▼ *Capabilities,* which tell the employer what you can do and what you plan to offer the company if hired.

▼ *Special Projects,* an especially helpful category for the prospective graduate. You can list school or internship projects that relate to your prospective job.

**Chart 3**

---

**Résumé Styles**

1. **Chronological**
2. **Functional**
3. **Targeted**

---

Many of Kristin's ideas were inspired by group brainstorming.

[3] Let's consider three basic résumé formats [Chart 3] that are used by job hunters today. [Show samples on posterboard] As you can see, each of these résumé types is divided into the subsets of information. Some of them, such as education, appear in each type, but might appear in a different place.

[4] The first type is the *Chronological Résumé,* which provides all of your pertinent information in reverse chronological order. You list all your employment, educational, and special achievements. You work backwards, keeping your most recent achievements at the top of each of the subsets.

[5] The second résumé format is the *Functional Résumé.* The functional résumé is designed to emphasize work experiences and is frequently used by individuals who have held a variety of positions. The functional format can be used effectively to minimize a record of different job changes. When creating a functional résumé, it is important to keep all job-related tasks at the top of each of your subsets. (For example, if you were applying for a management training position with a retail giant, and you had held lots of part-time jobs in retail stores while you were working your way through school, you would list them all here. . . . Emphasize your most powerful abilities and keep the education section at the end of the résumé.

[6] Finally, there is the *Targeted Résumé,* which is designed for one particular job opening. This one is used when you know the description of the job that you're applying for. It points to key words in that description and it emphasizes the capabilities that you know the company is looking for. A targeted résumé begins with the candidate's capabilities and it emphasizes what he/she can do in the future. The candidate's past accomplishments are the next subset, and education follows.

[7] Of course, you are not limited to these formats or these headings. When it comes to résumés, there is plenty of room for versatility. If you think it would be advantageous to be unique and create something new and different, go ahead. Employers often look for the "unique you." Ellen Jackson, author of many texts on résumé preparation, advises college students to "avoid standardized approaches that seem too uniform and conventional and don't allow for you to express your own uniqueness and determination. Take your own initiative . . . go beyond the normal." Most importantly, college students need to remember that employers are interested in

what you can do for them. To prove this, include any leadership roles you have held, part-time jobs, and interests that will make you the best candidate for the job.

8 I'd like to leave you with four important principles [Chart 4] to remember when writing your résumé:

▼ Brevity—Keep the résumé to one page, and avoid excess information. Some information, such as references, reasons for leaving past employers, and salary information will be requested later if the company is interested in you. And don't include a photograph, unless you are applying for a job in the theater arts.

▼ Clarity—Use bullets, underlining, and bold print to organize your subsets. Use the clearest, simplest language you can. Have your advisor and one or two professors or friends proofread a draft to make sure it's clear to others.

▼ Neatness—Keep the résumé neatly typed and clean. The image of the paper is a reflection of you. And don't bother with a fancy cover or binder—they just make it difficult for a potential employer to file your résumé.

▼ Persuasiveness—Sell yourself by accentuating your best qualities. Highlight your most recent experience and accomplishments. Make sure that you present yourself in the best possible light so that you stand out above the rest and so that you get the opportunity to speak with the employer in person.

9 If you are careful in following all of the résumé rules that I have explained, you are sure to increase your chances of winning that interview of a lifetime. Your résumé is well worth the time it will take you to complete it. Now we will move to the next step: circulating that résumé in order to continue a successful job search and ensure an interview appointment. Norman will now explain how you do that, through *networking*.

**Chart 4**

| Brevity |
| Clarity |
| Neatness |
| Persuasiveness |

Conclusion of her speech is combined with a transition to the next speech.

## 🔵 NETWORKING

Norman Benito

1 While you are in the process of preparing your résumé, you should be networking. Today I am going to tell you what networking is, why you should network, and how to network.

2 Networking is defined as discovering and using connections. Your first step to networking is to make a list of people who might be able to assist you in your job search. The list could include family members, past and present employers, people you know from school, or a counselor. The list could also include people you know from your hobbies such as people on a

Transition from last speech, introduction of main point of this speech.

Norman's organization has been worked out in group sessions.

sports team you belong to or a club member. You should also include anyone that your parents may know. You might even include contacts from your chat groups and interest groups on the Internet. The list doesn't have to be extensive to begin with; it is the nature of networking that each name on the list will help you add names to it.

[3] After you have made your primary list, you should establish a networking file by transferring the names from your list onto index cards or a rolodex or a database on your computer. The entry should include each person's name, address, and phone number, and any additional information such as career highlights or even hobbies. As you make each contact, you should update the card with the date and the content of that contact.

[4] There are two types of networking, called *systematic* and *opportune* networking. In systematic networking, you have two approaches. The first approach is called *referrals* and the second is called *cold calling*. If you are new at networking, you should use the referral approach. This approach entails making a connection from a person whom you know, to a person who may be able to lead you to a job.

[5] From the list you developed, choose the people you feel will be of most help to you and contact them for an informational interview. An informational interview is an arranged meeting between you and a person whose professional accomplishments and/or industry are of interest to you. (Katherine will have more to tell us about the techniques of interviewing in a moment.)

*Internal previews to the next speech.*

[6] If you are the type who is confident and assertive, you could use the cold calling approach. This is when you call someone whom you would like to know, but who has no idea who you are. Many people who are established in their fields are willing to help out people who are trying to break in. It helps to drop them an e-mail or snail mail note first, however. If you use this approach, be sure you are persistent but not obnoxious or irritating, and don't take it personally if you are rejected. That probably just means the person was too busy to help out at this time.

[7] The second type of networking is called opportune networking. This is the type of networking that takes advantage of the unplanned opportunities that arise. Opportune networking can take place anywhere people meet. For example, that person standing in line behind you at the movies, whom you happen to have a conversation with. Or a guest speaker who comes to your class and stays after to answer questions. They all are potential contacts. You can create your own opportunities by being in the right places at the right times. Some of the right places are:

*Theses examples evolved out of group brainstorming.*

▼ Civic group functions—Functions such as Chamber of Commerce events or Kiwanis meetings create opportunities for you to introduce yourself to professionals.

▼ Informational meetings—There are often guest speakers in class or on campus. Sometimes these speakers are sponsored by the companies themselves. These are excellent opportunities to meet people involved with your industry.

▼ Trade shows—There are trade shows for almost every industry. For example, in my field, the most important trade show is the American Stockbrokers Association annual conference. Not only do you meet the movers and shakers of your field, you catch up with the most current issues, controversies, and gossip in the field, so you have something to talk about.

[8] When networking, you should use personal networking cards. [Chart 5] These are handy because networking encounters may last for a short period of time. These cards look like ordinary business cards and they allow you to distribute your name and number to anyone you meet. The campus copy shop will make up 500 of these for you for $12.95.

**Chart 5**

# Elizabeth Mendoza
Murchison State University
Clark Hall - Box 207
Murchison, TX 75126
**(214) 336-2382**

[9] According to Nancy J. Hemenway, a networking expert and author of *Mastering the Job Hunt,* you should follow some simple tips to be successful at networking:

This book was found during group research.

▼ End every conversation by asking for a business card—and, of course, handing them your own card.

▼ Never ask a contact for an internship, an interview, or a job. This puts the person in an awkward position. If they're looking for someone, let them ask you. All you should ask them for is advice, to assist you in your job search or expand your network.

▼ Try to get as many people involved in the process as possible. Your goal is to let everyone know what your career interests are.

▼ Always send a thank-you note to any contact who has been helpful to you.

[10] To conclude, you should never stop networking because it is a lifelong process. It is important to keep your networking file up to date because one day you may find yourself looking for another job. Also, you may be the person who is looking for that perfect job candidate. Having a strong network in your industry will better enable you to fill the position efficiently and effectively. Finally, your network will contribute to your lifelong success. Your contacts will be a source of important ideas and opportunities throughout your career.

[11] As you begin networking, it is important to research prospective companies that you are interested in working for. Irving will now discuss the research techniques that will help you along the job-hunting process.

## ▼ RESEARCHING THE COMPANY

### Irving Lee

[1] Kristin gave you some great tips on designing a resume, and Norman showed you how to build up your industry contacts, and in a couple of minutes Kathy will give you some hints on interviewing. I'd like to tell you how to maximize the effectiveness of all of these activities. To do that, you have to find out as much as you can about the company: about its history, about its management, about its goals for the future. I am going to discuss some reasons why it is important to research a prospective company before the actual interview, and maybe even before you customize that resume. I am also going to discuss the kind of information that you should be looking for, and where you can find it.

[2] First, let me outline why you should research a company you think you might want to work for: When you come prepared with information about the company to an interview, it says two things to the interviewer. One, it says that you are serious about the job, and two, that you have the dedication and interest to help the company. This will leave a positive image of you in the interviewer's mind.

[3] Information about the company is also used in determining whether or not it suits your needs as an employee. For instance, the size of the company and its organizational structure may give you an idea of where you stand relative to the rest of the employees. It is then up to you to decide whether or not you want to go to a large company where the process of advancement might be slow and the competition might be fierce. You might prefer a small company where it is more likely that you will gain experience and advance through the ranks at a quicker pace.

[4] You should also have a clear understanding of the goods or services offered by a prospective employer. You do not want to get stuck in something

that you lack interest in. One of my friends jumped into a job in television programming, thinking that it would be exciting and glamorous, and then found himself behind a computer screen crunching numbers all day. By the time he realized that he couldn't stand it, he had family obligations and a mortgage payment to worry about. That made it a lot more difficult for him to switch jobs.

5 So if you agree with me that researching a company is important, you might ask, "Where can I find the information?" Well, if you think about the kind of information you should be interested in, it will give you a hint of where to look.

6 For example, you should know the company's history. There are numerous books written on every major company. Browsing the shelves in the campus library, I noticed a half-dozen books on Westinghouse Corporation and nearly twice that many on the Coca-Cola Company. Of course, it is more important to know the current events of a company than its past events. Remember that there is a huge business press that spends all its time reporting on companies. Check the newspaper and magazine indexes, as well as the computer databases, for any articles about your company. You'll be amazed at how much you can find, including the most up-to-date information on mergers or acquisitions.

Irving was the most reluctant speaker in his group. Extra group time was devoted to practicing his delivery.

7 If you want to find out what is entailed in a particular job description, you can consult the *Occupational Outlook Handbook,* which is published each year by the U.S. Bureau of Labor Statistics. This book includes three hundred occupational briefs which are grouped into thirteen clusters of related jobs.

8 If you want to know the company's strengths and weaknesses, and its position relative to its competitors, you can get all this information in the campus library. If it's a private company, you can look it up in Dun and Bradstreet's *Million-Dollar Directory,* which actually lists every company that does a quarter-million dollars or more a year in business. Of course, most companies today are public companies, so you can look them up in *Moody's Reports,* as well as *Standard and Poor's Stock Reports.* Other documents you might be interested in include the company's 10-K report, which is an IRS document detailing most of the company's finances. Our campus library has 10-K reports, and company annual reports, on the top 500 companies nationally, and most of our local companies. You can also get this kind of information at any career placement center. Here on campus the career center contains pamphlets and annual reports on more than a hundred companies that are currently expanding and hiring. If you would like your own copy of the company's annual report, just call Stockholder Relations at company headquarters. You can also ask them for the latest brochures and financial information available to the public. If you want to look into the benefit packages that they offer their employees, you can talk to the personnel office.

Group research was involved here.

⁹ You might want to know about the company's guidelines and regulations of behavior in the workplace. Different companies foster different job atmospheres. Sometimes, this is seen in the dress codes: IBM's employees tend to wear dark business suits with button-down collars, whereas Microsoft's tend to dress much more casually. To get this kind of information, you'll want to talk to employees of that company in your network. If you don't have the company's employees in your network, remember what Norman told you about finding them. You may find out information this way that cannot be obtained through secondary resources; however, the information could be biased, so it should not be the only information used as the basis of your decision on whether or not to take the job.

¹⁰ I hope I've given you some information you can use in researching the companies you might like to work for. And I hope you understand how important this research is. Besides helping you determine if a job is the right one for you, it will also increase your chances for a successful interview. Most of us will be interviewed in the future when we pursue our careers, and Kathy is going to talk to you now about that important aspect of the job search.

## ◉ THE INTERVIEW

Katherine Ramsay

*Review of previous speeches.*

¹ Okay, you've designed a dynamite résumé, as Kristin suggested. You've established a network according to Norman's guidelines, and your contacts have led you to what looks like the job of your dreams. You've researched the job and the position as Irving suggested, and you know that this is the job for you. You've got one more hurdle to jump over, and it might be the most important step yet. According to the Inroads Career Development Organization, "Every interview holds the potential for changing the rest of your life." I am going to discuss some considerations to keep in mind before, during, and after the interview.

*Preview of her own main points.*

² In many cases you will have to call the company to set up an interview. This call takes preparation. Be sure to have the name of the company as well as the name and number of the person with whom you wish to speak. There should be no background noise when you make this call. For example, the television or radio should not be on and you should try to be alone in the room. Speak clearly with a positive tone. Start off with a greeting, take notes during the conversation, making sure to write down the date, time, and location of the interview. No matter how the conversation may end, remember to say "thank you."

[3] Once you have set up an interview, your next consideration is your visual image [Chart 6]. Your appearance provides employers with their first impression of you. Make sure that you are well dressed and groomed, like the man and woman in this illustration. Distractions in your appearance such as extreme colors, outlandish jewelry, fashion prints or patterns, heavy makeup, and hair in the face should be avoided. Your clothes should be flattering. They should fit well. A classic design is always a plus. Conservative dress is favorable. Neutral colors are best. When the interview is over, the interviewer should remember your qualifications, not the outfit you wore to the interview.

Chart 6

[4] Communication is the key to a good interview. The interviewer's main goal is to get an impression of you as a person, as well as getting information from you. You don't have to prove everything you know, especially if you did the extensive research that Irving suggests. Let most of that knowledge sit in reserve, to impress the interviewer if it happens to come up in conversation. The main thing you should do is listen; according to Karen Lindquist, author of *The Anatomy of an Interview,* interviewers are most impressed with good listeners. Pay close attention to the questions that are asked so that you can give an appropriate answer. And don't be afraid to ask a question yourself. You should be prepared to

explain all your life experiences as positive factors in terms of your preparation for this job. For example, if the interviewer says, "I see that in two years you had four part-time jobs," you proceed to tell the things you learned in each job and why they were good experiences for you.

⁵ Follow the interviewer's lead in terms of the formality of the interview. If the interviewer is very formal, that's your cue to be formal also. If the interviewer appears relaxed, you can loosen up and be yourself.

⁶ Another important factor to consider is your nonverbal behavior. This involves eye contact, facial expressions, posture, the way you handle your hands and feet, and the tone of your voice. You should enter the interview with confidence and authority. Your eye contact should be strong, direct, and consistent. A firm, confident, immediate, and friendly handshake is appropriate. Try to avoid looking anxious or nervous—don't fidget. You want the interviewer to see you as a prospective employee, so you want to present yourself as capable and confident.

⁷ After each interview it would be beneficial to evaluate yourself. Identify your strengths and weaknesses that were apparent during the interview. Work on your weak spots to improve your interviewing skills for possible future interviews. Last but not least, there is the thank-you letter. This is a method of professional follow-through. In the letter you want to express your appreciation of their time and give them some positive feedback about the interview. For best results this letter should be sent within a day following the interview.

Chart 1 is displayed again. Conclusion for this speech is combines with the conclusion for the group presentation.

⁸ In summary, the rules for a good interview are: be prepared, be prompt, dress appropriately, watch your posture, and maintain good eye contact. Combine that with the brief, clear, neat persuasive résumé that Kristin suggested, the energetic networking that Norman outlined and the in-depth research that Irving suggested, and you'll be well on your way to the job of your dreams.

## ▼ SUMMARY

Group presentations are often assigned in public speaking classes to help students experience group process in an environment in which it can be analyzed.

Group work is becoming increasingly common in the media/information age because of the wealth of information that needs to be mastered in any area. Effectiveness in group work depends at least partially on your understanding of group process, which is defined as the way a group's product or output tends to be more than the sum of its parts. Group process consists of such components as group goals (which include individual and social goals), roles (which include formal and informal roles), norms (limits on behavior that are not explicitly stated), rules (limits on behavior that *are* explicitly stated), and leadership.

Traditional types of leadership include authoritarian (maximum control), laissez-faire (minimal control), and democratic (providing guidance and encouragement). The functions of leaders include traffic control (regulating who talks, and for how long), conflict control (to keep it functional), and maintaining an agenda (drawing up an outline of what needs to be accomplished, and reviewing the group's progress toward it).

Types of group presentations include the forum (an interaction between audience and panel members), the informal panel discussion (in which panel members interact back and forth), and the symposium or formal panel discussion (in which panel members present planned speeches).

## ▼ EXERCISES

1. Review the list of informal group roles on p. 427. Which of these roles do you think might reflect your own strengths as a group member? Which of them reflect your weaknesses? Explain.

2. Take any sample speech, from this book or any other source. How would you divide the content of this speech for a panel discussion with a three-person panel? Four people? Five? Demonstrate in outline form.

## NOTES

1. Adapted from a more extensive list of group roles in Ron Adler and George Rodman, *Understanding Human Communication,* 5th ed. (Fort Worth: Harcourt Brace, 1994), pp. 318–320.

2. Ibid., p. 320.

# PERMISSIONS AND ACKNOWLEDGEMENTS

**Chapter 1**

*Calvin and Hobbes* ©1994 Watterson. Dist. by Universal Press Syndicate.
Reprinted with permission. All rights reserved.

*Calvin and Hobbes* ©1994 Watterson. Dist. by Universal Press Syndicate.
Reprinted with permission. All rights reserved.

"Don't Call Them Dreadlocks," by Pearlita Peters. Reprinted by permission of
the author.

**Chapter 2**

*Calvin and Hobbes* ©1994 Watterson. Dist. by Universal Press Syndicate.
Reprinted with permission. All rights reserved.

*Calvin and Hobbes* ©1994 Watterson. Dist. by Universal Press Syndicate.
Reprinted with permission. All rights reserved.

"Speak with Style and Watch the Impact," by Carl Wayne Hensley. Reprinted by
permission of the author.

**Chapter 3**

*Dilbert* ©(9/18/94) reprinted by permission of United Feature Syndicate, Inc.

"Debunking the Vitamin Myth," by Darn Perino. Reprinted by permission of the
Interstate Oratorical Association.

**Chapter 4**

*Dilbert* reprinted by permission of United Feature Syndicate, Inc.

"Tragic Trilogy," by Glenn Martin. Reprinted by permission of the Interstate Oratorical Association.

**Chapter 5**

*Calvin and Hobbes* ©1994 Watterson. Dist. by Universal Press Syndicate.
Reprinted with permission. All rights reserved.

*The Far Side* ©1995 Farworks, Inc./Dist. by Universal Press Syndicate.
Reprinted with permission. All rights reserved.

**Chapter 6**

*Calvin and Hobbes* ©1992 Watterson. Dist. by Universal Press Syndicate.
Reprinted with permission. All rights reserved.

"Transracial Adoption," by Sarah Hessenflow. Reprinted by permission of the
Interstate Oratorical Association.

**Chapter 7**

*Calvin and Hobbes* ©1992 Watterson. Dist. by Universal Press Syndicate.
Reprinted with permission. All rights reserved.

"America's Youth in Crisis," by Rebecca Witte. Reprinted by permission of the
Interstate Oratorical Association.

**Chapter 8**

Cartoon reprinted by permission of Gahan Wilson.

"Superbugs: Scourge of the Post-Antibiotic Era," by Andy Wood. Reprinted by
permission of the Interstate Oratorical Association.

**Chapter 9**

*Calvin and Hobbes* ©1994 Watterson. Dist. by Universal Press Syndicate. Reprinted with permission. All rights reserved.

"Faceless Enemies," by Donald McPartland. Reprinted by permission of the Interstate Oratorical Association.

**Chapter 10**

*Calvin and Hobbes* ©1994 Watterson. Dist. by Universal Press Syndicate. Reprinted with permission. All rights reserved.

Figure 10-5. Reprinted from MacUser, December 1988. Copyright©1988 Ziff-Davis Publishing Company.

Figure 10-8. Reprinted from MacUser, December 1988. Copyright©1988 Ziff-Davis Publishing Company.

"Reasons to Consider Vegetarianism," by Jeanne Klafin. Reprinted by permission of the author.

**Chapter 11**

*Dilbert* reprinted by permission of United Feature Syndicate, Inc.

"EMS for Kids," by Amy Wong. Reprinted by permission of the Interstate Oratorical Association.

**Chapter 12**

"Myths about Artists and Their Work," by Diane Handloser. Reprinted by permission of the author.

**Chapter 13**

*Dilbert* reprinted by permission of United Feature Syndicate, Inc.

"Very Fake Badges- Very Real Guns," by Bond Benton. Reprinted by permission of the Interstate Oratorical Association.

**Chapter 14**

*Dilbert* reprinted by permission of United Feature Syndicate, Inc.

"Death by Federal Mandate," by Tai Du. Reprinted by permission of the Interstate Oratorical Association.

**Chapter 15**

*The Far Side* ©1995 Farworks, Inc./Dist. by Universal Press Syndicate. Reprinted with permission. All rights reserved.

Remarks made at 1995 Essence Awards. Reprinted by permission of *Essence* magazine, Bill Cosby, and Colin Powell.

**Chapter 16**

*The Far Side* ©1995 Farworks, Inc./Dist. by Universal Press Syndicate. Reprinted with permission. All rights reserved.

**How to Find the Job of Your Dreams.** "Introduction," and "Designing the Resume" by Kristin Liguori; "Networking" by Norman Benito; "Researching the Company," by Irving Lee; "The Interview," by Kathcrine Ramsey. Reprinted by permission of the authors.

# PHOTO CREDITS

# INDEX